Sterling Spero
and John M. Capozzola

The Urban Community and Its Unionized Bureaucracies

Pressure Politics
in Local Government
Labor Relations

The Urban Community and Its Unionized Bureaucracies

The Urban Community and Its Unionized Bureaucracies

Pressure Politics in Local Government Labor Relations

Sterling D. Spero

John M. Capozzola

DUNELLEN

New York

To Bertha
and
Shirley
and
Meg, Joan, and Nan

Table of Contents

List of Abbreviations

AFGE	American Federation of Government Employees
AFL	American Federation of Labor
AFL-CIO	American Federation of Labor-Congress of Industrial Organizations
AFSCME	American Federation of State, County and Municipal Employees
AFT	American Federation of Teachers
AGE	Assembly of Government Employees
ANA	American Nursing Association
BLS	Bureau of Labor Statistics
CIO	Congress of Industrial Organizations
CSEA	Civil Service Employees Association
FOP	Fraternal Order of Police
IAFF	International Association of Fire Fighters
IBPO	International Brotherhood of Police Officers
IBT	International Brotherhood of Teamsters
ICPA	International Conference of Police Associations
IUOE	International Union of Operating Engineers
LIU	Laborers International Union
NEA	National Education Association
NFFE	National Federation of Federal Employees
NLRA	National Labor Relations Act
NLRB	National Labor Relations Board
OCB	Office of Collective Bargaining
PBA	Patrolmen's Benevolent Association
PERB	Public Employment Relations Board
SCMWA	State, County and Municipal Workers of America
SEIU	Service Employees International Union
SSEU	Social Service Employees Union
TWU	Transport Workers Union
UAW	United Auto Workers
UFA	Uniformed Firefighters Association
UFOA	Uniformed Fire Officers Association
UFT	United Federation of Teachers
UPWA	United Public Workers of America

Preface and Acknowledgments

Labor Relations in the American municipal government services reached highly controversial proportions in the 1960's. The problem is not new. Nearly 60 years ago Nicholas Murray Butler called it "beyond comparison the most important which modern democracies have to face." One of the central concerns of this book has been to consider the impact of collective bargaining on public policies and administration, as well as its broader institutional, legal, and political implications.

This work, financed in part by a grant from the Twentieth Century Fund, is based on both documentary sources and first-hand observation in many communities. Scores of public officers, officials, and staff members of civic association and employee organizations were interviewed. Dozens of tape recordings have been made. Nearly all of this activity was conducted under pledges of "no attribution." Therefore, many statements and quotations could not be buttressed by annotations, so readers will be obliged to accept them on faith. The sources are all on record in our hands. We are indebted to all those who gave us this indispensable information, which we checked and double checked against other sources.

During the course of writing this book, we were constantly aware of Professor Kurt L. Hanslowe's remark that writing about labor relations is like "shooting at a moving target." Events in local labor relations have moved with extreme rapidity. We can only hope that we have succeeded in not being out-of-date.

Repeatedly, in the course of preparing our manuscript, we therefore found ourselves in need of additional data not available from any readily accessible source. In such cases, we requested assistance from Al Bilik and Mary L. Hennessey, of the American Federation of State, County and Municipal Employees; Henry Wilson, of the Laborers International Union; Richard E. Murphy, of the Service Employees International Union; Foster Roser, Personnel Director of Philadelphia, Pa.; W. Donald Heisel, former Personnel Director of Cincinnati, Ohio; Robert D. Krause, Personnel Director of Hartford, Conn.; Jean J. Coutourier, Executive Director of the National Civil Service League; and Elisha Freedman, Chief Administrative Officer of Montgomery County, Md. We are also pleased to acknowledge the generous cooperation of the Bureau of National Affairs in Washington, whose Government Employee Relations Reports were of great value.

This work could not have been carried out without the able assistance of our staff: Lawrence Bender, Claude Shostal, Ray Palombo, Fred Charap, Richard Rous, and Douglas Routh. Producing a manuscript requires a substantial office operation. We would be remiss not to acknowledge the devoted assistance of Louis Goodman, and the able typing of Miss Janice Riggs and Mrs. Joanne Goodman.

We are also indebted to Mrs. Frances Klafter and Mr. John Booth, of the staff of the Twentieth Century Fund, for helping us over many rough periods. To Dr. Isador Lubin, the Fund's economic consultant, we owe deep thanks for his constant support and encouragement throughout the course of our work and especially when it was needed most. To our old and close friend Professor Maxwell Lehman of Long Island University, former City Administrator of New York, who helped us unstintingly to put our work into final shape, we owe a debt of gratitude which no mere line of preface can pretend to repay.

Without the active cooperation of the late Dean Ray Harvey, Acting Dean, Troy R. Westmeyer, and Dean Dick Netzer, of the Graduate School of Public Administration of New York University, our work could not have been carried on to completion.

Finally, no mere word of thanks could possibly express our gratitude and appreciation for the kindness, generous help, and competent advice provided by Paule H. Jones and Eugene H. Nellen, of the Dunellen Publishing Company.

We have, in short, enjoyed the benefits of the advice, cooperation, and patience of many persons. Any actual errors, or shortcomings in ideas or emphasis are our own responsibility.

Sterling D. Spero
John M. Capozzola

Graduate School of Public Administration
New York University
April 25, 1972

We warmly thank William H. Fitelson, Esq. for his continuing efforts to remove roadblocks in our way. For their wise counsel and generous help we are deeply indebted to our colleague Professor Emanuel Stein and our co-workers in sister institutions: Professor Arnold Zander of the University of Wisconsin at Green Bay, and Professor Albert A. Blum of Michigan State University.

Errata

p. xiv: NAGE–National Association of Government Employees

p. 33: First paragraph: references to UBT should read IBT.

p. 37: Second paragraph, first sentence should read: I don't know how much support . . .

p. 63: Second paragraph, second sentence should read: . . . loaded by strike-breakers . . .

p. 118: Fourth paragraph, eighth line should read: . . . aggrieved employee . . .

p. 126: Second paragraph, second line should read: . . . black highway workers union . . .

p. 189: Third paragraph, last sentence should read: . . . above 30 . . .

p. 195: Note 4, first sentence should read: . . . stated that in half the cities and counties he investigated, standard management rights were reserved to the municipal employer.

p. 242: AUTHORS' NOTE. First full paragraph, last sentence should be amended as follows: By 1972, all public employee organizations affiliated with the AFL-CIO, federal and local, revoked their no-strike clauses. The independent NFFE is the only general federal employees organization which adheres to its traditional no-strike policy.

p. 262: Last paragraph, second sentence should read: These states . . .

p. 286: First word should read: news

p. 288: Last paragraph, fourth line should read: . . . after the decision is rendered . . .

p. 290: Third paragraph, first sentence should read: But undue emphasis may have been placed in these earlier decisions on the final and binding aspects of arbitration in the public service. Little more than a decade after the Mugford decision the New York City Department of Labor reported that: "In fact, voluntary arbitration has been the recourse in some governmental units . . ." citing the experiences of Detroit, and the Tennessee Valley Authority and Canadian municipalities reported, . . .

p. 317: Sixth line should read: communications . . . would have been affected . . .

p. 321: First paragraph, second line should read: . . . and labor . . .

p. 353: Immediately after the entry "American Federation of Labor-Congress of Industrial Organizations", insert "American Federation of State, Country, and Municipal Employees" under which all entries between "agency shop and," and "union security" fall.

p. 355: Third line from bottom should read: serious objections to . . .

1   Conflict and Changing Patterns

The Changing Characteristics of Public Employment

Problems of local public employment relations, once the concern of a few obscure scholars and government personnel technicians, have since the 1960's been catapulted to the center of the political stage. Every element of the traditional relationship between public employer and public employee has been basically altered. What was once regarded as impermissible, like the public employee strike, has become a common occurrence. What was once an article of faith, like the concept of sovereignty, has become a mere legalistic shibboleth. What was once unthinkable, like employee intervention in the processes of management, has become increasingly a feature of public administration. In the event that these trends continue, the influence of employee organizations will deeply affect the conduct of government business and even the shaping of policy. This indeed is now happening at an accelerating rate. The consolidation of organized public employee strength is projecting new issues of delicacy and significance into the governmental scene.

Since World War II municipal employment has experienced a dramatic growth. This growth is in part the fruit of a change in the American economy, which has shifted the major portion of the national labor force from the making of things to the dispensing of

1

services. There have been mounting popular demands for improved and additional local government services. These demands, together with new problems and complexities of local government, have compelled the employment of a variety of specialists, technicians, and professional workers, as well as skilled and semiskilled workers in large numbers.

The increase in municipal employment has been accompanied by an explosive expansion in employee organization. The unorganized have been energetically organized. Small, competing groups, long on the scene, have been displaced or absorbed by powerful unions utilizing all the techniques developed by unions in private industry. These unions press their demands with extraordinary militancy, ranging from intense political pressure to service-crippling strikes headlined in the printed media and given prime-time television exposure. Such unexpected activism was met with pained surprise by politicians, civic leaders, high senior civil servants, and editorial writers.

The public worker had been presumed politically passive, rendering services quietly and impartially and wearing the halo of political neutrality. Many restrictions on civil service conduct had reflected such attitudes. The restrictions are rooted in law and practice that placed the public employee in a class apart, denying him the privileges of legislative guarantees accorded to employees in the private sector.

In part insulated from the dangers of unemployment and the risks of the competitive economy, with a modest but secure salary and a small pension, the civil servant was supposed to be humble, docile, and grateful for the good fortune of his protected status. The leader of a British civil service union once quipped, "The civil servant lives in a state of abiding poverty, but thank God it's permanent."

Restrictions on the conduct of public workers sometimes reached absurd depths, as evidenced by provisions contained in certain teacher contracts. A Missouri school district required every male teacher upon receipt of his contract to sign a resignation to become effective at once should he "smoke a cigarette, cigar, or pipe at any time or place." It was frequently stipulated that teachers be "neatly and appropriately dressed." One North Carolina town included in its contract a commitment "to sleep at least eight hours a night" and "to abstain from all dancing." Another contract forbade teachers "to fall in love, become engaged, or secretly married."[1] Local school boards and the communities endorsing such provisions apparently regarded teachers as members of a quasi-monastic order taking vows of poverty, chastity, and obedience.

2

Employee Activism: Old Roots and New Forms

When the teachers both in large cities and in small towns began to rebel against the conditions imposed on them and other public employees and to challenge established ways, it was feared that a new and sinister force had come upon the scene, threatening the foundations of society.

Yet, this was only the newest wave of protest. Civil service activism began in the 1830's, a phase of Jacksonian revolution. Public employees in federal shipyards and municipal public works organized, demonstrated, and struck in support of a general movement for the 10-hour workday.

In locations where private employers had granted the shorter day, this embryonic attempt at collective bargaining in the public sector was successful, but it was unsuccessful where the movement failed in the private sphere. A pattern was set for the policy of making working conditions in public employment conform to those among "the generality of employers" outside.

Shortly after the Civil War, federal employees sought the establishment of an eight-hour day by congressional action, espousing a new principle of public employment under which government, free from the profit motive, should be a model employer establishing standards for other employers to emulate.

Whereas the doctrine of the prevailing standard has been widely accepted and written into federal, state, and local legislation, the principle of the model employer, while winning lip service from some public officials, has been opposed as an unwarranted drain on the public treasury.

Stimulated by the rise in prices following World War I, energetic unions of teachers, fire fighters, and policemen were on the point of achieving their objectives when their activity was brought to an abrupt halt as a result of adverse public reaction following the Boston police strike of 1919. Nevertheless, that strike was not without effect. Employing authorities forestalled the union movement by hastening to ameliorate the conditions that led to unionization. In Boston, for example, where the striking policemen were dismissed from their jobs, the new force hired to replace them was granted the improved conditions the union had sought.

At the end of World War II, prices rose sharply while municipal employee pay lagged. Unrest grew, reaching climactic proportions in the mid-1940's. At the same time, city employment, which had been virtually frozen during the war, began to expand, and many of the newer employees joined labor-affiliated unions. The thrust of this

3

movement carried members of conservative employee associations into the unions.

Strikes and strike threats occurred with increasing frequency in that decade. There were two general strides, one in Portland, Me., and another, even more serious, in Rochester, N.Y. In both cases, unions of private employees affiliated with the then rival American Federation of Labor and Congress of Industrial Organizations struck in sympathy with the public workers and joined them on the picket lines. In 1946 alone, there were 43 strikes in cities of over 10,000 and threats occurred in many more, along with mass demonstrations and heightened political pressures on legislatures and executives.

The momentum of the experience of these years accelerated a gradual shift in the determination of working conditions away from unilateral prescription by employing authorities through legislation or administrative order and toward collective bargaining along the lines prevailing in the private sector.

Collective Bargaining: Progress and Resistance

At the turn of the century, most public employers seized the opportunity to resist the development of unionism in public employment. Some municipalities specifically forbade any type of labor organization. But organization proceeded, so employers sought to influence, if not control, the existing organizations. Relying on the theory that the state occupied a sovereign relationship to its employees and that the government was the effective custodian of ultimate authority in the community, employers held that membership in labor organizations led to divided loyalty on the part of public employees.

President Theodore Roosevelt, attempting to push this doctrine to its logical end, issued an executive order forbidding federal employees to seek to influence legislation in their own behalf, "individually or through associations, save through the heads of their departments." For more than a decade, government employees were obliged to work under this order, which became known in the service as the "gag rule." President Taft supplemented the gag rule with a regulation of his own. The order not only prohibited appeals to Congress by federal employees, as the old order had done, but also provided that no employee or official should "respond to any request for information from either House of Congress, or any committee of either House of Congress, or any member of Congress, except through and as authorized by the head of his department."

4

While such regulations were supported by many political scientists and reform groups, in the interest of economy, efficiency, and a nonpartisan civil service, many administrative officials, taking their cue from the White House, proceeded to interfere with attempts of employees to join organizations of which the authorities disapproved. With the passage of the Lloyd-La Follette Act in 1912, labor achieved the nullification of the gag rules and organization gained momentum.

The burgeoning new movement was the culmination of a history of struggle against the opposition of determined public employers, who had regularly invoked the doctrine of sovereignty to rationalize their unilateral authority over their subordinate employees as necessary to preserve the integrity and legitimate powers of government. Their law officers armed them with legal opinions telling them that they lacked the authority to accede to union programs which they did not wish to accept. The whole issue of union recognition and collective bargaining thus came to be viewed as a question of law rather than an issue of public policy.

Public employers buttressed their refusal to accede to the demands of organized employees by citing a statement of President Franklin D. Roosevelt in a letter to Mr. Luther C. Steward, President of the National Federation of Employees, an independent union:

> ...the process of collective bargaining as usually understood, cannot be transplanted into the public service ...The very nature and purpose of government make it impossible for administrative officers to represent fully or bind the employer in mutual discussions with government employee organizations....[2]

This statement was included in official personnel handbooks and was constantly pointed to by public employers to prove that public collective bargaining was "impossible."

Despite the Roosevelt statement, despite the learned legal opinions, despite the invocation of the doctrine of sovereignty, public employee organization and collective bargaining continued to advance. Many municipal authorities finally concluded that employee demands for a direct negotiating voice in determining their working conditions could no longer be denied. Some municipal employers, casting aside the negative legalistic approach, held that the practical meaning of sovereignty was the power to decide matters of public policy. Thus, a decision to adopt collective bargaining as an employer-employee relations technique was a sovereign act.

Several municipal employers boldly proceeded to implement collective bargaining by formal action.

The most authoritative voice to assert that public collective bargaining was not "impossible" after all was that of President Franklin D. Roosevelt himself. Three years after writing his letter to Luther Steward, on Labor Day 1940 the President dedicated the Chickamauga Dam of the Tennessee Valley Authority. He began his remarks by praising the splendid new agreement between organized labor and the TVA, which had just been consummated, adding "collective bargaining and efficiency have proceeded hand in hand."

Many local government employers either were unware of these remarks or chose to ignore them, and these employers continued their negative stance, still quoting the Steward letter. The movement for collective bargaining, however, continued to accelerate. Various other municipal employers, desiring to meet the demands of employees, chose to effect collective bargaining by indirection. Sustaining the letter of the law as interpreted by cautious legal advisers, they negotiated agreements with employee organizations and issued them in the form of unilateral statements of policy, executive directives, or official memoranda. In some cities the accords took the form of resolutions or ordinances of the local legislative body.[3] Dr. Wilson R. Hart noted that by devices such as these, with little change in legal climate, collective bargaining was "bootlegged" into municipal labor relations.[4]

This legal or de facto recognition of collective bargaining greatly stimulated the activity of labor-affiliated unions. The American Federation of State, County, and Municipal Employees made steady progress in concluding contracts. Before the flowering of the militancy of the late 1960's, that union had negotiated contracts with over 400 state and local governments, 215 of which were exclusive agreements with dues check-off covering 80 percent of the federation's membership.[5] In the late summer of 1971, the AFSCME Research Department reported over 1,200 contracts on file, most of them containing exclusive-recognition clauses.

The expansion of collective bargaining on the municipal level was a stimulus to the issuance of President Kennedy's Executive Order 10988 on Employee-Management Cooperation in the Federal Service, issued in 1962. The order extended to federal employees a limited right to negotiate working conditions and, in turn, encouraged a further expansion of collective bargaining in state and local governments.

Greater flexibility of management was reflected in a more liberal attitude on the part of the courts and in the actions of legislative bodies. Pennsylvania and Hawaii enacted statutes in 1970 granting a limited right to strike. As of May 1971, 25 states had laws requiring the public employer to bargain. Eleven additional states authorized the employer to meet and confer or bargain. Yet, despite progress in recognizing bargaining rights, punitive antistrike legislation remains the rule, regardless of the fact that its futility or counter-productivity has been amply demonstrated.

The genesis of punitive legislation dates back to the militant activities of the 1940's, which saw some of the most bitter strikes in civil service history as well as the first federal antistrike legislation. In 1946 the schools of Buffalo, N.Y. were closed for a week by a teachers' strike. In a remarkable demonstration of solidarity, three rival organizations—the AFL, the CIO, and the independent Teachers Association—joined on the picket lines, carrying signs reading AFL—ASSOCIATION—CIO.

The strike, which ended in substantial concessions to the teachers, vexed Governor Thomas E. Dewey, who had made no direct effort to intervene in settling the dispute. In a Coolidge-like gesture, he sought and obtained the passage of New York's notorious Condon-Wadlin Act. This legislation provided that workers who violated the statute's antistrike provision automatically lost their jobs. Should dismissed strikers be rehired later, for a period of three years they would not receive more pay than they were getting when they struck. In addition, such workers were to be placed on probation for five years after returning to work, during which time they were subject to summary discharge. While strikes had been traditionally regarded as a concerted action involving a number of persons, under the terms of the law an individual act could be legally construed as a strike.

Passage of the law was opposed by not only trade unions and prestigious independent labor relations specialists but also so strong an opponent of civil service strikes as the leading civic organization in the field, the Civil Service Reform Association of New York.

The first test of the Condon-Wadlin Law came quickly, in a city-wide sanitation strike in Yonkers, N.Y. in 1947. The city government realized that if it attempted to enforce the law and discharge the employees, it would make the strike permanent and garbage would not be collected. An offer to reinstate the strikers, with the grave penalties legally required, would be futile, since the men obviously would not return to work under conditions worse than those which they were striking to improve. The city authorities therefore ignored the law, declaring that the strike was not a strike and that the workers had not been absent without leave but had suddenly become sick. The strike ended with concessions to the workers. This set the pattern. The law was unenforced in scores of strikes. Yet it remained on the statute books for years—a political white elephant, unenforceable and untouchable.

Other states, instead of learning the lesson of the futility and counter-productivity of punitive antistrike laws, passed legislation along the same lines—with the same results.

Despite the growing extent of permissive or mandatory bargaining legislation, antistrike provisions carrying severe penalties are still the rule. Simultaneously, there has been a steady increase in the number of public service strikes in all parts of the country. Gross statistics (142 strikes in 1946, 181 in 1967, 254 in 1968, and sharp increases in 1970 and 1971) do not tell the story as vividly as a report by Jerry Wurf, President of AFSCME, to the 1970 session on unionization of municipal employees held by the Academy of Political Science, Columbia University. Citing a report of the United States Conference of Mayors, he pointed out that every three days in the first twó and one half months of 1970, employees of an American city went on strike. Strikes that year lasted from three to 34 days and included almost every category of employees: white-collar workers, sanitation men, street repairmen, fire fighters, police. These strikes even affected the national capital, where despite punitive antistrike laws, striking sanitation workers went unpunished and won a generous contract with the District of Columbia government.[6]

The unionized public employee does not view his defiance of antistrike laws as a serious offense and challenge to public order. He sees it as a moral protest against being relegated to a class apart from other workers, as an act on a par with the defiance at the turn of the 19th century that had forced abandonment of the antistrike conspiracy laws. Refusing to be singled out as the only class of worker subject to a general strike ban, public employees raise the question: Are public employees' strikes really more serious than strikes in private industries, which may affect public health and safety and even the operations of government more severely than many public service strikes? Yet the right to strike in private employment is guaranteed.

The New Militancy

The militancy of the modern civil servant, like the activism of earlier times, is stimulated not only by internal conditions but also by outside factors. The successes of organized labor in private employment is an obvious factor. Much of the militancy was galvanized by the desire to eliminate legal distinctions, imposed on them over the years, that served as the basis for unilateral employer action. The reluctance of administrative officers to part with their so-called managerial rights irked the civil servant, especially professionals, desiring a more flexible approach to management. School teachers, in particular, objected to the autocratic structure of many school districts. While each employee group had varying goals, the objectives of higher wages, shorter hours, and improved working conditions were vital to public workers, who had until the 1960's generally lagged economically behind their brethren in private industry.

The municipal work force is becoming younger, more active, and more responsive to militant leadership. As in private industry, activism has been further stimulated by interorganizational competition, reflected by the upsurge of various groups seeking to out-promise and out-maneuver their rivals, by internal factionalism, and by leadership rivalry.

A more subtle influence has been the atmosphere of protest against traditional authority and social arrangements, which since the early 1960's has affected all segments of society, from the most exploited to the most stable and respectable. Some aspects of this protest, such as campus unrest, appear to be passing, but others, such as the civil rights movement, reflect really deep grievances, and the struggle to resolve them continues, although the style of the struggle may alter from confrontation to more conventional political action.

This militancy has been manifested in a variety of ways: against the public, against public officials, and against the employees' own leadership. Long-standing no-strike promises have been cast aside. The employees have struck in defiance of laws which expressly forbid strikes, both with and without the sanction of union leadership. They have exhibited no reluctance to threaten stoppages and staged a series of "job actions," a euphemism for strikes. The creation of militancy funds, the ousting of conservative leadership, and the election of young aggressive leaders have accelerated demands for the same rights possessed by all workers.

The strike, which has become as much a fact of municipal employment as it is of private employment, will remain a union weapon. Resort to political action will probably be intensified. The unions will doubtless continue to pursue those tactics that have already yielded significant returns and to press with all their powers for the removal of their basic grievance, the relegation of the public employee to a category apart from other workers.

Yet the strike is not without risks. Adverse public reaction is already apparent, especially in the form of rejection of budgets by the electorate. When schools do not open, when garbage piles up in the streets, when fire and transit services are interrupted, when the normal functioning of hospitals and other institutions is impeded, the shocked public often finds itself unprepared to accommodate to the breakdown of services. Adverse reactions are likely to follow.

Yet, why should not the public be equally shocked if the interrupted transit service is privately owned and operated, if private utility company employees cut off power and light, or if drivers of private oil company trucks strike and cut off fuel supplies in the dead of the winter?

While the strike issue makes the greatest immediate impact on the individual citizen, it is not the only issue raised by the expansion of collective bargaining. Observers of the political scene have begun to direct attention to the increasingly independent role of organized bureaucracies in public affairs. The traditional processes of personnel administration, in which the prerogatives of elected officials were carried on by their appointed deputies, are already giving way to the new bilateralism. Some personnel officers view this development as a threat to the merit system. Others welcome it as a stimulus to overdue change in a process "which long needed a fresh wind to blow new ideas into its encrusted routines."[7]

The interests of unions have gone beyond such internal processes as personnel administration and have extended to policy matters of broad public concern. The "new public worker" of the 1970's, particularly the professional, openly challenges the accepted way of doing things. He desires to participate in decisions affecting not only his job but also the clientele he serves and with which he frequently identifies. No longer content merely to implement policies handed down to him, he insists on becoming involved in the what, how, and why of the policy-making process as an active agent of change.[7]

These attitudes are reflected in union policies. It is not easy to draw a line between working conditions, now concededly in the scope of collective bargaining, and decisions regarding issues of public policy, the constitutional prerogative of legislative and executive authorities.

On the ground that issues heretofore regarded as policy matters directly affect working conditions, unions have been insisting increasingly on direct voice in their settlement. They have used their powers either through the route of collective agreement or by the exercise of their greatly enhanced political influence on officials with legal power to decide. In the latter case, the unions are merely resorting to a more effective version of their traditional tactics. In the former, they are directly exercising the prerogatives of elective authority. In either case, they are codetermining public policy.

10

Employees in client-oriented education, health, and welfare services have been the most articulate exponents of codetermination at the bargaining table, insisting that their status as professionals imposes a duty upon them to push the official bureaucracy into making long-ignored service reforms.

Policemen and fire fighters have used their powers in similar ways, claiming that their objectives are "the protection of life and limb of their fellow workers."

All of which presages increasing power struggles in "the new day" of public employment relations.

Notes

1. Sterling D. Spero, *Government as Employer* (New York: Remsen Press, 1948), pp. 299-301.
2. Letter from President Roosevelt to Luther C. Steward, August 1937. See Appendix for full text.
3. Spero, op. cit., p. 348.
4. Wilson R. Hart, *Collective Bargaining in the Federal Service* (New York: Harper, 1961), Chapter 8.
5. Arnold Zander, "A Union View of Collective Bargaining in the Public Service," *Public Administration Review* (Winter 1962), 7-8.
6. Jerry Wurf, "The Revolution in Public Employment," *Proceedings of the Academy of Political Science*, Columbia University, 1970, XXX, No. 2, 134.
7. Frank Marini, ed., *Toward a New Public Administration* (Scranton, Pa.: Chandler, 1970), Chapters 3, 6, and 9.

2 Municipal Employees Organize

The Public Employment Explosion and Union Growth

Public employment has increased to enormous proportions over the last few decades. As of October 1971, public employees constituted approximately one sixth of the nation's work force; and municipal employees are the most rapidly expanding segment, having more than quadrupled between 1945 and 1971. Furthermore, an annual growth rate of 5 percent has been projected for municipal employees, in contrast to an anticipated increase of slightly more than 1 percent at the federal level.[1]

Public Employee Unionism

Unionism in the public service, which had experienced a relatively slow growth until the mid-1950's, while not rising proportionately to the growth of government itself has nevertheless become the most rapidly expanding sector of unionized labor.[2] The general labor movement had achieved its greatest gains in the 1930's and 1940's, in the wake of militant action and the passage of the Norris-La Guardia Act of 1932 and the Wagner Act of 1935. These two legislative acts had largely removed the legal shackles inhibiting union growth and gains in private industry. Not since this surge of unionism in the 1930's has the labor movement or the country experienced anything comparable to the current explosion of collective bargaining. Less than a decade ago labor boasted of several hundreds of agreements covering tens of thousands of workers in public agencies. By 1970 the trade union movement had achieved thousands of contracts covering millions of public workers.

With the proliferation of government agencies, acceleration of regulatory and service activities by all levels of government, and the mounting demands of the public for greater services, public employment mushroomed. Federal employment approximated 435,000 when Franklin D. Roosevelt took office. Before the entrance of the United States into World War II and on the eve of the rearmament effort, federal employment had risen to about a million. While there was not a substantial increase in federal employment during the Johnson presidency, there was a sharp rise in local employment, owing to the Great Society legislation. Thus, while federal employment rose only 22 percent during the 1960's, state and local employment growth approximated 62 percent.

As the organizational momentum of the general labor movement peaked in the 1950's, specific AFL-CIO affiliated unions marked the municipal field as one for special organizing efforts.

The AFL-CIO, despite a decline in its own membership, had little interest in and had rendered inconsequential financial support to public employee unions until the late 1960's. Rather than visualizing public employees as "a new plum to be picked," it preferred, with the exception of teachers, a hands-off policy.[3] The AFL had a relatively secure membership, with well staked out jurisdictions. Individual unions, such as the International Brotherhood of Teamsters, the Laborers International Union, the Service Employees International Union, and the American Federation of State, County, and Municipal Employees, led the organizational drive. The International AFL, and later the AFL-CIO, preferred to avoid the inevitable jurisdictional entanglements. During the late 1950's and early 1960's, virtually the only national union which gave substantial financial help was the United Auto Workers. Nonetheless, individual unions engaged in massive organizing drives to tap the vast potential of public employees.

In 1944 only 540,000 public employees were members of unions; in 1955 those organized numbered 900,000; but by 1971 more than 3 million state and local public workers held union or association membership cards. While it may be argued that the greatest success in percentages organized took place within the federal government, unionism in municipal government made spectacular gains when local independent unions and professional association gains are considered.[4]

Within municipal government, individual unions and associations achieved large numerical and percentage increases. AFSCME reported an increase of 111 percent in membership from 1960 to 1970. During the same period the American Federation of Teachers claimed a 265 percent gain. Similarly, powerful independent associations, such as the Civil Service Employees Associations of New York and California, achieved major increases in membership. By 1971 some type of employee organization existed in 75 percent of the nation's cities and represented 64 percent of the personnel employed by local governments.[5]

Origins and Subsequent Growth

Employee organization among local government employees dates back to the beginnings of the American labor movement. As early as the 1830's, craft-type units of "laborers, workmen, and mechanics" organized both in federal shipyards and in municipal public works. The American Institute of Instruction, predecessor of the National Education Association, was established in 1830. Local police benefit societies and fraternal groups were also formed in pre-Civil War days. These earliest attempts to organize were sporadic, limited, and relatively ineffective. Such independent organizations found it difficult to exist, let alone grow in size and power.

The first serious wave of municipal employee organization took place in the 1880's and 1890's, mainly in the form of police and fire fighter benefit societies and fraternal groups. These efforts, along with the earlier efforts of state educational associations leading to the establishment of the NEA in 1857, paralleled the efforts of the general labor movement in forming the AFL in 1886 and the establishment of federal postal unions in the 1880's and 1890's.

Only during the early decades of this century did these organizations turn to activities designed to advance and protect their interests as employees. Even then, the political climate was not conducive to widespread organizational efforts. After the enactment of the federal Pendleton Act in 1883 (the civil service law) and of state laws introducing the "merit system" into government, such organizations as existed tended to work in close alliance with existing party machines. Largely confining their efforts to lobbying at state capitols and city halls, employee groups focused on the elimination of restrictions on political activities by public employees.

Probably one of the most effective public employee units was the

Civil Service Forum in New York City, founded in 1909. The Forum exemplified the old-line, independent employee organization which, when to its advantage, functioned as an adjunct of a political party or faction. Not having yet achieved the right to bargain collectively, public employee units chose the legislative route. The Forum was so committed to politicking that it actually opposed collective bargaining and only came around to accepting it after Mayor Wagner espoused it.

Organization and the Law

As a matter of law, the sovereign state could have forbidden public employees the right to organize. As a matter of fact, government employers merely attempted to discourage organizational attempts or efforts to affiliate with the general labor movement. The prevailing view in 1910 was that expressed by Nicholas Murray Butler, who declared that the right of government employees to organize should be limited to the formation of mutual benefit societies.[6]

Actually, the right of federal employees to organize existed prior to the passage of the Lloyd-La Follette Act in 1912. This legislation, which specifically aimed to nullify the so-called gag orders, was regarded as a general expression of congressional sentiment in favor of the right to organize without executive interference and improperly imposed obstacles. Nevertheless, some states and municipalities had, by law, forbidden organization.

Despite the fact that the National Labor Relations Act had excluded public employees from its protective provisions, by 1946 Charles S. Rhyne concluded that the weight of legal authority was that municipal employees could organize or affiliate "except where from the nature of their employment, union membership may be prohibited or limited as incompatible with the public duties which particular city employees must perform."[7] A decade later another significant study conducted for New York City's Department of Labor reached virtually the same conclusion—that in the absence of express legislative or executive provisions to the contrary, public employees had the same right to organize that other workers had long enjoyed.[8] By 1970 approximately 40 states had enacted legislation which explicitly or implicitly recognized the right of public employees to organize and be represented.

The current trend of judicial decisions is that public employees possess a constitutionally protected right to join unions, which right cannot be abolished by statute in the absence of a paramount public interest warranting a limitation.[9] In 1969, a Federal District Court in the Atkins Case struck down a North Carolina statute prohibiting membership of fire fighters and police in a labor organization "which is, or may become, a part of or affiliated in any way with a national or international labor union" having as one of its purposes collective bargaining. The ban was held "void on its face as an abridgement of freedom of association" and unnecessary to the protection of a valid state interest.[10]

A 1971 decision of a federal district court voided a 1953 Georgia law making membership in a labor union a misdemeanor for policemen. The State of Georgia tried to distinguish its law from the legislation struck down by the Atkins decision, pointing out that of all Georgia employees only policemen were prohibited from union affiliation, in the interests of "an impartial police force." The court stated that this did not outweigh the obvious impairment of constitutional rights, holding the statutory provisions fatally overbroad.[11] In conjunction with the passage of state legislation during the 1960's, the right to organize and affiliate appears firmly established.

Municipal Employee Organizations

Municipal employee organizations are of several types: craft unions, general or industrial unions, professional associations, and independent unions and associations. Some unions and associations are affiliated with national or international parent organizations, such as the AFL-CIO or NEA, and others remain independent or cooperate with similar type associations in some sort of loose confederation, such as the Assembly of Government Employees (AGE). Some are composed solely of municipal or federal employees; others are combinations of state, municipal, and federal employees. Most comprise solely public employees, but a few organizations also have a membership that includes employees in private industry. Among these "mixed unions" are the Service Employees International Union, the Laborers International Union, the International Brotherhood of Teamsters, and some 25 others.

American Federation of State, County, and Municipal Employees

Probably the fastest growing and most influential union in the municipal service is AFSCME, claiming a membership of almost 600,000, organized into 1,900 locals in 1971. It came into the field as an industrial-type union with broad jurisdiction over all city employees but teachers.

AFSCME evolved out of the Wisconsin State Administrative Association, established in 1932 with a membership of less than 100. Subsequently, under the leadership of Dr. Arnold Zander, the "Wisconsin Group" affiliated with the American Federation of Government Employees, an AFL affiliate whose jurisdiction over federal workers had been extended by the AFL to include state, county, and municipal employees. Functioning only briefly as a relatively autonomous unit of AFGE, AFSCME was granted its own charter in 1936 by the parent AFL, which feared defections to the rival CIO, which had been established in 1935 under the leadership of John L. Lewis. Within a year of receiving its charter from the AFL, a dissident faction of AFSCME, led by Abe Flaxer, established a rival organization, The State, County and Municipal Workers of America, and received a charter from the more militant CIO.

The vigor of the sharply competing AFSCME of the AFL and SCMWA of the CIO began to overshadow the small competing groups that had been functioning through political machines and acting as watchdogs of employee rights under the machinery of civil service systems. Members of older groupings drifted into the more powerful AFL and CIO unions, and AFSCME and SCMWA began to assume positions in many cities which no longer could be ignored and which resulted in informal but de facto bargaining.[12]

The progress of AFSCME was uneven. By 1950 it had attained a membership of some 68,000, nowhere fully organized, rarely recognized, and as one of its organizers has pointed out, "at worst harrassed, coerced, dismissed—or entirely ignored." Its strength was concentrated in a few state services; and lobbying, which especially suited the needs of state employees, rather than collective bargaining, was the order of the day.[13]

AFSCME's jurisdiction was broad, and its big break occurred in the cities, where it soon organized a wide range of municipal workers, from architects to zookeepers. Organized into locals, usually grouped into larger District Councils, AFSCME primarily operates on the municipal level. Its membership is roughly 70 percent white, 30 percent black, and 70 percent blue-collar and 30 percent white-collar.[14]

During the first decade of its existence, AFSCME's activities represented a compromise between conventional trade union objectives and union involvement in public policy questions, such as public power, navigation projects, prices, rents, and poll taxes.[15] Initially, AFSCME stressed support of the merit system and civil service legislation, relying heavily on lobbying to achieve its goals.

18

The right to strike was not renounced, but its use was deemed fatal to accomplishment of union objectives.[16]

Under the new leadership of Jerry Wurf, who assumed the presidency after a bitterly contested election in 1964, AFSCME questioned the adequacy of merit systems, stridently proclaimed its right to strike, accelerated its organizing efforts, and stepped up both its political and its collective bargaining roles.

The differences between Wurf and his predecessor, Arnold Zander, were rooted, not in the basic philosophy of the role of public employee unions, but more in style of leadership. Zander had built the organization from scratch into a national union of 220,000 members with locals throughout the country. He strongly supported collective bargaining and the use of the strike as an instrument of last resort. He ardently believed in the international character of the labor movement and represented the American movement in international conferences. He encouraged AFSCME's role in the Public Service International, a federation within the non-Communist wing of the international labor movement.[17] Zander also invested substantial union funds in housing projects for AFSCME members.

Jerry Wurf believed that these activities distracted the union's attention from the more pressing need to expand the organization and improve working conditions in American local government services. He also questioned the economic soundness of the housing program. His style was more vigorous and forceful than Zander's. Taking full advantage of the widespread emergence of collective bargaining and the demands by militants in the local affiliates to "catch up" with the economic advances of unionists in industry, he accelerated organizing, bringing AFSCME membership claims in 1971 to nearly 600,000.

AFSCME remains active in the Public Service International. Far from being uninterested in foreign affairs, Wurf openly criticized aspects of American foreign policy and openly differed with the positions of the AFL-CIO leadership. Nevertheless, by 1971 he had led AFSCME to a sufficiently important role in organized labor to be elected to a place on the AFL-CIO's Executive Council.

By 1971, AFSCME had concluded more than 1,200 collective bargaining agreements and had achieved exclusive recognition in a number of major cities. In 1966 the union's power and growth had already prompted *Business Week* to proclaim: "The one-time 97 pound weakling of the labor movement...is rapidly forcing a showdown over the future of collective bargaining and strikes in the public sector."[18] From 1960 to 1970, AFSCME had advanced from being the nineteenth largest AFL-CIO affiliate to sixth position. Its almost geometric progression of growth, national scope, and potential may possibly make it the largest single unit within the AFL-CIO within a decade.

At the meeting of the Academy of Political Science of Columbia University in April 1970, AFSCME President Jerry Wurf espoused federal legislation governing local government employer-employee relations. He declared that such legislation could become a Magna Charta for local government employees, doing for them what the National Labor Relations Act had done for employees in private industry.[19] This proposal was criticized in some quarters as promoting undesirable overcentralization and threatening to set up a lowest common denominator standard that might eliminate the gains local government employees had achieved in several states.

The next year Wurf clarified his position regarding federal legislation:

> I have trouble understanding those who support collective bargaining for public employees but oppose a national law providing for it. There should be no more difference between the job rights of a public works employee in Wisconsin and Virginia than there is between an aerospace worker in California and New York. The labor relations situation of public employees today is different in every city, county and state—not just between states. There is no more reason to justify fragmentation of labor relations between states and their cities and counties than there is to fragment any other system of dealing with problems on a national level.
>
> We are not asking for a federal takeover. It would be outrageous to take away from local units of government their rights and concerns. We are advocating a federal law that leaves the state and local government the authority to conduct labor relations....
>
> Our union's proposal for national legislation will permit a state to be master of its own fate and destiny so long as it has provided rights substantially equal to those included in the national law. If a state wanted to control its own arena of public sector labor relations, it could do so. The legislation provides for a uniformity of application, not for transfer of power....[20]

International Brotherhood of Teamsters

AFSCME, despite its great expansion, was not without serious competition and has been compelled to participate in several hotly contested representation elections with sister affiliates of the AFL-CIO as well as the IBT. The IBT has long been engaged in the public employee field as an independent industrial union, taking in all classes of workers, including clerks, sanitationmen, laborers, correction officers, sheriff's deputies, policemen and firemen, as well as professionals, including school principals, nurses, and physicians.

The teamsters have organized many municipal employees, attracted to the IBT because of its image of great power (1.9 million members in 1970). The IBT had a long history of ignoring jurisdictional lines, even before they were expelled from the AFL-CIO. Being outside the AFL-CIO, the Teamsters were further encouraged to ignore the jurisdictional claims of other unions and succeeded in organizing about 57,000 public employee members, mostly blue-collar workers.

Teamster's Local 237 in New York City, with 15,000 Department of Hospitals and Housing Authority employees, is the IBT's largest municipal affiliate. (Local 237's membership in 1971 comprised primarily Housing Authority employees. Originally, the organizing effort was designed to encompass both hospital and housing employees. AFSCME's organizing efforts have limited the extent of Teamster representation of hospital employees.) The second largest public employee affiliate is the powerful 12,000-member Uniformed Sanitationmen's Association of New York City, led by John DeLury.

In 1971 the IBT reported that nationwide it had established 170 locals comprising public employees, with 70 percent working for cities, towns, or villages. About 10 percent operated within county units. An additional 10 percent worked for special municipal authorities, such as housing, and state workers accounted for approximately 6 percent.

Several major work categories are involved: 28 percent perform sanitary services, 25 percent are engaged in street and highway work, 12 percent in noninstructional educational services, 10 percent in public welfare, and the remainder encompass the broad range of parks, police, fire, public utilities, hospitals, and transportation previously indicated. The aggressive efforts of the Teamsters to organize public employees at all levels of government continues unabated in 1972.

Laborers International Union

The Laborers International Union, established in 1903 under the aegis of the AFL, had 553,000 members in 1970, of whom 75,000 were engaged in public employment. Like the Teamsters, the Laborers organize all classes of workers but concentrate largely on blue-collar workers—50,000 of the LIU's 75,000 public employees are blue-collar, with the remainder involved in white-collar or service work. In the field of public employment its largest growth has occurred from 1963 to 1970.

As in the case of AFSCME, a large proportion, estimated at about 40 percent, of the LIU membership comprises blacks, Mexican-Americans, Puerto Ricans, and other ethnic minorities. The onetime "hodcarriers' union" remains largely a union of unskilled and semiskilled, many of whom are engaged in construction work.

Early in its history the LIU sought to organize city employees, particularly in the public works, water, and sewer departments. The present thrust of the union, previously considered craft oriented, is to become a general workers' union, "a haven for all sorts of blue-collar workers, including those in government."[21] Already having organized some state employees, the union established in 1970 a federal public service employees division, evidence of its efforts to broaden its jurisdiction. Besides providing bitter competition for AFSCME's attempts to organize black workers in the South, they have ranged far and wide—Pocatello, Idaho; Milwaukee, Wis.; Providence, Rhode Island; Philadelphia, Pa.; and Baltimore, Md.—in an aggressive campaign to organize public employees. The LIU has also utilized the merger technique to augment its membership. In 1968 it merged with the 60,000-member Post Office Mail Handlers Union. It is clear that just as the LIU has challenged AFSCME in local units, it will not hesitate to vie with the American Federation of Government Employees and the National Postal Union, which concentrate their organizing efforts on federal employees.

Service Employees International Union (SEIU)

The Service Employees International Union, another AFL-CIO affiliate, is apparently intending to make itself into a replica of AFSCME although, like the Laborers, it organizes both private and public workers. Known for many years as the Building Service Employees International Union, the SEIU had a membership of 435,000 in 1970 and claims that 150 of its 450 locals include 125,000 public employees. The BSEIU, chartered in 1921 by the AFL, always claimed jurisdiction over the maintenance, upkeep, cleaning, servicing, and operation of all public and private buildings. The changing of the name symbolized the expansion of its organizing horizons, although sister AFL-CIO affiliates have also claimed jurisdiction over social workers, police officers, court clerks, practical nurses, janitors, and service personnel recently organized by the SEIU.

As evidence of its renewed interest in public employees, the SEIU now publishes a magazine devoted to the interest of public employees, *SEIU Public Service News*. In the face of AFSCME opposition, it won election in July 1970 to represent 7,000 Los Angeles County Social Service Employees. That same year the SEIU also won bargaining rights for the Massachusetts State Department of Social Welfare Workers. In Boston the SEIU already represented more than 2,500 employees, including white-collar City Hall employees and public works and hospital employees. Like other AFL-CIO affiliates, the SEIU makes effective use of the merger route to increase its membership. It announced in 1971 its intention to merge with the 30,000 member Los Angeles County Employees Association, ending the latter's 60 years of independent existence. The SEIU is undoubtedly the second most powerful affiliate of the AFL-CIO presently engaged in organizing local public employees.

The SEIU also has a substantial federal membership, with 25,000 of its 125,000 public workers reputed to be federal employees. The federal segment of the SEIU consists of Post Office mail handlers and employees in some national parks.[22]

Transit Unions

The 135,000-member Transport Workers Union is not strictly a municipal employees' union, since most of its members, like those of the IBT, LIU, and SEIU, are not municipal workers. Most of its membership is involved in air, rail, and private mass transportation, with key locals in New York City, Philadelphia, and San Francisco. The rival Amalgamated Transit Union has strong locals in Boston, Detroit, and elsewhere.

In many instances these unions have become pace setters for municipal wage and working conditions. To some degree this is because unions whose membership consists primarily of employees of privately owned transportation systems do not have the same degree of inhibition against striking as do some public employee unions.

Craft Unions

The first municipal employee unions were the so-called craft unions, with members in both public and private employment. Until the upsurge in public employee organization, the craft unions, through their dominant position in the city central labor councils of the AFL, were the leading supporters of local government employees. Though largely outside the organized labor movement, they constituted a conscious and significant potential block of votes. Thus, the city workers and the politically active central labor councils found their mutually friendly relations useful.

A number of international craft and industrial unions beyond those already discussed played a significant role in adding to the total strength of public employee units. Among the organizations were the International Association of Machinists and Aerospace Workers, the International Union of Operating Engineers, the International Brotherhood of Electrical Workers, the United Mine Workers, the United Brotherhood of Carpenters and Joiners of America, and the United Association of Journeymen and Apprentices of the Plumbing and Pipefitting Industry of the United States and Canada.

Units such as these have members in both public and private employment, but accurate figures as to the public employee segment are not available. The overall importance of their role, however, cannot be overlooked; and in particular cities' individual unions on occasion played a major role in public employee unionism.

Independent Associations

The labor-affiliated unions' most serious competition comes from the independent state Civil Service Employees Associations, many of which are branching out into the county and municipal fields. Such associations exist in 37 states, with memberships ranging from a few hundred in Florida to 110,000 in California and 170,000 in New York, where the CSEA was founded in 1910.

These associations lay great stress on their independence. Their freedom from ties with organized labor, they claim, gives them the advantage of freedom of action without the interference or supervision of an international union outside the state. "Every cent of CSEA dues," declared the New York CSEA, "is spent on representing you—not on the international in Washington, D.C."

The affiliated public service labor unions characterize the independents as "company unions." Jerry Wurf, President of AFSCME, has castigated them as "weak and gutless and ready to jump through management's hoop," despite their "Madison Avenue efforts" to convince public employees that they have changed into militant organizations.

Nearly all of them admit supervisory or management officials to membership. In 1962 an investigator, in attempting to check the validity of the company union charge, asked, "Have there been any attempts by management to guide or influence the policies or programs of your association?" Four replied affirmatively.[23]

The unions play up the company union image of the independents. Despite the latter's attempts to emphasize their nonunion character, unions push their hand in a manner not unlike that in which the AFT has been pushing the NEA. The two largest and most influential NEA groups, in New York and California, repealed their no-strike pledge in 1967 and 1969, respectively. In 1971 the Maryland Classified Employees Association, comprising 22,585 mostly state employees, also voted to drop the organization's no-strike policy. The California group took the action during a struggle with Governor Ronald Reagan over slashing funds for a pay increase for California employees. The New York Association has also met the union challenge, in literature addressed to prospective members declaring: "Join New York State's No. 1 Civil Service *Union*, CSEA [emphasis added]."

The New York Association admits all state employees, including department commissioners and judges of the highest court. It maintains close relationships with legislative leaders and elected officials and has been able to maintain these good relations regardless of changes in party control in the executive or legislative branches. For years the President of the New York CSEA had his office in the state capitol, and it remained there as administrations came and went until criticisms from many sources brought about its removal to its own elaborate quarters, across the street from the capitol grounds.

Through the effective use of traditional public employee lobbying and other political activity, the New York CSEA has been able to produce a record of outstanding accomplishment for state employees, bringing salaries and benefits close to the highest level of any branch of the public service, until the federal government began to close the gap in the mid-1960's. For a considerable period of time association pamphlets, leaflets, and membership information were included in the material given every new employee entering the service. The association also introduced a very attractive group insurance program, acceptance of which is voluntary and not covered by organization dues.

Traditionally, the New York CSEA eschewed collective bargaining until state legislation endorsed the process. The association now attempts to take full advantage of the new tool. Very soon after the right of public employees to bargain collectively was legally recognized in New York in 1967, the Governor moved to conclude an agreement with the CSEA covering all 130,000 of the state's employees. After vigorous protests from AFSCME, which appealed to the State Public Relations Board and the courts, the state employees were divided into five bargaining units: correctional; administration; institutional; professional, scientific and technical; and operational.

Following a whirlwind campaign carried on through its official organ, the *Civil Service Leader*, and direct appeals, the CSEA won bargaining rights for four of the five units by substantial majorities. It lost in the correctional unit, the only one where AFSCME had a comparatively long record of activity.

Although most of the state associations still adhere largely to their traditional methods of lobbying and political action, in states where collective bargaining is recognized they are turning to it as an additional tool in their chests.

Most of the state and many local associations are now members of a loose confederation, the Assembly of Government Employees.[24] In 1969 the 32 state affiliates reported a total membership of approximately 500,000. In 1971 the AGE claimed a membership of "almost 600,000." Its President, Thomas C. Enright, Executive Secretary of the strong Oregon Association, which like several others has made effective use of collective bargaining, declared:

> You will be hearing more about AGE in the future because this organization is going to grow not only by affiliation of more state associations but also by the addition of local government and Federal groups. We feel we are much better equipped by attitude and experience than others to represent public employees and that developments in the representation field in recent years and at present justify this confidence.

Many of the AGE affiliates are strong and experienced organizations. Their present growth is in the local government field, where they have frequently defeated labor-affiliated unions in contests for representation as bargaining agents. This has been the case in several New York State counties. In California over half of the municipal employees belong to independent associations, which are active in at least 250 of California's 373 city governments.[25]

On the whole, the independent city associations may prove to be a fruitful and ready-made field for absorption by AFSCME and other labor-affiliated organizations. For example, in 1971 the executive boards of the 20,000-member Hawaii Government Employees Association and the 8,000-member United Public Workers of Hawaii voted in separate actions to affiliate with AFSCME. As

26

previously indicated, the SEIU absorbed a county association in Los Angeles. Undoubtedly, it was the inclination of some independent associations to merge with unions that motivated a spokesman for AGE to issue a statement in 1971 urging caution before sailing on the sea of "industrial unionism." The statement likened the mergers to shotgun marriages and advised the associations to think beyond the "honeymoon period."

Where the growth of state associations since 1964 has been most substantial, it has been in large measure due to the expansion of state employment in the more populous states such as Oregon, Washington, Ohio, and Maryland. In some of the small states, such as Utah and Nevada, where state employment is limited, percentage growth of the associations has been spectacular.

City associations, while having a numerical strength of 241,655 in 1968, have little of the organizational strength of state groups. (In 1971 the BLS reported the existence in 1968 of 662 municipal employee associations. The Middle Atlantic region reported 140; the East North Central 141; and the Pacific Area 217. These figures are changing rapidly as some associations merge with unions.) Most are composed of local police and fire fighter associations, which are not members of the international. Their white-collar membership is small and has been rather easy pickings for the International Association of Fire Fighters in particular. Professional and technical membership, while a little larger than the white-collar element, is also small. The likelihood is that as unionization grows the fire fighters will be absorbed into the IAFF, which now includes the overwhelming membership of the occupation.

Professional Unions and Associations

The IAFF chartered by the AFL claimed a membership of 150,000 in 1970, organized into 1,550 local craft unions representing more than 90 percent of the nation's uniformed fire fighters. In 1919 the IAFF had only 82 locals. Its membership has grown threefold since World War II. Organizing is easier for it than for most other unions, since fire fighters throughout the country have generally organized themselves and the IAFF representatives' main effort has been to negotiate the affiliation of these groups.

Unlike most unions, the IAFF does not exclude supervisory personnel, admitting Battalion Chiefs, Lieutenants, and other officers and usually excluding only the Fire Chief. (In the case of Michigan, the IAFF does not exclude Fire Chiefs in about one third of the cities. A decision of the Nebraska Court of Industrial

27

Relations in 1971 required that Battalion Fire Chiefs be excluded from units representing fire fighters. The Nebraska Supreme Court, the state's highest tribunal, went so far as to exclude Fire Captains and Lieutenants from fire fighter units.)

Originally organized in the 1880's as fraternal and benefit societies, because fire fighters were not considered good insurance risks, the fire fighter groups became more militant as city officials began to oppose further attempts to organize through the IAFF. As a result, some 30 strikes, mass resignations, and lockouts took place in 1918 and 1919. In the wake of the Boston police strike, militancy subsided, and a no-strike clause was inserted in the IAFF constitution in 1930. Despite the more conservative stance assumed by the IAFF during the 1950's, it continued to secure considerable gains by lobbying and de facto negotiations.

With the upsurge of militancy in the 1960's in most employee groups, the IAFF rescinded its no-strike policy in 1968. Deeply concerned with the fact that fire fighters have suddenly become the target of snipers and rock throwers, the IAFF has demanded more protective equipment and protection while steadfastly opposing any consolidation of police and fire fighters into safety officers or the arming of firemen.

Police groupings are more fragmented than those of the fire fighters. Unlike the fire fighters, rank and file patrolmen have zealously guarded their freedom from interference by higher police officials. Higher police officers —Sergeants, Lieutenants, Detectives, Captains, etc.—very often have their own associations, which function vis-a-vis their superiors in much the same way as do the rank-and-file organizations. (In large cities, such as New York, fire fighters in the higher ranks also maintain separate bargaining units, which are also affiliated with the parent IAFF.)

The oldest and one of the largest national groupings of police is the Fraternal Order of Police, with 620 local lodges in 19 states and a membership in excess of 81,000 in 1971. Primarily concerned with police pensions, improved working conditions, and greater professionalism, the FOP, like the IAFF, does not exclude supervisory officers.

In 1954, rank-and-file groups, suspicious of the role of officers, established a rival organization, the International Conference of Police Associations, which had a purported membership of 142,000 in 1971. Serving mainly as the Washington, D. C. representative of local police associations, it is a tough-talking organization. At its national convention in July 1970, its Vice-President, head of the New Jersey State Police Benevolent Association, declared:

We carry guns in defense of our lives and we will use them. . . .We are not going to stand idly by and watch our brother policemen murdered in the streets. Unless the governing bodies of municipalities look at the situation. . .and the judiciary gets tough with criminal elements, we have no alternative but to meet force with complete and superior force. . . .I don't believe in indiscriminate shooting, but we're going to protect lives and property.[26]

Until recently there has been little effort on the part of police to affiliate with the organized labor movement, excepting scattered AFSCME locals totaling 11,000 policemen in 1971 in 68 cities and even fewer locals affiliated with a few other unions, such as the IBT, in 14 cities. In 1970 two rival movements were underway to form a national police union, largely split over the issue of affiliation. John Cassese, formerly head of New York City's Patrolmen's Benevolent Association, has attempted to organize a national police union. The newly organized International Brotherhood of Police Officers has succeeded in organizing 8,000 of the nation's 400,000 policemen. The IBPO claimed the formation of 56 locals in 32 states as of March 1971. The likelihood is that for some time to come the police organizations will maintain both the relative independence and associational contacts and cooperation implicit in the work of the FOP and ICPA. In 1971 the AFL-CIO rejected the IBPO's request for a charter of AFL-CIO affiliation.

The American Nursing Association represented 205,000 members in 1969, about one third of the nurses in both private and public hospitals. A loose amalgam of state and local affiliates, the ANA was constrained to relax its no-strike policy or lose its hold on more militant affiliates, as exemplified by the New York and California units.

Another, more recently established professional association is the National Association of Social Workers, founded in 1955 by the merger of several groups, with a purported membership of 50,000 in 1968. Only a small proportion of social workers are organized, and those organized are often set up as independent local units, such as the Social Service Employees Union of New York City. Their survival rate has not been high and, as was the case with the SSEU, they have begun to merge into AFL-CIO affiliates such as AFSCME.

The undisputedly largest and most powerful professional association of municipal employees is the over 1-million-member National Education Association, with 50 state affiliates and approximately 8,000 local associations. Public school teachers constitute more than three quarters of the membership, which also includes an influential supervisory component known as the American Association of School Administrators.

The NEA is an association with strong roots in the educational establishment. For decades the NEA emphasized better schools, educational research, and increased professionalism. The organization gradually accepted "professional negotiations" backed by "professional sanctions," to meet the criticisms that had spurred the formation of a rival organization—the American Federation of Teachers, chartered in 1916 and affiliated with the AFL. By 1967 the NEA had announced the abolition of the Educational Policies Commission, which had been the ideological voice of both the NEA and its powerful AASA component. The same year, the NEA formally backed away from its position of a no-strike policy, finally endorsing officially the viewpoint of its National Secretary, who for nearly two decades had espoused the doctrine of "no contract, no work."

The formation of the AFT had been brought about largely as a result of complaints that the NEA was dominated by school administrators and had not forcefully sought to achieve long needed gains of its teacher component. The AFT has had its greatest success in large cities, including New York, Philadelphia, Boston, and Detroit. In 1970 its membership of approximately 175,000 constituted about 20 percent of the country's organized teachers.

The AFT is primarily a trade union for classroom teachers and thus excludes supervisory personnel, such as school principals and administrators, from membership. Nonetheless, in 1971 supervisory units in cities with a large AFT membership were seeking affiliation with the AFL-CIO, whereas administrative components of state educational associations were withdrawing to form separate supervisory units.

The AFT has stressed the use of collective bargaining, including the strike, but has not neglected political action. The NEA, in turn, to meet the competition, no longer shows disdain for the strike. The pressures of the urban educational crisis have forced the AFT to place more stress on professionalism.

While the competition between the two groups remains intense, as illustrated by the AFT's victory over the NEA by a vote of 690 to 684 in Springfield, Mass., in 1970, contacts to consider a merger have been initiated. In 1969 the first local merger of the NEA and the AFT affiliates took place in Flint, Mich., followed by Los Angeles in 1970 and New Orleans in 1971 and New York in 1972. While a temporary moratorium was declared by the AFT on future mergers, in 1972 the negotiating committees of the AFL-CIO United Teachers of New York and the NEA's New York State Teachers

Association reached agreement on the merger of the two organizations. The pending merger will make the proposed unit the largest state teacher organization in the country. The likelihood is that this tendency will assume national dimensions. Should the NEA and AFT unite on a national level, the power base of teachers would be enlarged, and the possibility of a nationwide teacher's strike within the next decade is not to be ignored.

Inter-Union Rivalries: The Race to Organize

Unions operate in a competitive market, and the race to organize and to maintain and increase organizational strength produces unusual conflicts and rivalries. The rivalry is not restricted to the struggle between affiliated unions and professional associations or independent groups but extends to competition between affiliates of parent international organizations. One high union official of the IBT, when interviewed by the authors, indicated that more money was spent by his organization in fighting rivals within the parent organization than in meeting external competition. In 1968 the President of AFSCME also bluntly declared to us, "There are other unions that have a hungry eye on our jurisdiction—unions inside the AFL-CIO and outside and a lot of nonunion associations."

On occasion the rivalry is settled by cooperative arrangements. In 1967 the Michigan Conference of Teamsters concluded a no-raiding agreement with AFSCME District Council 77. Each side agreed to withdraw pending court appeals, the Council specifically recognized Teamster jurisdiction over certain categories of workers, and the Teamsters agreed not to compete for, encourage, or represent all workers who were not specified as Teamster employees.

Similarly, in New York City in May 1968 AFSCME District Council 37 signed a "nonaggression pact" with Teamsters Local 237, permitting each union to concentrate on organizing specific groups of employees. Significantly, the New York agreement prohibited both parties to the pact from conducting campaigns in a manner that would "impugn the motives or attack the character of either union, its officers, representatives, or members." The accord also provided for joint legislative action, consultation, and agreement to respect the bargaining relationships each had with the city.

One consequence of AFSCME's broad jurisdictional claims has been its numerous disputes with unions, such as the Teamsters, that make equally broad claims. The struggle between Teamsters Local 237 and District Council 37 prior to the nonaggression pact was one of the longest, bitterest, and most important interunion battles that ever occurred in New York. From the standpoint of expenditures alone, during the period 1957 to 1968 the two organizations spent an estimated total of more than $5 million fighting each other for a dominant position in the Department of Hospitals. The contest was not always conducted by Marquis of Queensbery rules, with charges of vote buying, ballot box irregularities, and strong-arm tactics being hurled by both parties.

The organization that secures recognition constantly faces a challenge to its dominant position. For example, in 1961, after District Council 37's initial organization of both professional and nonprofessional employees in New York City's Welfare Department, a dissident faction organized as the Social Service Employees Union, an independent association. A bitter battle ensued between the two organizations until the SSEU bested AFSCME in a representation election, winning bargaining rights for nonsupervisory categories. The subsequent militant policies of the SSEU motivated a return to AFSCME's fold in 1969, when the City eventually was able to counter successfully the erratic though troublesome antics of the independent group of social workers.

AFSCME has also had strong competition from sister affiliates of the AFL-CIO, despite the Internal Disputes Plan of the parent organization, established to ameliorate such internecine conflict. In San Diego, Calif., AFSCME charged that the Service Employees International Union had encouraged an independent association to solicit AFSCME's members. In this instance, which occurred in 1968, the Impartial Umpire upheld AFSCME's claims and rejected the SEIU defense that its actions were justified because the bargaining relationship was threatened by a Teamster affiliate.

The same year, AFSCME also had problems with the SEIU in Illinois, but in this case the Impartial Umpire ruled that the SEIU could enroll former members of AFSCME. AFSCME had contended that unions in cities lacking a legal basis for exclusive recognition should be accorded protection against raiding by sister affiliates, since unions with exclusive recognition are protected under the Internal Disputes Plan.

AFSCME also had its problems with the SEIU in Gary, Ind., in 1971; the Impartial Umpire ruled that the former had "upset established collective bargaining relationships" of a sister affiliate by attempting to sign up secretaries of a school district already represented by the SEIU. Still another decision, in a Manchester, N. H., school district, went against AFSCME on the grounds that during a previous decade of activity it had never established a collective bargaining relationship for custodians. The Umpire ruled that the SEIU was free to organize the custodians and push for recognition.

A prior position of strength is, on occasion, insufficient to stem the tide of competition. AFSCME had long held a position of strength in Milwaukee. Early in 1971 the LIU represented only 260 garbagemen of the Sanitation Department's 1,000 plus workers. The LIU subsequently achieved the status of joint representation of the department's personnel, along with the UBT, who represented drivers who had been transferred to the sanitation department in a reorganization move, and AFSCME. Within six months a contract dispute erupted. As a result of a new election, the LIU defeated both AFSCME and the UBT, becoming the sole representative of the unit.

Just as AFSCME has had to compete with the LIU, it has also had disputes with the International Union of Operating Engineers. In one case the Impartial Umpire upheld AFSCME's right to organize in the Buildings and Grounds Department of the school system in Washington, D. C. Likewise, AFSCME has also faced strong competition, particularly in New York State, from the independent CSEA units, with survival depending on a continuous struggle for success after success. With the entry into the field of a federal union, NAGE, which extended its jurisdiction to state and local employees in 1970, it is likely that AFSCME's problems, especially with police units, will be further complicated. Already, at least eight units of the International Brotherhood of Police Officers have affiliated with NAGE.

The competition between the AFT and the NEA has deep roots. During the early decades of this century, Professors of Education in leading universities abetted the pleadings and threats of many school administrators and boards of Education that joining a union was unprofessional. (There were exceptions, such as John Dewey and George Counts, who espoused dual membership, in both the NEA and AFT, to establish a countervailing voice to the conservative NEA.)

Beginning in the 1960's, the AFT, with the assistance of Walter Reuther of the UAW, sought to recruit teachers and other professional school personnel to infuse new blood into the labor movement. The opening wedge was the recognition of the United Federation of Teachers, an AFT affiliate, as the exclusive bargaining agent of New York City teachers. The word "power," which had been taboo in educational circles, was soon accepted as the main tool of collective bargaining. The UFT and other affiliates of the AFT used large cities as their power base. The NEA was viewed as the chief obstacle to collective bargaining: apathetic, lethargic, inconsistent, and unable or unwilling to confront School Boards.

The AFT was the gadfly, chiding the NEA for its cautiously worded pledge of 1967 to support striking NEA affiliates. The AFT urged a militant acknowledgment that a strike threat was advantageous, and scorned "professional negotiations" and "sanctions," calling them ineffectual substitutes for free collective bargaining. Segregated locals in the South, long tolerated by the NEA, were denounced by the AFT, which further accused the NEA of having failed to dramatize the financial plight of the teacher. In 1967 the AFT audaciously called for a $5,000 raise in salary for each school teacher and sought the support of substitute teachers, stating that the long-term substitute should be paid the same amount as other teachers.

The AFT stridently demanded to know the role of the NEA in the work of the U.S. Central Intelligence Agency, charging that the NEA was linked to the Vernon Fund, allegedly a creation of the CIA. The NEA, maneuvered into a defensive position, counterattacked, rejecting any insinuations that it had been an unwilling handmaiden to the CIA. They not only took strong measures against segregated NEA chapters in the South, they urged that ghetto children be transported into white suburban schools, even if it meant crossing state boundaries. Reversing a position taken in 1964, two commissions of the NEA called for an end to restrictions on federal aid to public schools. It recommended that such aid be used for such purposes as the states saw fit, including teacher salaries.

In short, both the NEA and the AFT acted like politicians trying to outbid the competition. A review of the publications of the AFT and the NEA from 1967 to 1970 shows that each is deeply concerned with demonstrating how they have won representation elections. Despite the "war communique" flavor of the journals, the power structures of the two organizations have moved closer together. The most recent efforts of the NEA to demonstrate its militancy are implicit in its call upon the AFT to support a federal law authorizing teacher strikes after all efforts to resolve teacher impasses have failed. The AFT released a salary survey in 1971 to show that the pay rates of its members in seven AFT-represented cities were higher than in the seven largest cities represented by NEA affiliates.

Interorganizational competition is not restricted to the race to organize more employees. Nonetheless, sufficient membership is the major source of the political and financial strength necessary to enter the fray.

Affiliation and the Limits of Labor Solidarity

Civil service unions have sought affiliation with the organized labor movement as represented by its national center, the AFL-CIO, for both ideological and practical reasons.

Civil servants affiliate with the labor movement to demonstrate that instead of constituting a class apart from other workers, as public employers have traditionally contended, they regard themselves as wage earners who happen to earn their livelihood in public employment rather than in private jobs. They therefore consider themselves a part of the mainstream of American labor. Historically, affiliation with organized labor has served as a declaration of independence from official domination of their organizations. It is a demonstration of self-reliant action to defend and improve working conditions and a departure from the "stand-in" tactic of achieving organizational objectives by currying favor with the employing authorities.

The practical reason for affiliation is that it enhances the power of the unions and brings to their support the influence and political prestige of the organized labor movement. As one trade union officer of a public employee organization put it:

This union's operation has always been a bona fide trade union in terms of collective bargaining, political rights, and political action. We are part of a trade union movement. We're no different from any other union in the movement. We should take our place along with other unions, working with them, because we have in many of our people much to contribute to the rest of the movement.

Yet the labor movement is actually far from a monolith acting on the principle of "labor solidarity" in support of all affiliates. Individual private industry unions have at times given support to public employee unions. During the Cincinnati public workers' strike in the winter of 1970, "support for the strike," according to AFSCME, ran high among Cincinnati-area trade unionists. (See Chapter 3 for a detailed discussion of *The Cincinnati Strike*.)

In New York, the central labor body donated $50,000 to striking school teachers in 1967 in the face of protests from many black unionists that ended in a sit-in in the office of the President of the city central body.

During the various building service workers' strikes against the landlords in New York, the sanitation union refused to cross the strikers' picket lines to collect garbage. Although sanitation workers had no dispute with their city employer, their refusal to cross the private workers' picket lines brought added inconvenience and hardship to thousands of workers and their families, already inconvenienced by the strike.

The city central bodies, like the state Federations of Labor, are primarily political organizations, in which the interests of many unions are often in conflict. Thus, in Detroit, where the Wayne County AFL-CIO was dominated by the building trades components and the United Auto Workers, before its withdrawal from the AFL-CIO, it had not been possible to win support for the demand by a public union, particularly AFSCME, for a written contract.

The same situation that prevailed in Detroit also exists in other cities. The basic conflict arises when a city executive is "pro labor" toward private sector unions, a "hard-boiled employer" where his city employees are concerned, especially with respect to their economic demands.

Written contracts are not usually opposed on principle. Mayors have been willing to grant them when they are confined to grievance procedures and working conditions not having a substantial impact on the budget. But where wages and hours are concerned, some mayors are tough employers, interested in keeping down the tax rate. This is especially the case in cities where home-owning is prevalent and apartment-dwelling still exceptional. Increased public payrolls hit the private worker's pocketbook and lead him to be uninterested in or opposed to higher public payrolls. To private sector workers represented in city labor councils or state federations of labor, public officials are politicians with power to give or withhold "plums" on matters of interest to private sector employees, i.e., public contracts for building or purchase of supplies. This helps create a favorable atmosphere for private sector unionism. To public employees on the other hand, the public official is an employer, to be pressed like other employers for improved working conditions, which are often costly.

In New York, the 12-day transit strike of 1965 resulted in losses of pay for poorer middle-class and working-class New Yorkers who could not get to their jobs and a subsequent increase in transit fares. Four years later, another generous settlement resulted in another raising of transit fares, from 20 to 30 cents. The question might well be raised as to how long the users of busses and subways will continue to support the demands of the organized transit employees, which directly affect their living costs.

There is no overriding working-class interest in the United States, where there has been little implemented tradition of labor solidarity. Like Fourth of July orators, national labor leaders give the notion of labor unity due lip service, but fail to practice it as an operative principle. Conversely, officials of individual unions attack one another in public over differences in policy and over their respective "jurisdictional rights" but collaborate for their own ends. This is illustrated by the withdrawal from the CIO of the UAW, under the late Walter Reuther's leadership, and its strange alliance, in a rival labor federation, with the IBT, which was expelled from the AFL-CIO for corruption.

The cleavage in the ranks of the central labor body has been especially marked in Detroit, where the administration of former Mayor Cavanaugh turned a prolabor face to the private sector but played the part of unyielding employer to the city employees. The private sector delegations supported the mayor in his attitude toward them and assumed a modified "couldn't care less" role toward their publicly employed brethren. The following comment by one AFSCME officer expresses the reality of the situation:

> I don't get know much support beyond moral support we could get from the other unions. I've been in the labor movement long enough to know and understand that you fight your own battles. We're going to bring the bacon home for ourselves.

Notes

1. In October 1970, civilian public employees numbered 13 million. Of this total, more than 10.1 million were state and local employees, of which more than 7 million were local employees. See *Public Employment in 1970*, U.S. Department of Commerce, Bureau of the Census, GE 70, No. 1, issued April, 1971. It is anticipated that state and local employment will almost double, reaching a figure of 13.8 million, by 1980.
2. See *Labor Management Policies for State and Local Government*, Advisory Commission on Intergovernmental Relations Report A-35, Washington, D.C., September, 1969, p. 5; Everett M. Kassalow, "Trade Unionism Goes Public," *The Public Interest*, No. 14 (Winter, 1969), 122; David L. Pearlman, "The Surge of Public Employee Unionism," *The American Federationist* (June, 1971), pp. 1-6.
3. One interviewee drew a parallel between the AFL's prior pattern toward agricultural workers in the period 1919 through 1936, during which it had no interest in organizing "unorganized peasants" and its attitude toward public employees.
4. The ACIR report cited in Note 2 states that in 1968, 52 percent (1.4 million) of all federal executive branch employees belonged to unions, whereas only 9.6 percent (890,000) of state and local government employees belonged to affiliates of national unions. These figures do not reflect the million plus members of the National Education Association or the members of numerous other unaffiliated organizations which exist as associations.

5. The figures are changing almost daily. In a report issued in August 1971, the Bureau of Labor Statistics reported that public employee unions represented 2,317,000 government workers—1,370,000 in federal agencies, and 949,000 in state and local units. Employee associations in state and local units represent more than a million additional employees. See BLS *Municipal Employee Associations*, August, 1971.

6. See Sterling D. Spero, *Government as Employer* (New York: Remsen Press, 1948), pp. 2 and 16-42 for a detailed description of this issue.

7. Charles S. Rhyne, *Labor Unions and Municipal Employee Law* (Washington, D.C.: National Institute of Municipal Law Officers, 1946), p. 150.

8. City of New York, *Report on a Program of Labor Relations for New York City Employees*, 1957.

9. See AFSCME v. Woodward, 406 F. 2d. 137 (8th Cir., 1969); *McLaughlin v. Tilendis*, 398 F. 2d. 287 (7th Cir., 1968); *Keyishian v. New York Regents*, 385 U.S. 589 (1967); and *Reports of the Committee on State Labor Law, Report of American Bar Association Committee on State Labor Law*, Chicago: American Bar Association, 1969, 1970, 1971.

10. *Atkins et. al. and IAFF v. City of Charlotte*, 296 F. Supp. 1068 (1969).

11. *Melton et. al. v. City of Atlanta*, 324 F. Supp. 315 (1971).

12. SCMWA also had its factional split-offs. The remaining units merged with the United Federal Workers of the CIO to form the United Public Workers, which was subsequently expelled from the CIO for alleged Communist activities. The CIO later formed the Government and Civic Employees Organizing Committee, which in 1955 affiliated with AFSCME, becoming the first merger in the "new" combined AFL-CIO labor movement.

13. Al Bilik, Assistant to the President of AFSCME in an interview with the authors.

14. Article II, Section 1A, p. 4, of the AFSCME Constitution reflects the breadth of jurisdiction: nurses, dieticians, street cleaners, grave diggers, psychiatrists, and librarians carry AFSCME membership cards. A 1967 census revealed that 47 percent of the membership worked for municipalities, 28 percent for states, and 10 percent for counties, with the remainder working for school districts, universities, and special authorities.

15. See Morton R. Godine, *The Labor Problem in the Public Service* (Cambridge, Mass.: Harvard University Press, 1959), p. 130.

16. See the statements to this effect of AFSCME President Arnold Zander in *Public Management*, September, 1937, p. 260.

17. The PSI serves as an international forum for the exchange of ideas between public employees, and it studies and publishes materials related to civil service practices in scores of countries. It has regarded encouraging and assisting in the formation of free trade unions in developing countries as one of its most significant functions.

18. *Business Week*, December 3, 1966, p. 92.

19. Jerry Wurf, "The Revolution in Public Employment," *Proceedings of the Academy of Political Science*, Columbia University, April 1970, p. 143.

20. Remarks at the Secretary of Labor's Conference on State and Local

Government Relations, Washington, D. C., November 22, 1971.

21. *Wall Street Journal*, July 15, 1968.

22. See William J. Eaton, *A Look at Public Employee Unions*, (Washington, D. C.: Labor-Management Relations Service, 1970) for concise summaries of several principal employee organizations.

23. Joseph Krislov, "The Independent Public Employee Association: Characteristics and Functions," *Industrial and Labor Relations Review*, July, 1962.

24. A survey by the International City Managers Association indicated that in 1968 some 662 associations existed. The survey further indicated that one third of the associations were on the Pacific Coast. For a brief sketch of the general characteristics of independent associations, see Kenneth O. Warner and Mary L. Hennessey, *Public Management at the Bargaining Table* (Chicago: Public Personnel Association), 1967, pp. 28-31, 220-224.

25. Richard L. Harris, "Independent Municipal Employee Associations in California," in Kenneth O. Warner, ed., *Management Relations with Organized Public Employees* (Chicago: Public Personnel Association, 1963), pp. 194-202.

26. Cy Egan, "Police Talk Tough at Convention," *New York Post*, July 21, 1970.

3 The Evolution of Collective Bargaining in Selected Cities

The ways in which local governments organize for collective bargaining with their employees differ from place to place. While the mechanical or organizational arrangements have their importance, the essence of the arrangements actually lies not so much in the way in which the employing government is represented at the bargaining table as in the governmental structure, and in the politics and social fabric of the city, and in the legal basis of the bargaining system.

Philadelphia

When caught by a strike of unorganized employees in its Public Works Department early in 1939, both the City of Philadelphia and the striking employees found themselves in a quandary. There were no responsible employee representatives with whom the city could deal, and the employees had no responsible leaders to present their demands. Both sides urgently requested AFSCME to intervene in the dispute. The union's Local 222, responded immediately. It assumed leadership of the strike and quickly entered into negotiations with the city officials. The result was a formal collective agreement that remained in force on a year-to-year basis until 1944, when a new contract was concluded with AFSCME District 33. This contract expanded exclusive representation rights for Public Works Department employees and established a reformed grievance procedure providing for binding arbitration. The contract made wages a bargainable issue, at the same time stipulating that they were legally to be set by the budget ordinance: the contract provided that the union was to "present its wage requests to both the mayor and city council," who were "obliged to meet with the union to discuss their requests."

From Machine Politics to Professional Bargaining

Philadelphia had been governed for generations by an admittedly corrupt political machine. The city, in the words of Lincoln Steffens, was "corrupt and contented." According to Foster B. Roser, the city's Personnel Director,

> ...for 67 years prior to 1952, Philadelphia bore the dubious distinction of having probably the most discredited merit system of any large city in the United States. In spite of all the traditional civil service provisions, the system was completely emasculated by political influence and fraud.[1]

The citizens, however, were becoming restive under the old regime. A reform movement, using the Democratic Party as its instrument, was initiated in the late 1940's and finally brought about a dramatic political upheaval in the 1951 city election. Along with this reform victory, which elected Joseph Clark mayor, the electorate adopted a home· rule charter, effective January 1, 1952.

One of the charter's provisions authorized the introduction of labor relations program through the adoption of regulations by the Civil Service Commission. Pursuant to this authority, the Commission promulgated a regulation authorizing the Personnel Director to enter into collective bargaining agreements with AFSCME:

> *Authorization for Agreement With District Council 33, AFSCME, AFL-CIO.* The Personnel Director of the City of Philadelphia is . . . authorized to engage in negotiations and enter into agreements concerning wages, hours and working conditions with District Council 33, AFSCME, AFL-CIO, as collective bargaining agent for an appropriate bargaining unit or units of civil service employees, subject to the provisions of the Philadelphia Home Rule Charter and applicable regulations and Statutes.[2]

In accordance with the procedures outlined in the charter, the Personnel Director proposed for the Civil Service Commission's approval specific regulations embodying in substance provisions already negotiated with the unions. The first contract was negotiated under the new charter in 1953, and the contract was amended annually.

AFSCME Gains Exclusive Recognition and Modified Union Shop

Prior to 1956, District Council 33 had informal exclusive departmental representation rights with certain listed departments. In 1956 an agreement was signed whereby the city formally granted to District Council 33 exclusive bargaining rights for city agencies in which AFSCME members represented a majority status in the future. This agreement became effective January 1, 1957.

In February 1958 a "union recognition" clause was formally adopted whereby District Council 33 was recognized as the exclusive bargaining agent for the city as a whole, with the exception of supervisory personnel and the uniformed forces. The city had long maintained consultative relations with the fire fighters' local union and the local chapter of the Fraternal Order of Police. Every provision of the 1958 AFSCME contract, with exception of the exclusive bargaining clause, also appears in Philadelphia's Civil Service Regulations.

On April 4, 1961, Mayor Dilworth, who succeeded Clark, approved a City Council Ordinance which inaugurated a "modified union shop." For the purpose of union membership, the ordinance separated all city job classifications into mandatory, voluntary, and prohibited union membership groups.[3]

As a condition of employment, new employees in the mandatory category are obligated to join the union by the conclusion of their six-month probationary period. Employees in the mandatory category are permitted to withdraw from the union during the 15-day "escape period" between June 15 and June 30 of each year, providing they have been union members for at least six months. At the expiration of the escape period, the city guarantees maintenance of membership in the mandatory category for the remainder of the year.

Employees in the voluntary category can enter or leave the union at any time, and employees in the prohibited category are denied the right to union membership. Employees in the mandatory classification are primarily blue-collar workers; employees in the voluntary classification are mainly administrative, technical, and professional workers; and employees in the prohibited classification are supervisors and high-level administrators and the uniformed forces.

The Negotiating Team and the Mayor

The Philadelphia bargaining system has given the city the advantage of dealing with its general employees through a single union, rather than through a large number of bargaining agents as is the case in many cities. Although the pay provisions must be approved by the City Council in its budget ordinance, the nature of the bargaining process has been such as to make this practically a formality. A "family understanding" has grown up under which the agreement reached by the city's bargaining representatives and the union presents a united front to the City Council in behalf of their agreement.

Until 1971 the city's negotiating team consisted of the Personnel Director, the City Managing Director, the Director of Finance, and the Labor Relations Consultant. Before the early 1960's the Mayor, while kept informed of the proceedings, did not participate directly in negotiations. Since the mid-1960's the Mayor has chosen to serve as head of the city team after preliminary negotiations have been completed. This has altered the role of the appointed bargaining team, since the Mayor, for all practical purposes, has the power to commit the city. At the same time, however, the Mayor's presence has dominated the bargaining process and encouraged the other side of the table to ignore the appointed team and concentrate on the source of effective authority. It has also tended to politicize the bargaining process, at the expense of its earlier professional character.

With the end of the Clark-Dilworth era and the election of James H. Tate to the mayoralty in 1962, the tone of Philadelphia municipal government changed. Mayor Tate openly politicalized his relations with the public service unions.

In 1971 the city replaced its ex officio negotiating team with the Office of Labor Relations, headed by a director reporting to the Mayor.

Detroit

On July 23, 1965, Governor Romney of Michigan signed into law the Public Employment Relations Act of 1965 (PERA), thus amending the Hutchinson Act, which had been in effect since 1947.[5] The new Michigan law (1) applies to city, county, and school district em-

44

ployees but excludes state employees; (2) states that the public employer shall bargain collectively; (3) empowers the State Labor Mediation Board to handle procedures for representation petitions and disputes, mediation requests, fact-finding and unfair labor practices: (4) spells out unfair labor practices that apply only to public employers, including the refusal to bargain collectively with an exclusive bargaining representative; and (5) prohibits strikes by any public employee. The PERA is silent regarding unfair practices by unions.

Before the passage of the PERA the Hutchinson Act had also prohibited public employee strikes, but the punitive provisions of the Hutchinson Act demanded automatic dismissal whenever any public employee participated in a strike. Any striking employee could be rehired but only on the condition that his rate of pay could not exceed what he had received before the strike occurred. The PERA repealed the automatic dismissal penalties but retained the strike prohibition.

For 18 years prior to the passage of the PERA, approximately 48 labor organizations were dealt with in varying ways by the City of Detroit. The so-called bargaining pattern that existed between the city administration and the municipal labor organizations was dependent upon budgetary amd fiscal considerations. As the budget deadline approached, all of the labor organizations received notices to appear before the Review Committee set up by the Controller.

The employee organizations took advantage of the procedures at City Hall, which enabled them to appear before the Common Council and the Mayor at scheduled sessions. The labor groups, in the words of one union leader, "acting more as suppliants than as aggressive trade unions, merely indicated what they would like to receive in terms of improved wages, hours, and working conditions." The early stages in the evolution of collective bargaining were marked by a lack of rapport between management and labor, even though the city had "a working relationship" with the local employee organizations. By Common Council resolution, this included the check-off of dues in return for a small fee charged to the unions.

Establishment of the Labor Relations Bureau

In a systematic effort to stabilize municipal labor relations and establish machinery to implement the PERA, the City of Detroit enacted an ordinance in December 1965 establishing the Labor Relations Bureau and the post of Director of Labor Relations. The power and authority of the Director were defined as follows:

(a) To act as the agent of the city in matters within the scope of this ordinance.

(b) To have power to negotiate with duly accredited bargaining agents and units of city employees and make recommendations to department heads, Common Council and the Mayor.

(f) To have authority to act as the agent of the city in signing collective bargaining agreements subject to the approval of the Common Council and the Mayor as provided by the City Charter.[6°]

The ordinance, after describing the relationship between the Labor Relations Bureau and the other city departments, further provided:

> The *Corporation Counsel* or his designated assistant, the *City Controller* or his designated assistant and the *Secretary-Chief Examiner* of the *Civil Service Commission* or his designated assistant shall serve as an *advisory committee* to the director of labor relations.

The role of this advisory committee in the bargaining process, as management and civic leaders had predicted, proved a source of frustrating confusion. It trapped the Labor Relations Bureau and its Director in a crossfire of legal ambiguities, legislative-executive competition between the Mayor and the Common Council, and bureaucratic rivalries within the city administration.

In accordance with the provisions of the Detroit ordinance, all of the city's labor groups were to bargain with the Director of the Labor Relations Bureau. When an agreement was negotiated, the Director was to recommend it to the Mayor and Common Council for ratification. In effect, however, the Director and the members of the controversial "advisory committee" constituted the city's actual negotiating team.

With the passage of the 1965 state law and the municipal ordinance, the city, with assistance from the State Labor Mediation Board, proceeded to recognize 62 groups that represented approximately 21,000 out of the 27,000 city employees in some 40 departments. The Teamsters won city-wide recognition for truck drivers, and the International Union of Engineers and building trades unions were also recognized on a city-wide basis.

This extensive fragmentation of the organized labor force led the Director of Labor Relations to remark, "There aren't that many people or hours in the day to sit down with sixty-two groups." Yet organization in an umbrella-like coverage for all municipal employees presented no easy solution for the problem. In the words of one city official close to the situation:

If we do change an ordinance for something that a major union wants, it covers the whole city but the unions refuse to recognize this. It's a fearful job to try and bring sixty-two unions and organizations up to a level where they all think they're getting something individually.

A running dispute, sparked by the role assumed by the advisory committee, arose between the city unions, regarding the interpretation of the terms "power to negotiate" and "make recommendations" within the scope of the ordinance. In the words of the Labor Relations Director:

> The power of this particular department (Labor Relations Bureau) and myself is greatly limited. Living up to the Charter, the power of the Mayor, the Common Council and the department heads, they were only able to come up with a resolution forming our department to deal with unions across the bargaining table on the limitation that I would only be able to *negotiate* and *recommend*. My recommendations go back to the Common Council and to the Mayor.

One labor leader contends, however, that according to the ordinance establishing the Labor Relations Bureau the Director has the authority to negotiate a contract but that "he lacks the strong support at City Hall that is needed to get the advisory committee and the department heads into line."

Another factor undercutting the Director's authority to negotiate was the internal bureaucratic rivalries within the city administration. The department heads jockey with one another for favorable positions, thus stymieing the negotiations. These department heads, reluctant to surrender any of their authority or discretionary powers, keep pressuring the Mayor to tell the Director of Labor Relations to back off, at least as far as reaching any definitive agreement with the municipal labor groups is concerned.

In terms of governmental structure, the City of Detroit may be classified as a strong mayor-council form of municipal government. The Mayor possesses the power to appoint and remove his department heads without cause and to item-veto any acts of the Common Council although his veto may subsequently be overridden.

The Bargaining Contract Becomes a Political Issue

The major political issue of collective bargaining has been AFSCME's demand for a written contract with the City of Detroit. For AFSCME, as well as for other municipal labor organizations, the written contract is the symbol of legitimacy, acceptability, and equality with the municipal employer. According to the provisions of the PERA, if an agreement is reached, then, at the request of either party, the agreed-upon items must be included in a written agreement, ordinance, or resolution.

Negotiations between the City of Detroit and AFSCME "dragged on." In view of the above-mentioned provision, AFSCME could not legally demand a written contract until an agreement had been reached. The contention was over legal interpretations of the PERA provisions, union security, grievance procedure, and a management's rights section. The city's strategy has been to draw up first a general contract that would cover all of the basic municipal labor groups and then to draw up supplements to the general contract recognizing the peculiarities of the individual departments.

Administration officials repeatedly emphasized to the union negotiators that the City of Detroit was bound up with legal entanglements of charter provisions, the state law, municipal ordinances, and Civil Service Commission rules and regulations. From the union standpoint, the city officials were merely utilizing the legalistic approach as a device for rationalizing their reluctance to negotiate in good faith with the union and at the same time protecting themselves from an unfair labor practice charge under the provisions of the PERA.

AFSCME's leadership contended that the culprit responsible for the frustrating delay was Mayor Jerome Cavanagh. An AFSCME official commented thus on Cavanagh's attitude:

> Cavanagh would be the guy who would have to say yes; all of his appointees are here to take his word and run with it. He's not making any effort to finalize it; he really doesn't want to finalize. If an agreement is finalized, then the only issue is economics, and Cavanagh knows that people will fight over economics.

The issues of sovereignty, managerial prerogatives, and management's rights further impeded the signing of a written contract. It was evident that the city officials were fearful of being charged with "giving away the city" to the public employee organizations. Commenting on Detroit's "sovereignty syndrome,"a labor official pointed out:

> The city is so frightened that in every sentence they write their sovereignty in—as long as it doesn't conflict with the City Charter and other rules and regulations. They're not content with putting a management's rights clause in and saying, "Now that's it"; they want to put a management's rights clause in every section, paragraph and sentence.

48

In frustration the AFSCME decided to de-emphasize Detroit for a while and concentrate on seeking written contracts throughout the state of Michigan. An AFSCME leader thus defended the rationale for this strategy:

> We tried to be understanding with Cavanagh, that it was something new and that the city administration had to make a mental adjustment as well as an administrative adjustment. We really went through the rest of the state and said to ourselves, "Since they're playing around and there's all kinds of jurisdictional questions, let's concentrate on clearing up the rest of the state and then Detroit will have to fall into line as the pattern is set."

Another union official declared: "There is nothing wrong with the PERA or the bargaining process but that we've just run smack into a political situation in which everything Cavanagh touches has to turn into votes."

Before Mayor Cavanagh left office, a contract was signed governing working conditions, including overtime, but omitting the wage issue in the hope of better luck with a new administration.

The contract concluded with the new administration not only covered working conditions and wages but also contained a section dealing with a significant public policy issue, in which the city in effect pledged not to contract out work performed by civil servants.

Meanwhile, the issue of the committee had fallen into place. The committee has assumed a truly advisory role. The Bureau seeks the advice both of the committee as a group and of its individual members. The Bureau is well staffed with experts. It not only engages in high-level contract negotiations but extends its influence into the city's operating departments. It employs a number of staff members who have permanent assignments with the city departments. The Director thus describes its functions:

> Each man lives with and services approximately five or six city departments. He is available to the department heads. He guides and counsels with his assigned supervisors, and he works in concert with each department's personnel officer. His trouble-shooting abilities are continually brought into play. He plays an important role in each department's appearance at the bargaining table and a key role in his department's supplementary agreements. He is an important witness in labor disputes headed for mediation, fact finding, voluntary binding arbitration and now, under the amended Public Employee Relations Act, compulsory arbitration for police and fire fighting activities.

49

The Bureau as of 1971 was supervising the execution of 45 master agreements, covering all employees, and some 30 supplementary agreements applying individual provisions to various departments. Its functions extend to grievance cases from a given step through final appeal to the city's joint city-union Appeal and Review Board.

In short, the Bureau's influence permeates the labor relations activities of all the city services. In top-level negotiations, however, no economic proposal goes to the bargaining table without consultation with the Controller and responsible officials. The fact that it is an instrument of the elected city authorities is always recognized.

As in the case of other cities, the Labor Relations Bureau has its difficulties with the Civil Service Commission, which claims the sole right to set conditions for hiring and firing, and grant certain forms of union security.

The Director declared that the "duplication, claims of charter rights, past resolutions, and past practices of the Civil Service has created unexpected problems for Detroit."

In the contract referred to above, the Bureau, after a tussle with the Commission, succeeded in creating a new classification of sanitation laborers. It is the considered opinion of qualified observers that the Bureau is increasingly moving in the direction of assuming and taking to the table many functions that the Civil Service Commission now claims the right to exercise unilaterally.

The Labor Relations Director advises his colleagues in other cities to define clearly the true role of the Civil Service Commission and pass necessary resolutions to minimize jurisdictional conflicts. He also advises them to "keep elected officials insulated from bargaining table pressures and involvement."

Cincinnati

After years of rule by a typical city machine, bearing a Rupublican label, Cincinnati was formally liberated in 1942, when a reform movement known as the Charter Committee, under the leadership of Charles P. Taft, an independent Republican, won control of the City Council.

Adoption of City Wage Policy

Under Taft's leadership the City Council in 1948 adopted an ordinance giving city employees the right to be represented by unions and requiring the City Manager to deal with such unions.

Negotiation guidelines were provided. No mention was made of collective bargaining. The fixing of wages was to be guided by the prevailing-rate doctrine and salary scales were to conform as nearly as possible with a fixed ratio to union scales prevailing in private industry. These arrangements, largely informal, remained the city's labor policy until 1951.

In that year the City Council adopted a resolution, "Declaring a City Wage Policy," which formalized and extended the prevailing arrangements, in effect establishing a system of collective bargaining.[7] The resolution, however, neglected to define a union or to state whether a majority was required before a union achieved the right of representation. Nor did the resolution define the area in which the union could operate.[8]

By 1960 the policy of the city, set by ordinance, clearly established the right of employees to join a union of their own choosing and required management to deal with the unions.

Evolution of the Written Agreement

In 1960, as a result of a series of conferences between AFSCME and the city management, amendments to the 1951 policy resolution led to the signing of a written agreement. Under the new provisions a union, prior to receiving formal recognition was required to demonstrate to the satisfaction of the City Manager that it represented a majority of the employees in an "appropriate" unit. The appropriateness of the unit was to be determined by the City Manager. To obtain this "written memorandum of understanding," AFSCME agreed to exclude the following groups from the bargaining unit: (1) employees already represented by recognized organizations; (2) probationary employees; (3) personnel department employees; (4) confidential employees; and (5) supervisory employees above the first level. In addition, "collective bargaining" was defined as "the process whereby city employees, their unions and the City Manager and his designated assistants shall make every effort through negotiations to reach an agreement on wages and working conditions."[9]

Immediately after the agreement was signed, the City Manager issued a written statement of his union policies. In the introductory portion he defended his managerial prerogatives by limiting collective negotiations to those areas explicitly stated in the agreement:

> Willingness on the part of the administration to explain and to listen does not mean that the union is necessarily entitled to participate in

51

the decision-making process. Negotiation is proper in some areas; determination of these areas in a function of the written agreement. It is the opinion of the City Manager that formalization of our relationships with unions through the medium of a written agreement will help to clarify these areas of mutual concern. [10]

To assist municipal officials in interpreting the City Manager's policy, explicit ground rules were introduced into the negotiation procedures. The City Manager, under City Council policy, represents the City in all negotiations except those before independent boards and commissions. The personnel officer, who is responsible to the City Manager, conducts negotiations on city-wide issues, including all wage matters. Each department head is granted "full authority" to deal with unions on working conditions affecting the employees of his department. The results of these discussions may be reduced to writing, subject to approval by the Personnel Officer for "conformity with city policy."

The Issue of Managerial Prerogatives

Concerning managerial prerogatives, the City Manager admonished department heads "not to construe such a management responsibilities clause as providing a convenient escape from the responsibility of keeping union officials informed on matters affecting employees." In addition, the City Manager indicated that the administration will deal with "the single majority representative of the employees in any appropriate unit." In essence, AFSCME was granted exclusive recognition, thus preventing excessive fragmentation and eliminating interunion competition.

Copies of the City Manager's Policy, the resolution "Declaring a City Wage Policy," and the agreement itself were circulated to approximately 500 supervisory personnel. After attending some 30 odd meetings where the provisions of the agreement were explained in detail, the supervisors disseminated this information to their employees. As a result, the city labor policy is probably the best understood of all the personnel policies in Cincinnati. [11]

City Policies Under the Charter Party

Cincinnati has long a history of "nonpolitical" municipal government. The Charter Party succeeded largely in its objective of separating the admin—istative operations of the city from its political and legislative functions and strongly emphasized effective public management and professionalism through the establishment of professional personnel direction. This made the city ready to accept the concept of collective bargaining. Commenting on the evolution of collective bargaining in Cincinnati, a union official declared:

> There has been a gradual development of reasonably intelligent collective bargaining in Cincinnati. This development was slow but it was meaningful. This development did not require at any point since 1948 a strike in order to achieve another advance in collective bargaining rights. These things simply developed without political manipulation, without backdoor operating, and without the unnecessary demonstration of a threat of a strike. [12]

AFSCME's District Council 51 has exclusive bargaining rights for all municipal employees who were not represented by other unions at the time the 1960 agreement went into effect. The city also bargains collectively with the International Union of Operating Engineers. The building trades unions operate under a scale, determined many years ago by the City Council, that sets rates of pay at approximately 90 percent of comparable union wages prevailing in private industry. The Fraternal Order of Police and Firefighter's Association have parity legislation.

How Bargaining Proceeds

All in all, AFSCME negotiates on a city-wide basis for its entire membership: and then if there are inequities in a certain department or division, they are brought to the bargaining table individually. The union's negotiating committee consists of the Presidents of the local unions. The negotiating committee brings the city's offer back to the membership for ratification. Thus, the responsibility rests with the individual local union Presidents and not with the Director of District Council 51. When the negotiating committee makes a recommendation to the membership, it is their recommendation and not the Director's. The Director of the district council is appointed by an executive board elected by local union members.

Legislative-executive competition in employer-employee relations is less prevalent in Cincinnati than in Philadelphia or Detroit. This, no doubt, can be partially attributed to Cincinnati's "nonpolitical" city manager-council form of government and its "good government" political tradition. Another contributing factor is the favorable attitude toward collective bargaining of the City Council members, both individually and in terms of the policies of their

53

respective political parties. In short, bargaining has been removed from an area of contention between the political parties.

The impact of collective bargaining on local political institutions in Cincinnati has been minimal. Management is not normally faced with the problem of "selling" collective bargaining to a legislative body that has to pass on the final results. One city official explained that where the administration has reached agreement with an employee organization, no disputes have arisen. In his words:

> ...the legislative body has bought the agreement 100 percent; the only exceptions being when the administration also had to point out that revenues were not available and that the effective date of implementation was deferred either in whole or in part.

In Cincinnati the City Manager assigns the negotiating function to the Personnel Officer; however, the City Manager retains the final authority on what is or is not agreed to. From AFSCME's standpoint, the collective bargaining process suffers from a structural defect because the City Manager is "wearing two hats": he is the master of the budget, and he is, technically speaking, the chief negotiator. The union contends that the City Manager negotiates on the basis of what funds are available instead of the needs of the employees.

From a practical viewpoint this so-called structural defect in the bargaining process has not interfered with the Personnel Officer's authority to negotiate an agreement with the union. The Personnel Officer reports to the City Manager prior to the start of negotiations, gives him the results of the personnel department's studies, gives him an opinion of where the negotiations should end up, and receives broad guidelines from the Manager.

As Secretary of the Civil Service Commission, the Personnel Officer handles the routine administrative workload for the Commission, thus enabling him to funnel municipal employee problems to the Personnel Department or to the Civil Service Commission where required by statute.

Under Ohio law the Civil Service Commission has unlimited authority to determine whether a position is to be filled by promotion or by competitive examination. On the other hand, overall salary schedules are set through negotiations with the Personnel Officer. The Civil Service Commission does not have the right to change pay scales. Thus, according to one union leader, AFSCME has the complicated problem of dealing with "a twin-headed monster, when you have a City Manager who has broad authority over personnel matters and a Civil Service Commission which has rather limited but pointed authority."

Management in Cincinnati feels that several factors give it superior power at the bargaining table. First, there is the lack of a state statutory status for collective bargaining. Certainly, the union would be stronger under a law passed by the state legislature than it is having to rely on a local grant. Cincinnati has an "open shop" provision for municipal employment. There are still employees who are not union members, and the union has no guarantee of retaining the membership of those who are.

Similarly, Cincinnati's "tight" fiscal condition is an added source of management strength. The city is at its legal revenue limit except for those revenues which must be voter approved. To get an increase in the rate of any tax, the government must go to the people; this is not always an easy thing to do.

The tightness of the fiscal situation is known to the union and weakens its resolve to persist past the breaking point. According to the Personnel Officer, "Our tightness of money is an asset at the bargaining table. If I had more money, I would probably be easier to get along with." Assessing the city's strength at the bargaining table he said:

> We have a strong position through having a pretty good assessment of all the facts. We know this local economy and we have a good staff. We will not get conned with any misinformation, intentional or otherwise, coming from the union. [13]

Tightness of funds, which had so long operated as a strike deterrent, became one of the principal factors that brought the city's long era of labor peace to sudden end.

The Cincinnati Strikes

In 1969 Cincinnati experienced its first serious municipal strike. The cause, to a large extent, was the voters' rejection of a proposal by the City Council to increase local income taxes from 1 to 2 percent. [14] The police and firemen had received substantial increases, but the city claimed inadequate funds to accord like treatment to the nonuniform workers.

Influenced by a quarter of a century of excellent labor relations, both sides conducted the strike responsibly. The city obtained but refused to enforce an injunction and made no arrests, realizing that jailing strike leaders is no way to end a strike. "Experience elsewhere," wrote W. Donald Heisel, the city's Personnel Director, "shows that strike settlements are never made in the jailhouse." The city also refused to enforce the state punitive antistrike law.[15]

The union, on its part, Heisel pointed out, showed equal restraint. Picketing was peaceful, and squads were held in readiness to do emergency work if necessary.

No politician tried to break the solid, reasonable, and conciliatory front of the city government by interfering with the settlement process and attempting to "play the hero."[16]

Federal mediators played a leading role in bringing the parties together. Both parties understood the process of collective bargaining, the city recognizing the bilateral nature of bargaining as a decision making process. "It found over a period of years that it can make decisions bilaterally and still survive."[17]

But the lessons of the 1969 three-day strike, so persuasively described by Heisel, were entirely lost by the end of the year. In January 1970 the old controversy flared up again. When negotiations reached a stalemate, the waste collectors, waterworks employees, highway maintenance men, and several other AFSCME locals, struck. They were joined by the operating engineers. The unions exhibited none of the restraint and observed none of the niceties and considerations demonstrated in the original walkout of 1969. Said one worker, "This was an all-out affair with no legal holds barred."

The City's reaction, like the unions', was the antithesis of its behavior in the idyllic strike of the preceding year. The antistrike injunction obtained before the walkout, far from being held in abeyance as had been the injunction obtained the previous year, was vigorously enforced. The state's Ferguson Act, barring strikes and imposing severe penalties, was invoked. Thirty-seven arrests were made, according to the union's account, "for walking picket lines and at least 3 were held without bail—a treatment usually reserved for first degree murder. Two were sentenced to 20 days in the work house and fined $1000 each."[18]

The strike, accompanied by great bitterness, lasted five weeks. Despite cold winter weather the union boasted that its picket lines were constantly maintained. Describing the strike as "more than a work stoppage aimed at winning a wage increase," the union declared it was:

a reaffirmation of the right of public employees to participate fully in the collective bargaining process by striking, picketing, and demonstrating regardless of legislation or court order. The 1,800 strikers...successfully defied legal maneuverings based on the Ferguson Act, a repressive and outmoded piece of legislation prohibiting public employee strikes. Their defiance was the principal ingredient of victory.[19]

Despite the inconvenience and nuisance caused by the pile-up of garbage and the absence of street maintenance and repair, the strike won substantial support from local labor unions. The United Auto Workers ran an advertisement in the Cincinnati *Inquirer* strongly supporting the demands of the strikers, for good-faith bargaining, the release of the jailed strikers, the cessation of threats to five striking employees, and the dismissal of the City Manager. A laundry workers' union contributed $1,000 to the strike fund, and the city was unable to recruit drivers for its refuse trucks. Members of the AFSCME sanitation local across the river in New Port, Ky., collected food for the strikers, asking people to contribute a can of food for every can of garbage they collected.

Although the strike resulted in substantial wage increases and other benefits for the employees, the release of all the jailed union officers and a promise that all legal action against strikers would be dropped, the dispute left a residue of mutual distrust. It is ironic that Cincinnati, so long a city with a history of model labor relations, should have been the scene of what, with the possible exception of the New York City teachers' dispute of 1968, was the most bitter labor dispute in any large city.

A citizen's law suit held up implementation of the agreement. The penalties of the Ferguson Act, however, were not enforced, because the authorities ruled that the city had failed to post warning notices, as required by law. The court also held that the injunction did not "properly lie," and therefore no contempt penalties were executed.

Milwaukee

The Pioneering Legislation of 1961

In 1959 the Wisconsin Legislature adopted a major landmark law concerning municipal labor relations, a "declaration of rights" for municipal employees. Legally, however, no right to negotiate collectively was provided until amendments enacted in 1961 expanded the 1959 statute by establishing collective bargaining for municipal employees.[20]

All employees of political subdivisions of the state, exclusive of police, firemen, and county traffic officers, were considered to be municipal employees under the statute. Supervisors were administratively excluded, on the grounds that they are representatives of management and to include them in the same unit with other employees would constitute a conflict of interest.

The new statute was administered by the Wisconsin Employment Relations Board, which was responsible for determining appropriate bargaining units, conducting representation elections, investigating prohibited practices, and administering the mediation, arbitration, and fact-finding provisions of the act. In addition, the board had supervision over the secret-ballot election machinery, the determination of employee representatives in jurisdictional disputes, and the certification of the exclusive bargaining agent. On August 1, 1967, the Board became the Wisconsin Employment Relations Commission.

Where a majority of an appropriate unit voted for bargaining representative, the statute provided that the chosen employee organization represent all the employees of the unit. In 1966 the legislature passed an amendment that provided for an "agency shop" whenever two thirds of those voting favored it, provided they constitute a majority of the employees. Governor Knowles, however, vetoed the amendment.

The question of whether professional employees should belong to the same unit as other employees was to be determined by the Commission. The law's definition of a professional employee was similar to the National Labor Relations Act definition applicable in the private sector. Unit determination, however, has been complicated by the provision that employees in a single unit or craft may constitute a separate unit.

Although the Wisconsin statute prohibits strikes, it does not provide for automatic, inflexible penalties when strikes occur. Wisconsin, owing in part to its long pioneering in the field of general labor relations legislation, offers a flexible approach to the resolution of impasses. The Commission can function as a mediator in disputes, upon the request of both parties. The parties may select a mediator by mutual consent. If the parties are deadlocked after a reasonable period of negotiation or if a party has failed or refused to negotiate in good faith, either party may initiate fact-finding proceedings. The fact-finding procedure is not applicable to discipline or discharge cases when civil service procedures for appeal exist. If fact finding is requested, then the Commission appoints a qualified impartial person or panel to serve. These procedures are also available to police and other law-enforcement officers, who are excluded from coverage under the act. Local experimentation is encouraged by permitting municipalities to establish their own fact-finding procedures, as long as they are in compliance with the basic act.

Interestingly, the Wisconsin Municipal Employee Relations Act, which mandated collective bargaining, did not contain specific language stating that a refusal to bargain was a prohibited practice. In a split decision, the majority of the Commission concluded that a refusal to bargain in good faith by an employer is not subject to a prohibited-practice charge, even though the refusal to bargain was subject to the fact-finding procedures of the statute. Thus, the majority held that the legislature did not explicitly establish an enforceable duty to bargain in good faith on the municipal employers or employees. The minority argued that since the legislature had granted the right to engage in collective bargaining to municipal employees, "it necessarily follows that a corollary of such a right is the duty to bargain or negotiate with the majority representative of its employees."[21] The Wisconsin statute for state employees, however, makes the refusal to bargain a prohibited practice.[22] Under both statutes, the Commission is empowered to issue cease and desist orders under the procedures of the state Employment Peace Act applicable to the private sector.

The Milwaukee Tradition

Wisconsin's principal city, Milwaukee, quickly took steps to conform to the spirit of the new law.

Milwaukee has had a tradition of prolabor administrations. As long ago as 1910 the city elected a Socialist mayor, Emil Seidel. He was succeeded in 1916 by another Socialist, Daniel W. Hoan, who served until 1938. The city's last Socialist mayor was Frank P. Zeidler, who served from 1948 to 1960. Zeidler is deeply interested in the public employment relationship problem and has often spoken and written on the subject.

The city has weak Mayor-strong Council form of government. The Mayor's administrative powers are limited by the existence of a number of semiautonomous boards and commissions. His department heads serve for fixed terms and cannot be removed until their term ends. The appointment of the Police and Fire Chiefs is in the hands of autonomous boards. The Mayor lacks executive budgetary powers, although he chairs a budget committee of 11 members. Despite these legal limits on powers of the mayoral office, Milwaukee Mayors, because of their strong personalities and their long periods of continuous service, have exercised more influence over city affairs than formal powers would indicate.

As in the case in most large cities, public employees in Milwaukee had been organized since the early years of the century in small unions and associations, with which the city maintained loose and informal relations. Owing to the nature of the Mayor's office, the employee organizations' contacts were with the city's Common Council, which had responsibility for fixing wages and salaries. Employee representatives stated their case before the Finance Committee of the Council, with the Personnel Department serving the Committee in an advisory capacity. In short, the role of the organized employees was the same as that of any other pressure group seeking to influence legislation.

In 1955, the dues check-off had been initiated in Milwaukee and the City (Civil) Service Commission had instituted a grievance and arbitration procedure. These innovations were unsatisfactory to AFSCME's District Council 48, the dominant of the 14 unions with which the city dealt. Union demands in 1963 for a written contract, an agency shop, binding arbitration on grievances, economic benefits, and a reduction of City Service Commission involvement in personnel matters remained unsatisfied. As a result, the dispute was submitted to fact finding under the auspices of the Wisconsin Employment Relations Board. The issues at stake were so complex that the fact-finding panel did not release its report until November 1964. On April 20, 1965, the Common Council finally approved a labor contract with AFSCME District 48, to remain in effect until December 31, 1965. The city then negotiated a new, three-year contract with District 48, effective January 1, 1966.

How Bargaining Proceeds

The expansion of city employees' unions, beginning in the mid-1950's, gradually altered the method of dealing with the Council through the hearing route to a relationship akin to collective bargaining.

In an attempt to diminish the charges of conflict over the interpretation of this general allocation of functions, a more detailed allocation was spelled out in an official procedure memorandum, which declared it to be the "duty and obligation of the labor negotiator and the Personnel Department to cooperate, communicate and coordinate in the performance of their functions." To avoid conflict and duplication of effort, the following division of functions was agreed upon. The Personnel Department's field included responsibility for wage and fringe-benefit surveys and data; job analysis and position classification; job training; the setting of rules and practices of personnel administration under the jurisdiction of the City Service Commission; and a joint involvement with the Labor Relations Division in grievance procedures and contract administration.

The functions of the Division of Labor Relations included the investigation of economic, budgetary, and major labor policies of concern to the Mayor and Common Council; the conduct of studies and reports in areas of wages and fringe benefits; the responsibility for conducting the negotiations and having proper operating department and resource persons at the bargaining table; the drafting of the city's proposals and counterproposals and the contract language; and the implementing of Council ordinances and resolutions dealing with labor relations.

Under the city bargaining procedures, all contracts that expire December 31 contain a timetable for negotiations, requiring unions to submit demands by February 1 of the year in which the agreement expires and to plan to conclude negotiations prior to July 31. Negotiations must be definitely concluded prior to the statutory budget deadline of November 20. Early in negotiations the Council Committee on Finance, after private briefing by the negotiating team, calls a public hearing on union demands and subsequently sets confidential bargaining limits. By this point as one city negotiator declared, "I can go to the table armed with authority and enabled to participate in the give and take, within such limits."

Even the attempt at meticulous spelling out of the division of functions between Personnel and Labor Relations still allows plenty of room for continued differences, and it will doubtless be a long time before the mandate of the procedure memorandum that it shall be the "duty and obligation" of the heads of the two agencies to "cooperate, communicate, and coordinate" in the performance of their functions is entirely implemented.

Negotiations proved to be so arduous and time consuming to the Finance Committee, which was not technically equipped for the task, that it became apparent to both the council and the Mayor that the city required a full-time management agency to deal with the increasingly complex problems collective bargaining was presenting. The Mayor, in his Charter Message of 1965, declared:

> The recent negotiations (with the Common Council) . . . point again to the need for a full-time staff to work in this complex field . . . not only to conduct negotiations for the city but also to process grievances. While the department in its truest sense should reflect Council policy . . . I do not think it should be so rigidly controlled that it cannot perform ordinary administrative functions in this field. [23]

In short, the Mayor wanted the new City Negotiator to be, not a mere messenger of the Council Finance Committee, but an official with effective negotiating powers.

The Labor Negotiator staffed his Labor Relations Division with an assistant Negotiator, a labor economist, several personnel analysts, and clerical help. The Secretary of the City Service Commission and the Controller were named an advisory committee to the Division. In addition, because of the intimate involvement of the Personnel Department in labor relations processes, the assistance of some of its staff was frequently called upon at bargaining proceedings.

The enabling ordinance required every department of the city government to cooperate with the Labor Negotiator "to the end that he may discharge his duties and responsibilities as contemplated by the ordinance." Hardly had the organization of the new division been completed when problems arose in the shape of conflicting claims by the Negotiator's division and the City Service Commission.

"To avoid duplication of staff effort," wrote the city negotiator,

> there is an understanding that the Division of Labor Relations has primary responsibility in contract negotiations and the Department of Personnel has primary responsibility in day-to-day personnel and contract administration. [24]

The Labor Relations Division cites the following accomplishments since its creation:

> Bargaining elections have been won by 18 unions which have been certified by WERC. Fifty contracts running from one to four years were negotiated. These contracts contain no-strike pledges, strong management rights clauses and, except for police and fire operating under different laws, have grievance procedures terminating in either advisory or binding arbitration. Essentials of the merit system of hiring have been maintained. [25]

New York City

New York City has a history of active dealings with organizations of its employees that dates back to the first decade of this century.

Prior to 1910 the police and fire associations began to flex their political muscles at City Hall and the state capitol in Albany. These organizations began in the 1890's as mutual benefit societies. They gradually evolved into labor organizations to protect and promote the interests of their members. Their tactics were confined to the use of political pressure and lobbying. For the purpose of strengthening their political clout, the police and fire organizations formed an alliance and jointly hired a "social secretary" to coordinate their activities.

The clerical and administrative employees formed a society in 1909, which later became the Civil Service Forum. The associations were greatly strengthened by the support of an independently owned newspaper, *The Chief*, devoted to reporting and commenting on civil service employee affairs in New York.[26]

The organized sanitation employees staged a strike in the early 1900's. The city ran a number of horse-drawn garbage trucks loaded with strikebreakers, a policeman sitting alongside the driver. This strike was condemned in the most extravagant terms. The *Outlook*, a progressive weekly with Theodore Roosevelt on its editorial staff, called the strike a "mutiny."[27] *The Survey*, organ of the Charity Organization Society, headed its comment, "Desertion of the Street Cleaners".[28]

In the mid-1930's some city clerical, administrative, and technical employees formed unions affiliated with the organized labor movement and began to talk about collective bargaining and the right to strike. By the 1950's the affiliated union movement had grown to significant proportions, in the face of strong opposition from city officials.

Mayor Wagner Lays the Groundwork for Collective Bargaining

Taking account of the political implications of this development, Robert F. Wagner, in his first Mayoralty campaign, promised New York City "a little Wagner Act," both to meet the politically explosive demands of the city employees and to give the Mayor official machinery to intervene in private-sector of political potential.

He obtained legislation establishing the city's Department of Labor. Most employers and unions, however, refused to accept the good offices and dispute-settlement machinery of the new department, because they regarded it as "too political." They preferred to utilize the services of the well-established, ably led, and respected New York State Board of Mediation.

In 1954 Mayor Wagner issued an interim executive order that laid the groundwork for the city's subsequent labor relations programs. The order recognized the right of city employees to join organizations of their choosing and granted organization spokesmen the right to represent their members in joint consultation with department heads on proposals concerning conditions of employment. It also established grievance procedures within the departments. The following year the Mayor recommended a voluntary dues check-off, which was approved by the Board of Estimate in 1956. That year the order was further liberalized by authorizing union meetings during regular working hours.

While experimentation under this order was going on, union demands for the authentic collective bargaining continued to grow. The Mayor, acting on the advice of friends and political supporters in the labor relations field, called upon the services of Miss Ida Klaus, formerly solicitor of the National Labor Relations Board. Miss Klaus made a nationwide survey of municipal employer-employee relations practices.[29]

Wagner's Executive Order 49

On the basis of these studies, Mayor Wagner issued his Executive Order 49, a major administrative innovation which ushered collective bargaining into New York's civil service.

The order departed from the prevailing attitude of neutrality, if not active opposition, on the part of public employers toward collective bargaining. It declared it to be the city's policy to "promote practices and procedures of collective bargaining prevailing in private sector labor relations."

The city Department of Labor was given a role analogous to that of the National Labor Relations Board relative to the National Labor Relations Act. The Department was charged with responsibility for determining bargaining units and certifying employee representatives, making rules and regulations implementing the order, and rendering opinions interpreting it. At the same time, it was also charged with making provisions for handling grievances and mediating impasses—functions which, under both federal and many state labor relations acts, are assigned to separate agencies.

Placing both the administration of the order and the settlement of grievances and disputes in a single agency was one of the short-comings of the order. Its principal defect, however, was the assigning of regulatory and quasi-judicial functions to a regular administrative department under the control of the Mayor, who represented the city in its capacity as employer, instead of in the hands of an independent agency.

The Director of the Budget and the Personnel Director were designated as the Mayor's bargaining team. Bargaining units were based on civil service titles, which except in cases such as police, fire, and sanitation, cut across agency lines. For example, the city bargained with clerical employees on a city-wide basis; it negotiated with nurses employed by the departments of Health, Hospitals, and several other agencies. This excluded department heads from the bargaining process, although they were often consulted by the bargaining team. They also often played a preliminary role through the system of joint labor relations consultative committees, which under the order were set up in the various departments.

The city bargained only with unions which had won city-wide majorities for specific job titles. The result of the Wagner system was the certification of literally scores of separate job title bargaining units.

Lindsay's Reorganization

When John V. Lindsay succeeded to the mayoralty, the bargaining system underwent a thorough change. Under Executive Order 38, issued in 1967, the Office of Labor Relations was established in the Executive Office of the Mayor, headed by the Director of Labor Relations, who was directly responsible to the Mayor and who was to serve as the city's chief negotiator. The office was staffed by labor relations specialists, legal and fiscal aides, and a research staff. An advisory committee consisting of the Deputy Mayor-City Administrator, the Corporation Counsel, and the Personnel and Budget directors met every second week to advise the Director of Labor Relations on issues of law, personnel, finance, and management policy.

Late in 1967 the Office of Collective Bargaining was established, by an amendment to the city charter, to replace the city Department of Labor. The OCB was organized as an impartial tripartite agency, with city government, union, and public members. The agency was organized into two parts: the Board of Collective Bargaining, comprising the full membership of seven, whose functions included the handling of impasses and the arbitration of grievances; and the Board of Certification, comprising the three public members. The Chairman of the OCB serves as Chairman of both boards. The Director of Labor Relations represents the city at OCB proceedings.

Wagner and Lindsay: A Contrast in Styles

The contrast between Wagner's and Lindsay's handling of labor relations is sharp. Wagner took an intensely personal interest in the process. The organization of the system under one of the Mayor's departments made it easier for him to do this. He could not be accused of interfering with an impartial agency. He relished the role of mediator, and he played it with great skill. His influence was not confined to the government service. He played a leading part in the long newspaper strike of 1963 which shut down all of the city's papers for months. He also played a decisive role in settling the teachers' strike of 1962. He never hesitated to intervene openly or furtively in the processes of the city Department of Labor. Often, when certification of bargaining units was in process and seemed to be bogged down, he stepped in on behalf of some unions and in opposition to others. His influence was greatly strengthened through close personal and political contacts with the principal labor officials in the private sector, notably those in the building and needle trades. One writer referred to him as a mediator *extraordinaire*.[30] He deserved the title.

Lindsay refrained from intervention in the bargaining process if circumstances made it possible for him to do so. He preferred to leave matters to the impartial machinery of the Office of Collective Bargaining. The Lindsay administration readily accepted the recommendations of the OCB. In one important matter the administration refused to go along, namely, the pension recommendations for police, fire fighters, and sanitation workers in 1970. The city had a cogent reason here, because the approval of the state legislature is required for any increase that makes city pensions more generous than those covering state employees. The scope of city bargaining is defined, in the tripartite agreement, as covering only matters "on which the Mayor or agency heads under his jurisdiction has [sic] authority to make final decisions.[31]

Although management rights clauses that reserve to the city a large number of prerogatives are included in every contract, these reservations have in large measure been weakened by a subsequent statement that questions concerning the practical impact of decisions regarding the management reservations on employees come within the scope of collective bargaining. Grievances are processed under a multistep procedure culminating in final and binding arbitration by panels or single arbitrators selected from a list established by the OCB. Arbitration is limited to "the extent permitted by law," an inevitable restriction that nevertheless has caused confusion and wrangling over the issue of what is arbitrable. Constant controversies brought about the intervention of the OCB to settle the issue of arbitration along with the grievance which sparked the controversy.

In cases of impasse in contract negotiations, provision is made by the Board of Collective Bargaining for the designation of an impasse panel, with powers to subpoena witnesses and pertinent documents and "take such action as is considered necessary to resolve the impasse."[32] Although the city formally agreed to be bound by the impasse panel's decision, this understanding was not regarded by the unions as binding on them. In 1970 the OCB recommended that it be given authority to make binding impasse decisions. In December 1971 the City Council passed a compulsory arbitration law implementing this recommendation.

Professor Alice Cook of Cornell University, writing in 1970, called the record of the OCB in dealing with negotiations and disputes "fairly impressive." She then raised the question, "Why does New York City present the image of a strike-torn city?" She answers, "One reason is that the threat of strikes among employees is a real, not a staged, one."[33] At the time Dr. Cook wrote her article, the long sanitation strike had been the only one that had occurred in a service within the OCB's jurisdiction. Since then, there have been a series of job actions by police, firemen, and welfare workers; a strike of drawbridge tenders, impeding the flow of traffic into the city, accompanied by a strike of employees at sewage-treatment plants that allowed thousands of tons of raw sewage to flow into the city's rivers; and a serious strike of police, involving two thirds of a force of over 30,000.[34] The series of teachers' strikes in 1968 (outside OCB jurisdiction) appeared to threaten the social fabric of the community, although the passions have since seemed to cool. Doubtless, if Professor Cook had written later she would have found that New York City's reputation as a strike-torn city was justified.

Perhaps the greatest shortcoming in the New York collective bargaining system under the OCB is that it covers only departments under the Mayor's control. This leaves over 70,000 Board of Education and 30,000 Transit Authority employees outside its jurisdiction. It is in these agencies that the most serious labor disputes and strikes have occurred.

Formation of the Health and Hospitals Corporation to replace the former city departments of Hospitals and Health may well take additional thousands of workers out of the system, unless the new corporation and its workers voluntarily decide to participate.

Employees in all these agencies, whether or not in one of the Mayor's departments, are paid by the city.

Some idea of the complexity of the city's problem may be gathered from the fact that 129 certified unions are involved, through 232 bargaining units representing about 90 percent of the city's 400,000 employees.

Hartford

Connecticut has gone further than any other jurisdiction in the land

67

to give the municipal collective labor agreement a unique legal status. The Connecticut Municipal Employees Relations Act of 1965 states:

> When there is a conflict between any agreement reached by a municipal employer and an employee organization and approved in accordance with this act on matters appropriate to collective bargaining, as defined in this act, and any charter, special act, ordinance, rules or regulations adopted by the municipal employer or its agents such as a personnel board or civil service commission, or any general statute directly regulating hours of work of policemen or firemen, the terms of such agreement shall prevail. [34]

The specific reference of this law to central personnel agencies has had the effect of virtually stripping them of their traditional powers. All that is really left to them is control over civil service examinations and the policing of restrictions on political activity. This, however, has not spelled disaster to the merit system. The upshot of the new order of things has been to change the course of appeals on discipline and classification from the Personnel Agency to the state Board of Mediation and Arbitration, which according to Hartford's Personnel Director, has "upheld merit factors as much as the city's Personnel Board, if not more."[35]

Pre-1965 Collective Bargaining

Hartford began experimenting with collective bargaining in 1945, when a local ordinance authorized employees to defend and improve their working conditions. This immediately inaugurated conferences and discussions on working conditions between the employee organizations and the city administration, which developed into a relationship that the municipal administrators unhesitatingly characterized as collective bargaining.[36]

According to Elisha C. Freedman, the City Manager, the system rested on a few basic assumptions, such as:

1. When an individual chooses to work for government, he does so with the understanding that government employment is different from private enterprise and may require sacrifices, etc., in the interest of the "public good," whatever that might be.

2. Political activity on behalf of employees by either elected officials, employees themselves, unions, friends, etc., is a fact of life that should somehow be regulated but not eliminated, since it is a clear substitute for the strike.

3. It should be possible to develop guidelines, acceptable to em-

ployees and management, that relate public salaries and working conditions to the private market.

Impact of the Connecticut Municipal Labor Relations Act

The Connecticut Municipal Employees Relation Act of 1965, which mandates collective bargaining between municipalities and their employees, has instituted a system that, in the opinion of Hartford officials, hardly differs from the model of industrial collective bargaining.

The city bargains with three unions, one representing the police, one representing the fire fighters and one representing most of the clerical, blue-collar, and other general employees. The Personnel Director, working under the supervision of the City Manager, serves as the city's chief bargaining spokesman. The Fire Chief serves along with him for the Fire Department when the city bargains with the fire fighters' union. The Police Chief or his assistant serves in a similar way in negotiations with the police association. When the city bargains with its general employees, represented by an AFSCME local, the heads of either the Department of Public Works or the Department of Parks and Recreation and the representatives of other departments concerned join with the Director of Personnel and his staff to constitute the bargaining team.

Agreements are subject to the approval of the City Council for conformity to the law and official regulations. If the Council rejects the agreement, it is returned to the parties for further negotiation. If the Council fails to act, the agreement becomes operative after 44 days and the city is obligated to make the funds available to comply with the agreement.

The principal shortcoming of the Hartford labor relations system prior to the passage of the 1965 state law was the union practice of constant "end runs" to Council members, undercutting the Manager's authority as city executive.[37]

Although the state law emphatically placed responsibility for collective bargaining "on the chief municipal executive officer," attempts of some unions to go behind his back to members of the Council continued. This led Hartford's City Manager to remark, "Regardless of the fact that the unions sold collective bargaining as a substitute for politics, politics has not been eliminated from the system."

The law is so explicit, however, that these attempts at leap-frogging the executive were finally defeated. A ruling in 1968 by the state Board of Labor Relations in cases involving the town of Groton armed the Hartford Manager with an effective legal ruling to support his position.

In the Groton case the Town Manager stated during negotiations that he could make no financial proposals without prior approval of the Town Council. The Board of Labor Relations declared that "although it was understandable that the Chief Executive in fear of repudiation by the local council might seek to shift responsibility to it for making decisions regarding employment relations, the statute, however, places that responsibility on him and he cannot, out of political timidness or caution refuse to fulfill that statutory responsibility. He may," the Board continued, "in conducting other affairs of the Town act as an errand boy for the legislative council, but he is charged with exercising primary authority and responsibility and to exercise that authority is a failure to bargain in compliance with the statutes."[38]

When a few years after this ruling certain Hartford unions again tried to play the old games with the Council, the City Manager firmly asserted his authority and with the aid of newspaper publicity forced the Council to adopt a self-denying resolution taking its members out of the bargaining process and recognizing the primacy of the executive's role. (*This episode is discussed in Chapter 5.*)

Thus, Hartford has a system of labor relations with the responsibility clearly placed in the hands of the executive authority, with the role of the legislature severely circumscribed and the primacy of the collective agreement over existing enactments explicitly defined, and with funds for its implementation guaranteed.

Notes

1. Foster B. Roser, "Philadelphia Story," *The Public Employee,* April 1960.
2. Section 28.011 of Civil Serive
2. Section 28.011 of CIVIL Service Regulation 28—*Labor Relations.*
3. Council of the City of Philadelphia, Bill No. 646, An Ordinance to AFSCME, AFL-CIO, Philadelphia and Vicinity, regarding its representation of certain city employees.
4. "Philadelphia Gets Modified Union Shop," *The Public Employee,* September 1960, p. 9; and *1961 Annual Report of Civil Service Commission and Personnel Department, City of Philadelphia.*
5. Act 336 of Public Acts of 1947, as amended by Public Act No. 379 (1965).
6. Ordinance No. 140-G, Chapter 2, Article 7, *Labor Relations Bureau for City Employees Collective Bargaining.*
7. American Bar Association, Committee on Law of Government Employee Relations, Section of Labor Relations Law, *Report* (Chicago, 1960), p. 89.
8. W. D. Heisel and J. P. Santa-Emma, "Unions in Cincinnati Govern-

ment," in Kenneth O. Warner, ed., *Management Relations with Organized Public Employees* (Chicago: Public Personnel Association, 1963), p. 120.

9. City of Cincinnati, City Council, *Resolution Declaring A City Wage Policy,* passed April 6, 1960.

10. City of Cincinnati, *City Manager's Policy with Regard to Unions,* April 7, 1960, p. 1.

11. Heisel and Santa-Emma, op. cit., p. 121.

12. Al Bilik, Director of Ohio Council No. 8, AFSCME, in an interview with the authors, May 18, 1967.

13. W. D. Heisel, City of Cincinnati Personnel Officer, in an interview with the authors, May 19, 1967.

14. Heisel, "Anatomy of a Strike," *Public Personnel Review,* October 1969, p. 223.

15. Ibid. p. 222.

16. Ibid.

17. Ibid.

18. *The Public Employee,* February, 1970.

19. Ibid.

20. Wisconsin Municipal Employee Relations Act, Wisconsin Statutes Annotated, Subchapter IV of Chapter III, Section 111.70 (1959), as amended in 1961, 1963, 1965, and 1967.

21. *William E. Moes v. City of New Berlin, State of Wisconsin,* Wisconsin Employment Relations Board, Case IV, No. 9897 MP-17, Decision No. 7293, Memorandum Accompanying Findings of Fact, Conclusions of Law and Order, pp. 4-36

22. Wisconsin State Employment Relations Act, Chapter 612, Laws of 1965, amending Wisconsin Statutes, Subchapter V of Chapter III by adding Section 111.80 to 111.94, effective January 1, 1967.

23. Annual Charter Message by Mayor Henry W. Maier of Milwaukee, April 20, 1965, p. 3.

24. James J. Mortier, "The Experience in Milwaukee," *The City Prepares for Labor Relations* (Washington D.C.: Labor Management Relations Service, 1970).

25. Ibid.

26. Sterling D. Spero, *Government As Employer* (New York: Remsen Press, 1948), p. 205.

27. *The Outlook,* November 25, 1911.

28. *The Survey,* November 18, 1911.

29. On the basis of Miss Klaus's work in New York, the Secretary of Labor called her to Washington as counsel to President Kennedy's Task Force on Employee-Employer Cooperation in the Federal Service. The report of the Task Force provided the basis for Kennedy's Executive Order 10988, which introduced the beginnings of limited collective bargaining in the federal Service.

30. Raymond D. Horton, "Municipal Labor Relations in New York City," *Political Science Quarterly,* vol. xxx, no. 2 (December 1970), p. 73.

31. City of New York, Tripartite Panel to Improve Municipal Collective Bargaining Procedures, *Memorandum of Agreement,* March 31, 1966, p. 5.

32. City of New York, Collective Bargaining Law 1173-7.0 c (3) (a), 1967.
33. Alice H. Cook, "Public Employee Bargaining in New York City," *Industrial Relations*, May, 1970, p. 263.
34. Connecticut General Statutes, Chapter 113.
35. Robert D. Krause, memorandum to the authors, September 22, 1970.
36. Carleton F. Sharpe and Elisha C. Freedman, "Collective Bargaining in a Non-Partisan Council-Manger City," *Public Administration Review*, Winter 1962, pp. 13-18.
37. Ibid.
38. Quoted by Robert D. Krause and Constance M. Willard in their paper presented to the International Conference and Public Personnel Administration, New Orleans, La. Oct. 22, 1968.

4   Civil Servants and the Political Arena

The Political Environment of Collective Bargaining

Municipal collective bargaining quickly becomes a political contest. The city government, in its capacity as employer, is pitted against public employee units, whose members are taxpaying citizens and also constitute a sizable electoral bloc. Employees seek to advance their interests on a number of fronts: at the bargaining table, in the city councils and state legislatures, in the electoral arena, and in the courts. As a result, the bargaining process of necessity reflects the coloration of municipal politics, and the success of the process is closely related to the particular setting in which the contest takes place. The difficulty begins when one attempts to make generalizations applicable to all cities.

City Employees as a Political Bloc

The emergence of civil service voting power is becoming one of the more potent factors of American municipal and state politics. The obvious reason is that public employees, together with their families, close friends, and relatives, make up a sizable bloc of votes. In 1965 the *Civil Service Leader*, a weekly paper devoted to civil service affairs, concluded that nearly 20 percent of the votes cast in any New

York City election reflected the will of the civil service population. Three years later, the *Leader* noted that the importance of this vote loomed larger with each passing year.[1] By 1969 one out of every 27 of New York City's inhabitants was employed by the city, and union members constituted approximately 66 percent of the municipal work force. In 1971 New York City employed nearly 400,000 persons, who, together with their families, constitute an estimated population of more than 1.2 million. This would represent a powerful political and voting force.

Public employees also make up a sizable electoral bloc in smaller cities. Robert A. Dahl noted that the city of New Haven, Conn., was the fifth largest employer in the state; public employees, when combined with union members and their families, were estimated to total 36 percent of the electorate.[2]

The fact that there are a large number of civil service voters, however, is not as significant as the fact that they are increasingly well organized and that politicians now woo them with great ardor. As the extent of organization increases and unions merge or act in political coalitions, the total effect will be to solidify the civil servant population into a stronger political bloc than currently exists. In some cases they will certainly compete with, if not supersede, the traditional party machinery.

While public employees constitute a large potential bloc of voters, it is questionable whether the leadership of their organizations can "deliver" their votes. Rather, its power lies in the ability of the organization to give or withhold endorsements, to provide canvassers for bell ringing, and to contribute money or services in kind, such as leaflets, publications, and forums.

Restrictions on the Political Acitvity of Civil Servants

Municipal employees, in their role as citizens, are limited by restrictions on their political activities. The restrictions evolved from the civil service reform movement, which sought to protect both the civil servant and the public from the pernicious effects of partisan political interference with the operations of government. The result was the establishment of a complex of laws, executive orders, and administrative regulations that introduced the merit principle into public personnel administration and set forth restrictions on the political activities of public employees. Merit systems and political restrictions, first employed at the federal level and in New York and Massachusetts, were gradually extended to most states and to many of the larger cities.

One basic problem confronting the reformers was how to eradicate the spoils system, which had permeated the government from almost the earliest days of the Republic, and yet encourage the participation of as many citizens as possible in the political processes of the nation. The reformers sought a politically neutral civil service, wished to eliminate conflicts of interest, and desired to achieve both the appearance and reality of the impartial treatment of all citizens in their dealings with government.

Political restrictions were imposed on the civil servants for the dual purpose of protecting employees against pressure from political machines for forced contributions of either time or money and assuring loyal performance of duty to whatever administration the people might elect to office.

The term "political neutrality" has been used in different contexts. In the sense of the impartial rendering of governmental services, political neutrality is obviously a desirable element. Garbage must be picked up from households regardless of the political complexion of the occupants. Schooling must be provided without political indoctrination, and fire fighters and police provide protection to all shades of the political spectrum. In Mayor La Guardia's words, "There is no Democratic or Republican method of collecting garbage or regulating traffic."

Neutrality has also been held to mean that a civil servant will exercise all his talents with equal loyalty to politically elected representatives of the people. It is incumbent upon the civil servant that he "advise" his political chief and yield to him once the policy objective has been decisively fixed. Any other course would obstruct the implementation of public policy.[3]

Not all scholars interpret the doctrine of political neutrality as requiring that the bureaucracy blindly serve as an instrument of politically elected policy makers. Political power is deemed to be an important element of effective administration, with the bureaucracy appropriately participating in the shaping as well as the carrying out of policy. As Norton Long has said, the lifeblood of administration is power, the necessary precondition for the accomplishment of other objectives.[4] And the bureaucracy has not been and should not be a neutral instrument docilely executing the orders of political superiors. Because of the unprecedented measure of independence that civil servants have already achieved, the issue of existing restrictions on their political activities poses the question of whether the limitations should be strengthened or eased.

There were attempts to restrict the political activities of civil servants long before the civil service reform movement. George Washington recognized that to bring into office men whose tenets were adverse to those of the elected officials was a form of political suicide. President John Adams removed some subordinates for partisan political activities. As early as 1814, Daniel Webster, then Secretary of State, issued an order limiting political activity.

So called "gag orders," issued in the form of presidential executive orders, during the administrations of Cleveland, Theodore Roosevelt, and Taft had indirectly acted as a brake on the political activities of federal employees. In the Roosevelt administration the Civil Service Commission adopted Civil Service Rule I, whereby federal employees in the executive civil services were forbidden to use their official authority or influence "for the purpose of interfering with an election or affecting the results thereof."

The 3,000 decisions issued by the U.S. Civil Service Commission between 1907 and 1937 were adopted, by reference, into the Hatch Act in 1939, when Congress directly attempted to deal with the problem of political activity. Employees compensated in whole or in part from federal grant-in-aid funds were made subject to the restrictions set forth in the Hatch Act, which were extended to state and local governments by amendments enacted in 1940. Several state and local governments soon thereafter enacted restrictions of their own that largely paralleled those of the federal law.

The Legal Framework: Confusion and Ambiguity

The existing legal framework requires fundamental changes to bring some order out of virtual chaos.[5] Municipal employees may or may not. be subject to these federal laws and administrative rules, depending upon the extent to which their pay is supported by federal funds. (Of the 4.5 million employees now subject to the provisions of the Hatch Act, at least 1.5 million are state and local employees.) Furthermore, an employee in a specific city may be subject to state laws as well as the city charter, city ordinances, and administrative rules and regulations of the jurisdiction in which he works.

State and local laws show a considerable lack of uniformity. The laws and accompanying regulations may or may not distinguish between partisan and nonpartisan political activity, issues, and candidates for varying offices. Some cities impose restrictions on political action regardless of the government involved; other municipalities are concerned only with the local employing unit of government.

Some local governments forbid public employees to run for office;

others hold this right inviolable. Voluntary political contributions are authorized by some cities and restricted by others. Petitions, membership in political clubs, and holding official party positions are regulated in a variety of ways.[6]

Detroit has no specific ordinance regulating the political activities of unions and their members, nor are the restrictions on political activity incorporated in the Michigan Civil Service Law, always applicable to municipal employees. In Philadelphia employees are bound by City Charter provisions that ban political activity by all city employees except elected officials.

Cincinnati employees are subject to the provisions of both the City Charter and the Ohio Civil Service Law. The charter prohibits specified political activities by all employees within the administrative service; the state law is only applicable to employees considered part of the classified categories of the civil service.[7]

New York City employees are restricted in their political activities by provisions of the New York State Civil Service Law, the state Penal Law, and the City Charter. By virtue of the state law, city employees are not obligated to contribute to any political fund or to render any political service. The City Charter expressly forbids members of the police force to contribute money directly or indirectly to political funds. The police may not contribute to "any fund intended to effect an increase in their emoluments" or become a member of any political organization.

Civil servants are prohibited from using their official authority to coerce the political action of any other person or to interfere with elections. Employees are also shielded against inquiries concerning their political affiliations.[8]

Recent Trends

The lack of uniformity of federal, state, and municipal restrictions on political activity noted above parallels a reluctance on the part of city officials to enforce such regulations as do exist. To a lesser degree, the same attitude prevailed in federal employment.

The elemental wisdom—that excessive restriction of employee political activity is the country's loss and can't be prevented in any case—has percolated to the lower levels of government. As of 1967 there were at least 33 states with laws more lenient than the federal Hatch Act.

The clear tendency has been to ease restrictions in state and municipal governments. In 1967 Oregon enacted legislation that expanded employee rights, and the following year the Attorney

General of Wisconsin upheld the right of public employees to participate in political activities during nonbusiness hours. Such actions are in accord with the basic thrust of the *Report of the Commission on Political Activity* to expand the area of permissible activities for local employees administering programs financed with federal funds.

Because of the stepped-up pace of political activity, the U.S. Civil Service Commission issued a series of 39 questions and answers in 1968 to clarify some of the problems, noting that the restrictions applied to municipal employees whose principal employment is in connection with a federally financed activity.

The Courts on Political Restrictions

The right of legislatures to impose reasonable limitations on the political activities of public employees was upheld by the Supreme Court of the United States even prior to the widespread enactment of civil service laws. In 1882 the Court stated the rationale in the case of *Ex Parte Curtis*: to promote integrity, to maintain proper discipline in the public service, and to protect the employee against unjust exactions.

For decades the courts repeatedly rejected challenges to restrictions, relying on the classic distinction between public employees and other citizens made by Justice Holmes: "The petitioner may have a constitutional right to talk politics, but he has no constitutional right to be a policeman." From this dictum of Holmes's, courts and scholars built up a theory that there are few public employments for hire in which the worker does not agree to suspend his constitutional rights of free speech, as well as of idleness, by the implied terms of his contract. The employee could not complain, as he took the employment on the terms offered him.[9]

What was too often overlooked was the fact that Holmes was specifically dealing with the rights of policemen, a rather special category of public employee. More important, the exponents of restrictions conveniently overlooked the fact that Holmes explicitly stated, "On the same principle the city may impose any *reasonable* condition upon holding offices within its control [emphasis added]."

Courts show a marked tendency toward a more liberal posture regarding the political participation rights of public employees. They reject the absolute position that government may condition public employment on *any* terms it may choose to impose. Impediments must be rationally related to the integrity and preservation of the public service; only a compelling public interest can justify restraints; the restraints must not be broader than necessary; and the gains to the public must outweigh the resulting impairment of an individual's constitutional rights. Since basic constitutional rights are at stake, there must be an absence of alternatives less subversive of such rights. Finally, the courts are not inclined to abdicate their responsibility to determine the limits of constitutional protection in such areas by deferring to the wisdom of legislators.[10] Such criteria are in no way inconsistent with the Holmes test of reasonable restrictions. What is indicated is that some courts are obviously applying the doctrine of reasonableness to permit a wider area of political action.

Several recent decisions indicate the practical impact with regard to an employee's rights. A California court ruled that a nurse's aide had been improperly dismissed because she refused to stop participating during off-duty hours in a political campaign that involved the recall of some of the hospital district's directors. In a second case, the California Supreme Court ruled that a probationary employee who had not yet acquired civil service status could not be "summarily dismissed for political activities displeasing to his superiors." In still another opinion a court struck down a board of education rule against circulating petitions during teacher lunch periods.[11]

Employee Organizations and Political Restrictions

Before the Hatch Act was passed, many local employees had welcomed restrictions that tended to free them from the demands of city political machines. Depending upon the state and local law, city employees were subject to varying degrees of restrictions. As the organizational strength of city employees increased, a change in attitude toward legal restrictions occurred. City employees now believed themselves strong enough to pursue their own special political interests rather than carry out the broader interests of the dominant political machine.

Public employee organizations continue to question and challenge the existing broad limitations on their political activity as inimical to the democratic process and an unwarranted invasion of their constitutional rights. It must be noted that many public employees continue to desire restrictions. There is evidence in the Presidential Commission Report of 1968 that some employees disagreed with the position of their union leaders.

Employee organizations have sought court tests to challenge statutes that, according to AFSCME, "hold public employees as hostages of a halfhearted, legalistic approach alleged to protect them from the spoils system." On more than one occasion AFSCME has castigated the limitations as "sheer nonsense" and "oppressive measures" and proceeded to announce that they will seek a test case by having employees violate the rules and challenge a city to discipline the employee who committed the violation.[12]

The Connecticut State Employee Association voted in 1970 to seek the repeal of a state law prohibiting most state workers from involvement in politics. Under the present law, the Association stated, workers subject to the merit system were prohibited from political activity, whereas nonmerit employees and teachers were not subject to formal bans on political activity. Police organizations have also sought to eliminate legislative restrictions to political activity.

Not all public employee organizations, however, have welcomed the elimination of restrictions. In March 1968 the Executive Council of the National Federation of Federal Employees pledged to do all in its power to defeat proposals to weaken restrictions on partisan political activity. Change was viewed as opening the door to a wholesale return of partisan political pressures.

Political Restrictions: An Appraisal

It is clear that no employee should be forced to participate in political activities against his will or be subject to pressure for monetary contributions. In the main, however, the effect of the existing laws has been to hinder the employee in the exercise of his political rights. It has been argued that public employees, with their friends and families, would constitute a virtual "political army"; and through the simple exercise of economic coercion, the party in power would be able to turn loose the "troops" to win elections.[13]

There is a danger that the removal of all restrictions would perpetuate a party in power, erode the merit system, endanger the concept of political neutrality, and undermine the public's confidence in the government. Employees would be encouraged to seek out political influence, knowing that their tenure in office would ultimately rest upon willingness to cooperate and, so to speak, "maintain a clean file."

Nevertheless, political activity does not, ipso facto, constitute objectionable interference with the impartial or efficient administration of government. The current hodgepodge restrictions are inappropriate, ineffective, and inimical to conditions in the 1970's. The integrity of the service in no way depends on the contrived dichotomy of "partisan" and "nonpartisan" political activities.[14] Many of the so-called excesses and extremes of the past no longer have the pernicious effects they once had.

Restrictions on individual employees have become almost impossible to enforce in the context of modern employee organizations. The individual does not have to perform acts that the organization can perform for him. Unions often purchase tables at a political dinner, and laws can hardly prevent a superior from casually conveying to an employee that it is in his interests to attend or lend a hand in some chore having a political effect. Often the techniques are subtle; at other times the facts are "laid on the line." Legal bans do little about the more subtle devices and sometimes add to the confusion as to what is permissible behavior.

The current mode of restrictions could also diminish the advancement of the blacks, who constitute a large and growing number of employees in several cities. Political activity is essential to easing their plight. With many new and controversial programs being introduced, it is advisable in some cases to man agencies with personnel acceptable to the political forces that brought about the creation of the new programs.

Although it had little choice at the time, the activities of the American civil service reform movement resulted in the application of restrictions to lower echelons while their superiors remained subject to political appointment and partisan direction. British reform affected the higher echelons, who set the tone for the entire service without the necessity of legally imposing centrally administered, rigid restrictions on lower ranks. Without the rigid safeguards of the American system, the British have attained standards of nonpartisan service equal, if not higher, to those that prevail in the United States.

Unreasonable, unrealistic, and unenforceable restrictions should be modified to encourage, rather than bar, full participation in the American political process. The solution is one based on a working balance between merit and patronage. But myths die hard. And the myth that laws, as currently drafted, strengthened, and enforced will assure a civil service unstained by corruption or politics or the hard truths of life in major urban centers still lives on.

Political Tactics and Employee Organizations

While municipal employees have a continuing interest in combatting the evils of outside political interference, their organizations increasingly seek to alter or bypass the existing system of political restrictions. Since their inception they have engaged in political activity.

Traditionally, government employee unions on all governmental levels have used their political power to check or overrule administration labor policies to which they objected and to obtain legislation spelling out working conditions in detail. This greatly circumscribed administrative discretion, but it was exactly what the unions wished to do. They regarded the legislature as the buffer between themselves and their bosses, who with few exceptions refused to recognize and deal with them through their organizations. Thus, recourse to the legislature was their only alternative to unchecked executive control over their working lives. Even prior to collective bargaining, they felt that they were forced to use political tactics, although many regarded this as a threat to a nonpartisan service.

The more recent upsurge in direct bargaining, however, has in no way diminished organizational interest in the use of political tactics. An abundance of political weapons are available that may be distinguished from collective bargaining but have an impact on the form and scope of the bargaining that takes place.

The Choice of Tactics

Many forces and influences operate to determine the choice of political tactics and the object against whom organizational pressure will be directed. Smart leadership seeks out the political weak spots and eventually goes for the jugular, whether or not the initial ploy appears aimed elsewhere. Will the first thrust be toward the professional administrator or the political executive? Should there be an appeal to the legislature in the hopes of getting "two bites" out of the bargaining apple? And if so, at what stage of the negotiations? What kind of appeals to the public would enhance the opportunities for success? To what extent does the public understand the goals of the union?

Before such tactical decisions are made, even more complicated strategical choices are involved. The mere task of defining the organization's objectives is a difficult one and cannot be resolved by the slogan "More." Proposing a realistic economic package of wages, hours, and fringe benefits requires considerable research and planning.

There is also the problem of deciding what you should "demand" vis-a-vis what the organization can realistically hope to get and what will keep the membership happy. Even more complicated is the attempt to secure policy changes that arouse the watchdogs, who bark, "Management's prerogatives cannot be bargained away, because they belong to the people."

Still other influences are at work. The extent of unity within an employee organization—the influence of racial, ideological, and other factions—may well determine the choice of strategical objectives and tactical moves. The existence of competitive employee units and the degree to which they will cooperate have a definite bearing on all decisions.

The political I O U's that are outstanding along with the relationships with existing party machines; the organization's standing with the general labor movement and especially the Central Labor Council; the impact of the legal framework; the numerical power and financial stability of the union; the ability and skill of the union leadership as against their counterparts in government—all these and many other factors influence decisions made in a dynamic, shifting, emotion-charged context.

Much of the subsequent discussion of political activity dwells on New York City, which bears detailed exploration. As indicated by A. H. Raskin, New York City dwarfs all others in size; its problems are usually more elephantine; and the afflictions of the urban crisis assert themselves more virulently there.[15] To this comment by a distinguished New York editor may be added the words of an eminent Californian, Roger A. Freeman, economist at the Hoover Institution, Palo Alto, California: "While New York City is not typical of the rest of the country—fortunately, as some would say—it epitomizes and foreshadows trends and developments elsewhere. A look at New York City is enlightening." In one sense New York City is sui generis. Nonetheless, other major cities are confronted with similar troublesome bargaining relationships. And while variations, admittedly significant, influence the elusive political aspects of bargaining, it is difficult, if not impossible, to have sufficient insight to portray accurately the political nuances of many cities. Few profess such omniscience.

Lobbying: Formal and Informal

Unions may choose to lobby both formally and informally at all levels of government. Lobbying is conducted to obtain specific objectives favorable to employee organizations and to prevent the passage of legislation considered inimical. Much of the lobbying in recent years has been geared to expand the rights of municipal employees to bargain collectively, including the repeal of antistrike legislation. Collective bargaining is currently considered a more direct route to conventional bureaucratic goals, but the refusal of

legislatures to give chief executives authority to bargain over wages inevitably led to the politicalization of the public employee.

Originally, the lobbying conducted by municipal employee groups was a matter of deliberate choice rather than a matter of necessity. Despite the "gag orders" referred to previously, union leaders subordinated collective bargaining to lobbying, considered a more expedient and effective means to achieve their goals. This preference for the legislative route to employee goals motivated affiliation with the organized labor movement and especially the Central Labor Council of the AFL-CIO in cities with a large component of trade unionists.

The Government Employee's Council, composed of all AFL-CIO unions with members in federal, state, and local government services, serves as a clearinghouse for the consideration of common problems and the formulation of programs of political action. The Council is headed by a permanent executive assisted by a competent staff.[16]

The Goals of Lobbying

The extent and effectiveness of lobbying varies with individual employee groups. Teachers, for example, are in an excellent position to concentrate on the state legislature to secure detailed provisions in the state education law favorable to the teaching profession. State education departments, of necessity staffed by former educators, serve as an excellent means of access to the decision-making process. Teacher groups act in coalition with local economy groups to secure greater funds for education, including salaries. The residual power left to local boards of education remains highly susceptible to pressure by local teacher groups. Teachers increasingly recognize that power and politics count in education, as they do in all segments of society.

Police and fire fighter groups, despite local prohibitions on lobbying, have also sought state legislation with regard to pension benefits, manpower assignments, and other matters of interest. Lobbying came naturally to both the police and the firemen. The police were virtually "born into politics," having served a long apprenticeship as servants of the party organizations.[17] The firemen had a long history of affiliation with the organized labor movement, which strengthened their lobbying efforts. Indeed, because of the free hours available to firemen, the party organizations were fully cognizant of the advantages of close relationships with fire fighter organizations.

84

In the case of both police and fire fighters, a major effort was mounted at the state capitol and at City Hall to secure what in effect was a "closed system." The aim was to create a virtual citadel, in the sense of reducing the role of outsiders in the organization's decision-making processes. Supervisory and top-echelon personnel were to be selected from within the organization, at the least, any appointments of "outsiders" would be subject to the veto of the organization. At one time it was the practice of the Post Office to promote officers of subservient organizations as rewards for their support of administration policies.

Some employee organizations concentrate their lobbying efforts to secure changes in personnel policies or practices by legislation. For example, they may seek the filling of vacancies by promotion and transfer from within the career civil service; or they may urge that provisional promotions be based upon seniority in title, where provisional promotions are unavoidable. Other organizations endeavor to eliminate the contracting out of work normally performed by civil service employees. In most cases, however, these goals are also sought through informal bargaining with management.

The Lobbying Process

Lobbying as a communication process is a subtle blend of facts, persuasion, persistence, power, and pressure. Selling a controversial plan to the legislature is an intricate political process subject to "crisscrossing lines of influence." What one group wants another group opposes.

For several decades police organizations were able to frustrate the efforts of Mayor Lindsay's lobbyists to exempt the City of New York from regulations requiring that the same number of policemen be assigned to each shift. These regulations, which were later amended to mandate the exact hours of each shift, posed a considerable problem for the city Police Commissioner, who desired greater discretion regarding the disposition of manpower. Finally, in 1969 the Mayor received authority from the state to establish a "fourth platoon," which would go on duty during peak crime hours.

The issues of school decentralization and community controls in New York City clearly illustrate the pluralist aspects of lobbying and its political, and on occasion, racial overtones. As a condition for obtaining increased state aid for education, the 1967 legislature passed a bill requiring Mayor Lindsay to submit a school decentralization plan to the legislature in 1968. The aims of the 1967 legislature were threefold: (1) to put pressure on the city to restructure its school system; (2) to make the school system more sensitive to local needs; and (3) to make the school system more effective.

In accordance with the legislature's request, the Mayor submitted his proposal in January 1968. The plan was unacceptable to a legislature facing a general election in November. In its place a mild decentralization plan was put forth by Senator John J. Marchi, a Staten Island Republican. Initially this plan received the support of the United Federation of Teachers and its president, Albert Shanker. Senator Marchi's plan was sharply criticized by the State Board of Regents and Mayor Lindsay as being "meaningless."

Working behind the scenes, the Board of Regents formulated its own bill, which would have replaced the present city Board of Education with a paid three-member education commission and given local school boards within New York City virtually full control over the schools in their communities. Governor Rockefeller predicted passage of the Regents' strong decentralization bill, but the Regents' bill collapsed in the face of the combined opposition of the United Federation of Teachers, the New York City Board of Education, and the school system's supervisory groups, who favored a gradual decentralization that would retain some degree of central control.

The UFT, led by Shanker, was instrumental in scuttling the Regents' Bill. The Regents' plan was criticized on the grounds that it failed to provide for city-wide school hiring, nationwide teacher recruitment, and adequate school financing.

The lobbying on behalf of a watered-down school decentralization plan offers a classic example of effective lobbying tactics. Shanker organized a demonstration of several hundred parents and teachers, who traveled from New York City to Albany in a special train to "buttonhole" legislators for an entire day. He openly stated that the UFT spent between $125,000 and $255,000 to win public and political support for its views. The word was spread that the UFT would dip into its treasury to defeat any legislator who voted against the union's position, and the New York *Times* depicted Shanker as being "very visible in Albany today, huddling with aides in corridors, remonstrating with legislative officials in their offices, talking intently on hallway pay phones...."[18]

After derailing the Regents' bill, the UFT lobbyists worked out another decentralization plan, and the stage was seemingly set for legislative action. At the last moment Shanker attempted to strengthen the mild plan by prohibiting the Board of Education from delegating to local community school districts the power to hire and discharge teachers. The new demands raised the hackles of legislators, who explained that there was sufficient protection for teachers in the completed bill. Legislators also pointed out to Shanker that if his opposition prevented the adoption of a mild plan, the legislature might be recalled into special session to enact a stronger one.

In its final form the decentralization plan enlarged the city's Board of Education from 9 to 13 members, thus allowing Mayor Lindsay—a proponent of decentralization—to appoint four prodecentralization members. This enlarged board was then required to draft a detailed permanent decentralization plan within certain guidelines and to present it to the state Board of Regents for the approval of the 1968 legislature. In effect, the legislature voted to postpone any decentralization plan for at least a year.

The racial issue dominated the debate, as many legislators expressed concern about the growing dissatisfaction in the city's black ghettos over the effectiveness of local schools. The unrest in the predominantly black Ocean Hill-Brownsville demonstration district, where the local governing board ousted 19 educators without formal charges, dramatized the volatile issue of decentralization.

Mayor Lindsay emphasized that this predicament would never have occurred if a meaningful decentralization plan had been in existence, whereupon Shanker announced that it was a harbinger of what would come to pass elsewhere in the city if the Regents' plan was enacted. One thing is certain: Shanker's extensive lobbying campaign in Albany and his teacher boycott of the Ocean Hill-Brownsville demonstration district exacerbated the tension that had developed between the UFT and the black community as a result of the 1967 teachers' strike.

The end result, as described by A. H. Raskin, was that after 10 weeks of political manipulation over decentralization at Albany and City Hall, racial crosspulls within the Central Labor Council, and universal exhaustion, a settlement was arrived at that both the UFT and the black community could live with.

The amount of money actually expended on lobbying is not known. The UFT reported spending a total of $629,198 during fiscal year 1969 on activities related to legislation.

Two conclusions appear warranted: substantial sums are expended to further the interests of employee organizations, and no one has ever been prosecuted for a violation of New York State statutes governing expenditures for lobbying.

Methods of Lobbying

Many informal methods of lobbying are used to attain political results. The process is long and tedious work and ranges from the compilation of information to having a few drinks with people who carry weight in the legislative arena. Some employee organizations privately concede that committees are established to find out all they can about legislators and public officials, including their personal affairs and interests: Does he play bridge? Does he have a mortgage on a property? Does he have club memberships? Does he play golf? etc. One union leader candidly remarked:

> ...this technique works—"the contact"—and is far more effective than to appear before legislative committees. This kind of thing, in my book, is a lot more effective than waving banners and ballyhooing the strike. The new legislator, in particular, who is a stranger in town is interested in meeting people with similar interests. Your aims, however, have to be such that the people you recruit to do these things are willing to devote themselves to them—wages, pensions, in-service training, etc. They are not necessarily•done for idealistic reasons, but because they are very practical matters.

The annual record of gains through formal and informal lobbying is substantial. During the 1968 session of the New York State legislature, the Civil Service Employees Association claimed that it had won a pay increase, guaranteed half-pay retirement benefits, and a cut in the time required to draw such benefits from 30 years to 20 years and that state employees were no longer required to contribute to their pension plans.[19] Each year the goals are limited, and each year gains are made. The total progress over the past decade is astounding.

The Use of Coalitions

During the early 1900's the lobbying efforts of municipal employee organizations were characterized by divisiveness, intergroup competition, and inexperience. A recent tendency is the use of coalitions to exert added pressure on legislators. For example, a coalition of some 350,000 county and municipal employees in Michigan began to take shape in 1969. The proposed coalition includes membership from such diverse organizations as the International Brotherhood of Teamsters, AFSCME, the Building Trades Council, and the Michigan Federation of Teachers. By charting strategy, the combined efforts could muster the strongest "political punch" of any single lobby in the state. Intended eventually to include nurses, firemen, and police, the coalition will press for legislation to provide legal sanctions against city and county units involved in prolonged labor disputes.

The preceding year, a possible "union of unions" for Michigan police officers was in the process of formation, and by October 1968 at least 25 police unions in the state had joined the new Police Officers Association of Michigan.

The movement toward coalition lobbying is not confined to Michigan. Flushed with confidence over their use of the referendum technique to achieve a victory over the Mayor's opposition, St. Louis, Mo., firemen noted in September 1970 that they would be a potent political force working in combination with 8,000 civil service workers and 2,000 policemen.

At least as early as 1967, 20,000 members of AFSCME, the UFT, and the TWU gathered in New York City's Madison Square Garden and declared that they would bolster their resources to devote particular attention to political-legislative activity and "stand together in defense of one another" until the evils inflicted by the strike prohibitions of the Taylor Law, which replaced the Condon-Wadlin Law, were repealed.

The most recent plea of this nature is the statement of President Wurf of AFSCME. Wurf has recommended a coalition of AFL-CIO and independent unions representing federal, state, county, and municipal employees, to lobby jointly to change both federal and state laws. Such a coalition would tend to mobilize the power of unions, which is now fragmented.

During 1971 several steps were taken toward augmenting the lobbying strength of organized local government employees. Jerry Wurf entered into an agreement to engage his labor-affiliated AFSCME with the independent NEA in joint lobbying activities.

Albert Shanker, of the New York City UFT, has taken steps to join the AFL-CIO affiliated New York State Federation of Teachers with the New York State Teachers Association, affiliated with the independent NEA, in a new combination, under the suggested name of the United Teachers of New York. This, he declared, would be a first step toward national combination of the NEA and the AFT. On the national level, according to Shanker, such a union, with a potential membership of 3,000,000, would be the largest in the country and "could apply political leverage in behalf of teacher's interests."

The Electoral Activity of Municipal Employee Organizations

Municipal employee organizations have engaged in a variety of electoral activities, which include assistance to party organizations by providing manpower, information, money, and endorsements.

Manpower, Information, and Money

Several hundred newspapers and journals are published by the labor movement, and they are presumably read by perhaps one third of the households throughout the country. Other informational devices are utilized to make the public aware of labor issues. Union leaders speak before conventions and meetings of professional associations. If union leaders are not among the panelists, those most likely to engage in colloquy are other representatives of employee organizations. Typically, union members can be used to provide a built-in audience for candidates they prefer.

Money, as well as manpower, is an essential ingredient of political success. No reliable figures are available as to the amount of money municipal employee organizations expend in support of candidates. There are a variety of ways in which campaign expenses may be hidden, and much doubt has been cast as to the validity of studies in this area. Money expended for research, legal fees, and public relations in many cases directly benefits legislators who sponsor desired legislation.[20]

Union Endorsements

It has become commonplace for municipal employee organizations to endorse state and local candidates. Many factors influence the decision whether to endorse officially, to support but not endorse, or to play a neutral role. The prior history of negotiations is not necessarily a guide. In 1965 New York City's TWU endorsed Lindsay's opponent Abe Beame. Despite the prior bitter negotiations that had led to the jailing of TWU President Michael Quill, in 1969 Quill's successor opted to endorse the Mayor in his quest for re-election. Perhaps the composition of the TWU membership in 1969 partially motivated the reversal. The more than 17,000 nonwhites in the TWU probably preferred Lindsay to his more "conservative" opponents. Moreover, the new president, Matthew Guinan, had no history of personal clashes with Lindsay, as was the case with Quill. The TWU had also negotiated good contracts with Lindsay in 1966 and 1968, and where you have had success with an incumbent, why gamble with an unknown quantity?

There are sound reasons why public employee organizations should not officially endorse candidates. When the union supports the loser, it later finds itself dealing with the victor, who may have a long memory. Some individuals oppose the action as inconsistent with the concept of political neutrality of civil servants, who are, as discussed above, subjected to restrictions on political activity in order to avoid the slightest appearance of political motivation in their work. In reality, the mere exposure of a candidate's record may be tantamount to an endorsement or rejection. And surely the actions and statements of employee leadership, while short of official endorsement, are easily translatable into instructions as to how the membership should vote.

The recent divisiveness of society, accentuated by the war in Vietnam and the struggles of the civil rights movement, has tended to emphasize that the organized labor movement is not a monolithic bloc of votes or attitudes. There are many indications of fragmentation within the rank and file of several public employee organizations. In some cases the leadership of the Central Labor Council within a particular city is unable to present a united front, and even executive boards of individual unions are divided. Therefore, the effect of official endorsements is not clear. If, as is often the case, the leadership has been plagued by increasing membership rejection of bargaining contracts, the assumption that the members will vote along the lines of an endorsements cannot be taken for granted but will depend on the individual and the cohesiveness of the organization.

Labor and the Party Apparatus

The extent to which labor is involved in the party apparatus is also subject to wide variations. In some cities there is virtually an interlocking relationship; in others the employee organizations have limited themselves to the traditional acts of cooperation or alliances with entrenched machines. In still other cases the employee organization has openly fought the party machine and even attempted to replace it—or at least to elect union members to the position of precinct captain, to bring influence to bear on the party organization. Party machines are in disarray in some of the larger cities, and labor, which includes public employee organizations, has become a significant political force, from the precinct level to the apex of established party organizations.

"The best political machine in New York City is John DeLury's Sanitationmen's Union."[21] This accolade, delivered by a former leader of Tammany Hall, the Democratic party organization in New York County, is not likely to be denied by the leader of the Uniformed Sanitationmen's Association or to be ignored by city and even state officials. When Costikyan stated, "I would rather have John DeLury's sanitationmen with me in an election than half the party headquarters in town," DeLury proudly replied, "Only God can guarantee 100 percent delivery [of votes]. We are sure of 99 percent, based on past performance."[22] The belief in the enormous political power of the sanitation union was long fostered under the slogan of "We strike through the ballot."

Whether the claim of massive political power is illusion or reality is beside the point. While some critics of DeLury assert that such claim is exaggerated, the sanitationmen are certainly equipped to do the job. Manpower is available to distribute literature house by house, with two men per an election district of one to five city blocks, and 1,000 additional members are available for central services. Estimating that his union has "direct contact" with 150,000 voters, the union chief boasts of his card file on every member, former member, retired member, and deceased member's widow. The card system is arranged by both assembly district and election district.

The basic thrust of the organization has been political, and the few strikes that have occurred—in particular the major strike of 1968—resulted from rank and file pressure, with the press noting that DeLury "exhibited terror when his men bulldozed him into striking." Indeed, if the Mayor felt that he had cornered DeLury by temporarily isolating him from his membership, he was playing with dynamite. Normally, management should support responsible leadership's influence with the rank and file rather than chance the chaos that almost invariably results when it is challenged.

DeLury had pursued a policy of attempting to maintain influential relations at the state capitol, and there was much talk of "friends" in high state offices and boasting of legislative gains, including an excellent 20-year retirement plan and the right of the organization to manage its health and welfare plans. In fact, segments of the press during the strike of 1968 stressed the fact that DeLury was taken from jail by the Governor, who conferred privately with the union leader while the Mayor "cooled his heels" in another part of the building.

The sanitation union had ties with the Democrats during the days when a job largely depended on a "good word" from the "ward heeler." Despite these earlier ties, DeLury's ship moved with the political winds. His union was the backbone of Vincent Impellitteri's successful mayoralty campaign in 1950. In 1954 DeLury supported Robert F. Wagner, Jr., and he subsequently backed Wagner in his fight against Carmine DeSapio's regular party organization in 1961. These actions in no way deferred the sanitation chief from supporting the regular Democratic party organization and backing Averell Harriman for Governor in 1958 or from remaining neutral when Nelson Rockefeller ran for Governor in 1962 and becoming the first organized labor leader to announce support for Rockefeller in the gubernatorial race of 1966.

The flamboyant DeLury made sounds at every opportunity, but the orchestration of the political symphony never lost its basic melody. When Mayor Lindsay had his picture taken while sweeping the streets bordering his official residence, Gracie Mansion, DeLury chided, "If the Mayor wants to sweep, don't let him use a woman's broom; let him use a real broom." Maestro DeLury then waved his baton at the "Italian section" of his orchestra. Objecting strongly to Lindsay's appointment of Edgar D. Crosswell to the newly created post of Inspector-General in the Sanitation Department, DeLury scornfully announced: "We don't need a Gestapo to watch over us. ...We are not the Mafia." Mr. Crosswell, a former state trooper, had played a prominent role in the state police raid directed at the upstate New York meeting of the Mafia.

When the Mayor was considering the elimination of the Sanitation Band as an economy measure, Mr. DeLury vowed a slowdown during public hearings on the city budget. Despite the rhetoric and the subsequent strike, the sanitation union supported Lindsay in his 1969 campaign for reelection. In the interim DeLury had won substantial pay increases and other benefits for the sanitation workers.

In December of 1966 Commissioner of Sanitation Kearing, during attempts to reorganize his department, charged that the Sanitation Department was "the most politically dominated department" in the city. It was a well-known fact that some positions were filled by "clubhouse techniques," and doorbell ringing during campaigns was not the only politics. According to Kearing, "...politics have also been involved in a large number of religions and ethnic minorities in the department, all ... urging promotions and favors for members of the particular group."[23] When Kearing was dismissed some months later, DeLury reportedly commented, "My men love him." The union leader realizes that politics is the active principle, both within the department and in its relationships with the city administration. As he frequently reminds his members,

"You may be a garbageman, but you're not garbage." Mr. Costikyan has forcefully pointed out the power that Mr. DeLury possesses:

> ...the Department of Sanitation,...is run by the Sanitation workers.
> If the party is impotent to exercise control...it does not follow that the mayor and commissioner are similarly impotent. Indeed, they do have power which they exercise from time to time. And the Bureaucracy...obeys.
> But the mayor's and the commissioner's power flows largely from John DeLury's insistence that they have it. [24]

AFSCME District Council 37

Not all employee organizations have participated in political campaigns for as long as the New York sanitationmen. Some organizations lacked the cohesiveness necessary to acquire the reputation of political strength, even though they were much larger numerically. Within two years of the Madison Square Garden Rally of May 1967, however, a great transition had occurred, turning the political apparatus sought by AFSCME District Council 37's leadership into a powerful reality.

The Council created a political action and legislative department, specifically charged with the task of political action. There were two basic goals: to achieve enactment of legislation favorable to the union and to elect sympathetic and understanding candidates who would make such legislation possible.

The Delegate Assembly's Legislative Committee concentrates on securing the passage of legislation at the state capitol, maintaining a permanent, full-time lobbyist at Albany. A political and community-action committee has also been established by the Delegate Assembly, to evaluate the records of all candidates, make recommendations to the Executive Board, and directly aid candidates endorsed by the union. The Executive Director primarily handles the union's political relations with the Mayor and City Council.

In 1969 the newly established political units had their baptism of fire. District Council 37 volunteers helped man "street-front headquarters" for the incumbent Mayor. Other volunteers rang doorbells, distributed literature, and made thousands of phone calls urging support of Lindsay. Literally millions of pieces of literature favoring the Mayor were prepared and printed by the organization. Union personnel worked closely with the Citizen's Voter Registration campaign, assisting with special registration efforts at hospitals, schools, and other locations throughout the city. In addition, the union arranged for the use of sound trucks and cars and provided drivers and poll watchers. The purchase of tables at fund-raising dinners helped to attract needed funds.

Mayor Lindsay had created a broad based "fusion advisory committee" to advise and coordinate the efforts of the diverse groups supporting him. District Council 37's Executive Director, Victor Gotbaum, became a key member of the fusion committee. Immediately after his re-election, Mayor Lindsay praised the effective work of Gotbaum and the union, just as Mayor James Tate effusively had praised the efforts of District Council 33 in his behalf in the 1967 Philadelphia primary and general elections.

The Executive Director bluntly stated that District Council 37 would enter the political arena to insure that an administration that believed in "honest collective bargaining" remained in office. In remarks apparently applied to Lindsay's predecessor, Gotbaum declared that the leadership was determined that "the political fix would not return to City Hall."

AFSCME's relationships with the Lindsay regime are clearly more harmonious than those that existed between AFSCME and the city during the Wagner era. Indications are that AFSCME didn't do itself any harm by supporting Lindsay, notwithstanding Gotbaum's statement that "no political favors are sought or will be given when the organization's interests diverge from that of City Hall." However, the probability is that District Council 37 will not become too closely attached to the administration in power, for fear that such attachment would impair its ability, in Gotbaum's words, to "reward our friends and make our enemies terribly insecure."

Because of its previous political successes, District Council 37 formulated in plans in 1970 to organize on an assembly district basis. The organization claims that in each of New York City's 68 assembly districts there are 1,200 "Council families," which if properly organized could constitute a big and powerful grouping for specific political objectives.

AFSCME units have made several attempts, with varying measures of success, to engage in electoral politics. In 1961 the New York District Council had supported the unsuccessful candidacy in the primaries of State Comptroller Arthur Levitt against Mayor Wagner. The result might have been a disaster for the union had it not been for the political sagacity of Mayor Wagner, who continued to maintain good relations with the union as though nothing had happened.

Several local leaders of AFSCME have taken active roles in local and state politics. In the 1950's a local leader named Roth was elected to the Colorado State Senate, where he played an active role in support of the interests of state and local employees. Likewise, in Rhode Island a union official named Ambrose Raleigh ran successfully for public office.

In the early 1960's Al Bilik, who had served as Director of the Cincinnati AFSCME District 51, became President of the central labor body. In 1965 he ran for the City Council on the Democratic ticket. He was defeated in a campaign that oriented AFSCME to the Democratic party. Bilik's defeat, according to a prominent union leader, was due to mistaken tactics:

> ...you cannot run a Council campaign in Cincinnati on the basis of party ideology, it's got to be run on the basis of individuals. Al Bilik didn't agree with this; he was determined that the way you beat the Republicans in Cincinnati is to run a Democratic ideological campaign. The only way to get somebody is to knock somebody out on the other side. Al Bilik beat himself because he insisted on an ideological approach.

The unofficial alignment of AFSCME District 51 with the Democratic party was strongly opposed by several influential union spokesmen. One said that Samuel Gompers' maxim, "Reward your friends and punish your enemies at the polls," offered the most effective policy for political action in local politics by municipal unions. He reasoned:

> The formal alliance between labor and the Democratic party is a serious mistake. Very frankly, I feel that we've done rather well even with the Republican administration. The policy of the Council now, at least, is going to be that if the guy is going along with us, we're going along with him and forget party labels.

Conventional observation appears to indicate that unions are not actually able to "deliver" the votes of their members. They have certainly not been able to do so in hard-core Republican Cincinnati. Yet, politicians, who like all tightrope walkers are supercautious, seek and respect union endorsements. The influence of unions lies to a large extent on their power to give or withhold endorsements, to make willing members available for bell ringing, contributions, the distribution of campaign literature, and the sponsoring of meetings. The actual delivery of membership at the polls is another matter.

In the two elections in which the prominent Democrat Averell Harriman ran for Governor of New York, the upstate public employees were, like their neighbors, overwhelmingly Republican in sentiment. A reliable observer declared:

There is pretty good evidence that their level of political participation, measured by voter registration, was lower than the populace at large. This is an anomaly in the public sector, because it is also true that public employees are much more sophisticated about the political processes and the law than are most employees.

This remark, of course, preceded the days of the public union explosion and collective bargaining. Writing in The New York *Times* in 1971 Tom Kahn, Executive Director of the League for Industrial Democracy, noted that a couple of candidates for the party office of District Leader in Manhattan called a press conference to denounce the UFT for "interfering" in the leadership race. UFT President Albert Shanker had sent a letter to teachers in the district in which he pointed out that the candidates in question had been involved in attempts to break the 1968 school strike and were opposed to the union in other ways.

Declaring that labor must not retreat from politics and leave the field to its opponents, Kahn went on to say:

> Teachers and other public employees have a special stake in seeing that this does not happen. Indeed it is not accidental that the expansion of labor's political action programs parallels the growth of public employee unionism. Not only are such employees directly affected by government policies, but their jobs are such as very often to put them in the center of society's racial and class conflicts. What kind of schools teachers teach in—or whether they will teach at all—is decided by public officials and the political parties determine who these officials will be. Political unionism is a necessity. [25]

The Teachers

During the early decades of the 20th century, the teachers, while organized, were not active politically. The traditional opposition toward mixing education and politics militated against effective, concerted political action. In many school districts almost any overt political action was deemed cause for dismissal. The major exceptions were the limited number of truly professional administrators and those few teachers who comprised the union vanguard.

Despite the political naivete of the mass of teachers prior to World War II, teachers as a professional group had operated effectively as lobbyists at state capitols. These early lobbying efforts, however, were largely a low-pressure operation, in part a result of the ethos of the profession. The main thrust of the operation was a coalition of teacher associations, school administrator associations, and parent-teacher groups. Generally, the coalition was dominated by administrators, with exceptions in some key states, including California and Michigan.

Following World War II, both the NEA and the AFT endeavored to "educate" the mass of teachers in the use of the political process to enhance "teacher power." By 1962 the transformation into militancy was obvious. The NEA Citizenship Committee sent to each Congressman and Senator a reprint of the NEA Journal article of October 1961 entitled, "The Teaching and Practice of Politics."[26] None of the legislators' responses questioned the propriety of teacher participation in politics, as long as teachers "kept personal politics out of the classroom."

The teaching profession had extensive power assets at their disposal. For decades administrators and professional educators at the universities had controlled the profession through influencing teacher-certification legislation, by administering teacher-training institutions, and by the contacts they had developed with "education committees" of state legislatures and state departments of education.

Professional expertise facilitated "feeding information" to specific legislators, who soon acquired reputations as legislative experts in education. This technique became more significant in education, perhaps, than in other areas of social policy determined by legislative bodies. There was a natural growth of informal contacts between university personnel, public school administrators, professionals on school boards and legislative leaders and their allies on educational policy.

At one point a single university professor became the "center of gravity" for much educational legislation enacted in New York State. The professor, who had taught for many years, had an outstanding reputation, which was further enhanced by the simple fact that many of his students had subsequently acquired positions within the educational power structure of the state. Some had become school superintendents, many were school principals, others served on school boards, and still others had become university professors of education who either taught or became members of the research component of the state Department of Education.

The expertise and ability of these individuals, in conjunction with their continued formal and informal contacts, enabled them to hold and exchange posts in government agencies that influenced education policy. As a result, a game of "musical chairs" was played. Furthermore, legislatures were confronted with interlocking informal relationships not readily apparent to the public.

University professors, school administrators, teacher representatives, school board association representatives, state Education Department officials, and a few concerned parents would appear before legislative committees' in Albany to support or oppose various bills. These "independent" appearances were ostensibly objective in character. In the opinion of some close observers, however, both the legislation and the testimony show the stamp of professional administrators. Except when this "interlocking directorate" was confronted with the classical problems of "race, reds, religion, and money"—at these points they clashed with equally strong and competitive political forces—the established educational power structure could pretty well write its own ticket.

The AFT and the NEA

Because of the increasingly dominant role of professional administrators, the AFT has emerged as a strong rival to the century-old NEA. Both the AFT and the NEA have stepped up their political action, at times in coalition and at times in bitter competition. Both organizations have sought to eliminate strike prohibitions and have campaigned for increased wages and fringe benefits, improved retirement plans, measures to enhance organizational security, a greater role for professionals in the decision-making structure, and the appropriation of greater sums to advance and improve education.

The AFT has lobbied extensively at the nation's capitol and, assisted by the political efforts of its large affiliates, in major cities. In an attempt to counter long-standing charges of unprofessionalism made by the NEA, the AFT has sought to step up its research activity, at the same time steadfastly maintaining that its trade union activities are integral and indispensable elements of true professionalism.

The NEA's most effective political role is played in Washington. The political role of the NEA at state capitols is governed by its relationships with its affiliated state educational associations. The resultant interaction motivates the state unit to attempt to maintain the key decisions at the state level. In practice the actual flow of power is largely determined by the strength, composition, and quality of leadership of the state unit.

The NEA has other roles that, while technically nonpolitical, have a political effect or serve as the rationale for political action and even for the modus operandi that ensues. For example, to improve education the NEA conducts extensive research with regard to educational policy and teaching. Critics of the NEA insist that the purpose of pouring vast sums into education is sometimes not so much to improve education as to enhance an already entrenched bureaucracy. Certainly, the NEA has served a worthy purpose as a national forum on education, but critics respond that the so-called forum is really a "closed system" that perpetuates administrator power.

The Education Lobby in Action: A Classic Case

In January 1970 the NEA called for a "summit meeting" of educators in Washington to plot tactics to add $1.3 billion to the budget of the Department of Health, Education and Welfare in the face of a presidential threat to veto such a bill.[27] The intense and dramatic pressure by educational lobbyists led Senator Percy of Illinois to comment, "The kind of pressure I'm getting from Illinois is absolutely fantastic...I think I have heard from every school board and school district in the state."

The actions pursued by the lobby are a classic example of how to influence legislative policy making. Key education lobbyists participated in drafting the bill, which was a shrewd concoction designed to appeal to diverse groups. For example, there was the possibility of money for every Congressional District, and there was provision for substantial sums for 385 school districts with large concentrations of federal employees. Vocational education was to receive a sizable increase in funds, and more money was to become available for student loans.

The coalition concept was implemented, with over 80 education groups participating. The NEA and the AFT put aside their rivalry and engaged in a concerted effort to persuade teachers, school administrators, librarians, school boards, parent groups, and universities to send representatives to Washington. Even university presidents and trustees were enlisted to engage in the trial by legislative combat. The aid of organized labor was requested, and the AFL-CIO supported the action and lobbied extensively.

The coalition hired a special executive secretary to coordinate the efforts of the diverse groups and individuals involved. Teams were created, briefing sessions were held, and specific assignments were given, supplemented by the exchange of information and reports. The "interlocking directorate" was revealed when it was reported that the U.S. Office of Education was supplying much of the data favorable to the coalition's cause.

Cooperation, concentration, and coordination marked the drive.

Where persuasion failed, "coercion," in the form of threats of political retaliation, was to be employed without compunction. Washington was inundated with "imported educators," the goal being at least one for each member of Congress. The political burners were turned on high. Each legislator was informed that a record vote would be insisted upon, and the lobby warned that "observers" would be stationed to record the "teller votes." Legislators supporting the bill were visited in their offices to make certain that they voted; legislators opposing the bill were urged not to vote, on the grounds that if he were "absent" the legislator might be dealt with less harshly politically than if he were to cast a vote against the bill. Information was made available to the lobbying teams that enabled them to concentrate on legislators already in trouble with their home districts. The "floor manager" of the bill was briefed on resistance and progress.

Nor was the home front forgotten. The coalition had previously instructed both state and local groups to contact and to pressure legislators who were home during the three week congressional recess in December. Upon their return to Washington, these legislators were reminded that press releases would be issued explaining that any cuts might well result in higher local taxes. They were further admonished that any actions, inimical or favorable, would receive wide publicity. All considered, the major effort constituted a classic maneuver in the politics of education, a maneuver in which public employee organizations played the principal role.

Fire Fighters and Police

Fire fighters and police have adapted their political activities to the special requirements imposed by law in certain jurisdictions. For example, the City Charter in Denver, Colo., requires that the salaries of firemen and police can only be changed with the approval of the voters. Voters in Denver approved a 10 percent pay raise in a special referendum in 1967. Three years later, Local 109 of the International Brotherhood of Police Officers and Local 858 of the International Association of Fire Fighters again joined forces to place on the ballot a proposal to amend the charter to authorize collective bargaining on wages and other terms of employment.

In 1966 Detroit's fire fighters secured 51,000 signatures to place on the ballot a proposition authorizing a 12-hour reduction in the work week with no loss in pay. Similarly, the San Francisco Police Officers Association filed some 92,000 signatures on initiative petitions, demonstrating the political support that can be mustered for such matters as higher pay, a 10 percent night-pay differential, and time and a half pay for overtime work.

The same year, St. Louis, Mo., firemen used the referendum as a device to achieve pay equal to that of the police, the parity proposal being accepted by nearly 65 percent of the voters. During their campaign for voter approval of the proposition the firemen reportedly spent $50,000.

Economy groups have been tolerant of the demands of public safety forces, generally favoring increases in manpower totals even when they resisted wage increases. For such reason, a favored strategy, as early as the 1920's and 1930's, was for the safety forces to seek referenda on wage issues, and this tactic also transferred the political onus of costs to the people.[28]

For decades the police have used political tactics to secure their objectives. They have lobbied with regard to the number of platoons, the tours of duty, the right to "moonlight" on jobs not inconsistent with their police duties, and the right of "outsiders" to judge their performance. Much of the activity has been to maintain the relatively high bureaucratic autonomy they have achieved over the years.

Police have become more and more active in their attempts to nullify charter or legislative restrictions on their political activity. When lobbying fails, more direct tactics having political consequences have been employed. Detroit's police succumbed to a siege of the "blue flu" in 1967, and in 1968 New York City's police force was afflicted with an epidemic of "Hong Kong flu."

Some police departments undertook job actions constituting a "slowdown," others engaged in a "superenforcement" campaign to exert a different kind of political pressure. Members of the Milwaukee, Wisc., police bargaining team engaged in a 9-hour "sit-in, sleep-in" at City Hall in 1970, and no police were called to evict them. Members of the Knoxville, Tenn., Fraternal Order of Police drew attention by threatening to engage in a "pray-in" at Evangelist Billy Graham's meetings. Their leader commented, "As President of the FOP, I cannot advocate work stoppages, strikes, or sick call-ins, but I am a firm believer in prayer."[29]

Increasingly, fire fighter and police organizations are officially endorsing candidates for office who are sympathetic to the objectives of their organizations, the most recent example being the endorsement by New York City's Patrolmen's Benevolent Association and Uniformed Firefighters Association of James Buckley, the Conservative party candidate, in his successful bid for election to the U.S. Senate in 1970. A few years previously the PBA had openly cooperated with the same party to secure the abolition of the Civilian Review Board, an "outside" panel that had been established to judge police performance.

The most succinct statement of current trends is indicated in a 1970 statement by the President of the International Conference of Police Associations:

[The ICPA] will not just sit by and criticize, we shall actually support candidates and legislatures supporting law enforcement, and we shall work against candidates...who are anti-good law enforcement. We shall let the public know who are the judges that are letting the criminals go free....it's time someone spoke out and answered the bleeding hearts and sob sisters who have been fighting for the advantage of the criminals. [30]

The initial caution of the police induced by the disastrous effects of the Boston police strike is but a distant memory. Police in many municipalities have actively entered the political arena.

The Central Trades and Labor Councils

The Central Trades and Labor Councils of the AFL-CIO are important participants in the political life of cities. Including its membership delegate representatives of each of the local AFL-CIO unions, in a city's Council of course encompass affiliated public employee organizations. The Council thus serves as a useful source of strength in achieving the objectives of public employee unions.

Three major functions are performed by the Council: it is instrumental in adjusting jurisdictional differences between member unions; it combines the resources of the labor movement in disputes with employers; and it generally exercises labor's influence on the city's government and its politics. [31]

New York City's Central Council, headed by its elected leader, Harry Van Arsdale, illustrates the immense power that can be wielded by an association of more than 500 labor unions, with a combined membership of 1 million plus. Frequently, the Council's chieftains are called upon by city officials to assist in the resolution of the city's disputes with its employee organizations. Working sometimes openly and other times quietly behind the scenes, the Council has been of immeasurable help both to labor and to the city. When individual public employee unions threaten the broader interests of the total labor movement, pressure is brought to bear on employee leaders by the Council to cool the rhetoric and reach a settlement.

The influence of the leader of the Central Council will depend on his personal dimension of power within the organized labor movement, and his power base will shift in tune with time, the issues involved, the parties involved, and the political environment generally. Van Arsdale has long been the man to see when a union wanted action from the City of New York.

The niceties of union protocol got as much attention in Wagner's dealings with Van Arsdale as diplomatic protocol gets in U Thant's dealings with President Nixon or Premier Kosygin. Wagner's invariable question when his chief labor advisor, Theodore W. Kheel, came to him with a proposal affecting labor was, "Have you cleared this with Van Arsdale?" The only exception was transit. Then the question became, "Have you cleared this with Quill?" The result was that the union establishment was never caught off base by a Wagner move. [32]

During the New York City teachers' strikes in 1967 and 1968, influential Council members were aware that the seemingly unalterable stance of the union on some issues could bring the city to open warfare. The Council worked covertly with the union, Mayor Lindsay, and the Board of Education to bring about a compromise.

In other instances the Council may find it necessary to take a public stand. For example, during the sanitation strike of 1968 in New York City, (See Chapter 10 for a more complete discussion of the New York City sanitation strike.) The Council leadership issued the statement, "We will not tolerate the use of the militia against any workers." This was backed by a declaration of the Executive Board empowering a special committee to "take any action necessary—including a strike—if National Guardsmen are called in." The strike action referred to was a "general strike"; and some of Mayor Lindsay's aides implied that the talk of union-busting and a general strike was fostered by Governor Rockefeller to pressure the Mayor. When the Governor was criticized by the news media for not taking a stronger position against the sanitation union, Van Arsdale assailed "the filthy press for their stand against labor in New York," and praised the Governor for "having the kind of guts a public official should have."

The extent to which public employee unions will receive the all-out support of the Central Council in their battles with the city will depend on the city, the issues, and the personalities involved. Some public employee union leaders interviewed by the authors indicated that they had been around the labor movement long enough to know that the only support one could expect was moral support. Others interviewed made clear that the amount of support the Council gave was in part a response to how closely the public employee unit had cooperated with and supported the Council's activities.

While the Council by no means constitutes an irresistible monolith, it remains a powerful lobbying and mediative force in the labor relations of a city. Furthermore, while the Council has only limited ability to speak for the whole labor movement, it remains the most important political expression of the combined unions in a specific area.

Notes

1. *The Civil Service Leader*, April 16, 1968.
2. Robert A. Dahl, *Who Governs* (New Haven: Yale University Press, 1961), pp. 76, 253-54.
3. This point of view has been cogently stated in Herman Finer, *The Theory and Practice of Modern Government* (New York: Holt, 1949), pp. 614-17.
4. See Norton Long, "Public Policy and Administration: The Goals of Rationality and Responsibility," *Public Administration Review*, Winter, 1954. A leading authority, referring to the Administrative Class of the British Civil Service, states: "The duties of the administrative class include the formation of policy, the coordination of government machinery and the general administration and control of the departments of the public service," Frank Dunhill, *The Civil Service*, 1956, p. 221. See also H. E. Dale, *The Higher Civil Service of Great Britain*, 1941.
5. This point has been clearly shown in *Report of the Commission on Political Activity of Government Personnel* (Washington, D.C., 1968.)
6. See Pamela S. Ford, *Political Activities of the Public Service: A Continuing Problem* (Berkeley, Calif.: Institute of Governmental Studies, 1963.)
7. The above summary relating to Detroit, Philadelphia, and Cincinnati is based upon letters received from the Office of the Corporation Counsel, City Solicitor, and Department of Personnel, respectively.
8. Restrictions in New York are set forth in the Civil Service Law, Section 107.1; the State Penal Law, Section 772-a; and the New York City Charter, Sections 439, 1107, 1108, and 1109.
9. The Holmes dictum was cited in *McAuliffe v. Mayor of the City of Bedford*, 125 Mass. 216, 29 N.E. 517 (1892). See Arch Dotson, "The Emerging Doctrine of Privilege in Public Employment," *Public Administration Review*, Spring 1955, p. 77 and Dotson, "A General Theory of Public Theory of Public Employment," *Public Administration Review*, Spring 1956, p. 197.
10. See *Bagley v. Washington Township Hospital District*, 421 P. 2d 409 (1970) and *Fort v. Civil Service Commission*, 392 P. 2d 385 (1964).
11. *Los Angeles Teachers Union, AFT, Local 1021 v. Board of Education*, Case No. 29637, Calif. Sup. Ct., June 30, 1969. The decision indicated that neither the possibility of dissension nor the disturbance of work duties would outweigh the First Amendment protections in this area.

12. See *American Law Reports*, Vol. 163, pp. 1363-70.

13. See Whitney N. Seymour, Jr., "Must Civil Servants be Politicians Too?" *Good Government*, Winter 1967, p. 11. Mr. Seymour concluded that "Our nation's health and future as a democracy depend on prohibiting *all* active political campaigning by civil service employees on all levels of government. ..whether such activity is labeled as 'partisan' or 'non-partisan.' "

14. See Louis S. Loeb, "Public Employees and Political Activity: New Realities Require Fresh Approaches," *Good Government*, Winter 1967, p. 8.

15. A. H. Raskin, "Politics Up-Ends the Bargaining Table," Paper presented at the American Management Association Conference, March 22-24, 1971.

16. Harry A. Donoian, *The Government Employee's Council: Its Organization and Operations*, Washington, D.C.: Government Employees Council, 1968.

17. Wallace Sayre and Herbert Kaufman, Governing New York City (New York: Russell Sage Foundation, 1960), p. 428.

18. New York *Times*, May 25, 1968.

19. *Civil Service Leader*, May 21, 1968.

20. Alexander Heard, *The Cost of Democracy*, (Chapel Hill, N.C.: University of North Carolina Press, 1960) presents a significant study of expenditures incurred by private sector unions. Heard concluded that the $2 million or so of free funds that 17 million union members contributed in 1956 about equalled the reported voluntary contributions of $500 and over made by 742 officials of the nation's 225 largest business concerns. Heard also indicated that six sevenths of all electoral expenditures were incurred at the state, district, and local levels, being concentrated in ten states, whose populations include two thirds of all organized labor. See pp. 173-74, 183-84, 187-88, 196.

21. Edward N. Costikyan, "Who Runs The City Government," *New York Magazine*, May 26, 1969, p. 45.

22. Anthony Presondorf, "A Political Machine on Wheels," *New York Post*, February 24, 1968.

23. The New York *Times*, December 20, 1966.

24. Costikyan, op. cit., p. 47.

25. Tom Kahn, "Teachers Unions and Politics: Some Thoughts for Labor Day," The New York *Times*, September 5, 1971.

26. *NEA Journal* vol. iv, no. 3.

27. The following account relies heavily on an excellent summary by Norman C. Miller, "Lobby in Action," *The Wall Street Journal*, January 20, 1970.

28. Sayre and Kaufman, op. cit., pp. 431, 428-29.

29. *Government Employee Relations Reports*, No. 350, May 25, 1970.

30. *Government Employee Relations Reports*, No. 365, August 7, 1970.

31. Temporary Commission on City Finance, New York City, Staff Paper No. 8, 1966, pp. 13-14.

32. Raskin, op. cit.

5 The Bargaining Process

Collective bargaining is a technical process by which the terms of employment are negotiated by the parties to an agreement. While the process is technical and requires considerable negotiating skill, other considerations influence the nature of the contest. Psychological, institutional, and political considerations give a distinctive atmosphere to public service bargaining. Thus, the process includes more than mere preparation for negotiations, the bargaining sessions themselves, and the writing and administering of an agreement.

In some cases the strategy and tactics of the participants become fairly predictable, and negotiations assume the trappings of a highly competitive and belligerent process. Sometimes the process breaks down, and a painful strike must be endured. But in the overwhelming majority of cases agreement is achieved without resort to strikes. This is confirmed by the New York State Public Employment Relation Board, which reports that of the more than 8,000 contracts negotiated in the four-year period 1968-1971, over 70 percent were concluded without third-party assistance.[1] Negotiations are often conducted quietly, reasonably, and professionally, without carnival atmosphere. However, there are cases where agreement is not easily reached without considerable role-playing. What takes place is a highly ritualistic charade, sometimes referred to as the script.

The Script

The pattern of negotiations between the New York City Transit Authority and the Transport Workers Union in the days of the late Michael Quill is a classic illustration of the script. Along about May or June every other year, Quill, the TWU President, would summon members of the press to announce the demands of the TWU for justice, the 30-hour week and various other possible—and impossible—goals to be enshrined in the forthcoming contract with the Transit Authority. "Or else," Quill would thunder, "the trains won't run!"

After the rejection of the union's demands by the Transit Authority and possibly the breaking off of a meeting or two, quiet would descend upon New York for the balance of the summer.

In the fall a series of meetings, usually stormy, would take place, building up to a peak in early December, when someone, usually the TWU leader, would break off negotiations. Quill would warn that there would be no transportation for Christmas shoppers unless talks became serious. The Transit Authority would announce that there was no money to meet the union's "exorbitant" demands.

Just in the nick of time a third party would step in, at the request of the Mayor, to mediate the dispute. Shoppers would be saved, the negotiations would begin to build up to a New Year's climax. Both parties would be summoned to city hall; the mediators would move from the union to the Mayor to the union, building suspense as they went. Finally, a settlement would be announced—usually in time for late TV and radio news broadcasts and the morning papers, and Quill would declare that the embattled transit workers had been victorious.

That was "the script," as written, directed, and produced by Michael Quill. It was his genius that he could maintain the suspense long after the lines had become tiresomely familiar and the militant postures patently false.

From Psychological Warfare to Final Settlement

During the period prior to the announcement of union demands, discussions and studies are undertaken by both sides in preparation for the negotiations about to ensue. Each side marshalls its information, reviews its programs, prepares cost data, and considers

108

the economic and political feasibility of its position. It is not unusual for either side to leak information as a trial balloon for possible later moves.

The script normally begins with the announcement of employee demands, if they have not already been preceded by a flurry of statements by city officials that anticipated budget deficits would make any major pay increases impossible. While the city is claiming the cupboard is bare, the union announces demands that are usually exorbitant and carry an implicit threat of a stormy future. The union's militant but obviously false posture evokes either a stunned reaction by city representatives or utter silence. Both sides have begun the psychological warfare phase of bargaining.

The preliminary sparring is characterized by the city's response to the union's demands. "Incredible, impossible, and ridiculous" state the city representatives. "We are in grave danger," the union leaders retort, "and the city's talk of large impending deficits is nothing but a deliberate plan to stand in the way of justice for city workers."

Bargaining and political maneuvers have already begun, even though formal meetings have not been held. Both sides realize that the initial demands—sometimes several hundred of them, at an estimated cost of more than a billion dollars—bare little resemblance to what a union really wants.

Each side tries to make the other look unreasonable; each side tries to feel the other side out and gain leverage. An exchange of letters or statements may follow, and generally key excerpts find their way to the press. Union rhetoric evinces a feeling of invincibility, but the leadership is aware when the budgetary situation may or may not make the going rough.

The second stage begins with early meetings, sometimes raucous and frequently characterized by temporary breakdowns in negotiations. Both sides are cautious and fear being "boxed in" by a rigid stance. Each side appeals to reason in private and appeals to fears in public. Beginning with generalities, the bargaining shifts to specifics. The role-playing by the negotiators is accompanied by an external scenario, with numerous meetings, demonstrations, and rallies held by the membership. Trade unionists from both the public and private sector pledge support for the embattled employees.

The third stage of the script involves third-party intervention, necessitated, according to the Union, by the shameful, insulting, and provocative tactics of the city, which has caused the impasse. The public officials stress the emergency and crisis conditions faced by a fiscally starved city that is trying for an honorable settlement.

As the contract deadline nears, the serious bargaining takes place and the participants somberly engage in the numbing marathon process. The round-the-clock sessions, with their sense of drama and urgency, end in a "verbal settlement"—when the script works. The clock may even be officially stopped, to postpone the strike deadline. When the script breaks down, the strike is on, and the results are painful to the parties and the public alike.

Appearances and Realities

The ritualistic performance of the script makes for a certain cynicism in labor negotiations. One city negotiator interviewed by the authors stated that the procedure is "unfortunate and maybe a little stupid," since if both he and the union negotiator put their conclusions in a sealed envelope at the start of negotiations, they would not differ by more than half a percent from the figure they finally agreed on. Yet he insisted that the charade was essential to both the city and the union, concluding, "If we don't recognize this, we cannot understand the whole union operation."

An outstanding labor leader also stressed the danger involved in neglecting the script. He emphasized the point that there is a certain form the process must take, with all participants understanding the impact of the role-playing on the public and especially the rank and file of the union.

Even labor leaders opposed to the script as "an excuse for hard work and professionalized bargaining" did not discount the reality of the script, and perhaps its necessity. A union official who had negotiated with Mayor Fiorello La Guardia recounted the following incident:

> We had a meeting with the "Little Flower" which lasted approximately two hours. After much arguing and debating, we concluded an agreement, and I felt we had done quite well. As we were shaking hands and saying good-bye, La Guardia said to me, "You're not finished. You are coming back here tomorrow afternoon and we are going through all this again." I thought the man had to be fooling, but the fact is that we repeated the total performance in public the next day, and the same agreements were reached after the same type of counter arguments.
>
> We put two hours' time before an audience, with the Mayor of the greatest city in the world putting on an act. The significance attached to this performance by La Guardia underscores the significance of the script as a bargaining procedure.

The script can give a cutting edge, add color and a dash of drama to the negotiations. The union leader, constantly exposed to the glare of the press and public scrutiny, is caught in the crossfire of an unyielding management and an implacable membership. He is a double negotiator, who realizes that he may have to pare the demands of the membership, which is on "cloud nine" as a result of the pie-in-the-sky speeches union leaders often make to hold their positions.

A posture of defiance and militancy may be thrust upon him by other union leaders, who have successfully defied the city and came away with gains because they struck. He is pressured by such remarks as, "If it's the noisy wheel that gets the grease, then we are going to become a loud, noisy wheel from now on."

The script demands that the union appear to have won a large victory, wringing from a tough, hard-bargaining management the last cent possible. Indeed, a basic maxim of bargaining, according to a city official, is that the worst thing in the world is to hand a union something on a silver platter, since the leadership feels that if you have the power to give, you are, in fact, taking away their power to get.

Histrionics are a part of the script but are no substitute for results. Victor Gotbaum, Executive Director of District Council 37 AF-SCME, made this sensible appraisal:

> In all collective bargaining relationships, both in the public and private sector, there is a certain amount of histrionics.... But histrionics cannot replace producing for the guys. Merely getting into an argument and banging the table is really peripheral to the problems. Workers know their self-interest, and you really can't play around with them. They may like the idea that Vic Gotbaum bangs the table and gets aggravated, but if I labor and bring forth a mouse, they are not going to be impressed.

The script is far from purely opportunistic and is based on the in-stitutional needs of both sides. It serves a function and possesses a reality beyond rhetoric and histrionics. Far from being a certain, carefully structured, entirely predictable drama leading to predetermined result, it is a means of preserving the traditional form of bargaining when most needed. A strike-free climax is by no means guaranteed, as each side is only generally aware of the directions that negotiations should take. Especially useful where there is substantial prior agreement with regard to basic issues, it is least useful where each side honestly feels that it cannot compromise further. A strong union cannot be built where either side ignores the script. Rather than providing an exercise in duplicity, it serves as a set of psychological ground rules designed to avoid strikes by satisfying the institutional needs of both parties to the bargaining process.

The Private Arrangement

Sometimes the script calls for supplementary arrangements to make the formal agreement possible, such accords, based on unwritten understandings may or may not be made public. Michael Quill and Mayor Wagner brought many New Year's Eve cliff hangers to a peaceful conclusion by unrecorded deals. There were, for example, several so-called attrition understandings, unrecorded but hardly secret, which provided that certain vacant positions would not be filled. In this way enough money was saved to make a mutually acceptable contract between the union and the Transit Authority possible.

In time, of course, that tactic reached its natural limits. As a result, other private arrangements or political *quid pro quos* had to be found. One bargaining point, used to achieve a successful contract in the late 1950's, subsequently backfired. The Mayor objected to what he considered the inordinate cost of sick leave, which he claimed the records showed was caused by questionable one day absences. Since the sick leave privilege was guaranteed by law, new legislation was required to curtail the alleged abuse. The Mayor stated that he would request the state legislature to change the law so that the first day of absence would not be covered by sick leave pay. In turn, Quill agreed not to oppose such legislation vigorously, and the Mayor's bill was enacted.

Once the membership of the TWU felt the impact of the change a rebellion began, and in a comparatively short period of time the union lost an estimated 12,000 members. Quill resorted to increased militancy to recoup his losses. The climax of such militancy occured during Quill's confrontation with Mayor Lindsay.

Prior to the date that Lindsay took office, it was reliably reported that the outgoing Mayor Wagner had agreed on a gross increase for the new contract of $40 million. When the deal came to Lindsay's attention, he denounced it as an arrangement maneuvered by the "power brokers" and demanded "genuine collective bargaining." Quill's uncompromising attitude during the negotiations was sparked to some degree by Lindsay's refusal to adhere to the Quill-Wagner deal. The result was a 12-day transit strike and a contract that cost the city not the previously agreed-upon $40 million but an estimated $60 to $70 million.

112

The Union Role in the Bargaining Process

Many factors tend to complicate the union's role in the bargaining process. Employee organizations have experienced growing pains. They are confronted with the basic problems of effective leadership, factionalism, the difficulty of securing ratification of agreements negotiated by the leadership, and the lack of experienced negotiators. Each has a perceptible impact on the bargaining process.

The Union Leader

The union leader is faced not only with the day-to-day problems of running his organization but also the constant need to prove himself before a demanding, skeptical, and sometimes unruly and faction-torn membership.

"As a negotiator," said one union leader, "you are always looking behind you." The organization's position on issues, as stated by the leader, is circumscribed by the mood of the rank and file. This may limit the leader's ability to maneuver and to carry out preplanned strategic and tactical moves. He is at the mercy of clashing forces within his organization, and a fickle membership may neither understand nor appreciate his moves.

During negotiations the leader tries to keep himself flexible, able to give and take with management and still work out an agreement acceptable to the overwhelming majority of the membership, who may be sharply divided over the priorities of the various demands. For this reason some leaders advocate a "no comment" policy during negotiations, to prevent painting themselves into a corner by public statements.

When reporting to the membership on the progress of negotiations, the leader endeavors to isolate or placate the militant extremists, to safisfy the activists, and to arouse the support of the apathetic. This is not easily accomplished. Dissidents and would-be leaders are ever present, eager to sow the seeds of discontent, goading the incumbent with charges of "deal" and "sell out."

The leader's overriding objective is to produce gains. To achieve the gains he must be a sharp negotiator, a seasoned public relations man, and an astute politician with contacts in the right places, and he must be willing to endure a jail sentence to prove his courage to the membership.

The former head of New York City's UFA showed his mettle by stating, "Even if the Condon-Wadlin (antistrike) law were a workable piece of legislation, we would have to defy it." Albert Shanker, President of the UFT, demonstrated his toughness by bluntly stating, "Now we are beyond abstract lessons in legality; the city has taught us we have to strike to achieve gains." Mr. Shanker served two jail sentences within three years but rallied the support of his membership.

Gains cannot be achieved without effective research and able administrative assistance, which remains the broad responsibility of the union leader. "Some of our union people are extraordinarily inept," said Jerry Wurf, President of AFSCME, "We're working like hell to educate them, to give them expertise."[2] The leader, well aware of this situation, must know when to seek outside economic consultants and other experts to present his case.

The problem of the union's image is a major leadership problem. Conscious of the heavy burden of responsibility to ghetto parents, the UFT during its 1967 strike spent a considerable amount of money to explain their position. UFT teachers conducted classes in churches and storefronts in ghetto areas. It is estimated that the UFT spent at least $100,000 to get its message to the public by means of radio, television, placards in subway cars, and advertisements in the press.

When Floyd McKissick, head of CORE, condemned the teacher union's action as "a classic example of why black communities want to control their own school systems," the UFT leadership countered with telegrams received from such distinguished blacks as Dr. Martin Luther King, Bayard Rustin, and A. Philip Randolph. Rustin pointedly walked the picket line with the UFT President.

The union leader is like a juggler. He cannot antagonize his membership observing the projected image of the "good guy." One moment he is castigating the city with charges of bungling, stalling, and union-busting and subsequently pointing out that the union has been more flexible than the city. The script calls for a mixture of reason, explosive talk, threats, fear, justice, optimism, and pessimism.

Union leaders are also confronted with the problem of resisting the tendency to personalized leadership. As explained by one leader:

> Every success you have in benefiting the rank and file gives you that much more power, that much more prestige, and tends to build up a kind of egocentricity that is very difficult to defeat. This, to many, is the biggest curse of the labor movement; the more successful the leader is, the more difficult it is to maintain his equilibrium and remain immersed in the rank and file.

Probably the most serious problem confronting the union leader is securing membership ratification of agreements presented by the bargaining team. The consensus is that the harder you bargain—or at least appear to bargain—the easier it is to secure membership approval.

Contract rejections stem from many causes. The membership may resent the highly personalized leadership that has developed in some unions; they may be dissatisfied with the terms agreed to by the leadership; or the cause may lie in the internal politics of the union.

Where a highly personalized form of leadership has developed, with one man actually doing the negotiating, dissension is inevitable. Opposition develops inexorably and may manifest itself in the form of a contract rejection. The leader is apt to be accused of being too "cozy with management." If the leader thinks of himself as one who has personally negotiated a bountiful agreement and takes the attitude, "Look what I did for you fellows," this may well provoke the response, "We don't give a damn what you did for us, it's what we are doing." This type of reaction has been most frequent in unions with a high percentage of minority groups.

Dissatisfaction with the terms of the proposed agreement may trigger resentment. Where the leader's pep talks to the membership have encouraged high expectations, he is obviously in trouble when he returns for ratification with far less gains then had been anticipated. Resentment may also arise when the membership compares the gains of the pending contract with gains achieved in their earlier contracts or gains attained by other organizations.

Vincent D. McDonnell, Chairman of the New York State Mediation Board, has suggested that "everybody knows what everybody else is doing in our highly communicative society." Thus, the leader negotiates in the shadow of the ghost of his predecessor, the specter of his visible challengers, and the performance of leaders of other organizations. The challenger, especially, is in a good position to utilize the ratification proceedings as a forum in which to embarrass and test the incumbent leader.

The best of negotiated economic agreements also have to run the gauntlet of highly articulate professional groups. Where professionals are inclined to have gripes against the establishment, the ratification process is tempestuous. On at least one occasion the leader of New York City's UFT stormed off the platform, stating "The union constitution requires that I conduct a meeting, not a mob." On another occasion, the leader of a fire fighter's meeting became so enraged that he felt compelled to "deck" one of his

115

members who had leaped onto the podium—the leader in this incident just happened to be a former Golden Gloves heavyweight boxing champion.

The ratification process is especially difficult where factionalism is rife within the organization. Every employee organization has its factions, but where the dissident group exceeds 25 percent, one union leader considers it to be a danger signal possibly requiring the incumbent to beat a hasty retreat. It is more than mere percentages, however, with which the leader has to contend. Schoolteachers look upon themselves as the intellectual peers of the leadership and tend to insist upon being informed as to the progress of negotiations on an almost day-to-day basis.

Internal conditions of employee organizations inevitably spill over into the bargaining process and influence the climate of labor relations. Management sometimes does not know whom or what the other side of the table represents or finds itself in the position of taking the side of one union faction against another. In one instance management negotiators interviewed conceded that they deliberately held something in reserve, since they sensed that the rank and file were determined to strike. The reserve was utilized to buttress what officials bluntly appraised as "exceptional union leadership," which had informed them that the membership was "out of control."

Ratification of contracts by union membership evolved out of attempts to inject more democratic procedures into union operations. Alarmed by the rising frequency of contract rejections, some labor experts are now questioning the ratification process. Employers are reappraising their criticism of union "bosses," making such comments as, "Give me a boss, and save me from the rank-and-file," or "Who let these people speak for themselves?"[3]

The "rejection syndrome" shows no signs of abatement, and the law that diluted the power of the union leader to further democracy has tended to erode responsible leadership to the point where management may well refuse to negotiate with employee representatives who are sent to the well again and again to the tumultuous shouts of "More!"

It is obvious that the problems of the leader have become more complicated. That a solution or at least an amelioration of the problem is imperative in the interest of constructive labor relations is equally clear. Several ameliorative steps are in order. Since the labor leader who can guarantee ratification is an anachronism today, labor organizations must search for leaders who have the capacity, sensitivity, and flexibility to cope with the change in composition of the labor movement.

The lines of communication between the public employer and the mass of civil servants should be broadened by the creation of larger and more representative bargaining teams—even though the additional number will serve primarily as observers rather than negotiators. Indeed, it is as essential that the leader be as persuasive and communicative with his membership as he is when negotiating so effectively with management. The leader who cannot keep his finger on the pulse of his organization cannot remain sensitive to changing needs and loses touch with the membership.

If the labor movement cannot solve its own problems, a change in the law may well be the answer. One possible approach is to free an employer from his obligation to bargain in the absence of a rejection by secret ballot by the membership. Perhaps a more effective measure would be to invest the incumbent leadership with plenary power to conclude binding agreements. When coupled with more frequent, impartially supervised union elections, both a responsive and responsible system of accountability may be developed to fulfill the long range needs of the membership.

Implementation of the Agreement

"A contract we can live with" has been the repeatedly asserted goal of management-labor negotiations. The ultimate success of collective bargaining lies not only in the agreements reached at the highest levels, often after breathless cliff hangers, but in the implementation of these agreements at the place of work. Under the traditional pattern of the public employment relationship, conditions under which employees operate in "shop" or office were determined by rules and regulations that the employer made unilaterally and the local supervisors interpreted and enforced.

Perhaps the hardest adjustment public management has been obliged to make since the advent of the collective agreement has been the required sharing of the supervisory prerogative with the designated union representative in the shop.

Union representatives, usually known as stewards or shop or office delegates, are a link between the unionized employees and the managers on the scene. The arms-length adversary relationship that characterizes top-level bargaining, if projected into the place of work, would create an intolerable situation, in which effective performance would be difficult if not impossible. The steward-supervisor relation must be cooperative. As Warner and Hennesy point out:

> Effective administration of the contract calls for flexibility of attitude, and supervisors who previously regarded a labor agreement a per-

sonal threat must now accept the agreement as an administrative tool. [4]

The necessary function of the steward is recognized in private industry contracts by the granting to him of special privileges, such as free access to the work place and superseniority to protect him from layoff and transfer. The steward, as a matter of contractual right in public as in private employment, has a recognized role in grievance procedures and in reporting complaints regarding working conditions that may not constitute individual grievances but may often cause serious group dissatisfaction that requires higher management and union efforts for correction.

Some public union agreements provide for free access to the work place by union representatives to inspect physical conditions and observe the general administration of the work unit.

Perhaps the steward's most important function is to help prevent difficulties from becoming grievances. But if they do, his principal role becomes his functioning in the grievance procedure. These procedures, though they may differ in detail from place to place, are pretty well standardized. Many public agencies have long observed such officially prescribed, multistep procedures up the supervisory ladder. Provision was usually made in official procedures for the complaining employees to be represented by a union representative or other person of his choice, with a final appeal to a tripartite committee, whose finding was subject to review by the department head or designated high-level administrator. The procedure was basically management oriented.

Collective agreements are more and more displacing such official machinery. They usually provide for the presence of the shop steward or other union representative at the proceedings. In situations where there is no exclusive bargaining agent, provision is often made for the steward or another union representative to be present to protect the union's rights under the contract, even though the employee is not a union member and is represented by another person of his choice. Even under exclusive agreements the aggressive employee may be represented by a lawyer or any fellow employee of his choice, provided the representative is not a member of another union.

Contract grievance procedures are similar to the old official procedures in that they provide for time limits at each stage, so that delay will not become a denial of justice. The process usually begins with the employee's taking his case to the steward, who may iron out the difficulty in a talk with the immediate supervisor, without going

118

through formal procedures. Most contracts provide for shop committees, which handle grievance appeals to higher levels. Often the central city bargaining agency has a role at the higher steps of the grievance procedure.

Contracts indicate an increasing tendency to include clauses providing for arbitration as the final step in grievance procedures. Provision is frequently made for recourse to the rules of the American Arbitration Association for the choice of arbitrators. Sometimes single arbitrators are chosen under these rules. Under other circumstances, tripartite arbitration boards are set up, one member chosen by the union and one from management, with a neutral chairman, either chosen by the two selected arbitrators or designated under the rules of the American Arbitration Association. Contracts vary as to whether arbitration is final and binding or advisory and nonbinding.

It is desirable that appeals be as few as possible and that they be disposed of at the lower levels, to keep the agency running smoothly and to avoid the disturbance of a grievance that may become a *cause celebre* affecting not only the morale of the work unit but extending beyond it. Joint labor-management consultation at regular times holds promise for smoothing the implementation of a contract. A permanent impartial chairman, on the industrial model, is usually helpful.

State and local governments, with few exceptions, lag behind private industry in recognizing the positive and beneficial role of the steward. A large proportion of private contracts provide for full or partial pay for union representatives engaged in grievance work. Most state and local jurisdictions provide no such privileges, and about 40 percent provide that there will be no pay to union grievance officers for time taken from their regular job to attend to grievance work.[5]

To make the system work, both stewards and supervisors requir training. Carefully drawn manuals of instruction are often issued to both stewards and supervisors by their respective superiors. The supervisors often become the middleman, caught between the pressures of higher management, on the one hand, and the union, on the other. Careful training should help them to handle this dilemma. Contracts often contain time and movement controls on stewards, as well as other regulations that make it incumbent on both the union and the management to see to it that stewards do not abuse their privileges and stimulate grievances in order to promote their images as "effective union leaders." It is equally important that the supervisor be made to realize that "playing tough" is not always good management practice. In training both stewards and supervisors to perform their respective functions, the value of the human relations approach to public administration becomes apparent.

Factionalism and Race

No feature of public service unionism is of greater significance to the bargaining process than the internal divisions that breach the ranks of both local and national unions. The idea that employee organizations represent a united front is a myth that the parties to collective bargaining quickly discover.

Both unions and associations, being composed of subgroups having a power relationship to one another, are subject to internal stresses and strains. Ideological, political, and racial, as well as bread-and-butter, issues tend to divide a membership. Some observers believe that the underlying cause of the turmoil is the entry of younger, more articulate, more activist workers into the ranks. The younger group tends to emphasize pay-in-pocket increases and reduction of work schedules, whereas older members put more stock in pension improvements.

The factionalism is also triggered by an inherent conflict between the announced and unannounced goals of the union, a conflict that obscures the multiplicity of motives governing the actions of the leadership.

Perhaps the most abrasive factionalism that has become part and parcel of the internal politics of unions is racial in nature.[6] It is a long-standing problem and has recently become more visible as well as more critical. The broad-gauged impact on the bargaining process was described by a city official in this way:

> What has happened is that the blacks are saying, "By God, we can run our own shop. We want our own leaders." They feel that the Negro understands the Negro, so they have elections and knock out the white leadership. But, then the Negro, to prove his position, to show that he should have been elected, has to go out and win what had not been won by his white predecessor.

The New York Transit Workers

When Transport Workers Union Local 100 brings New York to the brink of a transit strike every alternate New Year's Eve, it appears to face the city with a solid front united to a man. Yet this union, has ever since it became a major factor in New York City's labor relations, been rife with internal factionalism, dissension, and defections. In its first dealings with the city, in the early 1940's, the

120

union was greatly influenced if not actually dominated by a Communist faction, with which its president, Michael Quill cooperated. When it became apparent that the CIO, under the leadership of Philip Murray, was planning a war on its Communist-infiltrated unions, the TWU, under Quill's leadership, changed its orientation and submerged the left-wingers, perhaps saving the union from expulsion from the CIO. Exhibiting similar dexterity, Quill was able to surmount threat after threat to the union's unity.

He experienced a major test in the mid-1950's, when a substantial segment of the subway motormen seceded and formed the Motormen's Benevolent Association, claiming that the TWU was giving insufficient recognition to the special skills of the group. The MBA called a strike, which was broken after a few days of Quill's skill in keeping the trains running on a limping schedule with loyal TWU members. Quill made concessions to the MBA, merging it into the union under special organizational arrangements to meet the secessionists' demands.

By the 1960's a decided change had taken place in the character of the transit system's personnel, which according to the Transit Authority had become at least 50 percent black and Puerto Rican. In the mid-1960's a group operating under the name Rank and File Committee for a Democratic Union charged that the old Irish leadership was not giving sufficient recognition in the union's affairs to the new workers. The Committee, denying that it was a black movement, declared that white participation in both its membership and leadership was welcomed. In 1968 the Committee contested the TWU's exclusive recognition as bargaining agent and actually obtained 7,000 signatures to its petition, a substantial figure but still short of the required majority of the union membership. A good deal of the steam was taken out of this effort for decertification by the very generous pay and retirement provisions obtained on New Year's Eve of 1969 and 1971, but the Committee continues to function.

The Teachers

Some unions have a tradition of officially recognized factions playing roles similar to those of political parties in government.

The AFT has tolerated and given at least semiofficial standing to established factions organized as caucuses. There are at least three nationally recognized caucuses within the AFT: one, called the Progressives, supporting the administration; a more conservative group opposing the administration; and a third group, more left in orientation, opposing the other two groups.

At the Federation's 1969 convention in New Orleans, a black caucus, which all blacks were invited to join, was formed to promote the special concerns of black teachers. Its purpose was not to break· away from the union but to work inside the organization. Its formation was accepted by the AFT leadership with good grace, since its purpose was not to disrupt but rather to promote a larger role for black members in the leadership and staff and to spur the organization to action in cases of discrimination.

The most serious issue affecting big-city school systems since the late 1960's has been decentralization of administration, with the transfer of control over curriculum and assignment of teachers and a large share in educational decision-making from the central Board of Education and its bureaucracy to local community school boards or to committees chosen by the people of the local areas in which the schools function. The AFT at its 1968 convention adopted a resolution approving decentralization and pledging support to communities seeking to run their schools within the frame of teacher tenure and due process.

A decentralization program was drawn up in New York City by the Ford Foundation, at the request of the Mayor. McGeorge Bundy, President of the Foundation, admitted in a radio statement that the plan had not defined the respective roles of the central and local school boards with sufficient clarity. The result of this failure was a series of three successive strikes by the New York UFT, which charged that teachers were being subjected to punitive transfers and assignments in violation of due process, the guarantees of the law, and their contract with the central Board of Education. The teachers also claimed that they were physically molested and that their safety was endangered. Several of the leaders of local boards claimed that the union was sabotaging decentralization, and the strike became a virtual black-white confrontation, with charges of antiblack racism and anti-Semitism flying back and forth.

So intense did feeling become in the black community that the leadership of New York District Council 37 of AFSCME was unable to pass a resolution backing the union teachers. After the strike (the three strikes were actually a single strike, since no more than a few days of work intervened between them) finally ended, a great deal of ill-feeling between strikers and nonstrikers continued for some time within the schools.

In the spring of 1970 the UFT went a long way to restore the confidence of the city's black workers by vigorously supporting demands of the paraprofessional school assistants for large wage increases. The union threatened to strike if its demands for the paraprofessionals, largely black and Puerto Rican, were not met. The Board of Education finally agreed to wage increases exceeding 100 percent.

The Afro-American Teachers Association (AATA), formed during the strike, was not intended to become a dual union. It appeared to concentrate its efforts on securing more objective teaching of the role of the black in American history and the institution of programs of black studies. Subsequently, some observers have accused the AATA's official publication, *Forum*, and the Association's leaders of being blatantly racist and anti-Semitic.[7]

Racial issues have also come to the fore within the NEA. In several Southern states the black and white NEA affiliates faced difficulties in effecting mergers into single organizations. The national officers have attempted to deal with the delicate problems sympathetically and constructively, at the same time firmly insisting on the carrying out of their policy to abolish racially segregated locals and to integrate the NEA.

In several cases mediators were sent to the troubled places to help iron out the difficulties. National Association for the Advancement of Colored People representatives aided in the Carolinas; and a fact finder was sent by the NEA central office to help solve the problems arising in Jackson, Miss., where the black association hesitated to surrender its independence. It felt that the role in the national association that its 9,000-member group could play might be lost if it merged with the 15,500-member white group. Yet it was the white Mississippi Educational Association that rejected the merger by a membership vote. The NEA reacted with a partial suspension of the white group, under which it was permitted to participate in regional activities, and the group was warned that this partial suspension might be followed by full suspension, with immediate loss of all rights and privileges, if its recalcitrance continued and that expulsion from the NEA would follow if the National Executive Committee found that progress toward merger continued to be unsatisfactory.

Interracial difficulties among NEA affiliates have not been confined to the South. In Indianapolis, where NEA's Representative Assembly had opposed a proposal for the mandatory reassignment of teachers to promote integration, a group of black teachers charged the NEA local with having a racist policy and staged a rally to oppose the local in a collective bargaining election. The black group also declared that it would not support the local of the AFT and could vote for no representative. Meanwhile, the AFT withdrew from the election on the ground that it was not being impartially

123

conducted but run by the school board, which had assumed the right to exercise the final decision in disputes between competing organizations.

In Trenton, N.J., the white teachers organized to oppose the demands of the Black Teachers Organization, which in conjunction with a newly formed sympathetic white group had succeeded in winning many concessions from the school board.

Police and Fire Fighters

Interracial dissension has been increasing in police and fire-fighting forces. Groups known as the Guardians have been formed in many city police forces, and the movement is growing so rapidly that the various independent local groups have joined in an informal national center for exchanging information and advising local Guardian groups who ask for assistance.

In Hartford, Conn., where the Guardians had functioned as a small fraternal organization, a three-day "sick-out" was called to protest alleged discrimination in the department. A long list of grievances was presented, including a call for complete desegregation of the service, the assignment of police to all divisions without racial consideration, more vigorous recruitment of blacks, and the inclusion in the union contract of a grievance procedure, set up within the police union, that would take account of the blacks' special grievances. However, the Guardians, showing little faith in the union, decided not to foreclose the taking of such independent action as they could muster. "I feel," declared their leader, "that this is a racial problem and that the union might not be able to handle it." The department took cognizance of the state of affairs and the Chief agreed to meet with representatives of the black group.

In St. Louis, Mo., the Negro police formed the separate Black Police Officers Association. The issue of whether the formation of such a group is legal has been taken to the courts. In both Hartford and St. Louis the dissident groups represent but a tiny minority of the force. But in view of the rising influence of the black community and the civil rights movement, these tiny black groups exercise an effect far beyond what would be expected from their strength in numbers.

In New York the Guardians have a substantial membership in the PBA. They broke with the official PBA policy of opposition to the Civilian Review Board and supported the Mayor's position in establishing such a board.

124

In Washington, D.C., blacks in Local 36 of the AFL-CIO International Fire Fighters Association formed an independent union called the Progressive Firemen's Association. The break with the long-established Local 36 was on the grounds of alleged discrimination in promotions and in representation in the union's management. All the Local's officers are white. Discontent had been apparent for a long time. The immediate cause of the break was the failure of the department to recommend noncompetitive promotions for seven men, five of whom were blacks. According to the leaders of the black union, the withdrawal from the old local was an attempt to show that Local 36 is not "our union." The PFA claimed that its secession was an attempt to pave the way for recognition of the black voice in collective bargaining. This appears to be a futile effort, since Local 36, with nearly 1,500 members, could easily win exclusive recognition under federal regulations, thus leaving the PFA out in the cold, with no representation at the bargaining table or voice in the affairs of the old union.

Many dissident black unionists, recognizing their minority position, have resorted to the promoting of black caucuses within the union to give them an effective voice, rather than withdrawing into isolated minority black unions.

AFSCME

The AFSCME has one of the most rapidly expanding black memberships among public employee organizations. Referring to this development in a discussion of the Memphis sanitation workers' strike, AFSCME President Jerry Wurf declared:

> Garbage in many sections of the country mainly is in the hands of black workers and their new militancy is part of the change taking place in the work force. The Memphis crisis had national impact. It never wore off. Now most strikes are signs of the new militance, not extremism, but the breaking through like the Irish, Italians and Jewish needleworkers broke through. This is a drive for wages and hours and we're not going to stop. It's a new force coming into its own.[8]

Among the signs of the breakthrough were demands by blacks for leadership in predominantly black locals and districts. In Philadelphia, where the area's District Council 33 had become, according to Wurf, at least 80 percent black, a demand for "changing the guard" from white to black was greatly complicated by an intraunion struggle between moderate and militant factions of the black power movement.

For 25 years the Council had been led by William J. McEntee, who since 1943 had been the moving force behind the extraordinary successes of the union. Despite the fact that his efforts had won him nationwide acclaim as one of the municipal employees' outstanding leaders, a demand for McEntee's displacement on the part of the black members became irresistible.

The opposition was led by Fred Lewis, militant, head of the predominantly black highway workers, union, who declared he would "retire McEntee to a rocking chair."

During the course of the controversy, the 25-year pattern of orderly collective bargaining in Philadelphia was so badly upset that the national office of AFSCME suspended Lewis for employing "irresponsible tactics" and fomenting a "racially oriented strike" by 250 Highway Department workers.

Lewis' suspension was reversed by a federal court order in time for him to run against McEntee for District President. Both Lewis and McEntee were defeated by a third candidiate, Charles Dade, a Negro and President of the Sanitation Workers Union.

In Cincinnati, where 25 years of good-faith bargaining relations were interrupted in 1969 by a strike sparked by the granting of generous salary increases to the uniformed employees, represented by their associations, than were offered to the nonuniformed workers, represented by AFSCME, some AFSCME members felt that the difference in treatment was due to racial factors. As one member put it, "Most of the uniformed men are Caucasian and most of the nonuniformed members are Negro. I feel this is the reason we are not getting the raise."

The national administration of AFSCME is very alive to the importance of adequate recognition for its increasing black membership. The leadership has stressed the common goals of the union and the civil rights movement. At the victorious conclusion of the Memphis strike, the black unionists cheered Jerry Wurf to the rafters, hailing him as a "brother."

At the beginning of 1970, Wurf designated an able black leader, William Lucy, a professional engineer, as his principal assistant.

Pressure Tactics

In municipal jurisdictions, where collective negotiations have become established procedures, a varity of pressure tactics are utilized by unions as part and parcel of the bargaining process. In each case the motive is to exert pressure on elected and appointed officials and the public, to gain an optimum settlement.

Mass Rallies and Demonstrations

Both before and during bargaining, rallies and demonstrations are frequently used to embarrass and harass politically elected and higher appointive officials. On May 23, 1967, at an historic rally, 20,000 public employees jammed Madison Square Garden in New York City in an impressive show of political force, sponsored by three of the most powerful unions in the city, with a total membership in excess of 100,000. The speakers vowed their intent to secure the repeal of the Taylor Law and to wreak political retribution on Governor Rockefeller and Speaker Anthony Travia of the New York State Assembly for their roles in the passage of legislation containing an antistrike prohibition.

As a prelude to the rally, over 2,000 members demonstrated at the capital, and other members later picketed a testimonial dinner in honor of Mr. Travia as the "first step in repaying" him for his support of the Taylor Act.

Mass demonstrations can be used for a variety of purposes: to excoriate city officials during the course of negotiations; to display union solidarity and rally the apathetic; to protest the jailing of union leaders; to emphasize that strike threats are not to be taken lightly; and to bring to the attention of the public the justice of the union's cause. In most cases the union Executive Board carefully plans the demonstrations to achieve a desired effect. Employees are described as being determined to gain their goals and no longer willing to be taken for granted or treated as second-class citizens. The entire panoply of public relations is used to maximize the show of political and bargaining muscle.

Generally, the Central Labor Council of the AFL-CIO will support the actions of public employee unions in times of crisis and members of the Executive Board are usually present at the demonstrations. When Albert Shanker of the UFT was jailed, the press called attention to the fact that other unions had more members on the "vigil" picket line than did the teachers.

Union Coalitions

Union alliances are not always easy to maintain, but if they are successful they add to the pressure on the public employer. The aim is to achieve a durable, effective, and productive alliance at the least cost to the union seeking the alliance. Very often the particular interests of a specific union will overshadow the common interest, and this means that such alliances are usually achieved only in critical periods and then only on limited issues.[9] While the fire fighters and police have from time to time worked in tandem, more often than not formal alliances are not achieved. The thrust is toward moral support. In 1967 a massive slowdown was initiated by the UFA in New York City. The President of the fire fighters consistently badgered the Mayor to intervene in the bargaining taking place. The same position was echoed by the leader of the police, and press headlines read, "Firemen, Cops Call for Lindsay." Other segments of labor, while not formally allied, also sought the direct and personal involvement of the Mayor. Local 3036 of the AFL-CIO Taxi Drivers Union publicly proclaimed its support of the "righteous claim" of the UFA to a "just and honorable contract."

The powerful Central Labor Council arranged a meeting with the Mayor to inform him of the Council's support of the UFA and the PBA. The information was leaked that there was no "public announcement," to avoid placing the Mayor in the position of joining the talks because of union pressure.

Strike Meetings

Strike meetings are run with all the hoopla a union can muster. Union halls reverberate to the sounds of shouts, whistles, and applause. Where no militant faction is challenging the proposed strike action, an effort is made to secure unanimous approval. Meetings are used as a showcase to provide the most devastating political impact possible. Although much of the trappings of such meetings may be discounted, the vote potential of a large, well-organized membership is not something city officials can lightly ignore.

Gestures of conciliation sometimes take place against the backdrop of thousands of city employees shouting down the wage offers of the city. For example, the union leadership may call for a strike ballot to be conducted by mail and defer immediate, drastic steps. This gesture of cooperation is extended "to offer the city additional time to arrive at certain cost factors."

Police and fire fighter organizations are especially adept in their use of the news media to explain their position and their adamant posture to the public. Both groups are very sensitive about their public image. The police repeatedly stress that they don't desire to speak in terms of a strike because the public safety is the paramount consideration. Even picketing is done by placard-carrying policemen in civilian clothes.

Firemen are equally adept at playing both sides of the street during strike meetings. While threatening a strike, they may engage in a job action to influence the course of bargaining. Giving the city time to reconsider their last offer, the firemen continue to respond to fire alarms.

Pressure on Elected and Administrative Officials

Public employee organizations have a sharp nose for the seat of real power and seek to pressure the focal points whenever it is to their advantage. It is the elected official who is most vulnerable to the political pressure noted above. Demonstrations and picketing are not limited to city hall but follow the movements of the Mayor, even to his home. The Mayor, the Governor, and the individual legislator can anticipate being lobbied, cajoled or politically threatened to intervene in negotiations initially conducted by appointed officials.

In some cases, elected officials react vigorously and pose as the defender of the rights, safety, and pocketbooks of the public against unreasonable and unnecessary aggression. In others, they may take a firm public position but quietly instruct their administrators to compromise further. The course of action dictated will depend on so many variables that few generalizations have any predictive value.

When New York City's Mayor was confronted with the possibility of a simultaneous job action by both the police and fire organizations, the Mayor reacted with immediate anger to the fire fighter's plans but withheld an equivalent comment with regard to the pending police action. The Mayor took a "Coolidge-like" stance in the sanitation strike, calling for the possible use of the National Guard to collect garbage. With remarkable inconsistency, he demanded that striking Welfare Department employees return to work before bargaining was resumed but dealt with other striking employee groups who had not returned to work, such as the teachers and transit workers.

In most cases the administrative official responsible for negotiations is "the man in the middle." Union tactics vary with the situation. They may extend beyond attempts to embarrass the official, claiming that he is arbitrary and unreasonable in his attitude. When they believe he has been ordered to be tough the unions may seek to bypass him as rapidly as possible and seek to bring the issue as quickly as possible before the elected political official whose electorate is directly concerned with the process. In such an instance, the union may find it strategic to destroy the appointed official's effectiveness through attacks on his ability, and claims that he is "fouling up" the negotiations.

The administrative official will be charged with distortion, irresponsibility, inefficiency, and incompetence. When he appears at press conferences and in scheduled television broadcasts to defend the city's position, the administrator will take the fire really aimed at his political boss. Some negotiators are given the full backing of the political leadership that appoints them to do a professional job. Less fortunate are those who act as puppets whenever it suits the political objectives of elected officials. It appears that the front lines of the cities' bargaining defense are quickly breached during election years. One method of penetration is a direct or indirect appeal to the City Council.

The Legislative "End Run"

Employee organizations are reluctant to abandon the legislative route even where collective bargaining procedures are available and they sometimes employ the "end run" as a tactic. The union negotiators will reject the position adopted by management and attempt to bargain directly with the legislative body. This approach, where an employee organization exhausts the possibility of greater gains from the management team and still persists in trying to get more from the City Council, has been criticized as "double-deck" bargaining. In essence, the union tries to get two bites from the governmental apple.

Some union negotiators disapprove of the end run, because it tends to complicate straightforward bargaining. As one union leader argued,

> Our position has been to deal with management and reach an agreement, with the understanding that the legislative body will put it into effect. It's not that we are being altruistic, but it is bad for our position to play tiddlywinks with the politicians (the Councilmen), so we ignore them.

City negotiators, to a man, tended to condemn the end run as a technique that would eventually destroy professionalized collective bargaining. Their resentment, however, is directed more toward the politician who abets the process than toward unions.

Few union leaders categorically reject the end run, which has become exceedingly tempting. The Mayor may be politically beholden to the union, making an end run to his office productive indeed. In other cases, a true deadlock in bargaining with the administrative team may exist and an appeal to the Mayor or City Council may be the only substitute for strike action. Even those union officials who try to avoid use of the end run concede, "It would be unrealistic to say that you don't try to feel these guys (the Council) out because they have the final say on whatever is going to happen or not happen." In the case of pensions and retirement plans, however, these benefits normally lie within the province of the state legislature. Therefore, while bargaining is conducted with the city, the more effective route for strong unions would be lobbying.

In New York State, the constitution makes pensions a contractual obligation. The involvement of Albany in the pension process taught the city unions long ago that there were advantages to be gained from making occasional end runs to the state capitol to obtain pension adjustments they could not wring from City Hall.[10]

The police negotiations of Cincinnati, Ohio, in 1966 remain a classic example of how the legislative end run works and how it may complicate the bargaining process. When the neighboring city of Dayton had granted its police and firemen a substantial pay hike, Cincinnati police ignored the established administrative channels and submitted a direct demand to the Council for an immediate increase. The Council referred the demand to the City Manager. Negotiators for the police, in effect, told the City Manager, "Look, if you don't want to give us the thousand (dollars), say so now, so that we can go right back to the Council." Refusing to grant the increase without further direct negotiations, the City Manager referred the dispute to the Personnel Director, who at the time was engaged in negotiations for a new agreement with AFSCME, which had traditionally avoided use of the end run tactic. As the Personnel Director quickly recognized, the AFSCME leadership could not go to its membership with what the city bargaining team was offering if the police were successful in getting a thousand-dollar increase through bypassing the normal bargaining channels. After an unsatisfactory meeting with the Personnel Director, the police again turned to the Council and obtained their increase. To preserve the integrity of the bargaining process, the Personnel Director was constrained to devise a new formula for the city's offer to AFSCME.

There is no pat solution to the end run. Except in extreme cases, politicians should insist that bargaining be conducted by the administration's bargaining team. To do otherwise complicates bargaining and could eventually undermine the process.

In the spring of 1967, when the city of Hartford, Conn., was preparing to go to the bargaining table with its unionized employees, the firemen's union, a local of the IAAF, decided to deal directly with the City Council, through traditional political methods, instead of utilizing the procedures of the collective bargaining law.[11] In the fall of 1967, just prior to the city elections the Council reduced the fire fighters' workweek from 56 to 48 hours without change in pay. At the same time, the council expressed support for the institution of a 42-hour week at a later date.

Meanwhile, the policemen's union turned to the bargaining table. It demanded a 17 percent pay increase to maintain the established practice of parity with firemen's wages. The union contended that the 17 percent figure represented the equivalent of the fire fighters' hourly increase resulting from the reduction in their workweek without a reduction in pay.

During the negotiations the union's business agent made continuing reports to the negotiators that Councilmen were speaking privately to union officers and policemen, assuring them of Council support for major pay increases beyond the city's offers. The negotiations, nevertheless, continued. At the point where they were inching toward a settlement, the Republican members of the City Council issued an anticrime program that included police salary increases above those contemplated by the city's negotiators. Council Democrats let it be known that they were ready to better the Republican offer. The City Manager declared in an angry statement that the councilmen's activities "made a mockery of the whole collective bargaining process."[12]

Finally a contract meeting the police union's wage demands and modifying some insurance provisions to make more funds available to meet the pay increases was signed. The contract was concluded amid jubilation by the union representatives, who invited press photographers to take pictures of the signing of the agreement.

Then the Council's activities bore unexpected fruit. Opposition to the contract developed among the union membership to such an extent that the union President reversed himself and recommended that the contract he had negotiated be rejected. He was supported by a majority of the union's Executive Board. Several union members resigned, however, including the Business Agent, on the grounds that the union had not negotiated in good faith and that its action threatened the stability of collective bargaining. These critical voices were sufficient to send the union back to the bargaining table. A new police contract was signed and ratified. It contained a few comparatively minor improvements for the union, and its cost to the city was only slightly higher than that of the rejected instrument.

The firemen, however, continued to rely on political pressure on the Council. Invoking the plea of maintaining parity with the 17 percent increase in police wages, they obtained a 17 percent cash boost, thus bringing the total of their settlement to 34 percent.

As a result of the pace-setting by the uniformed forces, the city was obliged to concede a substantially greater pay increase to the nonuniformed personnel, represented by AFSCME, than it had initially been prepared to grant.

Determined to preserve the integrity of collective bargaining, Elisha Freedman, the City Manager, armed with a memorandum of the city's Corporation Counsel and a decision of the state Labor Relations Board, pressed the City Council for a resolution defining the respective roles of the executive and legislative in the bargaining process.

The Corporation Counsel pointed out that under the state law contract negotiation is solely an executive responsibility and that the role of the instrument submitted by the executive—in Hartford's case, the City Manager. If the contract is rejected, it must be sent back to the City Manager and the union for further negotiation. [13]

A memorandum from the City Manager to the Council cited a decision by the state Labor Relations Board involving the City of Norwich, saying,

> The chief executive is empowered by the statutes to sign a binding agreement unless provisions of that agreement conflict with provisions of the city charter, ordinances or regulations or unless additional appropriations are necessary to implement the agreement.
> . . . the legislative body has no role in the bargaining process except where one or both of these exist. [14]

The council, relying on its own advisers, conceded that "involvement by a member of the legislative body prior to submission of (a) contract . . . may constitute an unfair labor practice and may cause a breakdown in collective bargaining procedures . . . "

This language was included in a Council resolution, which further declared:

> No member of the Court of Common Council either individually or collectively shall take part in, discuss, negotiate or in any way interfere in any present or future bargaining activities involving the City of Hartford and its employees or the Board of Education and its employees prior to the submission of said agreement for consideration in its role as the legislative body of the city and that any such interference shall be subject to censure by this Court of Common Council. [15]

The passage of this resolution not only constituted an orderly basis for collective negotiation but also restored the city government to the classical Council-Manager model, which the earlier interference by the Council in the management process threatened to destroy.

"Leapfrog"

"Leapfrogging" is a bargaining maneuver in which one union attempts to negotiate a contract that is better than one previously negotiated by another union, which must then increase its original demands. The use of the tactic is stimulated by the mutiplicity of bargaining units that plagues some city governments.

Both internal union politics and interunion competition encourage the use of the tactic, which is deeply bound up in city politics. Union leaders are impelled to compete with rival unions that have secured a particularly good agreement. The union that has settled in prior negotiations keeps a watchful eye on what the city does in subsequent negotiations. If another bargaining unit settles for more money, the union's members will be disgruntled.

After the Uniformed Sanitationmen's Association settlement of 1968 in New York City, the fire fighters' leadership commented, "We played the Boy Scout and got hit. Now what do we tell our guys. They can read." The result was galling to the fire fighters and to the police, who believed that a strike accompanied by a flamboyant display of political muscle had been the key to the sanitationmen's success.

Thus, settlements achieved by one employee group become the goal of other employee groups, bent on surpassing their rivals. For example, at the conclusion of the transit negotiations in New York City in 1967, the leaders of other units were "licking their chops" at the excellent pension plan negotiated. The resultant cries of "Me too!" were a signal that the city would be faced with even greater demands in forthcoming negotiations. In this sense, the transit negotiations took place in an atmosphere where both sides knew that other employee groups would quickly study the contracts and try to better them.

The city is placed in a position of trying to mediate the needs of rival employee groups. Each settlement made not only has an impact on wage guidelines within the city but also exerts a "ripple effect" extending beyond the city's boundaries. The disastrous effects of leapfrogging have led to various proposals to deal with power plays motivated as much by competition as by the needs or interests of employee organizations.

Professor Herman Gray, an esteemed labor consultant, has suggested that city bargaining must be radically changed in form to serve the special conditions of public employment. In essence, the "Gray Plan" favors bringing all the city employee groups to a single bargaining table, where their differences could be resolved with due weight given to their several interests. As in the legislative process, there would be the continuous reconciliation and adjustment of diverse interests, keeping any one group from overreaching the other.

Philadelphia, Cincinnati, and to a lesser degree Milwaukee and Detroit, already have in operation a type of bargaining similar to that proposed by Professor Gray. New York City has desperately overcome the impact of leapfrogging by minimizing the number of bargaining units, the multiplicity of which hampered city bargaining during the Wagner administration and the early years of the Lindsay administration.

There is no simple solution to leapfrogging. Employee organizations may sometimes support each other in a common cause, but the prime concern of individual union leaders is, "What can we do for our guys?" While the city or state agency responsible for the determination of bargaining units may help by discouraging unnecessary fragmentation, reliance must also be placed on the unions, realization that preserving the fiscal solvency of the city is in their interest. Since an inner sense of union responsibility is not likely to be effective in the present climate of labor relations, the city will ultimately have to rely on knowledgeable, experienced, and realistic bargainers who are given the support essential to professional negotiations.

Notes

1. *PERB News*, vol 5, no. 3 (March 1972).
2. *A Look at Public Employee Unions*, Labor Management Relations Service, Washington, D.C., September, 1970, p. 6
3. Damon Stetson, "Rebellion on Contracts," New York *Times*, December 2, 1968.
4. Kenneth O. Warner and Mary L. Hennesy, *Public Management at the Bargaining Table* (Chicago: Public Personnel association, 1967), p. 212.
5. Joseph C. Ullman and Jane P. Begin, *Negotiated Grievance Procedures in Public Employment, Industrial Relations Library, no. 25 [1970], 14-15.*
6. See W. Ellison Chalmers and Gerald W. Cormick, eds., *Racial Conflict and Negotiations: Perspectives and First Case Studies* (Ann Arbor, Mich.: Institute of Labor and Industrial Relations, University of Mighigan, 1971).
7. See Albert Shanker, "The Failure of Nerve in the Fight for Civil Rights," New York *Times*, April 16, 1972.
8. New York *Post*, July 21, 1970.

9. Wallace S. Sayre and Herbert Kaufman, *Governing New York City* (New York: Russell Sage Foundation, 1960), p. 407.

10. See A. H. Raskin "Politics Up-Ends the Bargaining Table," Address to the American Management Association Conference, New York City, March 1971.

11. General Statutes of Connecticut, Chapter 113.

12. Hartford *Times*, April 17, 1968.

13. Letter from the Hartford Corporation Counsel to the Court of Common Council, October 26, 1970.

14. Quoted in a memorandum from the city Manager of Hartford to the Court of Common Council, October 8, 1970. (Cf. Chapter 3.)

15. Resolution by the Hartford Court of Common Council, October 20, 1970.

6   Basic Preconditions and Problems in Bargaining

Before there can be any meaningful collective bargaining, preconditions must be established determining the setting in which the bargaining process takes place. In private industry these preconditions are determined under law by such regulatory agencies as the National Labor Relations Board and, in some states, similar state boards. The primary precondition is the determination of the employee bargaining unit with which the employer negotiates.

Unit Determination

Unit determination has a considerable impact on what is to follow. It is "more than picking a field on which to play before the game begins; it can have very significant implications for the game itself."[1] The interests of employees, their organizations, the public employer, and the public are involved. Excessive fragmentation may create headaches for unions, as well as for management and the public. A single, large bargaining unit may fail to accord proper recognition of the needs and desires of skilled crafts and professional groups. If the public employer takes the easy way out and plays a completely passive role, the rivalry he encourages and the subsequent strife that follows may result in strikes rather than amicable labor relations.

Statutory Criteria of Unit Determination

It is the function of both the public employer and the state agency charged with administering the law to foster the logical development of unit determination. Administrators, however, are faced with a thorny problem when trying to implement statutory criteria related to such decisions, because most statutes grant considerable discretion to administrative agencies in determining the appropriate unit.

Oregon's statute does not set forth specific criteria to guide public employers; New York's Taylor law states three basic criteria; the Minnesota statute lists seven standards; and Connecticut and Delaware provide four basic tests by which unit determination is judged.

A closer examination of state laws, as administered, however, reveals the influence of the basic criterion so long utilized by the National Labor Relations Board to decide the matter of unit determination in private industry.

The National Labor Relations Act sought to give the National Labor Relations Board power to assure employees the "fullest freedom" in exercising the rights guaranteed by the law. The Board basically operated under a standard known as the "community of interest." When administering the standard, the Board used its discretion to probe such factors as the wages and working conditions of public employees, the prior history of bargaining relationships, the relationship to the employer with which the unit would bargain, the desires of employees, and the impact on the public interest.

When the Kennedy Executive Order 10988 on Employee-Management Cooperation in the Federal Services was issued in 1962, it stated that bargaining units might be established on a plant, installation, craft, functional, or other basis to assure a "clear and identifiable community of interest" among the employees concerned. The Order also restated restrictions that had been established by the Taft-Hartley amendments as applied by the National Labor Relations Board in the case of managerial executives, professional employees, and specific categories of personnel workers. Nor was a unit to be established solely on the basis of prior organization.

The order allowed exclusive agreements with organizations representing the majority of the employees in recognized bargaining units. Since, however, it provided for no central agency comparable to the NLRB in the private sector, the determination of bargaining units and judgments regarding unfair labor practices were left in the hands of the employing department or its bureaus or installations and were limited only by voluntary nonbinding arbitration.

Union criticism of these arrangements led to a review by President Johnson, and in 1969 President Nixon issued Executive Order 11491, which liberalized the Kennedy order, removing final authority from the employing agency and placing it in the hands of central agencies. These agencies, however, were organs of management rather than neutral bodies such as those existing in several state and local governments. The Nixon order continued the union membership restrictions in the old order and declared that the basic guideline for the determination of bargaining units should be the promotion of "effective dealings and efficiency of agency operation."

The Community of Interest Standard in Municipal Government

Although the term "community of interest" is somewhat vague, it has played a major role in unit determination in state and municipal jurisdictions. New York, Connecticut, and Massachusetts statutes employ the phraseology in their statutes. Other statutes, including those of Delaware and Minnesota, state criteria that incorporate factors embraced within the community of interest concept.

When New York State's Public Employment Relations Board issued a statement of procedures, it regarded the concept as follows:

> *Community of interest*—this is a most significant element that must be considered in determining the appropriate unit in a particular case. The following will be important in this regard: whether the employees sought to be grouped together are subject to common working rules, personnel practices, environment or salary and benefit structure. A helpful question to ask might be whether any real *conflict of interest* exists among the employees in the proposed unit.

After discussing two additional criteria set forth in the statute, the Board stated:

> To summarize, the following criteria, among others, will be considered in determining the appropriate negotiating unit in each particular case: (a) the manner in which wages and other terms of employment are determined; (b) the method of job and salary classification; (c) inter-dependence of jobs and interchange of employees; (d) the desires of employees (this is indicative of a *felt* community of interest); (e) past practices regarding organization and

negotiations; (f) the manner in which the employer is organized to do his job; (g) occupational differences; and (h) the number of employee organizations with which the employer might have to negotiate.

New York's Advisory Commission suggested at least four different approaches to determine community of interest. Conditions of employment within an occupational group, department, plant, political unit, or classified service could be considered. Likewise, the agency could consider the existence of a prior negotiating pattern, make note of the occupational characteristics of crafts and professions with a recognized status and skill, and investigate the manner by which some groups, such as fire and police, exercise their representation.[2] Other state advisory commissions, such as those in Michigan, Illinois, and Minnesota, have shed little more light on how the community-of-interest standard or other guidelines will be employed in practice to make unit determinations.

New York's Taylor Law not only embraced the community-of-interest standard but sought to match the "power of [officials] to reach agreement" or act effectively concerning the terms and conditions to be negotiated. The statute also required consideration of the joint duty of the employer and employees to assure service to the public. Delaware's law incorporated the history of bargaining, and the extent of organization, as well as the desires of public employees. Minnesota's guidelines included efficient administration and geographical location. In both Oregon and Rhode Island statutes did not specify criteria, and broad authority is vested in the administering agency, which in practice has more impact on the actual form of unit determination than general standards laid down in statutes.

Craft and Professional Units

One of the greatest difficulties besetting those charged with making unit determinations is the rivalry between craft and industrial type unions. Several considerations are involved. Management naturally seeks to avoid a proliferation of the number of units with which it must bargain. Employee organizations are afraid that they may be effectively destroyed if the unit determination adversely affects their chance to be designated the bargaining representative. Professional groups and skilled crafts with unique problems often object to being swallowed up in a large bargaining unit. And the public, aware that picket lines are generally respected, feels that a small group of employees on strike may paralyze a large municipal activity.

Under the original NLRA in 1935, the National Labor Relations

140

Board was empowered to use its judgment in establishing craft units for bargaining. Board decisions tended to oppose the severance of craft units where an established more-inclusive unit was already bargaining. Congress amended the law in 1947 to provide easier means of severing craft units. The Board did not necessarily interpret the amendment as a mandate to carve crafts units out of pre-existing industrial units. For example, the Board considered the steel industry so integrated as to weigh against craft severance. During the Eisenhower administration there was a greater inclination to authorize the establishment of craft units. Abandoning its earlier policy of trying to set up definitive criteria, the federal agency now operates on a case-to-case basis.

Some state laws, such as those enacted by Wisconsin and Minnesota, are extremely lenient in tolerating craft units. The Wisconsin law states that where a proposed unit includes a craft, the Board shall exclude the craft from a unit.[3]

In Wisconsin a craft employee within the meaning of the law...must have a substantial period of apprenticeship or comparable training. Employees will be considered to be engaged in a single craft when they are a distinct and homogeneous group of unskilled journeymen or craftsmen, working as such together with their apprentices and/or helpers.[4]

Statutory amendments in 1971 directed that the Wisconsin Employment Relations Commission may not hold a unit to be appropriate if it includes both professionals and nonprofessionals, unless a majority of the professionals vote for inclusion within the larger unit. The same principle holds true for other craft employees.

The wording of the Minnesota statute would even allow for the possibility of a one-man bargaining unit, since it states that when a craft exists composed of one or more employees, then such a craft shall constitute a unit appropriate for collective bargaining.

Other statutes specifically provide for the exclusion of crafts or professionals from larger units. For example, the Massachusetts statute excludes firemen, and as in Connecticut, unless professionals vote to be included they are placed in bargaining units separate from nonprofessionals. Oregon allows professionals to choose whether they wish to be represented separately. A number of states, among them Connecticut, California, Washington, Rhode Island, and Oregon, have enacted special legislation that clearly recognizes teachers (and less frequently nurses) as separate bargaining units.

One unresolved problem that can have a major impact on the bargaining process is the fundamental conceptual distinction between *the* most appropriate bargaining unit and *an* appropriate bargaining unit.[5]

While some statutes delegate considerable discretion, the Wisconsin statute gave very little discretion:

> If the employee organization petitions for what would appear to be an appropriate unit, they are entitled to an election . . . regardless of whether the administrative agency or the employer feels that the establishment of such a unit will enhance the bargaining process, or will merely lead to additional fragmentation.... [6]

The question arises whether other administrative agencies are limited to this extent, and when dealing generally with the "most appropriate unit," the agency may define a unit that it deems appropriate although such a unit was not sought by any of the parties. Joseph R. Crowley, a member of New York State's Public Employment Relations Board, has concluded that it had such power based upon its statutory grant of authority to resolve disputes concerning representation cases.[7] Unlike the Wisconsin Board, which has gone so far as to authorize an election in a unit of one employee,[8] The tendency will be to avoid the rivalries engendered by a multiplicity of bargaining units. In 1970 New Jersey's Public Employment Relations Commission rejected a unit it found to be gerrymandered and acknowledged that the new unit was not the *most* appropriate unit or the *only* appropriate unit.

Fragmentation of Bargaining Units

Craft unions, professional associations and unions, industrial unions, and a variety of ad hoc employee organizations vie with each other for employee loyalty. Splintering of the work force is a consequence. Until the basic organizing pattern is established and union survival, security, and power are assured, logical groupings yield to the basic drive for a larger membership and representation status.

The presence of an excessive number of bargaining units creates difficulties for administrators who have to deal with them. Multiple units become time-consuming and frustrating. Moreover, leapfrogging, end runs, and jurisdictional fights are encouraged and may eventually become so disruptive and costly as to provoke repressive legislation inimical to the public employees' long-term interests. It is also disastrous for the employee organizations, which in the long run, will not receive the attention and time indispensable to fruitful bargaining.

The tendency toward fragmentation is exemplified by figures from Detroit in 1965. Of the city's 27,000 employees, 21,000 were

142

organized into 52 employee organizations, ranging in membership from 4 to 4,200. The degree of fragmentation led one city official to comment:

> There isn't much rhyme or reason to some of the organizing that is going on. They are scattered on approach and it makes it extremely difficult to negotiate....We feel this fragmentation hurts because you just can't physically cater to their needs. There aren't enough hours in the day to sit down with 62 groups.

By 1970 Detroit's bargainers were dealing with 157 units, ranging in size from a 5-member craft group to the 10,000-member AFSCME Council 77.

Although in Milwaukee the situation was less fragmented, there were 17 recognized bargaining units, including police and fire. AFSCME District Council 48 bargained for some 3,600 members, approximately one half the city's work force.

New York City, however, represented the clearest example of the chaos that results from the fragmentation of bargaining units. Prior to the establishment of the city's Office of Collect Bargaining the city negotiated with approximately 95 units and annually entered into some 200 contracts with public employee organizations. Employees were represented on various issues by different employee organizations—one organization may have handled grievances, and a second the negotiation of wages and fringe benefits. The result was organizational chaos. As one city official observed in an interview:

> When organization started in the city, just about anybody who came in to be recognized was recognized. Somebody would come in with cards for a half dozen employees and the city would begin to check off dues. When someone came in to be certified as representative of a small group in a department, the city would determine if that was an appropriate unit, would hold an election, and issue a certificate permitting representation on grievances for this group.
>
> Many union representatives managed to pick up certificates, but none had the right to bargain on wages. When a union believed that its various certificates constituted a majority of clerks, say, throughout the city, this union was recognized as having majority status city-wide for clerks. This empowered the particular employee organization to bargain with the city on wages and fringe benefits for all clerks. This union, then, continued to represent, by virtue of its departmental certificates, individual groups on matters of grievances, but bargained only on a horizontal slice across the city with regard to wages.

The administrative difficulties created by this unit-determination policy were aggravated by political considerations. The Democrats, the party in power at the time, did not wish to offend any powerful union allied with the Central Labor Council.

After the establishment of the Office of Collective Bargaining, the Lindsay administration attempted to simplify unit determination by issuing new majority city-wide certificates of recognition when the city determined that a union had achieved majority status. The new certificates invalidated certificates previously issued and thereby eliminated the recognition of minority unions within specific city departments. The union with a majority status was granted exclusive bargaining rights and the dues check-off. Bargaining units were also regrouped in order to establish more coherent and logical relationships. Mayor Lindsay issued an executive order in 1967 directing that bargaining units for municipal employees be set up on a city-wide basis where possible, but departmental units were still permitted under certain circumstances.

In Philadelphia the 10,000-member AFSCME District Council 33 has exclusive bargaining rights for the city's 19,000 nonuniformed civil service employees (excluding supervisors.) With the exception of police and fire fighters, there is only one major bargaining unit with which the city must negotiate.

In Cincinnati police and fire fighters also bargain separately, but under a parity arrangement, and craft trades automatically get 90 percent of the prevailing rates negotiated in private industry without having to bargain. With these exceptions, AFSCME District Council 51 is virtually the exclusive bargaining agent for all nonuniformed employees.

There is no simple solution to the problem of fragmentation; but determining the bargaining unit is a fundamental consideration, and the initial decision should be carefully considered, as it is not easily reversed. Administrative convenience should not be the goal, but administrative discretion may minimize excessive and irrational fragmentation detrimental to the bargaining process without, however, tampering with the rights of the employees freely to choose their representatives. The wording of the statute should grant wide latitude to the administrative body charged with the determination. Judicial review is always available to check capricious or unreasonable determinations.

From experience to date, it is clear that many jurisdictions are working feverishly to reverse the past trend toward over-fragmentation. This includes the federal government, where by 1970 some 3,000 units had been established, mainly under E.O. 10988. Nixon's E.O. 11491, issued in 1969, tried to deal with the problem by encouraging more national units. There is also a clear lesson provided by Wisconsin's experience over a decade. The 1971 amendments provided that whenever possible fragmentation should be avoided by maintaining as few units as practicable in keeping with the size of the total municipal work force.

The Role of Supervisory Employees

The question of whether supervisory employees should be included in the same bargaining unit as subordinate employees has received considerable attention in the public service. The overriding issue is whether such personnel have a community of interest with employees they supervise that might conflict with their responsibility to direct the work force. The difficulty is compounded in the public sector—and in white-collar employment generally—in that the line between supervisory and nonsupervisory personnel is tenuous. Governmental units, as is well known, are generous in awarding the title of "supervisor," often in lieu of greater compensation. Furthermore, in the public sector some distinctions made in job classifications are not always closely related to actual supervisory responsibilities.[9]

Who is a Supervisor?

Supervisory personnel—especially blue-collar foremen—pose no comparable problem of identity in private industry. The Taft-Hartley Law excluded supervisors from the definition of employee.[10] Supervisors are not necessarily excluded from membership in a union, as long as they are not in a bargaining unit.

In the public sector, sprawling bureaucracies make empty shells out of many impressive titles. This situation prompted the Wisconsin Employment Relations Board to look behind the titles to determine whether the employees were actually supervisors. WERB considered the effective authority vested in an employee to recommend hiring, promotion, transfer, discipline or discharge and to direct and assign the work force; the number of employees supervised and the number of other persons exercising greater, similar, or lesser authority over the same employees; the level of pay and whether the supervisor is paid for his skill or for his supervision of employees; and whether the individual is primarily supervising an activity or employees. The amount of independent judgment and discretion exercised in the supervision of employees is also considered.[11]

More recent statutes, enacted in 1970 and 1971, incorporate definitions of supervisory personnel that are virtually identical in verbiage. Most use this phraseology:

> Any individual having authority in the interests of the employer to hire, transfer, suspend, layoff, recall, promote, discharge, assign, reward or discipline other employees or responsibly to direct them or to adjust their grievances; or to a substantial degree effectively recommend such action, if in connection with the foregoing, the exercise of such authority is not merely routine or clerical in nature but calls for the use of independent judgment.[12]

Inclusion or Exclusion of Supervisors

State law varies with respect to the inclusion of supervisors in bargaining units. Although the Wisconsin statute did not specifically prohibit inclusion, in June 1968 the renamed Wisconsin Employment Relations Commission reviewed and reaffirmed the policy it had applied since 1962 that while the statute did not expressly exclude supervisors from the definition of "municipal employee," supervisors and their organizations are not covered by the statute. As a result, supervisors did not have the rights of bargaining conferred by the Wisconsin Statute.

Wisconsin's law was amended in 1971 to permit supervisors to remain members of the same organizations as their subordinates until 1974. The supervisors, however, are forbidden to participate in the determination of the collective bargaining policies of the organization. The amended statute no longer precludes police and fire supervisors from establishing separate bargaining units. The Wisconsin Employment Relations Commission is given authority to determine the levels of supervisory employees to be included in such units, which may affiliate with the same national parent organizations as their subordinates.

New York's Taylor Law did not mandate a specific course of action regarding the inclusion or exclusion of supervisors within employee bargaining units. The law defined "public employee" broadly, to permit inclusion of supervisors within employee units or allow the establishment of separate supervisory bargaining units. In 1971 the law was revised to exclude, upon designation of the Public Employment Relations Board, "persons who may reasonably be designated from time to time as managerial or confidential." Upon designation, such employees—"those who formulate policy or directly assist in collective negotiation or who have a major role in

146

administration of agreements or in personnel administration"—are excluded from the coverage of the Taylor Law.[13]

At the close of 1971, the paucity of decisions makes it impossible to state definitively whether the Legislature's choice of the term "managerial" indicated a clear intent "to delineate a category of personnel with other than supervisory functions." The only substantive decision issued in 1971 appears to answer the question in the affirmative.[14]

Michigan has permitted supervisors to form their own bargaining units. Pennsylvania employees at the first level of supervision cannot be included with other units of public employees, but the statute permits first-level supervisors to form their own separate, homogeneous units.[15] While Connecticut refused to allow the Hartford City Employees Association to participate in an election because it admitted supervisors, the State of Washington refused to recognize an AFT affiliate because it did not accept administrators [16] In 1968 the Attorney General of Indiana stated that professionals and supervisors may join the union of subordinates; but New Jersey's statute specifies, as does the Baltimore city code, that no unit shall be deemed appropriate if it includes both supervisory and nonsupervisory personnel.[17]

Minnesota revised its law in 1971. The amendments provide that the term "appropriate unit" excludes supervisory and confidential employees.[18] Another provision of the law states, "Supervisory and confidential employees . . . may join and participate in employee organizations and may form their own organizations, provided, however, that nothing in this section authorizes supervisory or confidential employees . . . to be included in an appropriate unit.[19]

No definite pattern has as yet emerged, and the above illustrations demonstrate that laws related to the role of supervisors are characterized by diversity.

Most labor experts, however, tend to concur in the desirability of excluding strictly supervisory employees from rank-and-file employee bargaining units. Several study groups, including the American Bar Association and the Illinois and Michigan advisory commissions, have recommended that supervisors be excluded from employee units.[20]

There is less agreement on whether supervisors should be authorized to form their own bargaining units. The Michigan report suggested that supervisors should have the same rights as the rank and file but be in separate units. [21] The Illinois report took a different view. It did not recommend supervisory bargaining units and also favored the exclusion of supervisors from bargaining units of employees. [22] Where the employing agency had no objections, the

147

Illinois report did not advocate prohibiting supervisors from holding membership in those employee organizations.

The Rationale for Exclusion—Evaluation

The common element in opinions favoring exclusion is concern over the basic loyalty of supervisory personnel as representatives of management. In the case of education, for example, to include supervisory personnel, and especially the superintendent of schools, in employee units would deprive boards of education of their most effective potential support in the bargaining contest.

The assertion is also advanced that if the statute encourages close association between supervisors and the rank and file, supervisors will tend to adopt an employee-oriented stance. When singled out, separated, and clearly identified as representatives of management, their allegiance will be management-oriented.

State employee associations in New York, California, and Oregon have long opposed the exclusion. The NEA has long had an administrative component. In the case of the AFT, however, many teachers voluntarily chose to exclude supervisory ranks. Supervisors in some welfare worker unions have established separate units, and the police and fire fighters have traditionally maintained separate units for all officers above the rank of patrolman.

The practice of excluding top-level supervisors and confidential employees from employee bargaining units is as appropriate as it is in the private sector. The dilemma is how to make the separation effective. The existing close ties between the ranks of teachers, firemen, police and their supervisors have often made them collaborators. The Michigan proposal to authorize supervisors to form their own, unaffiliated units appears to maintain allegiance and yet affirm the basic rights of supervisors to bargain. For the present, statutes should authorize exclusions where state agencies find separate units desirable, to benefit from experimentation and experience.

Selection and Certification of Employee Representatives

Once collective bargaining rights have been granted and the appropriate bargaining unit determined, there remains the problem of which employee organization shall be accorded the right to represent employees. The issues that confront public employers are similar to those faced by private employers: How does the employer know which organization has been freely chosen by employees? What procedures must the employer pursue to grant recognition to a particular group? What type of recognition shall be granted?

Voluntary Recognition or Certification?

There are two basic ways by which an employee organization may be recognized as the bargaining representative of employees: voluntary recognition or certification following an election. When a public employer wishes to recognize an organization, it may rely on dues-deduction cards, payroll signatures, or union authorization cards. Essentially, management safisfies itself by evidence presented that the employees desire that organization to represent them.

Such informal procedures conjure up several problems, including the validity of the evidence. Timing may also be a factor, in the sense that at certain periods a high proportion of provisional or temporary employees may have signed cards. Finally, there is the possibility that some employees may have been coerced into signing authorizations.

When management is in doubt or conflicting evidence is presented by competing organizations, the employer or one of the unions may request a secret election, pursuant to the statute or rules and regulations of the agency administering the bargaining law. Following the election, and depending on the type of recognition authorized or mandated by law, the administering agency "certifies" an employee bargaining agent.

Forms of Recognition and Representation

Several types of recognition are possible. An organization may be granted exclusive recognition, in which case it is required to bargain for and represent all employees in the unit, whether or not they belong to the employee organization. In some jurisdictions joint or proportional representation is authorized. "Informal recognition" is also permissible in some cases, for employee organizations representing less than 10 percent of the employees in a bargaining unit; and "formal recognition" may be granted to an organization representing more than 10 percent but less than 50 percent of the employees.

Depending on the jurisdiction, each type of recognition carries both differing and varying responsibilities. Both informal and formal recognition afford little more than the right to present the organization's views or to be consulted regarding policies and practices affecting employees. Only exclusive recognition carries with it the right to bargain for all members of the bargaining unit and to negotiate contracts. Thus, the type of recognition granted will directly affect the scope and level of the relationship, as well as the efficacy of the employee organization in the bargaining relationship.

State Legislation and Practice

State law and agencies treat the principle of employee representation in a variety of ways. California's 1965 law pertaining to public school employees provided for joint or proportional representation. Minnesota's law permits both formal and informal recognition, but the statutes of Wisconsin, Connecticut, Massachusetts, and Michigan, with minor variations, directed that an organization receiving a majority vote shall be the exclusive representative of all employees within a unit.

New York's Taylor Law, enacted in 1967, did not mandate exclusive recognition, leaving the issue for determination by the parties involved. The alternatives under the law included representation of members only, proportional representation, and exclusive representation. Following the suggestion of the Taylor Committee, the statute empowered the state Public Employment Relations Board to study the problem of representation in the light of experience.

Recently, the trend has been toward granting exclusive recognition. The 1971 revision of California's law permits exclusive recognition of employee organizations formally certified pursuant to a vote, although the statute specifically acknowledges the right of an employee to represent himself. The Hawaii and Pennsylvania statutes of 1970 allow exclusive recognition, and other major jurisdictions, including New York, Massachusetts, Michigan, and Wisconsin, authorize exclusive bargaining rights.

In some instances, the statute mandates the granting of such rights; in other cases, the employer may voluntarily negotiate such rights and even impose conditions. For example, in 1971 the Nebraska Court of Industrial Relations ruled that the statute did not require a public employer to grant exclusive recognition and that any lawful condition could attach to a representation election. The court upheld the right of the City of Lincoln to require that a minimum of 80 percent of the unit ballot in determining the majority representative.[23]

150

In private industry, when a union wins an election in an appropriate bargaining unit it is standard practice to accord the union exclusive bargaining rights. Exclusive recognition in public employment, however, has posed some legal doubts, although these doubts are rapidly being surmounted. They have usually taken the form of the argument that a citizen's constitutional right to petition his government makes exclusive representation inappropriate in the public service. Exclusive bargaining in no way prohibits a person's right to so petition, and there is a vast difference between having a right of a municipality to grant exclusivity rests on a policy decision of "sovereign" states.

President Kennedy's Executive Order 10988, issued in 1962, provided for three types of recognition for federal employees—informal, formal, and exclusive. Only organizations granted exclusive recognition were authorized to negotiate written agreements. As of November 1967, more than 1.2 million of the nearly 3 million federal employees were in organizations that enjoyed exclusive recognition. This was an increase of 18 percent over August 1966.[24] The apparent success undoubtedly played a role in the elimination of informal and formal types of recognition by Nixon's Executive Order 11491, issued in October 1969. In 1971 approximately 58 per cent of organized federal employees were represented by unions operating under exclusive recognition.[25]

On balance, the study commissions, while concerned with the protection of minority rights, favor authorization of exclusive recognition. Among the advantages found were the elimination of the possibility of playing off one employee group against another; the elimination of interorganization rivalries; discouragement of the splitting off of factional groups; simplified administration; and increased effectiveness of the no-strike policy—all of which were closely related to placing responsibility for the conduct of all employees within a unit on one organization.

The Presidential Task Force report in 1961 accepted the view that exclusive recognition "in appropriate circumstances is wholly justifiable" and would permit development of stable and meaningful relationships.[26] The Illinois Commission in 1967 also stated that exclusivity was "essential for stable employee relations;"[27] The Michigan Commission concluded that the rights of an employee to petition his government and have his grievances presented were not in conflict with exclusivity. On balance, the Commission stated that municipal governments would gain by encouraging its use.[28] New York's Taylor Committee, however, did not believe there was sufficient evidence available to make a definitive judgment and urged the Public Employment Relations Board to make exclusivity the focus of continuous study. "In the meantime," stated the report, "it is wise to leave the matter of exclusivity to agreement between the parties and to fact-finding boards."[29]

There are sound and practical reasons why the public sector is increasingly accepting the concept of exclusivity, which has proved its worth in the private sector. Nor is it contrary to democratic processes. When a person votes in society, the official elected may not have been his choice. Yet, the official represents his entire constituency. Statutes can adequately protect minority rights and still authorize exclusivity. The law should be drafted to authorize individual employees or groups to meet, confer with, and present proposals to agency officials. Although this is not equivalent to the right to bargain, it provides an adequate measure of protection in that their viewpoints may be considered when the agency bargains with the exclusively recognized agent of the bargaining unit.

Revision of the Wisconsin law in 1971 was intended to protect the rights of individual employees and minority groups to present grievances. In such cases, where the exclusive representative's right to be present was guaranteed, the results of the conference could not be inconsistent with the contractual rights of the exclusive representative.

Union Security

Public employees are aware of the need to protect their status. The institutional nature of unions motivates them to defend themselves against not only the public employer but also rival employee organizations. Instinctively and deliberately, they seek to enhance their strength and secure their position as a power bloc. To strengthen union security, they seek contract provisions already generally accepted in the private sector, such as the dues check-off, the union shop, maintenance of dues and maintenance of membership, the agency shop, and exclusive bargaining rights.

Relationship to the Strike Issue

Often overlooked is the indisputable fact that union security is inextricably related to the strike issue. Any possible solution to the problem of strikes must rest to a considerable degree with strong, secure, and responsible unions. Indeed, only a financially secure union is really free to act with responsibility. Where unions are fighting for recognition, they are prone to strike. The strike for recognition in private industry is now rare, but a survey of the period 1960-1965 makes it clear that strikes for recognition were the second largest cause of public employee stoppages. [30] Even where a union has only recently been recognized, it is encouraged to use militant tactics, sometimes culminating in strikes, to develop cohesion, solidarity, and generally prove its strength.

In many instances strikes are more an indication of union weakness than manifestation of strength. This simple point is clearly illustrated by the Memphis, Tenn., sanitation strike in 1968 and the Charlotte, N.C., hospital strike of 1969, both caused in part by the desire for recognition and bilateral negotiations. Similarly, the 1962 strike of New York City school teachers was more an attempt to augment strength and consolidate position than the 1967 and 1968 strikes, which were, in part, "defensive." Although both strong and weak unions engage in strikes, the elimination of the large number of strikes over recognition will diminish the number of strikes used to establish bilateral bargaining.

Union Security in Municipal Employment

Municipalities have been the pacesetters on questions of union security. Many jurisdictions have already demonstrated their ability and willingness to live with various types of union security. In 1964, 30 percent of AFSCME's agreements contained union security provisions; four years later, the figure had risen to 40 percent. [31] By 1970 AFSCME had negotiated approximately 800 agreements; 42 percent had union security provisions: 26 percent provided for a union shop or a modified union shop; 8 percent provided for maintenance of membership; 8 percent had an agency shop clause, and 90 percent of the contracts provided for exclusive recognition.

The Dues Check-off

The most widespread and least controversial union security provision is the dues check-off, under which the employer agrees with the union to deduct dues, fees, or assessments from an employee's pay and periodically turn over to the union the sums deducted. The record-keeping is the responsibility of the employer, who generally receives a small payment for the increased accounting costs. This method of withholding money from an. employee's pay has long been an accepted method of collecting union dues in private industry. (A check-off that does not require the specific

153

authorization of the employee is known as an automatic or compulsory check-off. If the written consent of an employee is required, the system is referred to as a voluntary check-off, which may be irrevocable for a specific period or revocable at will, depending on the contract's provisions.)

Despite the earlier decisions of a few courts,[32] the check-off is now commonplace in municipal jurisdictions. Some judicial decisions have discussed the benefits of the check-off to an efficient civil service. [33] New York State's highest court acknowledged that the check-off had become commonplace in both private and public employment. Widely utilized and long tested, the check-off was found by the court to be in accord with both national and state labor relations policies. Therefore, the check-off was held to be not unrelated to the city's legitimate purposes nor to lack a reasonable basis in law.

As of 1962, AFSCME reported that a check-off of employees' dues had been authorized in 38 states and that more than 80 percent of AFSCME members paid their dues through this method.[34] Since then, additional states and municipal jurisdictions have either legally authorized the check-off or permitted it in practice. From 1965 to 1968, 16 states enacted statutes granting the check-off to recognized or certified employee organizations.

Of the 54 cities with over 250,000 population in 1967, 46 cities (85 percent) authorized the check-off of dues. In 35 cities (76 percent) the administrative cost of the check-off is borne by the municipality. In the remainder, the administrative cost is paid by the employee organization. [35] In 1971 all cities with populations in excess of 1,000,000 provided for dues check-off; more than three quarters of the cities with populations between 500,000 and 1,000,000 also had check-offs; and more than two thirds of the remaining cities with populations over 100,000 permitted check-off agreements.

New York's Taylor Law granted the check-off but provided that it could be suspended for up to 18 months if unions struck in violation of the statute. The impact of this provision was apparent in the 1967 strike of New York City's United Federation of Teachers. Prior to the suspension of the check-off, the UFT paid the city $28,000 yearly to deduct and remit the dues of its members. The amount of annual dues collected was approximately $3 million. When the check-off was suspended, the union resorted to a private computer service to bill teachers directly. It has been estimated that during the first eight months of the suspension, the computer system cost the union some $500,000.[36]

The check-off has several advantages for public employee organizations: it insures a steady income on a year-round basis; it provides for the collection of dues from employees without pressure, coercion, or the engendering of occasional individual resentment caused by direct requests; it eliminates the much larger expense of direct collection by the union; and it reduces the likelihood of membership withdrawal. Union stewards, freed from the onerous task of dues collection, have more time for other union activities.

Still, some public employee union officials—a minority—privately concede that the check-off system has serious drawbacks. The withholding technique may lessen the individual member's feelings of responsibility to the union. More important, the check-off system may lessen the responsiveness of union officials to the needs of the rank and file.

The Union Shop

In private industry the closed shop (now outlawed), in which a person was required to be a union member before he could be hired, prevented antiunion employers from introducing workers into their establishments to undermine the union. But the closed shop also made it possible for unions to exclude those whom they did not wish to admit into the union—sometimes members of minority groups—and an employee could not withdraw from the union without quitting his job. Thus, the closed shop was a potent instrument of control over employees by the union. Union members in closed shops were also apt to be considered by political machines as a bloc of votes deliverable by the union. In return, politicians might promise leaders of powerful unions such favors as exclusive employment of union members on certain work. These were some of the reasons advanced in Congress to justify the banning of the closed shop.

In the public sector the closed shop has no meaning. Personnel in a closed shop are either supplied by the union or selected solely from union ranks. Since legislation generally requires that the selection of public personnel be made on an open, competitive basis in accordance with an effective merit system, the closed shop is impossible.

Because of the incompatibility of the closed shop concept and open, unrestricted employment, public employee unions have tended to favor the union shop, which requires employees to join the union within a given period after hiring, usually 30 days. The chief legal barrier to the union shop in public employment is the traditional concept of unrestricted employment in the civil service. Statutes such as that of Vermont, interpreted as authorizing the union shop, have to be carefully drafted to assure that union membership is not a prerequisite to hiring. This point has been stressed by the New Hampshire Supreme Court, which noted that the security agreement it upheld was "qualified and limited by its terms." [37] Furthermore, no state law prohibited a union shop in New Hampshire, and the city and the union had concluded it was a "reasonable requirement."

The union shop is not authorized in federal employment under either the Kennedy order of 1962 or the Nixon order of 1969. Modified union shop agreements have, however, been negotiated by municipal governments. Philadelphia's modified union shop agreement with AFSCME District Council 33 covers approximately 20,000 of the city's 30,000 employees, dividing them into three classes for purposes of union membership—mandatory, voluntary, and prohibited.

In the mandatory category, numbering some 14,000 employees, are all persons who were union members in 1961, when the union shop was established, plus all new employees who joined the union subsequent to employment, in accordance with the union shop agreement. These new employees had an "escape clause," by which they could resign from the union each year between June 15 and June 30 if they chose. Employees who were not union members in 1961 were not required to join. Within the voluntary category of nearly 5,000 employees, union membership is optional; and union membership is prohibited to approximately 1,000 persons considered management and supervisory personnel. Significantly, Philadelphia's experience with the union shop has not impaired the merit system or the bargaining process. Indeed, it has helped keep the city relatively free of strikes.

An AFSCME affiliate in Hartford, Conn., negotiated an agreement in 1968 containing a union shop clause for labor and trades employees. Modified union shop agreements were also negotiated that year in Lansing, Mich. Paducah, Ky., and Vernon, Conn.

The Amalgamated Transit Union has negotiated union shop agreements with the transit systems in Chicago, Boston, Pittsburgh, St. Louis, and other cities. Union shop agreements are also common in police and fire departments in Rhode Island and Connecticut. Where union shops and other forms of union security have been established, labor stability appears to have been enhanced. [38]

Nationwide, the drive for union security in the public service has faced difficulties. Michigan's Smith Committee spurned the closed shop and rejected the union shop, and a 1968 decision of the Michigan Labor Relations Board reflected the continuing division of opinion over various types of union security. [39] New York's Taylor Committee recommended granting of the check-off and of unchallenged representation status to unions for a specified period but reached no conclusion on such issues as the union shop, agency shop, and maintenance of membership. A fact-finding report issued in June 1968 stated that each of these security proposals were of "doubtful legality" under the Taylor Law.[40]

A 1971 contract negotiated by AFSCME with the city of Baltimore provided for a modified union shop. All employees hired after July 1 who completed their probationary periods were required to join the union; employees who had not joined the union prior to the execution of the contract were not required to become members. Despite this and sporadic other successes, similar attempts to institute a union shop in Toledo, Ohio, and Bay County, Mich. were frustrated by court decisions.[41]

Maintenance-of-Membership and Dues Clauses

To gain public acceptance of security provisions for public employee unions, the unions have stressed other demands in addition to or as a substitute for the union shop. Chief among these is the maintenance-of-membership clause, which provides that all employees who are union members at the time the contract is signed or who become members while the contract is in effect must, as a condition of continued employment, remain in good standing with the union for the duration of the contract. Another refinement, the maintenance-of-dues clause, requires the check-off of a worker's dues for the duration of the contract, even if he withdraws or is expelled from the union.

The Agency Shop

The agency shop concept is an important facet of union security. Because of the resistance, legal and political, to the union shop in the public sector, many unions have concentrated their efforts on securing the agency shop, in which a worker must pay either dues or a fee for services, sometimes equal to the dues, but need not join the union. The 1968 AFSCME convention stressed union security in general and the agency shop in particular as a means of protecting and consolidating gains made by the union. AFSCME President Jerry Wurf stated the union view at AFSCME's 1968 convention: "The agency shop is the high road to union security. And it is the road we ought to be taking in this modern era of collective bargaining in government."

The agency shop concept dates back to the 1950's, when unions in private industry, unable to secure a closed or union shop, sought an effective alternative. It did not suffer from an inherent defect of the union shop: Union employees who crossed picket lines during a strike were subject to expulsion from membership in the union and could lose their jobs if union membership was required. The agency shop also served as an effective device to circumvent "right to work laws."[42]

Unions argue that they should receive payment for services rendered to the nonmember (often referred to as the free rider) who reaps all the benefits won at the bargaining table. The union, which is the certified bargaining agent of the unit, is required to bargain for all employees in the unit, and there are costly functions related to bargaining. Unions maintain research departments to prepare economic and other studies essential to knowledgeable and effective bargaining. A staff is needed to negotiate agreements and to assure implementation.

In addition, the majority representative in municipal employment is generally charged with the duty of processing employee grievances, whether or not the employee is a union member. This duty requires augmentation of the legal department overseeing contract negotiation and implementation. The Grand Rapids Educational Association in Michigan noted that about half of the 52 grievance cases it handled in 1969 concerned nonmembers.

There are additional costs related to bargaining, such as publishing contracts and explanatory statements clarifying complicated contract provisions. Finally, there are the normal operating costs—rent, salaries, supplies, travel, etc.—implicit in the routine maintenance of the organization.

Unions point out that it is plainly fair, equitable, and entirely consonant with democratic values that all employees should share the costs. All Americans, they argue, are taxed for the costs of government and the benefits received therefrom. [43] Since the agency shop does not compel anyone to join a union or engage in organizational activities as a condition of employment, no coercion is involved. The reality is that if a nonmember can enjoy the fruits of bargaining without paying for it, this fact alone may actually discourage union membership.

From the legal standpoint, unions contend that the agency shop concept is fully consistent with constitutional or statutory requirements that a person may freely join or refrain from joining a union, or participating in its activities. Sharing the cost is not equated with participation. In jurisdictions prohibiting firing except for misconduct, the unions contend, the problem would not come up where the law provides for the automatic check-off of the fee, since no positive action on the part of the employee would be required.

Unions strenuously disagree that the agency shop is inconsistent with the "merit principle," on which public personnel administration is based. They point to many personnel policies that have nothing to do with "merit"—age and citizenship requirements, veteran preference, and mandatory pension deductions—and ask, "Why not an agency shop?"

Public policy considerations are also adduced to support the agency shop. The basic policy objective of labor legislation is to balance the bargaining power of the parties and thus enhance the very bargaining that has been declared to be in the public interest. In strengthening the ability of the bargaining representative to carry out his duties and responsibilities, equitable and stable labor relations are promoted and acrimony between union and nonunion members is minimized.

In sum, the advantages of the agency shop to unions are many: There is virtual elimination of "free riders"; the union treasury is strengthened; there is diminution of potential pockets of opposition, less friction, and an overall increase in union security. There is also increased incentive for nonmembers to join the union, since they are already paying a fee and are therefore more likely to develop interest in the organization's activities.

Opponents of the agency shop in the public service field affirm that the agency shop introduces new, nonmerit factors into the employment process. They ask, "Are we ready to exchange demonstrated character and fitness for union support as a requirement of public employment?" In doing so, they ignore the patronage and nonmerit aspects that presently exist or rationalize the exceptions as sound policy decisions, as in the case of veterans.

One approach is to contend that public employees do not need the same protection and benefits characteristically accorded unions in the private sector. The timeworn arguments are repeated: public employees are a secure, privileged class; they are well paid, and pay raises are a logical result of public awareness; people would be deterred from seeking public employment; and the agency shop is just another form of compulsory unionism, with all its attendant ills. These are essentially antiunion arguments rather than arguments against an agency shop.

Nonetheless, the point is made that our traditional concepts of public employment do not require a person to support financially someone to represent him:

By winning exclusive representation, a union incurs the obligation to speak for all in their bargaining units. This by no means obligates employees to contribute to an organization for which they never voted, in the attainment of benefits they didn't especially solicit, and which might have occurred otherwise.[44]

A variety of legalistic arguments—in some instances supported by case law—are presented. Forced unionism is clearly contrary to federal law. New York State's Taylor Law states, "Public employees shall have the right to participate in, or refrain from . . . participating in, any employee organization . . . . "[45] And a New York City Executive order uses similar wording.[46]

Legality of the agency shop is also questionable under state constitutional and statutory provisions. Article V, Section 6, of the New York State Constitution is cited, and opponents state that under Section 75 of New York State's Civil Service Law the only grounds of dismissal from the public service are conviction of a crime, errors of judgment, failure to report for work, false statements or reports, incompetency, intoxication, insubordination, or other violations, none of which involve the financial support of a union. One New York judicial decision stressed the need of voluntary action on the part of the employee:

> ...agency shop agreements are not applicable to Civil Service employees who do not voluntarily subscribe to such agreements..(they) would violate both the letter and spirit of Article V Section 6 of the Constitution of the State of New York and Section 75 of the Civil Service Law...[47]

An opinion of the Attorney General of Michigan (where many agency shop agreements exist and are being currently tested in the courts) ruled that it was contrary to law to deduct the wages of an employee without authorization, since the employee would be subject to dismissal. State tenure laws invariably authorize dismissal only for stated causes, as indicated above, and only after official notice has been given, specific charges stated, and a hearing held.

When Governor Knowles of Wisconsin vetoed agency shop legislation in 1965 he, too, stated that it would "establish in public employment a principle of compulsory financial contribution which has not been established by any other state or the Federal government . . . . "

Some employees do feel that an agency shop is a form of "taxation without representation," in that they must pay a fee but have no concomitant right to choose the leadership. They visualize themselves as second-class citizens, discriminated against and subject to pressure to join. Furthermore, where the fee established is equal to the amount of union dues, an employee could plausibly argue that this gives him no protection against involuntarily supporting a union he may not like or union activities—particularly political action— with which he may not agree. Nor would the employee necessarily be entitled to all the benefits that the member receives. Presumably an employee unable to work because of a strike would not be entitled to strike benefits; and union health and welfare benefits are intended for the membership. Some defenders of the union shop respond that the nonunion employee would only pay his pro rata share of "bargaining costs" and therefore is not discriminated against.

Not all unions are enthusiastic about the agency shop. Nor is the opposition based solely on the idea that the concept is antithetical to the goals and objectives of professional groups. When legislation is pending before a state legislature, it is not unusual to find an affiliate of the NEA endorsing the agency shop at the same time an affiliate in another state is opposing it. The *realpolitik* is that the union holding the dominant position tends to favor the legislation, since its position will be strengthened. An employee organization seeking to supplant the recognized bargaining agent realizes that employees are not inclined to pay dues to a minority organization in addition to the dues automatically checked off to a majority organization.

In general, state and federal legislation is relatively silent on the subject of union security. Bills proposing the agency shop are pending before many state legislatures, and the Massachusetts legislature has authorized the agency shop for the city of Boston.[48] In 1970 the Hawaii law also authorized the negotiation of agency shop provisions. The following year Wisconsin amended its statute to allow negotiation with regard to agency shops. New York City has concluded an agency shop agreement with AFSCME District Council 37, contingent on the passage of authorization legislation by the state legislature. Mayor Lindsay has urged the legislature to match traditional penalties by affirmative steps in the interest of labor peace, considering the approval of the concept of the agency shop "clearly such an affirmative step."[49] Similarly, the reconvened Smith Committee in Michigan recommended that the agency shop be authorized by statute.[50]

The agency shop has become well established in Michigan, where in 1969 thirteen boards of education, three cities, a county hospital board, and a board of road commissioners had contracts that included agency shop provisions. Even more extensive adoption was reported by the Inkster Federation of Teachers, which stated that 100 out of 500 contracts negotiated by the Michigan Education Association contained such clauses. AFSCME District Council 77 negotiated an agreement with Detroit that gained the union fees in lieu of dues from 4,000 city employees. Under the terms of the agreement, all employees represented by the Council were required to become members or pay a fee equal to dues, beginning August 1, 1968. The agreement negotiated by the Grand Rapids teachers effected a "compromise." The presently employed "free riders" were allowed to continue, but new teachers were not to be given that privilege. [51] In recent years a number of fact-finding, labor board, and court cases have considered the agency shop. Although all the legal issues are far from resolved, it is likely that the agency shop will spread as collective bargaining grows in the public sector. In dealing with bargaining impasse in Inkster, Mich., the fact finder declared that the proposed agency shop would not be "coercive." Prior to this report a Michigan Circuit Court had ruled a challenge to the agency shop "premature" in a case where the plaintiff contended that the agreement to discharge nonparticipating employees violated the teacher tenure law. [52]

It was inevitable that the Michigan courts would become deeply involved when a hotly disputed decision was handed down by the Michigan Labor Relations Commission in January, 1968, holding that an agency shop provision would not violate state law and was a mandatory subject of bargaining. [53] Within a short period, four fact-finding opinions upheld agency shop provisions.

In *Simgel v. Southgate* a Michigan Circuit Court sustained an agency shop provision for teachers. The court observed that the agency shop "has been a bargainable issue in the collective bargaining process for many years," stabilized bargaining, and served the purpose of allocating the cost of bargaining by eliminating free riders. The court said common unified goals precluded an interpretation of the tenure act as being in conflict with the Public Employment Relations Act. [54] A second Michigan Circuit Court failed to find an agency shop clause in conflict with the tenure laws in *Clampitts v. Board of Education.* [55] The purpose of tenure, according to the court, was to remove teachers' jobs from the spoils system, protecting them from the "whim and caprice of changing office holders." A subsequent circuit decision, *Nagy v. City of Detroit* in 1969 upheld the AFSCME-Detroit agreement as a proper subject for collective bargaining. The court, however, ruled that where civil service employees were involved, the Civil Service Commission was a necessary party to the negotiation of such agreements. [56]

As of 1971, the issue had not reached Michigan's highest court. Michigan's first Appellate Court decision in December 1969, however, refused to hear an appeal from a Circuit Court decision. The trial court refused to enjoin the discharge of nurses who failed to comply with the agency shop provision. The Appellate Court simply noted that the plaintiffs, discharged nurses, had "failed to demonstrate an abuse of discretion by the trial court."[57]

In 1971 the Michigan Employment Relations Commission expanded its prior ruling of the Oakland Case, where it had held the agency shop to be a mandatory subject of bargaining. The Commission ruled that since the contract's benefits applied retroactively to all members of the bargaining unit, the agency shop provisions should be given equal retroactive effect.[58]

In New York State two key decisions, *Ritto v. Fink*, discussed above, and *David v. Scher*,[59] precluded the involuntary withholding of agency fees, the former case being decided after the passage of the Taylor Law. Other jurisdictions have also thwarted the development of numerous agency shop contracts. Ohio's Supreme Court issued a 1971 opinion upholding a lower court ruling that prevented the implementation of an agency shop agreement between AFSCME and the city of Akron. An opinion of the Attorney General of Oregon was less severe. While declaring that no state agency could enter into the traditional form of agency shop, the opinion suggested that "agreements providing that any future nonrevocable dues deductions signed by employees shall be regarded as nonrevocable without the consent of the labor organization.[60]

Two successive opinions of the City Attorney of Trenton, N.J. in 1971 have also prevented implementation of agency shop clauses negotiated by AFSCME. To support his thesis, the City Attorney noted that decisions in the courts of Florida, Maryland, Ohio, and New York had found agency shop provisions to be illegal.[61]

The really troublesome issue is likely to develop in the case of statutes similar to that of California. In this instance the law clearly gives employees the "right to represent themselves in their employment relations" with a public agency.

No one should be required to join a union in order to secure public employment. The introduction of the agency shop concept into public employment, however, appears to be a reasonable and proper step toward stable labor relations, as well as an essential element of union security. Thus, in the absence of legislative prohibitions, it is a proper subject of collective bargaining.

There are advantages for management, too. If a union places a high enough premium on the agency shop, it may be willing to make important concessions to management in exchange. Furthermore, once such a shop is established, the union becomes a more effective force for discipline and the enforcement of contract provisions. In private industry, security clauses such as the check-off and union

163

shop have proved the contention that the greater a union's security, the more stable are labor-management relations.

The crux is not whether the agency shop violates traditional principles of government employment but whether it is a worthy device to improve labor relationships, whether it will improve government operations, and whether it will promote the public welfare.

No individual should be forced, however, to subsidize union activities not directly related to the costs of bargaining or the processing of grievances. Nathan Feinsinger, a distinguished mediator, suggested an alternate way of handling payments by nonmembers to overcome objections that the payments would be used for political and lobbying purposes. He proposed that employees have the option of allocating that proportion of the fee that might be so used by the union to a recognized charity.[62] Perhaps a more simple solution would be for the city to negotiate what is considered an equitable pro rata fee, which would be somewhat less than the usual amount of union dues. A 1971 decision of the Hawaii Public Employment Relations Board recognizes this principle by its ruling that rejected a contention that service fees were in all cases to equal union dues. The Hawaii statute incorporated several provisions pertinent to the problem. The statute requires an automatic check-off of service fees. This tends to surmount the legal barrier of the problem of unlawful discharges. Furthermore, the law expressly limits such fees to a pro rata share of the costs of contract negotiation and administration. An additional safeguard is the interpretation that the fee negotiated is subject to review by the PERB.[63]

The real long-run danger is that the agency shop fee might eventually weaken the labor movement by encouraging "business unionism," chiefly preoccupied with collecting dues and providing routinized services. This would tend to widen the gulf between the leadership and the membership. There appears, however, to be no justification for maintaining the fiction that the agency shop is appropriate only in the private sector. As the operation of the Taylor Law has proved, rights granted to unions can be suspended in the event of irresponsible union action.

Administrative Machinery

Well-constructed administrative machinery is of inestimable value in developing rational collective bargaining relationships. Experience has demonstrated that general policy statements concerning employee self-organization and the rights of representation and collective bargaining have little practical value unless effective administrative arrangements are provided to implement legislative and executive policy declarations. But the best of machinery and procedures can be neutralized when there is an attitude or persistent aversion to the bargaining process on the part of state or local officials.

The State Agency

The first question when setting up administrative machinery to handle public employee labor relations involves the nature and responsibilities of the state agency that is delegated overall authority in this field. While legislatures encourage the adoption of locally designed procedures and, in some cases, the establishment of local agencies, the necessity for a state law and agency is not a matter of dispute.

Whether the state agency should be a separate body or housed within an existing state board that handles the private sector has not been universally agreed upon. New York's Taylor Law established an autonomous Public Employment Relations Board within the Department of Civil Service. [64] This action implemented the reasoning of the Taylor Committee that an agency exclusively concerned with the public sector would be in a better position to cope with the nuances of public employment than a group accustomed to dealing with private industry. The Taylor Committee wanted to avoid superimposing private industry's doctrines and rules on the public sector, stating, "The arrangements developed for private industry cannot be literally transferred to the public sector without meeting the special requirements for exclusive negotiations in the public sector."[65]

The Illinois Advisory Commission also recommended the establishment of an independent board, which would report to the Governor. The Illinois group reasoned that the prestige of an independent board would assist in attracting high-caliber professional employees needed for the successful administration of the law.[66]

The Smith Committee favored a special public employment relations panel to handle mediation and fact finding but made no mention of removing unit recognition and certification from the jurisdiction of the existing State Labor Mediation Board. When the Michigan law was enacted, the jurisdiction of the SLMB was extended to the public sector.

Wisconsin, Massachusetts, and Connecticut also decided against creating a special agency to administer newly enacted public employee relations statutes. Only the titles of the agencies change. The Wisconsin Employment Relations Commission, the State Labor Relations Commission of Massachusetts, and the State Board of Labor Relations in Connecticut are the agencies charged with handling both public and private sector labor relations.

To date, experience indicates that the effectiveness of the administrative machinery in each state has not been determined by whether it is a separate body or housed within the agency responsible for private industry as well. Competent commissioners, respected by all the parties, with terms conducive to professionalism are, however, universally accepted for whatever type of administrative machinery chosen.

The Twentieth Century Task Force on Labor Disputes in Public Employment flatly concluded, however:

> Responsibility for the administration of public employment relations policies should be placed in an independent agency. It should be a legislative creation with the legislature retaining only budgetary control through its constitutional power over appropriations.[67]

Unfortunately, the report does not provide us with a definitive answer or even present evidence of any sort to bolster its recommendation. Presumably, the task force would have its "independent" agency vested with jurisdiction only over the public sector. But could the task force demonstrate that the New York Public Employment Relations Board has been more or less effective than the Wisconsin Employment Relations Board or the Michigan State Labor Mediation Board, which also exercise jurisdiction over the private sector? No doubt because of its extreme brevity, the report makes no mention whatsoever of the elementary principle that it is possible to have a single labor agency so organized as to provide internal separation and specialization of functions. If we are to be successful in our efforts to achieve labor harmony, we must rid ourselves of the spurious public-private dichotomy that has been the major cause of much of labor strife. A single agency with jurisdiction over both public employment and private industry is both necessary and feasible.

Responsibilities and Functions

One of the most difficult legislative determinations is the precise nature of the responsibilities, functions and authority that should be delegated to the state agency. For example, the vague generality,

166

"The agency should be empowered to impose penalties on public employees and their unions that engage in illegal strikes and on public officials who violate the law," doesn't really add anything new or give much guidance. What kind of penalties? How far can an agency act in the absence of any legislative guidelines? [68]

The prime legislative objective is to enhance the collective bargaining process so that it promotes labor harmony that is in the public interest. Any agency established will, of necessity, be vested with such functions as an appellate body to consider questions of unit determination, recognition, and activities related to the preservation of labor peace, whether by mediation, fact finding, or arbitration. Legislative restrictions should be designed to encourage flexibility but assure responsibility, to improve communication between the bargainers, to increase mutual understanding, and to foster responsibility.

Notes

1. Andrew W. J. Thomson, "Unit Determination in Public Employment," *Public Employee Relations Reports* (Ithaca, N.Y.: Cornell University, 1968), p. 1.
2. Final Report of the Governor's Committee on Public Employee Relations, State of New York, Albany, March 31, 1966 (cited hereafter as Taylor Report).
3. *Wisconsin Statutes Annotated*, 111.70 (4) (d) (Supp. 1968). The subsequent sentence, however, directs the Board not to order an election among employees in a craft unit except on a separate petition initiating representation in such a craft unit. A Wisconsin Employment Relations Board ruling in 1966 was subsequently construed to cover nurses, teachers, and other professional groups as craft units.
4. *Digest of Decisions of the Wisconsin Employment Relations Board*, Madison, 1966, Vol. 1, p. 207 (cited hereafter as *Digest of Decisions*, WERB.
5. Arvid Anderson, "Selection and Certification of Representatives," Address to the Twentieth Annual Conference on Labor, New York University, April 18, 1967, p. 3 Mimeographed.
6. Ibid.
7. Joseph R. Crowley, "The Resolution of Representation Status Disputes Under the Taylor Law," *Fordham Law Review*, May, 1969.
8. *Digest of Decisions*, WERB, p. 226.
9. It has been noted that some titles fail to distinguish between one who supervises other employees in the popular meaning of the term and one who supervises "activities," such as a playground "supervisor," Anderson, op. cit., p. 7.
10. Section 2 (II) defines a supervisor as one who may exercise the employers authority to hire, transfer, suspend, lay off, recall, promote, assign,

direct, discharge, or reward or discipline other employees. The use of independent judgment and the ability to adjust or recommend the resolution of grievances is also mentioned.

11. *Digest of Decisions,* WERB, op. cit., p. 206.

12. See Pennsylvania, Act 195, Sec. 301 (6), 1970; Hawaii, Act 171, Sec. 2 (18), 1970.

13. New York State, Public Employment Relations Act, Sec. 201 (8), 1971.

14. *PERB News,* Vol. 5, No. 3 (March, 1972).

15. Pennsylvania Public Employment Relations Act, Sec. 604 (5).

16. Thomson, op. cit., pp. 17-18.

17. See *Board of Education, West Orange v. Wilton,* 57 N.J. 404, 273 A. 2d 44 (1971); Baltimore, Md., City Code, Article I, Sections 110-124.

18. Minnesota, S.B. 4, L. 1971, effective July 1, 1972. See Sec. 3 (17).

19. Ibid., Sec. 5 (6).

20. *Report of the Committee on Law of Government Employees.* American Bar Association, July 1966, p. 138. New York's Taylor Committee recommended further study of the issue.

21. Advisory Committee on Public Employee Relations, Report to Governor George Romney, Lansing, Mich., February 15, 1967 (cited hereafter as *Smith Report*).

22. Governor's Advisory Commission on Labor Management Policy for Public Employees, Report and Recommendations, Springfield, Illinois, March, 1967., p. 13 (cited hereafter as *Illinois Report*).

23. *IBEW Local 1536 v. City of Lincoln,* NCIR, *Case No. 48,* October, 1971.

24. News release, U.S. Civil Service Commission, Washington, D.C., February 26, 1968.

25. U.S. Civil Service Commission *Bulletin,* No. 711-22, February 24, 1972

26. President's Task Force Report on Employee-Management Relations in Federal Service, *A Policy for Employee-Management Cooperation in the Federal Service* (Washington, D.C., November, 1961),, p.15

27. *Illinois Report,* op. cit., p. 19.

28. *Smith Report,* op. cit., pp. 23-25.

29. *Taylor Report,* op. cit., p. 39.

30. U.S. Department of Labor, Bureau of Labor Statistics, and Illinois. *Legislative Coucnil Report,* Proposal 637, August 10, 1966.

31. D. S. Wasserman, AFSCME Director of Research, in a letter to the authors, July 11, 1968.

32. In 1947 an Ohio court denied the check-off on the grounds that it served "merely to promote the private interests of a non-public organization" and was *"ultra vires* and invalid," *Hagerman v. City of Dayton,* 71 N.E. 246 (1947), p. 258.

33. In April 1968 the New York Court of Appeals noted that the Mayor and Director of Labor Relations of New York City had declared the check-off would assist in stabilizing the collective bargaining process. *Bauch v. The City of New York,* 285 N.Y.S. 2d 263 (1967).

34. Arnold S. Zander, "A Union View of Collective Bargaining in the Public Service," *Public Administration Review,* Winter, 1962, p. 7.

35. International City Managers Association, *Municipal Year Book*, 1967, pp. 166-67.

36. *The United Teacher*, October 1968.

37. *Tremblay v. Berlin Police Union*, 66 LRRM 2070, 237 A. 2d 668 (1968).

38. See I. J. Gromfine, "Union Security Clauses in Public Employment," Twenty-Second Conference on Labor, New York University, June 11, 1969. Mr. Gromfine's address is an excellent exposition of the union security issue.

39. *Oakland County Sheriff's Department and Oakland County Board of Supervisors v. Metropolitan Council 23, AFSCME*, Michigan Labor Relations Board, January 8, 1968, MERC Lab. Op. 1, p. 43. This lengthy decision probes intensively the issue of union security, especially the issue of the agency shop.

40. *Government Employee Relations Reports*, June 24, 1968.

41. *Sheehy, et al. v. Ensign, et al.*, Lucas County, Ohio, Common Pleas Court, February 16, 1971; *Judges of the 74th Judicial District v. Bay County MERC Allied and Technical Workers Local 15157*, Michigan Supreme Court, Case No. 53278, September 30, 1971.

42. In 1963 the United States Supreme Court, in *NLRB v. General Motors Corporation*, 373 U.S. 734, upheld the validity of the agency shop in the absence of a legislative ban on its use. While courts were inclined to rule that employers refusing to bargain over the agency shop committed an unfair labor practice, most of the states that had banned the union shop also outlawed the agency shop. As a result, the agency shop concept had less significance in private industrial relations, where the union shop was a higher goal.

43. John D. Corcoran, "An Agency Shop for Public Employees in New York City," District Council 37, AFSCME, 1968, p. 3. Mimeographed.

44. William B. Pressman, "Place of the Agency Shop," *The Chief*, March 5, 1969, p. 4. Mr. Pressman is President of the Scientific and Engineering Professionals for New York City Service.

45. Section 202.

46. Executive Order 52, Section 3 of New York City states, "Mayoral agency employees shall have the right to . . . assist employee organizations . . . and shall have the right to refrain from any and all such activities."

47. *Ritto v. Fink*, 297 N.Y.S. 2d. 407 (1968).

48. Law of Massachusetts, Chap. 335, Secs. 1 and 2, May 22, 1969. The legislation also permitted specific suburbs to negotiate agency shop agreements.

49. Richard Bodenhimer, "D.C. 37 Wins Agreement," *The Chief*, March 5, 1969, pp. 1-2.

50. *Government Employee Relations Reports*, No. 289 (March 24, 1969), B-2.

51. The variation in the vast number of agreements in Michigan was pointed up by the analysis of the Michigan Labor Relations Board, concluding that only seven school districts had "full" agency shops while 58 other agreements cited by the teachers contained lesser forms of union security. See *Government Employee Relations Reports*, No. 289, B-12, 1969.

52. The court's decision did not deal directly with the legality of the agency shop clause, being based on evidence that the plaintiff had not exhausted other available remedies under the agreement before resorting to the judicial process, *Government Employee Relations Report,* Agust 5, 1968.

53. *Oakland County Sheriff's Department v. Countil 23, AFSCME,* Case No. C66-F-3, State of Michigan Labor Relations Commission, January 8, 1968. The decision and the concurring and dissenting opinions present a detailed analysis of the issues.

54. 70 LRRM 2042 (1968).

55. 70 LRRM 2996 (1968).

56. 71 LRRM 2362 (1969).

57. *Pullen et al v. County of Wayne and AFSCME, D.C. 23,* Michigan Court of Appeals, No. 8201, December 2, 1969.

58. *Swartz Creek Community Schools v. Jackson,* Michigan Employment Relations Commission, Case No. C69 G80, decided July 29, 1971.

59. 52 Misc. 2d. 138, Supreme Court, 1966.

60. Oregon, Attorney General Opinion No. 6858, September 13, 1971.

61. Trenton, New Jersey, Memorandum of City Attorney, November 23, 1971.

62. Nathan P. Feinsinger (Chairman, Milwaukee Fact-Finding Panel, appointed pursuant to Sec. 111.70 (4) of the Wisconsin Statutes, 1964), *Report of the Milwaukee Fact-Finding Panel,* 1967.

63. *In re Hawaii State Teachers Association,* Case No. Sf-05-1, October 27, 1971.

64. New York Civil Service Law, Section 205.1.

65. *Taylor Report,* op. cit., p. 22.

66. *Illinois Report,* op. cit., p. 18. Illinois, as of 1969, had not yet established such a board.

67. "Pickets at City Hall," *Report and Recommendations of the Twentieth Century Fund Task Force on Labor Disputes in Public Employement,* New York, 1970, p. 27.

68. Ibid, p. 28. The Twentieth Century Task Force statement that the agency "should have access to the courts for the enforcement of its rulings when it deems necessary" is hardly profound. All agencies and every person has access to the courts.

7 Employee Organizations and Public Policy

Public employee organizations have augmented their power to such an extent that they may be said to codetermine many facets of public policy. In practice they greatly influence "what the city government does, for whom, how quickly, by what methods, and at what cost," through their participation in the political process.[1] As Sayre and Kaufman have noted, their basic strategy has been to build their prestige and legitimacy by organization, to control the city personnel system, and to maximize their bureaucratic autonomy. They have succeeded to such an extent in some cities that it may safely be stated that they are rapidly moving toward a preponderance of political power in municipal governments.

The growth of bureaucratic power has raised serious constitutional issues, since the policy-making function is legally vested in politically elected public officials. In fact, interest groups are recognized as integral elements of decision-making in a democracy. We expect pressure groups to exert influence on our officials. Yet we often condemn the same officials for submitting to the influence.

Bureaucracy and Power

The increased power of the city bureaucracies stems in part from the efforts of civil service reformers to create a politically neutral civil service. The unintended result has been the development of an impersonalized and routinized bureaucracy, with ever increasing power to run city governments. Politically elected officials remain completely dependent on the votes and tolerance of their constituencies. Seeking to isolate the bureaucracy from politics, the reformers have to a considerable degree removed bureaucrats from political control. The "permanent bureaucracy," however, stays on, regarding the elected official as a temporary apparition to be contended with for a period of time.

The extent to which the bureaucrats have gathered actual power, if not legal authority, to govern led Edward N. Costikyan to argue that the civil service reform movement delivered New York City to the bureaucrats, leaving the city "uncontrolled, unmanaged, and ungoverned."[2] Costikyan proceeds to tick off example after example of how the bureaucracy actually runs the city.

He noted that a mayoralty candidate was asked to sign a statement that ended, "I pledge that there will be no outside interference in the Police Department," as a condition precedent to endorsement by a former Police Commissioner.

The candidate refused to accede to the demand, reading the statement as tantamount to abdicating his responsibilities as Mayor. He stated, "If I'm not going to be the Mayor of the Police Department, who will be?" He attempted to redraft the statement to read "I pledge that, *under my direction as Mayor*, the Police Department will be free of outside interference." The endorsement never came.

New York City's "nonpolitical" Board of Education is viewed as no match for the educational bureaucracy, which has grown to such an extent that there is one nonteacher for every two teachers. Under the guise of keeping politics out of education, the teacher's union has become part and parcel of the professional bureaucracy, dominating the civilian board.

After examining additional city functions, including welfare, sanitation, and health, Costikyan came to the conclusion that what it all adds up to is that "the City, when it is run at all, is run by its bureaucracy. This is . . . the objective . . . fondly sought. But the results leave much to be desired."[3]

Aside from the implications as to the debilitated state of most urban political machines, the question remains: How can we hold the policy-makers politically responsible in the face of the growing power of a bureaucracy that should be kept "politically responsible but not politically subservient"? The advent of collective bargaining and the development of public employee unionism has clearly altered traditional employment relationships.

172

Public employees have acquired a formalized voice in matters beyond the traditional areas of union concern. Unions have had a major impact on the personnel system, demanding a greater role in areas of recruitment, selection, position-classification, promotion, training, discipline, and career development. (*See Chapter 8.*)

Nor has the financial plight of the city been eased by a greater union role in fiscal choices, which has on occasion bordered on pre-empting the budgetary authority of those legally charged with the responsibility. Union concern has expanded to include the very "output" of an agency, as the union attempts to exert pressure concerning the programs, policies, practices, goals, and basic mission of the agency.[4] The impact of each of these moves on municipal finance is apparent, since the decisions reached are all translatable into dollar terms.

Policies are also inevitably affected when the basic pattern of decision-making itself changes. Not only is there the relentless drive to expand the number, type, and scope of negotiable issues; the codetermination concept has included reducing many decisions to contractual terms. The trend toward codification of policy decisions into contractual terms has far-reaching implications for management practices, including the possibility that the bureaucracy will have the backing of the law in preventing needed changes in our administrative system. Matters previously subject to consultation or handled by informal pledges, memoranda, and understandings are frequently entrenched in contracts. For example, conditions such as class size, sick leave, teaching load, and transfer policies are set forth in teacher contracts. Other issues, such as leaving early during the summer months, which was initiated prior to widespread air conditioning in municipal offices, now have become bargainable affairs.

Professionalism and Policy Making

Professionals in Government

Professionalism has introduced a new note into municipal collective bargaining, and one without an exact counterpart in the private sector. Doctors, lawyers, engineers, economists, accountants, and other groups have banded into professional organizations in the private sector, but some professions, being self-employed, do not engage in collective bargaining. In municipal employment professionals are frequently involved in broad-based white-collar bargaining units. Other professionals and quasi-professionals, such

173

as teachers, nurses, welfare workers, correction officers, fire fighters and the police, however, are, organized into distinct craftlike units. These units are nearly congruent with their employing agencies or departments.

Individual professions provide a substantial number of government employees, as well as a significant number of the leaders of individual agencies. Since World War II the interrelationships between the professions and government have become numerous and varied. The census report of 1960 indicated that approximately one third of all government employees were engaged in professional, technical, or kindred pursuits.[5] Unofficial 1970 census figures show that this percentage is increasing. Also, our governments directly employ over one third of all professionals working in the United States and hire a good many more through grants or contracts. Many of them exert a considerable influence over public policy.[6] Professional workers have expanded the scope of bargaining, intervened in policy-making, and reinforced the autonomy of their professions and, incidentally, of their specific bureaucracies.

Nearly every professional has his or her own definition of what constitutes a profession. Behavior attributed to one occupation may be observed in some degree in all lines of work. At least two traits, however, may be considered essential: a prolonged, specialized education in a body of knowledge and a collective or service orientation. Other derivative characteristics are common. Most of the "recognized professions," such as medicine and law, have determined the standards of education and training within the profession. Furthermore, they have achieved legal recognition through licensure, with admission boards manned by members of the profession and relative freedom from lay evaluation or control.

Within a given profession some groups may be more specialized or "professional" than others, with the potential for stratification seemingly endless. Whether they are considered members of "true professions" or "emerging professions," the teacher, nurse, social worker, fire fighter, and policeman have begun to bring into play their own perception of the employing agency's role.

"Teacher Power"

Professionalism has often been equated with the responsibility to exercise independent judgment on the basis of expertise. Seeking a greater voice in decision-making, public school teachers have effected a virtual revolution in their economic and social status. Teacher unions and associations have become so aggressive in their pursuit of a greater role in policy-making that many people have become alarmed.

174

Legal responsibility for education is vested in the state, which in turn delegates a large measure of authority to local boards of education. The authority of such boards is restricted by state education laws and the rules and regulations of state departments of education. Despite this complex legal framework, teacher organizations have changed substantially the character of the decision-making process, impinging on the so-called concept of lay-controlled education. Both legislative lobbying and collective bargaining have contributed to the changes.

Collective bargaining controls now openly proclaim the teacher's role in policy-making. For example, the preamble of the Huntington, N.Y. contract notes that "the members of the teaching profession have a special expertise which entitles them to participate in determining policies and programs designed to improve educational standards."[7] The same contract establishes an educational development committee, formed "for the purpose of establishing major goals in the District, setting priorities, and making recommendations." One half the membership of this committee is designated by the teacher's association. When combined with a clause wherein the Board of Education formally agreed that "the professional staff is and should continue to be a major source of developments and innovations in improving educational programs," the policy role of the teaching profession is recognized officially.

Philadelphia teachers, as well, have been provided access by contract "in the areas of educational policies and development." District principals and the Superintendent are required to meet regularly with the teacher's union to discuss "district policy and operations," and a "building committee" of teachers is in continuous contact on any proposed policy or procedural change.

Still other contracts use such phrases as "attainment of the objectives of the educational program" and "advancement of public education" to guarantee formally that school boards will encourage a participatory "exchange" regarding educational policies, in terms that recognize the professional pre-eminence of the teacher.

A recent teachers' contract concluded with the Board of Education of Chicago specifically stated: "The Board and the Union recognize that they have a common responsibility to work together toward the achievement of quality education," and, "It is recognized that teaching requires specialized qualifications."[9]

Contract phraseology is not confined to matters a layman might consider strictly "educational" in nature. The Philadelphia contract of 1969 asserted that teachers have a role extending to matters of "social justice," and provided for equal representation on a committee to effectuate faculty transfers to assure "quality integrated education."[10] Similarly, the Inkster, Mich., contract provided for mutual recognition of the civil rights movement, agreement to purchase "integrated" elementary textbooks, prompt and full integration of the teaching faculties, elimination of class-oriented achievement and intelligence tests, and the establishment of a community action committee to eliminate de facto school segregation.[11]

The 1970 contract between the AFT affiliate and the Chicago Board of Education also contained a section entitled "Integration—Quality Education," which stated that it was the "joint policy" of Board and union "to work affirmatively to give each child the advantage of an integrated school." Teacher transfers to schools with faculties comprising 80 percent or more of a different group were to be encouraged, along with the extensive use of curricula, texts, and supplementary materials that represent contributions made to civilization by all elements. The contract also stated:

The Board and Union agree to urge the publishers of standardized tests for pupils to include questions on the contributions of Afro-Americans to World and United States history as appropriate.[12]

The transfer policy provisions of the East St. Louis, Ill., school district contract of 1967 also contained several provisions relative to "integration." In general, no tenured teacher could be transferred without his consent, "except where necessary for purposes of integration," and no voluntary transfers were to be given "if it defeats the purpose of the District 189 integration policy.[13]

Teacher organizations have not been content to rely on contractual phraseology. City of Los Angeles teachers staged a one-day walkout in 1969 to protest lack of action on "special education" programs. Two years earlier the New York City teachers had struck, in part over the failure of the School Board to expand the More Effective Schools (MES) programs, which were geared to improving the education of culturally deprived children. In 1968 the same teacher group acted to stem the movement toward school decentralization and "community control" as inimical to long-established rights, including due process.

A number of other contractual provisions that have been secured relate to policy and practices once deemed to be clearly within the mangerial and legal prerogative of the school boards. Contracts more and more spell out teacher rights regarding class size, curriculum planning, and the textbook selection. A number of provisions that may be considered by one person to be "working conditions" are considered by another to be matters of educational policy. In fact, there is no clear-cut line, as in the case of "class size."

The teachers have successfully achieved an increased number of free-time periods for preparation, a greater freedom from clerical duties and nonprofessional supervisory duties, and a limit on the number of teaching hours. The East St. Louis, Ill., contract of 1967 clearly stipulated, "No change in teaching conditions shall occur within a building unless a majority of teachers desire the change." The desire of the majority was to be expressed through the Union Building Committee, which met with the Principal.

Some contracts are rapidly moving in the direction of giving teachers the right to elect department heads and to review their performance. The Huntington, N.Y., contract gives such election rights, subject to the Principal's veto. The Huntington contract also gives teachers the right to participate in recruitment screening. Two teachers serve on the five-member Personnel Selection Committee, which is charged with developing "job descriptions," setting "minimum requirements," for each promotional position, and recommending candidates to the Superintendent, who must submit names to the Board from the list provided by the Committee.

The 1970 contract negotiated by teachers in Gary, Ind., provided that departmental and grade-level chairmen would be elected by teachers rather than appointed by administrators. The School Board accepted the concept that departmental and grade-level chairmen "represent teachers rather than the administration."[14]

Teacher contracts also contain a variety of clauses dealing with recognition, grievance procedures, teaching load, freedom from nonprofessional tasks, transfers, professional development, academic freedom, physical facilities, and even the school calendar. All these are in addition to the usual provisions dealing with wages, promotions, retirement benefits, leaves of absence, and fringe benefits.

The amount of detail going into contracts is strikingly illustrated in the fact that the UFT contract with New York City, which totaled 38 pages in 1962, had increased in size to 114 pages in 1969. The East St. Louis, Ill., contract of 1967 contained the following provision:

> There shall be free athletic passes for all teachers to all athletic events except the Thanksgiving Day football game, the Lincoln-East Side Senior High Schools football game, state tournament games, and the Christmas holiday basketball tournament. Pictures for these passes shall be taken within two weeks after the beginning of each semester.

Expenses of the photography shall be divided equally between the Board and the Union." [15]

Several teacher negotiations during 1970 further illustrate current trends. The School Board and the union in Superior, Wisc., agreed to accept the recommendations of fact finders as to the length of the school day. The Lincoln, Neb., School Board yielded to a proposed evaluation process for teacher performance. Philadelphia teachers fought the implementation of a plan to investigate teacher absenteeism, despite the fact that the cost of hiring substitutes had risen from $1.8 million in 1965 to $5.1 million in 1968. Boston teachers demanded the restoration of their rights to use "hickory stick" discipline. They also demanded the appointment of school psychiatrists.

Indeed, the policy inroads made by teachers had gone so far by 1970 that one school board (Huntington, N.Y.) instituted a court action that, in effect, challenged its own authority to have agreed to five specific provisions in a contract it had concluded. Yet, in the face of criticisms that teachers are obstructing reforms to enhance and to preserve their power, the national organizations—the NEA and AFT—have encouraged their local affiliates to seek a greater voice in educational policy-making.

Nurses

The American Nursing Association takes little time, except in its recruiting literature, to talk of service to humanity, the joy of aiding the ill, and other humanitarian aspects of nursing. The Florence Nightingale legend of devotion to duty militated against trade union tactics; but in recent years the nurses have used all the techniques of collective bargaining, including strikes, to improve their economic position and share a greater role in policy decisions affecting the profession.

In New York City the State Nursing Association demanded "increased authority for nursing service at local institutions by establishing nursing service's right to have an effective voice in determining when staffing is at a safe level.[16]

It is to be anticipated that contract negotiations will more and more deal with such "policy matters" as "patient load" and the assignment of persons to tasks that nurses believe are beyond the present competency of such persons. Nursing associations have sought to assure by contract that nurses may recommend needed changes, be consulted on matters within their professional competence, and criticize without fear of reprisal.

178

Many matters traditionally considered the right of administrators have already been diluted in contracts. Examination of collective bargaining agreements in several jurisdictions revealed that all agreements provided for paid holidays, vacation time, and premium pay for evening shifts. The 40-hour 5-day week, health programs, and the posting of work schedules in advance were common features. Several agreements prohibited split shifts, unless mutually agreed to, and provided leave time for reasons of illness, maternity, and education.

For the present, the nursing associations are busily engaged in improving salaries, fringe benefits, pensions, and working conditions. This has militated against their showing the degree of basic policy concern that has been evident in teachers contracts. The pace at which collective bargaining has proceeded is demonstrated by figures from the ANA for 1960 and 1968. Only 75 agreements, involving 115 institutions covering 8,000 nurses, had been negotiated throughout the nation by June 1960. Four fifth's of these agreements were in private hospitals and all 75 had been negotiated by only six state associations. By December 1968 the ANA had negotiated 227 agreements, involving 352 employers covering 30,200 nurses. Eighty-five of the agreements were in municipal hospitals, and 18 state associations had participated in the agreements negotiated.

Social Workers

When any large group of professionals claiming the right of self-regulation works for a large, semiautonomous bureaucracy, then the process of adaptation and reform must somehow affect the institution as well as the profession. Already discernible in the teacher negotiations, this process is also clearly seen in the struggle of social welfare to bargain collectively. The activities of the once independent Social Service Employees Union in New York City is perhaps the best illustration of militant, emerging professionalism among social workers.[17]

Reform of the social welfare system and re-evaluation of the profession were as intrinsic to the SSEU demands and struggles with the city as were the traditional demands of labor. In 1965 the contract of the SSEU, its first, could only be understood in the context of the circumstances and forces that brought it about. The SSEU claimed that the welfare workers were held in "the same low esteem as the clients they serve, both by the public and by the employer." [18] Arguing that the city used public apathy to justify its own ineptitude in bringing about the necessary administrative changes, the SSEU President also charged that Local 371 of AF-SCME had failed as a vehicle of change and had even attempted to justify the status quo. Local 371 was described as a company union, and the SSEU organized and in October 1964 ousted Local 371 in a representation election for caseworkers, children's counselors, homemakers, and economists. After fruitless bargaining, on January 4, 1965, the longest strike in the history of the city to that date occurred.

One of the major factors in the strike of 1965 was the city's position that most issues were "not bargainable." The SSEU President's statement concluded that "the contract provides that in future negotiations all union demands, no matter how inclusive or far reaching, shall be considered appropriate matters for collective bargaining.[19]

Henceforth, the SSEU made determined efforts to bargain on such policy matters as case standards, physical conditions, rental of new office space, facility refurbishing, and acquisition of computerized data-processing machinery, as well as training programs, caseloads of welfare workers, recruitment, selection, promotion, and hiring of reserve staffs in each welfare office to assist field investigators.

By 1967 the SSEU was not only insisting upon such items as a reduction of caseload but demanding that specific programs, such as the hiring of 500 new trainees per month, be written into the contract, guaranteeing that the program would be carried out. Still other demands incorporated the SSEU's conception of the meaning of "welfare," which was held to include the right to telephones for all clients and the right of clients to be allowed to keep the entire income from the first month of employment rather than take a commensurate reduction in their welfare grants.

The union also demanded that the Department of Welfare make down payments and pay maintenance charges so that clients might move into cooperative housing. Increased and automatic twice-a-year clothing allowances, improved facilities, Spanish-speaking interpreters, and the establishment of residential treatment centers were also sought. Each of the demands, said the SSEU, would lighten workloads, "streamline" working procedures, improve operations, and benefit the public as well as the client.

Astounded officials refused to bargain on many of the issues, the 1965 contract notwithstanding. Some of the demands, said the city, would violate federal or state law and were thus nonbargainable. In both 1967 and 1968 the city and the union were moving toward the moment of truth. The strikes were emotional and intense. SSEU pickets on strike lines and outside City Hall carried the slogans,

"Money Talk—Not Double Talk," and "Let us Bargain on Standards of Service." The Welfare Commissioner framed the issue when he retorted, "We feel strongly that labor-management contracts cannot be the vehicle by which reform in public welfare is accomplished."

The city partially yielded during a short strike in January 1967, concluding an agreement on wages and a few other issues, but it refused to accede to many of the demands. Later in the year, the SSEU resorted to sporadic "job actions," short of an all out strike, and adopted the work-by-the-book tactics of the Transport Workers Union. SSEU President Judith Mage stated, "We'll think about our cases, think about our problems, and talk about them with our coworkers until the time when the Department comes to its senses." Union members reported to work but were instructed, "Do not answer phones. Do not pick up pen or pencil. Do not go to intake. Do not go to the field." Some caseworkers indulged in the free time to hold seminars on job related topics —including karate.

The "work-in" failed when the city responded with 622 suspensions and 28 arrests. Even Mrs. Mage's dramatic offer to have each welfare worker send the city a "pint of blood" could not stem the tide running against the SSEU. Excessive turnover of personnel had stopped its union solidarity. Any cohesion the organization might have had was hindered by radical left-wing factions. There was an almost total lack of support from the organized labor movement, including the AFSCME unit that represented welfare case supervisors. The city was in a perfect position to "pick off" an unaffiliated union that had got too far out in front on policy issues. With a welfare budget in excess of $1 billion, two thirds of which came from federal and state jurisdictions, the city could have its showdown. In 1969 the SSEU was absorbed by the organization that had left several years before, AFSCME District Council 37.

With the return to AFSCME, the social workers have nevertheless continued their movement toward areas deemed the right of management. Locals 371 and 1549 of AFSCME negotiated an agreement with the city in 1969 to reduce social service personnel solely by attrition rather than by firing or transfer. Increased caseloads were balanced by pay increases and the establishment of a joint council of union and Welfare Department representatives to work out changes in workload or reorganization.

The "new" Local 371 has continued to keep a watchful eye on the City's efforts to reorganize the Department. In January 1969 Locals 371 and 1549 objected to a plan to turn over some of the case workers' investigative and bookkeeping chores to clerical workers. In March 1970 it was agreed that the caseload average "shall be maintained at or below seventy-five cases." For the first time the City conceded that "no permanent employee shall be laid off, demoted or lose employment." In addition, the Department agreed to recommend to the state and to the Civil Service Commission provisions giving equal treatment to all hospital care investigators, whether or not they have Bachelor Degrees.[20] Without doubt, social workers' demands will remain an impediment to stronger managerial controls—but without the frenetic approach characteristic of the "old" SSEU. The demands of the employees, while not achieved by contract, may well have an educational effect on administration and the public.

Police Autonomy

The classic case of union-reinforced autonomy is, of course, the Police Department. The police benevolent associations, the police unions, are among the most vociferous proponents of police independence from City Hall and oppose any real or imagined "political interference." Such freedom is deeply rooted in tradition and has been vigorously seconded by some police commissioners and other high department officials.

Almost invariably it is pressure from police organizations that constrains City Hall to acknowledge police independence, to increase the number of men on the force, and to increase police budgets. The police, even more than other employee groups, seek to maximize bureaucratic autonomy and control their personnel system. Any City Hall move that even vaguely appears as interference with internal administration and manpower deployment is suspect, and reaction is swift.

New York City's Police Department is not the exception to the rule when it responds to executive action that might erode its authority. In 1954 Francis W. H. Adams became Police Commissioner and secured from Mayor Robert Wagner a guarantee of "no hindrance" from City Hall. The hot-and-cold, start-and-stop, on-and-off war between City Hall and the police organizations accelerated once the Lindsay administration assumed command of the city government in January 1966.

In December 1967, when Mayor Lindsay ordered two youthful aides to march with antidraft demonstrators to try to reduce friction between the police and the protesters, the antagonism became plainly evident. The Policemen's Benevolent Association called for the resignation of the Mayor's aides and accused Lindsay of violating a 14-year tradition of noninterference in police affairs. The

182

Mayor issued a statement to the effect that he considered his relationship with the Police Commissioner analogous to that of the President of the United States to the Joint Chiefs of Staff. The Mayor's assertion that he had a role to play in the fixing of policy in all matters in the city was interpreted as the strongest claim in years of a Mayor vis-a-vis the police department.

The police bureaucracy is likewise concerned with who becomes the commissioner and top administrators. Chill winds began to blow when Mayor Lindsay went outside the "system" to appoint a Philadelphian, Howard Leary, as Commissioner—especially when the outgoing Commissioner, Vincent L. Broderick, indicated that the real issue in his departure was "Who's going to run the Police Department, the Mayor or the Commissioner?" During the course of a television program, Mr. Broderick had stated that the city charter was "clear as crystal" in bestowing responsibility for the conduct of the department on the Police Commissioner. When Sanford Garelik was chosen to be Chief Inspector, the PBA chided the Mayor for "dictating his selection."

The PBA's first opportunity to demonstrate its political power occurred when Mayor Lindsay appointed a controversial, independent Civilian Review Board to replace "internal review" of the Police Department. Working from the premise that "only policemen could judge police in the performance of their duty," the PBA President, then John Cassese, denounced the action as the "death knell for the Police Department." In conjunction with other groups, the PBA filed a petition with the Board of Election to have the issue put to a city-wide referendum in the November 1966 election.

The PBA waged a mammoth public relations campaign to force the Mayor to dissolve the newly appointed independent board. The theme of many advertisements in the press and on television was fear. People were reminded of their reluctance to walk the streets to go into the parks at night. The implication was that the police were being hampered in their work, and the new board was pictured as further encouragement to the lawless elements in society as well as hindrance to effective police work.

The scare campaign played upon the real fears of many people and was enough to deal the Mayor a stunning blow. The efforts of Mayor Lindsay, Senator Robert Kennedy, and Senator Jacob Javits in support of the civilian board were unsuccessful against the combined efforts of the PBA and the Conservative Party. Unofficial estimates of the cost to the PBA of the saturation coverage in the mass media ranged from $250,000 to $1,000,000.

The PBA repeatedly issued statements alleging City Hall interference in police matters. Typical is the statement of former PBA Community Relations Counsel Norman Frank:

> In the days of previous mayors, there was an absolute statement that politics and interference from City Hall would stay out of the Police Department. I think that today we are suffering from the Police Department virtually being an arm of City Hall. I think that City Hall is actively calling policy, working administration, has participated in the deployment of troops, policemen, around the City of New York, and has involved itself in all other areas of Police Department activity, and I want to underscore this, in the face of professional objections in the Police Department, because the people who are interfering at the highest level have no background in law enforcement.

Such already strained relationships were aggravated whenever the PBA believed that the Mayor was attempting to block legislation sought by the PBA at the state level. For example, in 1967 the Mayor had initially opposed a police "Moonlighting Bill." This special legislation would have authorized New York City police to accept part-time work to supplement their salaries, as long as the outside job did not conflict with their police duties.

The PBA and its allies were again successful. Lobbying extensively in Albany, they secured passage of a bill authorizing all local policemen in the state to "moonlight" up to 20 hours a week. The final bill, however, permitted local police commissioners to decide what types of employment would be permitted. Presumably, police would be barred from holding jobs as bouncers in bars and nightclubs, where force might be required.

Police groups have a professional interest in entrance requirements to the service. Again the Lindsay administration ran into opposition from the bureaucracy. In an effort to increase the number of jobs available to minority groups (a policy highly favored by the Mayor), the Civil Service Commission proposed revoking a regulation that automatically barred persons convicted of petit larceny from jobs as policemen or firemen. The PBA Community Relations Counsel quickly affirmed the intention of the PBA to oppose vigorously that change "or any other dilution of entrance requirements for police service." [21] Subsequently, the PBA objected that prior to their appointment 62 new recruits had been charged with crimes ranging from burglary to murder. In 1969 the New York City PBA passed a resolution requesting the Department "restrict recruitment to those men and women who have demonstrated their ability to serve as examples of the highest ideal of dedication to good citizenship." Predictably, the fire fighters also opposed the proposed changes in entrance requirements.

The police bureaucracy is keenly interested in the manpower requirements of the department. With most urban centers having high crime rates, it is only natural that New York City's PBA annually calls for 3,000 to 5,000 more policemen. When the Mayor calls for quantitative analyses of "cost-effectiveness studies" and suggests better deployment of personnel, he inevitably incurs the wrath of the police. The PBA response cited statistics to show that "virtually every precinct in the city has two radio patrol cars which stand idle all the time due to lack of manpower." The rising crime rate along with the anticipated "hot summers" of the contemporary scene led Mayor Lindsay to announce that 710 patrolmen would be added to the force in January 1968. In May 1968 the Mayor stated that an additional 3,000 men would join the force within a year. The PBA quickly replied that 3,000 extra police were inadequate.

Deployment of the police force is considered a matter for professional judgment, and the PBA opposed the Mayor repeatedly on this issue. Objecting to the practice of "flying," in which police are transferred from one precinct to another in order to accommodate temporary needs, the PBA objected to Lindsay's proposal to employ one-man patrol cars in low-crime areas.

In May 1970, the Mayor was again locked in combat with the PBA when he caustically referred to an appalling "breakdown" in the police function—construction workers had assaulted youthful antiwar protesters in a dramatic confrontation in the canyons of Wall Street while police allegedly stood by, uninterested in containing the melee. The PBA denounced the Mayor's characterization of the incident and hurled a salvo of its own—the Mayor was at fault in issuing inconsistent "political directives" in the case of demonstrations. And in any case, the manpower of the Department was simply stretched too thin to cope with the unanticipated events. Within the week the Mayor was giving accolades to the Department for the way in which it successfully handled subsequent confrontations.

Just prior to Memorial Day 1970 Federal District Court Judge Constance Baker Motley issued an injunction commanding the police to protect peaceful antiwar demonstrators. The City Corporation Counsel immediately sought the revocation of the injunction by the Second Circuit Court of Appeals and was successful.

In the spring of 1970, the New York *Times* published the findings of an investigation it had made of alleged widespread corruption in the New York City Police Department. When an independent committee was appointed by the Mayor to investigate the charges, the PBA objected that the investigation would result in "great expense, harassment and inconvenience" to policemen. Furthermore, the police union contended, the action constituted a violation of a provision of the city charter reading as follows:

> . . . neither the Mayor, the Police Commissioner nor any other administrator or officer of the city may authorize any person, agency, board or group to receive, investigate, hear, recommend, or require action upon . . . civilian complaints (against policemen).

Seeking a court action to block such investigations is but another example of the interest of police in policy matters. The police have always been one of the most thoroughly organized and cohesive groups of public employees. The natural strength accruing from the nature of their work, when combined with the power of the fire fighters, has led them to a pre-eminent position in the movement toward bureaucratic independence.

The Fire Fighters

Union fire fighters, who have often worked in tandem with police organizations, also play a similar role in the fortunes of their departments. They, too, seek to increase the size of the total fire fighting force and control the operable size of fire fighting units. In 1969 New York City fire fighters and the Uniformed Fire Officers reached an agreement that resolved a year-long dispute over workloads and manning.

The same year the International Association of Fire Fighters, like many local of its affiliates, opposed the lowering of "educational and physical standards" for fire service recruits. With regard to recruitment policy, however, the Executive Board of the IAFF declared that the fire services should hire "any person...without regard to religious affiliation, political party membership, or racial origin" who meets proper civil service or personnel department standards.

Both the Uniformed Firefighters Association and the Uniformed Fire Officers Association in New York City have opposed policies transferring men and equipment about the city. For example, in 1971 the two organizations condemned as "unilateral" a departmental decision to assign a ladder company from the financial district to night duty in a congested residential area. Both police and fire organizations insisted that the only feasible way to meet increased fire hazards in overpopulated areas of the city was by providing more personnel and additional equipment. In 1967 Mayor Lindsay announced that more fire fighters would possibly be transferred to areas having a high fire incidence. The President of the UFA made no attempt to conceal the legitimate annoyance of the fire fighter organization, which had not been consulted:

> This union has continually urged the Fire Commissioner to discuss department problems affecting manpower before implementing such problems. More often than not, we learn about new procedures from the newspapers in department orders."(21)

To prevent transfer of personnel from their base stations to stations in high-risk areas during high-risk hours, the UFA in 1971 staged a long job action carrying a potential threat to public safety. Charges were made that in view of the assignment pattern of long duty hours extending over several days balanced by compensatory days off, many fire fighters moonlighted on their time off and objected to reassignment away from the neighborhoods of their moonlighting jobs. 22

Although there is nothing in the union contract to prevent the city from changing its assignment patterns, three factors have stood in its way. They are the need for union cooperation in operating the department; pressure from the neighborhood that believes it is being short changed on protection (a sentiment which the union is capable of feeding); and the all-important fact that firemen's working hours are fixed by the state constitution. 23

Like the police, the fire fighters have not been hesitant to employ the safety argument. The union president warned that disaster threatened the city unless additional men were added to the force and obsolete apparatus replaced. Most unions, however, traditionally include safety matters in their negotiations. Obsolete equipment creates a safety hazard and is clearly a legitimate bargaining issue, involving working conditions as well as policy matters.

Other Employee Organizations

Teachers, social workers, police and fire fighters are not the only employee groups manifesting interest in policy decisions. When New York City and its sanitationmen's union disagreed over air-pollution laws requiring the shutting down of incinerators, on the grounds that the department was not equipped to handle the additional garbage, the sanitation men prevailed and air pollution laws were changed.

In Philadelphia, Mayor Tate appointed James P. Halferty as Streets Commissioner in February, 1970. Two AFSCME locals responded with a slowdown in trash collection, contending that

Halferty, a former police officer, was not an engineer and was therefore not qualified to run the Streets Department. After several weeks the union won its victory and the slowdown ended after the resignation of the Commissioner.[24]

Detroit in 1971 signed a three-year contract with AFSCME in which it retained certain forms of authority regarding contracting out of work, at the same time circumscribing its powers with a series of restrictions. The contract reads:

> The city is genuinely interested in maintaining maximum employment for all seniority employees covered by this agreement consistent with the needs of the city. Therefore, in making these determinations the city intends always to keep the interests of the city employees in mind.
>
> The right of contracting and subcontracting is vested in the city.
>
> The right to contract and subcontract shall not be used for the purpose or intention of undermining the union nor to discriminate against any of its members nor shall any seniority employee be laid off or demoted or caused to suffer a reduction in overtime work as a direct or indirect result of work performed by an outside contractor. In case of contracting or subcontracting affecting employment covered by this agreement the city will hold advance discussions with the union prior to letting the contract. The union representative will be advised of the nature, scope and approximate days of work to be performed and the reason (equipment, manpower, etc.) why the city is contemplating contracting out work.[25]

Professionals and Management Prerogative

Collective bargaining procedures require that administrators deal formally with their bureaucracies and negotiate on hosts of issues heretofore dealt with informally or indirectly. Unions seek to insert contract provisions related to personnel policies, including job descriptions, position classification, work schedules, examination and promotion procedures, recruitment policies, and training programs. Many decisions long regarded by public employers as part of management's prerogative have become bargainable issues. (*See Chapter 8*)

The bureaucracies have penetrated the administrative process to such an extent that the line between the matters that affect working conditions and the public policy issues has become difficult to draw. This is especially the case with the professional employee groups, which consider that the standards of their professions are involved.

Management has insisted there are certain aspects of its authority that are exclusively management's domain and not bargainable.

Despite such claims, the kinds of issues brought to the bargaining table and the scope of the ensuing bargaining has made the concept of management rights increasingly mercurial in nature.

In law, public policy decisions are the sole prerogative of duly constituted authorities. Yet, the National Education Association strives to bargain "on all matters which affect the quality of the education system." The American Federation of Teachers remains concerned with "anything that affects the working life of the teacher." An AFSCME leader takes the pragmatic view that "any matter is bargainable if the union can get it to the bargaining table"; and the 1965 contract of social workers in New York City excluded virtually no issue from bargaining. (In subsequent social service negotiations the city regained many of its prerogatives.)

The problem is further complicated by the tendency of some municipal authorities to state that although a specific demand may be "not bargainable," it is "discussable." Assuming that today's discussable issue becomes tomorrow's bargainable issue, one wit commented, "There is one function that is solely management's—the right to coordinate the city's agreements with everyone on everything."

Working Conditions or Policy Decisions?

There is no clear-cut line between bargainable working conditions and public policy decisions that are legally vested in public officials through legislative delegation. Is class size in a school a matter of public policy or a teacher's working condition? A renowned educator concluded: "Below 30, class size is a matter of policy; above 38, it becomes a working condition."

Similarly, the police negotiate as to the number of patrolmen to be assigned to a patrol car. Welfare case workers negotiate as to case load, and fire fighters bargain over the size of operating units. Other employee groups also negotiate on work quotas, duty assignments, promotional practices, and numerous other issues held to be within the context of a flexible labor relations system.

Not all city employers have felt obliged to yield on union demands for the inclusion of policy issues in collective agreements. Hartford, Conn., in a situation similar to New York's, resisted union demands to negotiate on policy matters. The city's Personnel Director-Labor Negotiator declared:

> We have had some efforts on the part of unions to negotiate on policy matters, although this seems less prevalent with our unions (Police, Fire and AFSCME) than in the case of the teacher unions. The Fire Union, for example, has attempted to negotiate minimum manning

levels in the department, which we have thus far resisted. The Police Union attempted to negotiate, certain revisions of the Police Manual. We also resisted these efforts, although we agreed that the Police Chief would discuss any reservations with the union.[26]

Here the city won significant victories in keeping matters on which it deemed it needed a free hand from being imbedded in an enforceable contract. At the same time, the police union won a significant and legitimate concession, giving it the influence it desired without impairing the city's legal authority.

Settlements similar to that made with the Hartford police are not uncommon. They demonstrate that the sharing in decision-making is not all accomplished by formal contractual arrangements. Many policy demands made at the table are actually not intended for inclusion in the contract. They are intended rather to exert pressure on administrators to effect at least a portion of the demanded changes through decisions by their own legal authority. In the same way, the unions, by use of political pressure, now enhanced by bargaining rights and the power to strike, can exercise effective persuasion on the political authorities to make policy decisions along lines of the union's desires.

One of the most far-reaching and precedent-shattering employer-employee agreements in government was made through a grievance procedure between the Commissioner of Correction of the State of New York, with the Governor's sanction, and AFSCME State Council 82. The agreement followed the Attica Prison tragedy, in which 43 persons, 11 correction officers held as hostages and 32 prisoners were killed by the gunfire of the state police in an effort to quell a prison rebellion.

The agreement, in addition to a number of personnel items regarding the hiring and training of correction officers, including the setting up of a Correction Department training academy, contained the following two precedent-breaking items:

1. Provision for a special institution for incorrigible inmates to be put into operation within 30 days.

2. Improvement in the provision for inmate needs such as clothing, shoes, and shower facilities. On food service $689,000 is slated for the preparation of meals on the basis of nutritious diet rather than on current daily per capita cost. On clothing, a special $34,000 fund will provide a clothing ration at Attica, an additional $2 million is planned to implement the new clothing ration with appropriate laundry service.

The new clothing will include drastic improvements in material, style and tailoring for both summer and winter issues with wearability, appearance and comfort also improved. Toilet and shower facilities will be remodeled and relocated.27

Management-Rights Clauses

Management rights clauses, usually modeled after the clause in federal contracts required by Kennedy Executive Order 10988, are frequently included in municipal collective bargaining contracts. The management rights clause in New York City's contracts with employee unions is typical of clauses used in several other cities:

> . . . standards of service offered by its agencies and standards of selection for employment, to direct its employees, take disciplinary action, relieve its employees from duty because of lack of work or other legitimate reasons, determine methods, means and personnel by which government operations are to be conducted, determine the content of job classification and take all necessary actions to carry out its mission in emergencies and exercise complete control . . . over its organization and technology by performing its work.

Although the city declares that its reserved powers "are not within the scope of collective bargaining," it then proceeds to vitiate its reservations by declaring that "questions concerning the practical impact that decisions on above matters have on employees, such as questions of work load of manning, are within the scope of collective bargaining." [28]

The use of such clauses has been of minimal value in thwarting employee actions to broaden their autonomy. On occasion, as in Milwaukee, the city was upheld by the Wisconsin Employment Relations Commission in its right to make unilateral changes in job duties. The Milwaukee management rights clause clearly recognized the prerogative of the city to operate and manage its affairs in all respects in accordance with its responsibilities. Such authority, which the city had not officially abridged, delegated, or modified by agreement, was held retained by the city. AFSCME Local 831 had requested the Commission to rule on the issue when AFSCME wanted to renegotiate wage rates, contending that the city's unilateral action had materially increased the responsibilities of inspectors.

In still another Wisconsin decision, a WERC arbitrator ruled that contractual language guaranteeing an employee organization all rights provided by the state's bargaining law is no protection against the abolition of a position by the city, nor did the contractual provision act as a bar to the assignment of an employee outside the bargaining by a public employer armed with a "catch-all" management rights clause. [29]

The terminology of some clauses is so vague as to suggest that any possible reconciliation of contending positions lies in sound and responsible bargaining. Collective bargaining will undoubtedly foster further inroads into areas previously considered management's prerogative. Cities should continue to bargain on legitimate issues and consult employee groups on all matters that have significant effect on employee interests.

It is difficult, if not impossible, to lay down, a priori, precise areas as to bargainable and nonbargainable issues, especially where professional employees consider themselves knowledgeable. Willingness to consult, to discuss, and to act in a cooperative manner in no way implies a surrender of the authority entrusted to public officials by the public. In the final analysis, any accommodation will depend largely on the bona fide efforts of both sides to find agreement. Continued reliance on management rights clauses is likely to degenerate into mere ritualistic expressions, protecting neither the rights of the employer to manage nor those of the union to include certain legitimate bargaining issues in collective agreements.

Long-Range Impact on Public Policy

The country is being governed increasingly by large hierarchical bureaucracies that the public finds it harder and harder to penetrate. The question may well be raised as to whether unionization will so entrench the bureaucracy as to make it even more impenetrable or whether affiliation with the organized labor movement will bring the bureaucracy closer to the people.

The growth of professionalism has made it more and more difficult for outside elective officials, representing society as a whole, to impose policies on tightly knit, specialized groups. The issue of whether municipal employees are moving in the direction of workers' control of local government or at least toward formal joint participation in management is fundamentally more significant than the issue of the strike, which attracts public attention because of the immediacy and dramatic nature of the confrontation.

In the publicly owned and operated industries and other branches of the civil service in various European countries, there is a movement on the part of some unions toward what Harold Laski called "administrative syndicalism." [30] Employee representation is provided for on the governing boards of French nationalized in-

192

dustries. In Britain the Union of Post Office Workers has a proviso in its constitution calling for the reorganization of the service as a post office guild.

No such specific demands based on syndicalist or guild socialist ideology have been made in the United States, but there is some fear that practices already begun could move in such directions. AF-SCME officials emphatically deny such an objective, and the manifestations of syndicalist tendencies, i.e., worker participation or control, that have occurred do not have the conscious revolutionary implications of similar tendencies and practices abroad.[31] American unions have no revolutionary ideology. European counterparts, no doubt, were astounded by the signs carried by American construction workers on Wall Street in May 1970 reading "God Bless the Establishment."

The British Trades Union Congress has specifically gone on record against worker control or union participation in management.[32] When unions become responsible for the operation of industries or public services, their basic function changes. If union leaders become bosses, the question is raised: Who will defend the interest of workers vis-a-vis management? Would it become necessary to develop a new, independent union for this purpose? And who, if special interests dominated the services, would represent the public for whom the services exist?

Bureaucratic Autonomy

While the strike is the most dramatic issue growing out of the unionization of public employees, the rise of collective bargaining, especially in municipal employment, has begun to direct attention to the increasingly autonomous role of the organized bureaucracies in public affairs. Matters that have been regarded as belonging in the realm of official discretion are being placed on the bargaining table. Some public officials have succumbed and permitted public policies to be written into contracts. Others have resisted such demands as threats to the erosion of responsible representative government involving the surrender of public authority to nongovernmental organizations having no legal responsibility to the people.

Tendencies toward bureaucratic autonomy are especially dangerous in the case of the police. The police associations demand that only policemen be allowed to judge policemen and that the department remain free of civilian political control, referred to as "political interference."

In the case of schools, bureaucratic autonomy would lead to the establishment of educational policies without the voices of parents and taxpayers being heard. To ignore teachers when school policy is being formulated, however, is equally untenable. In sum, modern employer-employee relations involve a cooperative relationship of which collective bargaining is a part, not a whole.

The adoption of the process of joint consultation as practiced in the British nationalized industries might prove a constructive step. All matters affecting the welfare of the service of the staff are subject to formal joint consultation, with the right of decision reserved to management on all matters that do not fall within the scope of "negotiation," i.e., collective bargaining. Many matters handled by consultation often eventually become matters for collective bargaining.[33]

The Dilemma of Codetermination

The rising extent of codetermination of policy in the public administrative process, now widely referred to as participative decision-making, has led to a questioning of the trend as a threat to the integrity of responsible political democracy.

In the words of Frederick C. Mosher:

> . . . there has already developed a great deal of collegial decision-making in many public agencies, particularly those which are largely controlled by single professional groups. But I would point out that *democracy within administration*, if carried to the full, raises a logical dilemma in its relation to *political democracy*. All public organizations are presumed to have been established and to operate for public purposes—i.e., purposes of the people. They are authorized, legitimized, empowered, and usually supported by authorities outside of themselves. To what extent, then, should "insiders," the officers and employees, be able to modify their purposes, their organizational arrangements, and their means of support? It is entirely possible that internal administrative democracy might run counter to the principles and objectives of political democracy in which the organizations of government are viewed as instruments of public purpose.[34]

Defending the "trend toward participative decision-making in public agencies," Michael M. Harmon takes issue with Mosher:

> The dilemma which Mosher sees between administrative and political democracy is subject to serious question. The narrow professionalism in public agencies which he rightly fears is apprently assumed to be the result of a movement toward a more participative form of public

management and greater self-actualization of professional public employees. But it is just as reasonable to assume that self-centered professionalism which ignores public needs is likely to manifest itself in organizational systems which rely on quite authoritarian, highly centralized methods of decision making . . . The vision of professional administrators pursuing their own interests at the expense of the public . . . assumes that administrators will act selfishly and irresponsibly unless forced to act otherwise by vigilant guardians of the public trust. [35]

All employer-employee relationships are not rooted in collective bargaining. Consultation, accompanied by informal understandings, is a way in which to handle issues where responsibility for decision rests with legally designated public authorities.

Consultative practices have proved to be mutually satisfactory and educative. If adopted by local governments, consultative machinery could enhance legitimate managerial authority and give employees a constructive role without interference with the function of management to establish and control policy.

Notes

1. Wallace Sayre and Herbert Kaufman, *Governing New York City* (New York: Russell Sage Foundation, 1960), p. 446.

2. Edward N. Costikyan, "Who Runs the City Government?" *New York*, May 26, 1969, pp. 40-47.

3. Ibid, p. 47. Costikyan is not alone in his sadness over the decline of the political machine. Mayor Richard Hatcher of Gary, Ind., stated, "However well or poorly Mayor Daley may use his authority, the actions of America's last great political machine, in Chicago, demonstrate convincingly that patronage politics provides a way to get things done." *Time*, June 1, 1970.

4. David T. Stanley, addressing a symposium on the impact of unionism on public administration, stated that in half of the cities and counties he employer. "In most of 'my' cities and counties . . . bargaining concentrates on pay and benefits and the unions disclaim any ambition to say how government shall be run." But, he went on to point out, "in more active 'union towns,' however, the unions are concerning themselves increasingly with the content of so-called management prerogatives." Published by Bureau of National Affairs, Washington, D.C., May 10, 1971.

5. Fredrick C. Mosher, *Democracy and the Public Service* (New York: Oxford University Press, 1968), p. 108.

6. W. Henry Lambright, "Public Administration is Public-Policy Making", in Frank Marini, ed., *Toward a New Public Administration* (Scranton, Pa.: Chandler Publishing Co., 1971), p. 302.

7. Contract, Associated Teachers of Huntington, N.Y., June 10, 1968, Preamble.

8. Contract, Philadelphia Federation of Teachers, AFT Local 3, June, 1969, p. 94.

9. Contract, Chicago Teachers Union, AFT Local 1, January 1, 1970.

10. Contract, Philadelphia, Pa., p. 105.

11. Felix Nigro, "The Implication for the Public Administrator," *Public Administration Review*, March-April, 1968, p. 143.

12. Contract, Chicago, Article 46-5.

13. Contract, East St. Louis, Illinois School District 189, August 28, 1967, Article VIII.

14. Contract, Gary, Indiana.

15. Contract, East St. Louis Federation of Teachers, AFT Local 1220, Article IV Section 25, p. 9.

16. *Government Employee Relations Reports*, No. 239 (April, 1968) B-3.

17. The SSEU merged in 1969 with AFSCME, becoming Local 371, from which it had broken in the early 1960's.

18. *SSEU Contract, 1965*, Introductory Statement by Joseph Tepedino, President, August, 1965, p. 1.

19. Ibid, p. 4. Article XVI of the contract uses a slightly different wording: "The purpose of this provision is to effectuate collective bargaining on all *legitimate* issues involved in presently established areas for collective bargaining, and the City should take steps to eliminate its previous positions of 'not bargainable' or 'not bargainable at this forum' on questions bargainable in the accepted collective bargaining procedures . . ." (emphasis added).

20. *The Public Employee*, vol. 35, no. 3 (March, 1970).

21. New York *Times*, July 14, 1967.

22. Dan Cordiz, "How Come it Costs So Much To Run the City?," *New York*, November 22, 1971, p. 59.

23. Ibid.

24. See the *Public Employee*, Vol. 35, No. 3, March, 1970.

25. Contract between the City of Detroit and AFSCME, Art 20, July 1971.

26. Robert D. Krause, in a letter to the authors, November 9, 1971.

27. For full agreement see *The Public Employee*, November 1971, p. 4. AFSCME, in announcing the agreement, stated, "For the first time in American history a labor union has induced government to institute major reforms in its penal and correctional system."

28. City of New York, Executive Order 52, Sec. 5c., 1967.

29. See *Government Employee Relations Reports*, December 29, 1969.

30. Harold Laski, *Authority in the Modern State* (New Haven, Conn.: Yale University Press, 1918), Chapter 5.

31. The distinguished British political scientist Brian Chapman has noted that the wave of syndicalist sentiment that reached its height in the first two decades of the century affected the public sector more than the private. *The Profession of Government* (London: Allen and Unwin, 1963), pp. 37-38.

32. British Trade Union Congress, *Interim Report on Public Ownership* (1953), p. 495. This report, in opposing worker control, referred to the sentiment for it as "out of date ideas about industrial relations."

33. Acton Society Trust, *The Framework of Joint Consultation*.

34. Frederick C. Mosher, *op. cit.,* p. 18.

35. Michael M. Harmon, "The 'Dilemma' of Administrative and Political Democracy," in Frank Marini, ed., *Toward a New Public Administration* (Scranton, Pa.: Chandler Publishing Co., 1970), pp. 177-178.

8 The Merit System and Collective Bargaining

There has been a noticeable tone of alarm concerning the impact of collective bargaining on merit systems of personnel administration in municipal governments. The current trend of enshrining into collective bargaining contracts many facets of personnel policy or practice hitherto regarded as the prerogative of public officials has led to forecasts that soon public employee unions will control personnel systems, with eventual abandonment of the merit principle in public employment. In its place some fully foresee a new form of "spoils," rooted in public service bargaining.

Since the end of World War II, the entire concept of spoils versus merit has undergone remarkable change. Distinctions are made between what are considered the essential and nonessential elements of a merit system. The primary question is no longer how to prevent spoilsmen from taking over the jobs in government but how to induce qualified people to enter the public service and how to achieve effective implementation of public policy.

New forces are impinging on merit concepts previously considered sacred: the changing labor market; the rise of former underclasses into the decision-making process; the necessity of achieving consensus among clashing societal groups; differentials between pay in private industry and government; and emerging highly professionalized bureaucracies, which will profoundly affect the traditional modes of personnel administration in the years to come.

The Traditional Merit System

Public personnel administration in local government operates under a complex of laws and regulations that fall into two broad categories. The first stems directly from the civil service reform movement and was intended to eliminate partisan political spoils, under which appointments were rewards for party service. Legislation enacted under the leadership of the civil service reformers created a system of appointment and promotion, substituting for partisan service "merit and fitness" measured by objective standards, usually determined by competitive examination. Frequently regulations followed whose purpose was to insulate the employees from partisan pressures and, in a few jurisdictions, such as the Ohio home-rule-charter cities, these regulations were supplemented by restrictions seeking to bar employees from political activity. The regulations regarding political activity in Ohio cities, especially Cincinnati, are more stringent than the federal rules.

The policing of the service was put in the hands of civil service commissions, usually bipartisan and operating in substantial independence of the chief executive. The commission's mandate was to keep the system free from partisan influence and assure fair and impartial treatment for the individual employee.

As the civil services of the states and cities became larger and more complex, a second category of laws and rules was added to project the reform principles into the internal administration of the service. The attainment of this end was sought through a system of position classification based on duties and responsibilities meticulously described. Position classification was often accompanied by a compensation plan based on the principle of equal pay for equal work, so that jobs of the most varied nature could be compared to assure incumbents fair and equal treatment. For example, a budget examiner, a child psychologist, a nurse or a biochemist could be classified in the grade that included all employees whose duties, as determined by classification technicians, represented the same relative degree of qualification and responsibility.

The function of classification and pay administration was performed by specialists, supervised by the civil service commission. Their techniques, greatly influenced by the concepts of scientific management in private industry, led them to claim a quality of "scientific" objectivity for their practices.

As a barrier against favoritism and possible unfairness, advances in the service were usually made through promotion examinations. These examinations are frequently so constructed as to give advantage to employees in the agency over outside candidates. Indeed, the tests are not always open to anyone but agency employees. Outsiders as a rule often suffer further disadvantage by a grading system giving credits for work in the agency. This procedure of keeping outsiders out and reserving employment to the employees already in the agency is justified as encouraging a career service. The result of the effective barring of lateral entrance to even highly qualified outsiders has been the creation of a virtually closed service manned by self-contained bureaucracies and largely denied the infusion of fresh blood and innovative ideas.

Services in some states, such as New York, sought to encourage the entrance of college graduates and holders of appropriate graduate degrees, through the avenues of special examinations held each year. Yet these specially sought, well-qualified young persons frequently found themselves, after a year of careful in-service "internship," bucking the stone wall of the classification and promotion system. Instead of being able to move ahead quickly in accordance with their abilities, they either were mired in a lower-grade position or, frustrated and disillusioned, were impelled to leave the service.

The following case of a young applicant is not atypical. The candidate had qualified and was highly recommended for a challenging job. After waiting for many weeks, the state training officer of the internship program and one of the candidate's professors who had induced him to enter the state service were informed by the Personnel Director of the department in question, "We can't appoint your candidate. He is too good! Why, in a year he'd be ready for promotion, but we couldn't promote him and he'd become a frustrated and dissatisfied employee. We couldn't promote him because we have a promotion list with at least a dozen eligibles."

In the far more flexible federal services, interns have been able to rise rapidly to high posts. John Macy, who became executive director of the U.S. Civil Service Commission and then served as its Chairman under Kennedy and Johnson, entered the service as an intern.

This system of public personnel management was devised and administered by devoted specialists highly trained in the complex techniques of the craft. It was also strongly supported by the employees, who were organized in numbers of local unions or independent associations that, although usually small, were active and influential. They did not hesitate to utilize the complex machinery of appeal to the civil service commissions or special review agencies when they believed the regulations intended to protect them were not properly applied. Often groups of individual employees would band together and hire a lawyer to contest their complaints regarding aspects of the system that they claimed affected them inequitably.

The result was to handicap seriously the managerial powers and administrative discretion of agency executives. But this is exactly what the system was intended to do, in the name of a nonpartisan civil service guaranteeing fair and equal treatment to all. The executive was regarded with suspicion as a politician, untrustworthy if not actually "unclean."

Civil service reform in this country, unlike that abroad, began at the wrong end, concentrating on the clerks rather than the administrators who set the tone and character of the service. Top positions that were not properly in the domain of political appointment long remained rewards for partisan service, and the appointees were expected to administer their agencies accordingly. The "science of personnel administration" was the answer of the reformers and the employees. The bipartisan quasi-independent civil service commissions that policed the merit system were not always certain whether their function was to protect the employees and job candidates from partisan political pressure and guarantee the individual employee fair treatment or to act as a central personnel arm of the public employer. Was its business the promotion of innovative, efficient performance for the benefit of the public or were its activities confined to the task of protecting the employee from possible abuses of administrative authority? So confused had the situation become during the 1950's that civic and professional organizations concerned with public administration seldom met without programming panels or round table discussions devoted to the question, "Civil Service: for employee protection or for efficiency?"

In its attempt to eliminate partisan spoils and provide fair treatment to the individual employee, the system's complex regulations hamstrung the effective use of administrative discretion and initiative. Administrators hesitated to exercise their responsibilities in evaluating, assigning, disciplining, or removing employees. The administrative actions most frequently appealed were unsatisfactory performance ratings and requirements to "work out of title." Many supervisory officials in widely separated jurisdictions declared that they preferred to "make do" with an unsatisfactory employee rather than spend hours before appeals agencies justifying their actions and being made to feel as though they were on trial for exercising what they believed to be their administrative responsibilities.

In addition to appeals and reviews by administrative bodies, the civil services of state and local governments became highly judicialized. Appeals have been taken to the courts on almost every facet of personnel administration, to the extent that judgments of the courts have more than once been substituted for the discretion of public administrators. A huge, complex body of court-made law has either tied the hands of administrators or pushed them into undesired actions, with the result that personnel administration has become to a large extent operation by the rule book. Not only have the courts intervened on the initiative of organized employees but they have even, in action brought by candidates, ruled on the validity of examination questions.

Thus, the traditional merit system, operating on a semiautonomous basis and largely insulated from executive control, brought about a counter movement for the recognition of personnel administration as an executive responsibility. Specific endorsement of this proposition was given in the *Report of the President's Committee on Administrative Management* in 1937. The federal government suffered far less from the disabilities which afflicted state and municipal administrations. Yet complaints regarding rigidities of position classification and appeals from unsatisfactory ratings (with their attendant demands on administrators' time and energy), coupled with the purely negative system of recruitment through the posting of notices of examination for positions to be filled and then waiting for desirable applicants to show up were enough to stimulate the recommendation in the 1937 *Report.*

After World War II, as the civil services expanded to compensate for the virtual freeze on their activity during the war, the idea of personnel administration as an executive responsibility began to take root in state and local government. Instead of a surplus of applicants competing for comparatively few openings, as in prewar and especially Depression days, the economic prosperity of the postwar years saw the reverse of this situation. There were actually more job vacancies than qualified candidates, particularly in the larger cities and more populous states. It became apparent that the need was not for continuation of the traditional negative role of the civil service commissions but rather for positive approaches that would attract able men and women to fill the complex responsibilities of local government in the postwar era. In addition, the necessity of retraining incumbents took on new urgency.

To meet this situation, local governments moved toward the recommendations of the 1937 *Report* and created central personnel departments headed by single commissioners or directors responsible to the chief executive. The development assumed many forms. The civil service commission usually remained, its chairman designated by the chief executive and holding office at his pleasure. He served as the head of the central personnel agency, with the commission's functions limited to those of a servicing and appeals body. In some places the commission continued to have rule-making or rule-approving powers; and in a few cities it designated the personnel director, thus effecting a compromise between the old and new order.

John J. Couturier, Executive Director of the National Civil Service League, has proposed abolishing the civil service commission system and replacing it with a citizen's advisory board headed by an ombudsman with authority to hear grievances and appeals from decisions on questions as to management activities. The civil service commission would be replaced by a personnel director, who would be a member of the cabinet of the governmental jurisdiction and have the power and duty to engage in collective bargaining with organized employees.

With the decline of the old-line political machines and the change in the job market, and with the example of earlier successes of the civil service reform movement, active citizen reform associations did not hesitate to expose spoils abuses and go to the courts for assistance. The New York Civil Service Reform Association, under the militant leadership of H. Eliot Kaplan, brought hundreds of successful suits to combat the spoilsmen. All this led to the assumption that the spoils system was on the way out.

However, despite the accomplishments of civil service reform, the system of political spoils still persists in many areas. According to Couturier, fifteen states still function without any merit system except for those categories of employees who are in services receiving federal grants or aid and who are therefore required to be covered by a merit system. The League's study found that while most large cities have "some sort of system," the extent and quality in many places leaves much to be desired. Couturier declared:

> We have a long way to go, because *less than half* the local government employees are in merit systems and many of these systems are bad. There are still rascals using public jobs for political pay-off . . . The curse of patronage and political manipulation of public payrolls still run rampant wasting our tax dollars, warping our payrolls and weakening our government services. [1]

Yet despite this persistence of spoils, the major function of personnel administrators in the post-World War II years has been how to attract qualified candidates for the many vacant places. Thus, the standard personnel functions of recruitment, position classification, performance ratings, promotions, training, fringe benefits and all the factors intended to make the service attractive and promote the career concept became the province of the personnel department head, representing the chief executive.

While necessary to meet the demands of the times, the new authority of the executive over personnel matters tended to arouse employee suspicion and became a factor in stimulating the demand for collective bargaining to give the employees a recognized countervailing role to balance any abuses of authority that they feared the new dispensation might threaten.

Reactions of Personnel Administrators to Collective Bargaining

Many personnel administrators viewed the coming of collective bargaining with alarm, insisting that an adversary relationship that features collective bargaining has no place in the public service and would endanger the merit system. They objected to the various forms of union security as "substituting extraneous factors for the prime consideration of merit." They opposed the injection of outside third parties as arbitrators empowered to decide issues formerly within their province. They expressed fears that affiliation with organized labor would endanger the nonpartisanship of the service because of the labor movement's concern with politics, although both federal and local government workers had been affiliated with the trade union movement for generations before there were even whispers about public collective bargaining. They also stressed concern that seniority would replace the procedures of the merit system, as though seniority were not a cardinal feature of conventional merit systems.

Many personnel officers have found it hard to adjust to the changes in the functions brought about by collective bargaining. "The government personnel officer," wrote Randall M. Prevo, an experienced member of the craft,

> . . . has been experiencing something resembling a trauma in employer-employee relations in the past few years. For a long time he practiced his art relatively free from employee dissatisfaction. His success fully represented management and he was often considered the spokesman for employees so far as he was able to both protect employees from management misdeeds and, at the same time,

convince his bosses that he was protecting their interests as well as the civil service or merit system restrictions would permit.[2]

He added, "If the personnel director could not please both camps, his own predilection tempered by the prevailing local power structure generally guided his decision on which camp to favor."

Not all members of the personnel craft view the new order as calmly as does Prevo. Some view it as spelling the doom of the merit system. Holding that it was impossible to accommodate collective bargaining to the civil service, one critic declared:

> The decision is not where to draw the line. The decision is about two kinds of personnel systems . . .. They are different. They employ different principles, and they have different concerns. We can no longer believe that we can have half collective bargaining and half merit system.[3]

Another critic, the City Manager of Eau Claire, Wisc., thus posed the issue: "The decision we must really make is whether the personnel administrator and the merit system are to survive."[4]

These hand-wringing statements equate the merit system with the unilaterally administered traditional functions and concepts of the practitioners of the personnel craft and prophesy doom when new elements to which they are not accustomed disturb their preconceptions and habits. But not all members of the craft are so loathe to change what W. V. Gill, Executive Director of the Federal Labor Relations Council, referred to as "the old rituals."[5] Robert D. Krause, Personnel Director of Hartford, Conn., where collective bargaining has been required by state law since 1965, refused to view the assumption of several central functions of his agency by the bargaining process as a threat to the merit system. He stated:

> Job classification has been considered a part of the merit system. The present agreement requires that any new job class be subject to negotiation with the union to establish a mutually acceptable salary prior to establishment of a new class. In addition, disagreements over the classification of individual positions are subject to arbitration by the State Board of Mediation and Arbitration rather than the determination of the Personnel Board.
>
> Prior to collective bargaining, employees who were disciplined could appeal to the Personnel Board. Under the agreement, the appeal is now to the State Board of Mediation and Arbitration.
>
> Similarly, theory holds that a personnel board or civil service commission will uphold merit principles on reviewing appeals affecting discipline and job classification. As a practical matter,

however, it could be argued that the State Board of Mediation and Arbitration has upheld merit factors as much as the City's Personnel Board, if not more. [6]

Not all personnel directors are given the opportunity to learn the art of collective bargaining. Data accumulated by the National Civil Service League reveals that only about 40 percent of the heads of personnel agencies in major jurisdictions that operate under collective bargaining are involved in the bargaining process. Many personnel officers strive both to keep their traditional functions and to remain or become the public employer's professional bargaining representative.

W. Donald Heisel, who served with distinction for a long time as personnel officer of Cincinnati, said in referring to the city's many years of constructive and strike-free collective bargaining relations:

> Both parties understand the process of collective bargaining and accepted it. The city recognizes the bilateral nature of bargaining as a decision making process. It has found over a period of years that it can make decisions bilaterally and still survive. This acceptance of the process helps to accept the results even though at times the process becomes difficult. [7]

Perhaps the most significant effect of collective bargaining on personnel administrators will be to end their role as impartial friends of both management and employees and lead them to act as representatives of management. This should arm management with technical assistance enabling it to defend its prerogatives instead of having to wind through the maze of rigid civil service rules constructed out of administrative rulings, legislation, and judicial decisions, carefully trying to please everyone and avoid challenges and appeals.

Unions and the Merit System

Most union leaders believed that one of the best guarantees of union stability was support of existing merit systems and extension of the merit system into other jurisdictions. This support was based both on principle and on realization of the fact that reliance by individual employees on outside political influence for favors or for the correction of grievances diluted member loyalty and weakened the union as spokesman and protector of the workers it represented. But the unions vigorously rejected the proposition, sometimes articulated, that civil service status gave the employees all the protection they needed and it was not necessary for them to join and support labor organizations. In the words of the counsel of the Laborers International Union:

> Our union views the merit system as the hiring halls in the public service. My experience in the federal field and most state and local governments is that in the absence of a strong union representing employees, public officials have distorted the merit system principles or have ignored them completely in the broad areas of hiring, promotions, discharges, etc. In fact, our union did have a law suit against the governor of the state of Ohio, which we withdrew, challenging the right of the governor and state officials to collect political money from state employees in return for a promise of jobs, overtime pay, and promotions. [8]

Until the late 1960's AFSCME actively supported the personnel policies and practices of the merit system reform movement and concentrated on lobbying to effect changes. In 1940 Arnold Zander, the national president, expressed skepticism concerning the efficacy of contracts and agreements with municipal employers compared with the benefits to employees of legislation covering job security, wages, hours and conditions of employment. He noted that "enactments by legislative bodies are, in a sense, contracts between the government and the citizens and are enforceable in courts of law. We have our unions to force compliance with such enactments."[9]

By 1962 Zander, who by then had been a pioneering leader of the movement for collective bargaining for almost a quarter of a century, had come to the conclusion that civil service legislation required collective bargaining to promote its effectiveness. He declared:

> It (AFSCME) found early that statutory regulation of conditions of employment was inadequate in the complex operation of government. AFSCME advocates the merit system at all levels of government and the promotion of civil service legislation and career service in government as one of the objectives stated in its constitution. But civil service laws and rules were found too broad to care for the day-to-day problems of employees. Even a good civil service system must be policed through the collective bargaining process.
>
> Collective bargaining and the civil service merit system are complementary. [10]

With the election of Jerry Wurf to the presidency of AFSCME in 1964, the position of the organization, as expressed by its leaders, became increasingly critical of the traditional merit system: ". . . the merit system alone is not the answer to their problems as workers: in fact, the merit system frequently acts as an impediment or handicap to their progress and development."[11]

Another AFSCME official, Victor Gotbaum, Director of the New York District Council, declared that the workers "were tired of being reformists in the civil service area and wanted a trade union that would fight like hell for their rights, not a do-nothing merit-system-minded association."

Several union officers offered specific criticisms of the inadequacy of merit system implementation without the force of a strong union behind them. A union spokesman in a Midwestern city complained that "no one has enforced any civil service rules and regulations in this city except us." Another official in the same city conceded that the civil service agency had not reviewed job qualifications for over 20 years, and in another major city a high official admitted that "until we were forced into action by the union, this city had done very little in the field of training and equitable promotion practice, and even now our system is woefully inadequate."

Despite all their criticisms of inadequate administration of the civil service regulations and their insistence on a key role in position classification and salary administration, hitherto the sole province of the personnel agency, unions jealously guard those elements of the system that protect their tenure and their rights to hearings when violations of law are claimed and that shield them against political exploitation. Claiming that the abolition of "civil service," here used as a synonym for "merit system," would spell disaster, an official statement in a union paper declared:

> There are those who would have us believe that all we have to do is abolish civil service and presto!—we have a system that assures merit, fitness, and all the other virtues we admire in government employees.
>
> The alternatives to civil service, however, are political patronage, large-scale corruption, and less merit, fitness, and personal initiative. The alternatives are systems which demean and degrade employees, leaving them bereft of security and at the mercy of shifting winds.
>
> It is no accident that the very worst systems are those where civil service is either minimal or absent altogether. [12]

Union policy, in short, is to keep the protective features of the merit system but transfer position classification, wage administration, some aspects of grievance procedure, and several other unilaterally administered personnel functions to the bargaining table.

In New York, which has long had perhaps the most meticulously regulated merit system in the land, the failure to achieve merit and efficiency has been noted by several scholars.

Blanche D. Blank, Executive Director of the Mayor's Task Force on City Personnel, found the rule-ridden personnel system of New York a barrier to effective administration. Calling the city a "victim of the system," which she charges paralyzed the services' initiative and high sense of urgency, she wrote:

> In most organizations this essential "high sense of urgency" is elicited by a skillful mix of two parts positive incentive and one part effective discipline. Unfortunately, this formula cannot now be used effectively in the New York City public service.
>
> The usual lure of reasonably speedy promotion based on job productivity and accompanied by imaginative and relevant career training is snarled by legal, budgetary and procedural restraints.
>
> The second part of the formula, a dignified discipline with reprimands and dismissals judiciously but adequately distributed, has apparently atrophied. [13]

In their study conducted for the Brookings Institution, David Stanley and his staff were equally critical of the failure of the city's rigid system to attract high-quality technical professional, and administrative personnel. [14]

Although New York for many years has had a "scientific" classification system, known as the Career and Salary Plan, the growth of unionism has shifted implementation of the plan to the bargaining table. Thus, collective bargaining on wages and salaries has been an integral part of New York's labor relations program since the issuance of Mayor Wagner's executive order on collective bargaining in 1958. The appropriateness of a class of positions assigned to an occupational group was a subject of bargaining as early as 1961. In a 1967 order issued by Mayor Lindsay, the management-rights clause specifically prohibits bargaining on position classification, declaring, "It is the right of the city to determine the . . . content of job classifications." However, the order makes claims by employees that they are performing duties substantially different from those applying to their actual classification a grievance subject to appeal through the established grievance procedures.

Municipal bargaining representatives and personnel agencies must realize that both collective bargaining and the merit system are here to stay. The unnecessary competition between the two for supremacy must give way.

Collective bargaining has effected great changes in the functions of the central personnel agency. Its original function of selection on the basis of merit determined by objective standards will very likely remain. The promotion process by examination will probably also remain essentially intact, although subject to consultation with union representatives. The functions more recently assumed in personnel administration, which include almost all conditions of employment, will, there is little reason to doubt, be taken over by the collective bargaining process. The establishment of new forms of patronage through union-employer deals is always a possibility. (The Post Office long followed the practice of playing favored employee organizations against more militant unions and rewarded "good" local union officers with supervisory jobs.) A personnel office or perhaps an impartial civil service commission might be revived to protect employees from abuses and to represent that elusive factor called public or citizen interest in the preservation of an impartial patronage-free civil service.

By freeing the personnel officer of a great part of the burden of personnel transactions, collective bargaining should enhance rather than diminish his functions. Liberated from the routine of detail, he can assume a new role as the staff arm of management, using his expertise in the implementation of the bargaining agreement and advising management regarding areas of success or failure. He can stimulate and encourage a system of regular consultation on problems of agency concern, where policies clearly falling within the sphere of management's prerogatives but which affect the employees can be discussed and made understandable and acceptable to the workers. The department head, occupied with carrying out the mission of the agency, cannot pay adequate attention to these matters without expert staff help. Such help in personnel matters has contributed tremendously to the successful administration of the Tennessee Valley Authority and the U.S. Department of the Interior, both of which have a long history of genuine collective bargaining, with bilateral determination of personnel policies.

Training and Career Development

Without in-service training, blue-collar employees from minority groups are sometimes placed at a severe disadvantage in competing against outsiders for higher-level positions. Because of difficulty in securing employment in private industry, many culturally deprived individuals seek public employment. Government has evolved into the "employer of last resort," and some are suggesting that the public sector should become the employer of "first resort." The introduction of such concepts into public employment spurs the need for adequate additional training for disadvantaged persons, in order to prevent their being trapped in a multitude of dead-end jobs with little or no opportunity for advancement. There are some

211

entrance requirements, of long standing and adopted in good faith, that minority groups charge have become de facto discriminations against them. An example of such requirements is the minimum-height standards in public safety appointments. The average Puerto Rican and Mexican American is too short to meet them.

Similar charges have been made by minority groups in Great Britain against the Metropolitan Police. The service groups in both countries have resisted changing established standards, on the grounds that they are in the public interest and are necessary to maintain the efficiency of the services.

Generally, municipal governments have not done an outstanding job of in-service training. Limited by small staffs, inadequate funds, and (too frequently) inefficient administration, training programs have failed to solve a problem contributing to the urban crisis— meeting the needs of a desperate segment of the urban populace.

New York City's 1969-1970 budget provided only $207,350 for in-service training of all city employees, and only 21 employees were assigned to such training and development programs. As a result, unions have exerted pressure on the city to train lower-level employees even at the expense of cutting back training of professional categories. Surely, this "robbing Peter to pay Paul" approach is not a way to obtain adequate training programs.

Several hospital-career-development training programs initiated in 1969 are geared to prepare people for new avenues of promotion. The Cleveland Metropolitan General Hospital, the Boston City Hospital, the New York City public hospitals, and the Maryland state mental hospitals are participating in programs to upgrade hospital administrations. Trainees attend high-intensity classes during working hours at full pay, the goal being to allow a trainee to move from entry level to "professional" status.

Local 420 of AFSCME District Council 37 is cooperating in a program affecting nearly 1,000 employees who seek promotions to nurse's aide and licensed practical nurse.[15] While the New York City Department of Personnel retains legal responsibility to administer such programs, contract provisions state that the Department "shall consult, on a regular and continuing basis, with the Union on its plans for all such programs and the Union shall participate in the selection and recruitment of employees receiving such training."[16]

By mid-1970 AFSCME had joined with two professional employee organizations—the New York State Nurses Association and the Committee of Interns and Residents of New York City—to pressure for large-scale training programs to alleviate the critical shortage of nurses. City hospitals, as of March 1970, had a total of 4,151 registered nurses, although 7,996 were authorized.[17] The three groups were seeking a commitment by the City Hospitals Corporation prior to the date the newly established unit officially assumed responsibility for running the city's 18 public hospitals. The proposal was intended to train 1,200 nurses aides and technicians each year—and included a one year program to train 50 aides to become registered nurses, the remaining 900 aides would be trained as technicians. The proposal also called for the expansion of training for existing registered nurses, creation of 650 "unit administrator" positions, and a special revolving fund to provide housing quarters.

AFSCME District Council 37 also negotiated another precedent-setting agreement in 1968, involving school employees. Under the agreement the New York City Board of Education agreed to accept the union as a referral agency for half of the 1,000 newly created "educational assistant" positions in public schools.[18] By 1970 New York City's public school system had more than 10,000 paraprofessionals, for whom the UFT was bargaining to secure, among other gains, training programs whereby some of the paraprofessionals could eventually become licensed teachers.

Even those who resist "encroachment on merit principles" recognize the benefits of training proposals. In some instances unions have initiated their own training programs to aid members in passing promotional examinations or high school equivalency tests.

Personnel departments no longer possess the autonomy or discretion they once had in the area of training. Unions will tend to emerge as an equal partner if not a "major stockholder" in training, promotion, and career-development programs. Too few personnel departments have effective training programs, and even fewer have comprehensive programs appropriately staffed.[19] To date the increased participation of unions cannot be said to have affected training programs adversely. The activities of unions to alleviate critical shortages in areas such as hospitals, to open new sources of skilled manpower, to provide more efficient operations by better-trained personnel, and to free professionals for more specialized care are all on the plus side of the ledger. Such programs as exist should prove assets rather than dangers to the merit principle.

Notes

1. Jean J. Couturier, "Patronage Versus Performance—The Balance Sheet of Civil Service Reform," *Good Government,* Fall 1967, p. 14.

2. Randall M. Prevo, "Unions and the Personnel Officer," *Public Personnel Review*, April 1970, p. 83.

3. Muriel M. Morse, "Shall We Bargain Away the Merit System?," *Public Personnel Review,* (October 1963), pp. 239-43.

4. Douglas Weiford, *Public Management*, May 1963.

5. W. V. Gill, "Public Unionism," paper presented at the Seminar on Public Unions held at Louisiana State University, New Orleans, March 6, 1970.

6. Robert D. Krause, Memorandum to the authors, September 22, 1970.

7. W. Donald Heisel, "Anatomy of a Strike," *Public Personnel Review*, October 1969, p. 232.

8. Letter to the authors, October 9, 1970. Restrictions on political activity by city employees in the Ohio home rule charter cities go beyond those of the federal government. However, in some states employees have actually been encouraged to participate in politics.

9. Arnold Zander, letter to President Green of the AFL, January 23, 1940.

10. Zander, "A Union View of Collective Bargaining in the Public Service," *Public Administration Review*, Winter, 1962, p. 6.

11. Jerry Wurf, "Personnel Opinions," *Public Personnel Review*, January, 1966, p. 53.

12. *Public Employee Press*, vol. 9, no. 2 (January 30, 1970).

13. Blanche D. Blank, "Topics: Civil Services as a Victim," New York *Times*, March 4, 1967.

14. David Stanley, *Professional Personnel for the City of New York*, Washington, D.C.: Brookings Institution, 1963.

15. "Nurses's Aides: Up, Up, Up the Career Ladder," *Public Employee*, vol. 9, no. 5 (May 8, 1969).

16. See Contracts, *City of New York and D.C. 37, AFSCME, Covering Certain Clerical-Administrative employees,* January 1, 1969 to June 30, 1971, p. 9; and *City of New York and D.C. 37, AFSCME, Covering Certain Hospital Aides and Technician Employees, January 1, 1969 to June 30, 1971, p. 11.*

17. John Sibley, "Training Program Is Urged to Put More Nurses in City Hospitals," New York *Times*, June 10, 1970, p. 35.

18. "New Opportunities Greet School Lunch, School Aides," *Public Employee*, vol. 9, no. 5 (May 8, 1968).

19. David T. Stanley observed, "Training continues to occupy a continually low position in the union scale of values, as in that of management," "What unions are Doing to the Merit System," *Public Personnel Review*, April 1970, p. 111.

9 Collective Bargaining and the Urban Financial Crisis

Unionization, whether accompanied by collective bargaining or using traditional forms of political pressure, has introduced a significant new element into the municipal budget-making process. Public employee organizations have negotiated contractual gains that have contributed to soaring municipal budgets. Unions, both affiliated and independent, have had a direct, substantial impact on the costs of city services and have become almost a dominating force in municipal wage-setting. The virtual epidemic of budget crises affecting many of the nation's largest cities in the early 1970' raises the central issue as to whether union power has pre-empted the budgetary authority of public officials legally vested with the power to decide how, when, and for what purposes city funds shall be spent.

No authoritative studies show whether the ratio of personnel costs to total expenditures is higher in jurisdictions with "strong" public employee organizations or whether the proportion of funds allocated to personnel is accelerating at a greater rate than other categories of expenditures. Individual cities differ in their governmental structures, taxing powers, political leadership, and the almost infinite number of variables, which diminishes the usefulness of existing figures for purposes of comparison. Valid, reliable mathematical models are needed before definitive judgments can be made.

215

Collective Bargaining and the Budgetary Process

The rise in municipal expenditures attributable to unionization is but one aspect of the financial plight of the city. Other forces and pressures have also fed the insistent demand for new revenues. City officials have stressed the need for increased federal and state aid, at the same time advocating greater fiscal autonomy for the cities. Several additional factors have stimulated expenditures beyond the capacity of the cities' tax system, among them the urgent need of increased services; the spiral of inflation, which has increased the prices paid by municipalities for goods and services purchased from the private sector; the needed expansion and modernization of physical facilities; and greatly enlarged welfare rolls.

The woes endured by the city in housing, education, traffic, pollution, and public safety are obvious. Less obvious is the condition summarized by Dick Netzer, Dean of the New York University Graduate School of Public Administration, in referring to New York City's problems, which are analogous to those of other large cities:

> In nearly every year during the 1960's the nominal budgetary balance required by law has necessitated one or a combination of changes in statutory provisions, such as increases in the rates of existing city taxes, the adoption of new city taxes, revisions in state-aid formulas, or simply temporary borrowing and raids on reserves.
>
> Each such action involves the expenditure of political bargaining power and, in the case of city tax increases, the using up of another slice of limited tax-paying capacity, thus making the resolution of the following year's budgetary problems that much harder.

Legal Strictures and the City's Budget

Legally, cities are "creatures of the state." Thus, the city is in the position of a vassal, having no inherent powers of taxation. With the legal authority to grant to or withhold from a city the power to bargain or levy taxes vested in the state, and with control of federal funds centered in Washington, D.C., the ability of the cities to cope with the urban crisis is limited. They are heavily dependent on the federal government. It has been estimated that less then half of most cities' budgets is made up of city-raised revenues. Most city revenue is increasingly derived from state and federal sources.

Officials confronted with major employee demands involving substantial sums of money are bound by constitutional, statutory, and in some cases, charter restrictions on their power to tax and to incur further indebtedness. Cities remain largely tied to the comparatively inflexible real estate tax, which accounts for approximately two thirds of the revenues from taxes directly levied by them. Moreover, a great percentage of the cities' revenues from grants-in-aid from the federal and state government are earmarked for specific purposes.

Welfare costs, debt service, and pension costs are to a substantial degree beyond the cities' control, and the cities are already encumbered by additional state-mandated expenditures, some of which were achieved by the lobbying of unions in state legislatures. In those jurisdictions where state law or the city charter requires a balanced budget, city officials are occasionally pressured to seek loopholes or engage in questionable management practices to cope with employee demands.

In 1970 New York City, Detroit, Pittsburgh, Newark, N.J., and Washington, D.C., discharged employees and initiated the cutting of some services as economy measures. During negotiations with key employee groups, New York's Mayor dismissed 500 provisional employees, postponed the hiring of police and firemen, and spoke in terms of a general job freeze. The same year, Cleveland laid off over 3,000 of its 13,000 employees and Detroit dismissed hundreds. Emulating the New York City Mayor's talk of "payless pay days," the Mayor of Pittsburgh spoke of the possibility of closing City Hall for a few weeks; Newark's Mayor warned that the school system was running out of funds and might have to shut down.

These events were in part a city bargaining ploy. They were also a token gesture to indicate that the number of layoffs could escalate. For example, the dismissal of 500 provisional employees in New York could lead to the dismissal of the remaining 15,500 provisionals. Throughout the nation cities utilized various pressure tactics to accomplish two objectives: (a) counter demands of employee unions and (b) speed up initiation of a flexible plan of federal revenue-sharing to rectify the existing fiscal imbalance. Actually, cutting services temporarily, short-term job freezes, replacing higher-paid retiring employees with new employees at lower starting salaries, leaving vacancies unfilled, and selling "budget notes" were not new ploys; they had traditionally been used as emergency fiscal measures by cities.

Wages and Salaries

Since personnel costs range from 50 percent to 80 percent of a "typical" city budget, it is obvious that collective bargaining is potentially a major factor in driving up the costs of city government. During the period to 1950 to 1968, employment in local government increased 113 percent and payrolls increased by 402 percent.[1] But such figures reveal little concerning the impact of collective bargaining, which before the 1960's had been a minor factor. The expenditure patterns in large urban centers differ considerably from those in smaller local units of government. Differences are in part due to the type and extent of services provided, the degree to which commuters use city services, varying state legal requirements, and the extent to which a specific city has become a concentration point for impoverished minority groups.

From 1962 to 1967, the number of city employees grew by 19 percent and municipal payrolls rose 46 percent.[2] The changes were more the result of the adjustment of pay rates than the increase in the number of individuals employed.

During the period 1960 through 1968, the salaries of police, fire fighters, sanitationmen, and other categories of municipal employees showed heavy percentage gains. The average salary of school teachers from 1960 to 1968 increased by 65.5 percent. The pay of fire fighters and police in cities with over 100,000 population increased by 38 percent during the period 1964 to 1969.

In determining the compensation of municipal employees, negotiators, arbitrators and political officials have tried to maintain recognizable relationships between the wages of various occupations. The oldest specific relationship, long in effect in most larger cities, is parity between police and fire salaries. The fire fighters have insisted on maintaining this practice in the face of tendencies in some places to raise police pay above fire pay, to attract recruits to enlarge the police force in response to law and order sentiment. Resulting disparities have been a leading cause of fire fighter militancy and strikes.[3]

Tampering with established parities in New York gave rise to an imbroglio that cost the city more than $150 million and sparked a major strike. Parity has existed between police and fire fighters in New York since 1898, with established ratios between the pay of rank-and-file employees and higher officers. During the administration of Mayor Robert F. Wagner, the city agreed to establish the ratio of patrolman to police sergeant, the first promotion grade, at 3 to 3.5, fixing the ratio of fire fighters to fire lieutenants, the first promotion grade, at 3 to 3.9, presumably on the grounds that lieutenant is a more august title than sergeant.

Protests by the police were immediate. Successive efforts by leading arbitrators to end the disparity between police sergeants and fire fighter lieutenants disrupted the established ratios between

218

patrolmen and fire fighters, on the one hand, and the sergeant and lieutenant, on the other.

The PBA continued to assert its "contractual right" to a 3 to 3.5 ratio between patrolmen and sergeants. It based its claim on a memorandum by the city Director of Labor Relations, stating that it was the city's "intent" to preserve the 3 to 3.5 ratio.[4] The astronomical cost of the adjustment to the city, already plagued by a multimillion dollar budget deficit, failed to deter the PBA. It took its case to the court. The lower court and the Appellate Division, the first tribunal of appeal, upheld the policemen's claim, noting that courts cannot be expected to rewrite contract provisions that on reflection proved to onerous, expensive, and sometimes the result of miscalculation. The city, announcing that it would go to the "barricades" in subsequent negotiations in order to end the parity spiral, appealed the decision to the Court of Appeals the state's highest court. This high court sent the case back to the lower court for "trial," to determine whether the PBA in fact had a valid contract with the city. While the matter was still under adjudication, an estimated 20,000 policemen, two thirds of the total force, went on a five-day wildcat strike. The nonstriking force was so well managed and so effectively deployed that the city's life went on normally, without any of the disorder that accompanied the police strikes that had taken place a short time before in Montreal and Stockholm.

The trial court found that a valid contract existed. This decision resulted in payment to the patrolmen of a $1,200 increase to restore the 3 to 3.5 ratio. The merry-go-round continued, with the fire fighters saying that they were contractually entitled to whatever the police got. The city, to avoid a round of dangerous strikes, entered into agreements giving each employee $2,700. The additional $1,500 was for retroactive pay for the period of negotiation and adjudication, from October 1968 through December 1970.

The sanitation men then asserted their claim under their contract to 90 percent parity with the protective services. The city, to avoid the risk of a further expensive defeat in the courts that might have required retroactive pay for pensions and other benefits, granted the sanitationmen's demands. The rides on the merry-go-round cost the city more than $150 million.

The United States Bureau of Labor Statistics has made intensive studies of the wages and benefits of municipal employees in 22 large and middle-sized cities in each of the Bureau's ten administrative regions from coast to coast. In a report covering 11 of the large cities studied (Atlanta, Boston, Buffalo, Chicago, Houston, Kansas City, Los Angeles, New Orleans, Newark, New York, and Philadelphia), the Bureau found that in nine cities government workers in clerical occupations held pay advantages over their private industry and federal government counterparts. A smaller majority of the 11 cities showed higher pay for employees engaged in data-processing and in maintenance and custodial jobs. Only Kansas City, Mo., and New Orleans paid city workers less than employees in private industry received for similar work.[5] Inquiries at the BLS showed that city employees in skilled and semiskilled blue-collar jobs had annual earnings in excess of those received by their counterparts in industry. Although they were paid a prevailing hourly wage, they worked throughout the year, without interruptions for weather or movement from completed to new jobs. Some cities try to take the steadiness of city jobs into consideration by setting their pay at a fixed percentage of the rate in private industry. Cincinnati sets its rates at 90 percent of the prevailing industry rate.

In all its published studies, the BLS includes only a brief reference to the role of unionization in setting pay scales. The researchers, when questioned, declared that they had no evidence regarding various types of union operation, i.e., formal or informal collective bargaining or traditional political pressure, on the relative extent of wage increases and benefits.[6]

The influence of unions, whether utilizing formal or informal bargaining or relying on the older forms of political operation, drives wages up faster and higher than they would rise if left to the normal pressures of supply and demand and other factors determining the labor market. Elements other than collective bargaining have played a role in the setting of municipal salaries and wages. Collective bargaining has, however, created a different configuration than would otherwise have developed.

The competitive nature of collective bargaining is demonstrated by the fact that in 1968 the minimum base pay of New York City patrolmen, ranked in seventh place nationally, had reached a first-rank figure of $10,950 in 1970; and the Patrolmen's Benevolent Association was demanding a hike in base pay to $16,000 for the contract period beginning January 1, 1971. Both Los Angeles and San Francisco had paid a higher base salary to patrolmen than had New York City in 1968. As each city negotiated subsequent contracts, their police associations, playing the game of one-upmanship, argued that they had fallen behind "other cities."

Schoolteachers have been even more militant during the 1960's. At the beginning of the decade, the base pay of teachers averaged $5,174. By 1968 they had achieved an average base salary of $8,194, representing a 65.6 percent increase. As in the case of police and fire fighters, the percentage rise was far less in terms of real added purchasing power, because of inflation.[7]

Sanitation workers in 14 large cities earned widely varying hourly rates of pay in 1968.[8] Refuse collectors were paid hourly rates ranging from a minimum of $1.62 to a maximum of $3.70. In nearly all the locations surveyed, refuse-collection employees worked a 40-hour week. In Cincinnati the minimum rate was $2.51 per hour; in Detroit the rate was $3.50; Philadelphia paid $2.11; and New Orleans paid $1.62 per hour. These rates differ from the annual base pay of $9,871 in 1970 of New York City sanitationmen, where the job is held not comparable to jobs elsewhere, since the position requires a motorized equipment operator with some workers assigned as truck drivers and others as refuse collectors. In each of the cities other than New York, sanitation truck drivers received from 26 to 37 cents per hour more than the rate paid refuse collectors.

The above figures require considerable elaboration to reflect the actual total compensation paid. In the case of police personnel, salaries related to patrolmen are only a part of police personnel costs. Motorcycle officers, police corporals, sergeants, detectives, lieutenants, captains, inspectors and other superior officer ranks receive higher wages and salaries, often tied in by a stipulated ratio to the pay raises negotiated by police patrolmen. In the case of teachers, each school district has a scale whereby salaries are increased each year over a specified number of years. Teachers' compensation is also related to the type of university degree the teacher possesses or the extent of postgraduate credits accumulated. School administrators usually receive higher remuneration by a fixed ratio as teachers negotiate their increases. In short, the *averages* cast only a dim light on the problem of understanding the real costs of negotiated contracts.

The annual rate of growth in personnel costs has increased; but there are few reliable indices as to whether municipal productivity has kept pace. Some occupational groups, such as the sanitationmen, have characteristically presented an "analysis of work performance" to justify salary raises. Since there are no adequate measures of productivity in many categories, the question of whether productivity has kept pace with salary increases must go unanswered.

Municipal services remain high-cost items, but services provided by private industry have become high-cost items too. With the basic purpose of municipal governments being to provide services, the high cost of service is a phase of the general rise in service costs prevalent in the entire economy. Collective bargaining may contribute to the rise in the cost of services but it cannot change this economic fact unless the increase in labor costs constrains the city to automate more of its services (and even this is doubtful).

Charles M. Rehmus and Evan Wilner, of the Institute of Labor Relations, Ann Arbor, Mich. analyzed the economic impact of employee benefits achieved through collective bargaining in 12 Michigan school districts. The bargaining appeared to have given teachers 10 percent to 20 percent more in pay increases than unilateral school board action would have provided, at an estimated cost of from zero to 60 percent over school board estimates prior to the contracts. Per pupil costs rose 14 percent and 11 percent respectively during the school years 1966-67 and 1967-68, compared with the average 4 percent annual rise during the four years prior to bargaining.

Manpower, Hours, and Working Conditions

The impact of collective bargaining on municipal personnel costs is not limited to wages. Many employee groups have negotiated with regard to the size of the work force. Where the size of the work force grows, costs increase commensurately. Teachers, police, fire fighters, sanitationmen, and social workers consistently seek increments in manpower. Social workers in New York City demanded that the specific number of employees to be hired be written into their contract. When job freezes are declared, employee groups such as sanitation workers strive to have their category exempted, and police and fire fighter organizations quickly raise the spectre of danger to the public safety.

Teacher contracts that stipulate a reduction in class size entail not only additional teachers but more classroom space, which in turn, may require construction of more school buildings. Likewise, teacher contract provisions related to expansion of special projects, such as the More Effective Schools programs for disadvantaged children, add to the size of the staff as well as to the cost of operating the school system. More sick-leave time generates the hiring of a greater number of substitute teachers, and temporary replacement of teachers on sabbatical leave increases costs.

Working conditions and hours worked also affect the cost of personnel. Where teacher groups attain more free periods, increased class-preparation time, the assistance of teacher aides, the elimination of clerical and monitoring duties, and restrictions on extracurricular assignments, the changes in working conditions result in the hiring of more administrative and paraprofessional personnel. As teaching manpower grows, the bureaucracy to manage the school system is enlarged.

As a result of such contractual terms, per pupil costs increase.

Collective bargaining undoubtedly was a significant cause in the rise in per pupil costs in New York City from slightly over $500 in 1960 to more than $1,500 in 1970. In the case of school budget outlays, these increases ought to be weighed against the educational gains to pupils. This is difficult to measure. The community, it would seem, should benefit from such changes. Nonetheless, there is the difficulty of pinpointing in financial terms the public's gain in "cost-benefit" terms from the increased investment in education that has evolved out of collective bargaining.

Fringe Benefits

Bargaining has resulted in vastly increased fringe benefits for municipal employees. In 1970 fringe benefits added $26.75 for every $100 of salary in the New York City budget. The latest survey conducted by the Bureau of Labor Statistics of the U.S. Department of Labor reported that the value of fringes in private industry during the period 1963 to 1966 rose from 23.8 percent to 24.5 percent of basic salaries and wages. In 1967 federal employees received fringe benefits equivalent to 23.8 percent of wages and salaries, as against 23.5 percent in 1963.[10] BLS data current to 1968 showed that private employers contributed 25.1 percent of basic wages toward the cost of fringe benefits whereas the federal government's figure was 24.3 percent. Studies accurately portraying fringe benefits in municipal jurisdictions are sparse, and no general reports comparable to those of the BLS are available.

Fringe benefits include a variety of items. Some benefits available to many categories of city employees include vacations; civic and personal leave; sick leave; health benefit programs; life, accident, and health insurance; retirement programs; and unemployment programs. The uniformed services receive clothing allowances not applicable to other departments of the municipal service.

Recent items sought by most employee units include leaves to attend conventions, funeral leaves, jury duty leave, and time off to go to union meetings. Some organizations have attempted to negotiate special plans for employees on bargaining teams or steward assignments.

Additional paid holidays, premium-pay holidays, stand-by pay, "wash-up" pay, increased health insurance, and dental and optical benefits will become more widespread as bargaining expands.

A survey conducted by AFSCME in 1968 indicated that city employees received far better vacation benefits than state and county employees. None of the 47 counties or 28 states surveyed authorized more than four weeks' vacation, whereas 10 of the 156 cities reporting provided five weeks' vacation after periods ranging from 10 to 25 years of service. Of the cities granting three weeks' vacation, nine granted the vacation after one year of service, one after five years, four cities after seven years, 58 after 10 years, 18 after 15 years, three after 20 years, and two after 25 years of service.

One of the most thorough studies issued prior to 1968 was a survey of fringe benefits in Connecticut. It revealed marked stability from 1959 to 1966. Collective bargaining by municipalities was not mandated until 1965. More than half the municipal employees receive two weeks' vacation after the first year's employment and at least a week of accumulated sick leave, and employees are granted 10 to 13 paid holidays, in addition to pensions and partial payment of medical insurance.

Benefit programs in Connecticut ranged from less than 5 percent, the most common amount reported, to 40 percent. The study further revealed that changes occurred mainly in smaller cities, that variation in the scope of benefits was wide, that retirement plans were the most costly benefit, and that employees tended to view benefits as part of the compensation package and not as a salary substitute. Perhaps more significant was the anticipation of a refinement in city fringe benefit programs authorizing the transfer of retirement credit from one municipality to another, especially within metropolitan areas.[11]

The reaction of one city administrator interviewed was a quip that "the range of benefits may well be limited only be the ingenuity of employee representatives to devise them." The Comptroller in a major city warned that "requests for increased wash-up time, rest periods, and coffee breaks pose a threat to the public service day." One Finance Director, who had watched the amount of his city's fringe payments climb 131 percent from 1965 to 1967, suggested doing away with fringe benefits. He advocated an increase in take-home pay, "since the employee only appreciates the first year's benefits, and from there on relates them as part of employment."

Thus, the impact of collective bargaining on personnel costs can only be understood when a range of costs beyond wages and salaries are considered. New York City's Budget Director estimated that wages and benefits sought by patrolmen during the 1970 negotiations would cost the city $35,000 per year per man.

To basic wages or salaries one must add the cost of overtime, premium pay, standby pay, shift differentials, and hazard pay. Direct compensation is sometimes augmented by cost-of-living escalator clauses, which are rapidly emerging as a popular feature of wage agreements. These escalator clauses, generally based on the

224

Consumer Price Index of the Bureau of Labor Statistics, complicate the budgetary process by making the extent of labor costs during the contract term unpredictable.

Vacations, holidays, a variety of paid-leave provisions, shorter work hours, and fringe benefits, when added to the standard retirement systems, make snap judgments relative to base pay an illusory way in which to evaluate an employee's actual compensation.

Where contracts stipulate new special programs or expanded physical facilities, the resulting financial package can become a major problem of administration. Involved, too, are economic and political considerations.

Employee organizations do not achieve gains in each of these areas every year. In Philadelphia wage increases were granted in only seven of the 13 years from 1953 through 1966. Each of the several years resulted in pay increases for all major categories of city employees, except for 1965, when only policemen and firemen gained higher base pay. But in the remaining six years, while no wage increases were contracted, employee gains were achieved in different areas, adding to overall personnel costs. Pension and social security benefits were augmented in five of the 13 years; working time was reduced on four occasions; sick leave, vacations, and other leave benefits were improved in seven of the years; cash payments for standby time, callback pay, clothing allowances, and shift differentials were negotiated in nine separate years; pension and social security benefits were increased five times. The fact is that except for the single year 1962, the bargaining process yielded gains in every 12 month period.

Pensions

Pensions are likely to prove a major area for innovation and improvements in the coming years. Policemen and firemen have enjoyed exceptional pension programs in some cities. In New York City, for example, a policeman may retire after 20 years of service at half pay based on his last 12 months' earnings, including overtime. That is, it is possible for a policeman who worked a great deal of overtime in his last 12 months on the job to draw retirement pay of up to three quarters of his base pay. In October 1969 a patrolman with 20 years of service was receiving $11,150, entitling him a minimum pension of $5,575 a year.

The tendency of pension programs in police departments to provide for retirement at half pay after 20 years further aggravates the city's financial problem, by virtue of the fact that pension benefits are generally tied in to salary increases, including overtime, negotiated in future contracts.

Other city employees seek similar retirement benefits. The agreement reached in the New York transit negotiation of December 1967 provided for the vesting of pension rights after 20 years of service, retirement at age 50 with reduced benefits, and full benefits for retirement at age 65. In exchange for the generous pension plan, transit workers accepted a wage increase of 6 percent in lieu of the 10 percent they had demanded. The contribution of the transit workers to the pension fund was increased from 3 percent to more than 6 percent of their pay.

Although the reduction in benefits below age 65 was designed to prevent a mass exodus to jobs elsewhere by men receiving transit pensions, during the two years that followed the new contract between 7,000 and 8,000 of the system's 35,000 employees exercised their retirement privileges. Of these, the Metropolitan Transit Authority states, some 1,400 were skilled and specially trained workers from a maintenance staff of 4,000.

The transit workers' agreement was followed by a similar one reached in negotiations between New York City and AFSCME District Council 37. The pension plan calls for a pension of 55 percent of the final year's pay or 55 percent of the average pay for the three highest years, whichever is greater. Minimum retirement age is 55 (50 for employees doing heavy work) after 25 years of service.

More of the cost of increased benefits is likely to shift from the employees to the municipalities. Eventually, most if not all of the costs will be borne by the city. One interesting consequence of the new interest in pensions is the growing role of pension consultants in the bargaining process. In the transit negotiations alone, pension experts developed some 175 computations on various pension formulas.

Aside from the vast overall costs of pensions, the most important consequence of new agreements is the "reorientation of the pension concept of into something closer to a voluntary severance pay system."[12] A. H. Raskin, Assistant Editorial Page Editor of the New York *Times*, likened the new agreements to a lifetime subsidy of $4,000 a year to workers desirous of moving on to new jobs at the age of 40 or 45. This danger has led to stepped-up benefits "designed to keep too many 20-year men from grabbing their pensions and rushing out the turnstile in search of a well-paid job somewhere else."

The drive for increased pension benefits and earlier retirement is not confined to New York City. Philadelphia, Milwaukee, Detroit,

226

Cincinnati, Los Angeles, San Francisco, and other urban center employees have made analogous demands. The initial breakthrough by police, fire fighters, and transit workers is now being capitalized by other employee groups.

Pensions have become a major factor in the cost of local government, as a result of rising employment and increasingly generous benefits. State and municipal employment has more than doubled since 1960, reaching more than 10 million in 1971. During this period municipal employment alone has increased more than one third and average pay of municipal employees increased two thirds. The highest pay raises have been in the large cities, where employees are most strongly organized. Since pension payments are tied to wages, sometimes including overtime pay as well as the basic wage, the cost of pensions rises with every wage increase. The contractual pension obligations of many municipal governments amount to 10 percent to 20 percent of their payrolls. In Detroit and New York, pensions in some services have reached half of payroll costs. It is estimated that the expenditure for public service pensions could triple by 1980, with accumulated pension funds reaching over $200 billion.[13]

Pension demands have become major items in collective bargaining contract negotiations and have often been used as trade-offs for immediate salary increases. In Philadelphia in June 1971, a strike by thousands of employees was averted by an agreement to lower the minimum retirement age from 60 to 55. The cost to the city was estimated at over $21 million. In New York, the deadlock in the 1968 New Year's Eve transit negotiations was broken by an agreement vesting pension rights after 20 years of service and allowing retirement at age 50 with reduced benefits and at 65 with full benefits. The trade-off for this generous plan was a reduction in the wage increase from 10 to 6 percent. At the same time, the union agreed to an increase in employee contributions to the pension fund from 3 percent to over 6 percent.

Early retirement in the protective services, where strength and alertness are prime requirements, has been justified as promoting the effectiveness of the services. What has been happening in these and other services, such as sanitation and underground transport, is that the worker retires at his prime with the equivalent of a substantial lifetime endowment and increases his guaranteed income by taking other jobs. The generous New York transit settlement led to the retirement during the two-year span of the contract of many employees, including skilled maintenance workers and supervisors. The cost to the system in money, efficiency, and safety were tremendous. Delays and breakdowns due to undermaintenance

227

became common. The first subway accident in 40 years to result in fatalities was attributed by some sources to undermaintenance of trained personnel and especially to the retirement of 270 of 326 supervisors.

Cities large and small have been sloppy about funding their pension obligations. A knowledgeable Connecticut financial officer said, "I believe that there is hardly a single municipal pension fund in this state that is not in actuarial trouble." Many jurisdictions do not have enough money in their retirement funds to meet more than a few years' obligations. This means that when the funds run short, pension obligations would have to be met by current funds or default. In the state of New York, pensions are made a contractual obligation by constitutional provision. This makes it impossible to reduce or avoid pension payments on the ground of lack of funds. Most funds are financed by government and employee contributions. Employee organizations are seeking full funding by the government concerned. It is interesting that when the federal government was considering the adoption of a civil service retirement system, prior to 1920, the conservative unions supported full government funding whereas the progressive unions strongly favored employee contributions, on the ground that if the employees had a withdrawable equity in the fund it would give them a greater degree of freedom to change jobs and not tie them to their governmental employer in the way a noncontributory pension would.

The importance of the pension issue to the employees and the degree of pressure they are ready to exert to obtain favorable arrangements was demonstrated in New York in the summer of 1971. District 37 of AFSCME, representing 120,000 employees, negotiated a contract, with OCB assistance, granting a credit of 2.5 percent for every year of service, half pay after 20 years, three-quarter pay after 30 years and full pay after 40 years. Blue-collar workers could retire at age 50 and white-collar workers at 55.

The city objected to the arrangement on the ground that the state law required legislative approval of municipal pension plans more generous than that provided by the state retirement system for state employees. When after a series of maneuvers the legislature withheld approval on the ground that the District 37 proposal had exceeded the provisions for state employees, Victor Gotbaum, head of District 37, denounced the action as a violation of the concept of contractual collective bargaining. He also denounced the legislature's action as a breach of faith because the legislature itself had for three years been operating under a retirement system for its members and their staffs that was practically the same as the District 37 demands. Through this cynically conceived arrangement, the legislators (part-time officials who keep their private employment and sit in Albany for but a few months a year, usually only for a few days a week) had provided themselves with benefits based not only on their salaries but also the "lulus," payments in lieu of expenses. The legislative pension had not been given the degree of publicity it deserved.

Gotbaum, despite the fact that the law clearly required legislative approval of his agreement and despite the fact that he is not given to extreme statements, declared that the legislative failure to approve his program would result in "the biggest, fattest, sloppiest strike" in the city's history. When the legislature withheld approval of the agreement, the teamsters union demonstrated its disapproval and opened and locked the city's drawbridges and removed essential equipment, blocking the flow of traffic into the city. Although the strikers protested that their action would not affect the city's poor but only inconvenience the well-to-do commuters from the suburbs, their action cut off the delivery of school lunches for needy children. They also shut down garbage incinerators, causing the discharge of millions of tons of raw sewerage into the city's rivers. The strike ended in two days, with the unions accepting a "settlement" providing for the appointment of a legislative commission to review the state's entire pension problem.

"Our members are just beginning to realize," declared AF-SCME's pension specialist "that pensions can be negotiated." When asked where the money for higher pensions is coming from, he replied, "That's government's problem. Just because it is pinched for money is no excuse to make the employees do without."

While fact-finding panels have refused to accept inability to pay as a valid reason for withholding salary increases, the wave of rejections of school budgets by the electorate indicates that after all, the taxpayers have the last word.

Expenditures for Capital Improvements

It is difficult to assess the extent to which the expenditures for employee benefits have influenced expenditures for capital improvements. Officials may have been constrained in some cases to give priority to pay and fringe benefits and to postpone capital improvements. Benefits gained at the expense of necessary capital improvements may well come back to haunt the public employee, as well as the public, since the deterioration of the physical plant not only increases costs in the long run, but also contributes to a poor working environment.

An example of the difficulty of measuring the impact of collective bargaining on capital expenditures is the request of Mayor Lindsay to earmark more than $14 million for fire-fighting apparatus, communications equipment and building in the capital budget for fiscal year 1969/70. This was several million dollars more than the City Planning Commission had suggested. It may be that the Mayor's action, taken in January 1969, was partially in response to pressures of the firemen's organization in an election year. Yet, the decision to replenish and modernize facilities and equipment was a constructive one.

Employee groups more and more seek to affect decisions on capital improvements. Teacher organizations are keenly aware of the impact of capital items on the educational process. Social workers have sought to have specific capital expenditures written into contractual terms. Sanitation workers in major urban centers have long fought to modernize equipment as part of the never ending fight against refuse. Hundreds of millions of dollars are involved in the efforts of the larger cities to initiate incineration projects.

Nurses, doctors, hospital workers, and their clientele pressure and attempt to negotiate the improvement of municipal health facilities. Cities are besieged to construct new facilities to cope with the mounting drug problem. Employee organizations have used sustained pressure on city officials to move with greater speed. While collective bargaining is only peripherally related to the problem, it is an influential force in the allocation of more funds to health programs.

Mayors who operate with capital budgets, as distinct from expense budgets, often urge that overriding priority be given to items directly affecting city residents. New schools, health centers, and sanitation equipment are highly visible and dramatic. Not infrequently the proposals are a direct result of public employee demands.

The Search for Additional Revenue

With costs of city government rising steadily, the search for new revenue sources is intensified. This entails vigorous efforts to increase the taxing powers of local units. Cities seek greater flexibility in floating new bond issues. Heavier pressure is being exerted on the state and federal governments to increase financial aid to municipalities. Where there is marked resistance to higher local taxes, there may be efforts to transfer specific costly local functions to state or federal jurisdictions. In other instances, cities attempt to contract out services to private industry, create independent authorities to handle specific functions previously performed by government, or establish self-sustaining government corporations to circumvent existing restrictions on the city's authority to raise taxes.

The search for new revenues has its political overtones. Indeed, the entire budgetary process reflects political maneuvering. Aaron Wildavsky pointed out the role of pressure groups; and employee groups constitute one more type of pressure:

> We must deal with real men in the real world for whom the best they can get is to be preferred to the perfection they cannot achieve. Unwilling or unable to alter the basic features of the political system, they seek to make it work for them in budgeting rather than against them.[14]

Financial problems are not confined to the cities. California's Governor announced in 1970 what amounted to a state of fiscal emergency. New York's Governor made a trip to Washington to appeal for greater federal aid.

A major change in the pattern of distributing revenues is under consideration. While one group advocates more freedom for the city, the likelihood is that states may assume a larger role not only in channeling federal funds but in directing precisely how the additional funds will be utilized in providing specific services—firefighting, police, and sanitation—long considered the primary role of the city. The political struggle for control has begun.

Rejection of Referenda

Appeals to the electorate for additional funds are not always well received. In Youngstown, Ohio, the electorate refused to approve a tax increase on six successive occasions in 1967 and 1968. The result was that the public school system was compelled to close on November 27, 1968, for the balance of the calendar year because the school board had exhausted its funds. In 1969 the Youngstown Teachers Association pursued its drive for greater gains, despite the urging of the school board that a moratorium be declared because of the school district's financial problems.

The extent of the taxpayer revolt was illustrated when Ohio school districts were denied 61.2 percent of the operating funds proposed in local levies and bond issues during 1969. The failure of the levies constituted the greater percentage rejection of school money issues in a single Ohio election.

Taxpayer revolts have spurred municipal officials to seek new forms of revenue that are less likely to encounter taxpayer hostility. A three-man panel in Pike County, in Kentucky, recommended a 3 percent tax on utilities as a way of financing teacher pay increases. In September 1968 the Board of Education of East St. Louis, Ill., and Local 1220 of the AFT negotiated a novel contract providing that part of a salary increase granted teachers should be withheld and placed in a special fund if the board could not find sufficient money to finance the pay increase. The union agreed to buy $300,000 of tax-anticipation warrants to make up the difference if no other buyer could be found for the warrants. The intention was that the "loan" would be repaid from future tax revenues.

By and large, solutions have been the expected ones. A Michigan study summarized the methods for financing increased salaries in ten school districts as follows: two districts relied on newly voted millage, one on increased state aid, and two on growth in assessed valuation; three levied previously authorized millage; and two liquidated surplus funds and incurred additional interest charges.[15]

Many metropolitan areas have created ad hoc groups to study the cities' fiscal problems, to advise on new sources of revenues, or generally to give advice on budget problems. New York City's Temporary Commission on City Finance in 1966 had a task force on collective bargaining. In 1968 Mayor James Tate announced that Philadelphia was considering the creation of a citizens' committee to be appointed as consultants on the city's fiscal problems. Whether such units act as official arms of the city government or as independently operated tax-research organizations, the trend has been to give increased attention to the activities of public employee organizations.

Unions generally evidence a growing distrust of legal ceilings or restrictions on appropriations, debt limits, and tax levels. Whether the unions will exert their political strength to change revenue patterns remains to be seen. Significantly, the Colorado Education Association Delegate Assembly voted on March 15, 1968, to invoke sanctions to increase state financial support from 24 percent to 40 percent of the total cost of local schools. In addition, the CEA argued that the major school financial burden should be carried by a graduated income tax rather than by property taxes.

Fact Finders and the City's Inability to Pay

While cities search out sources of funds, employee organizations suggest that where the money comes from is not their problem. Fact finders seem to support the view that city employees should not be expected to carry a city's financial burden on their backs alone. A fact-finding panel in Rochester, N.Y., in 1968 refused to accept the "inability to pay" argument raised by the city and recommended a pay increase of $900 for teachers. The panel, while sympathetic to the city, reasoned that teachers and school children should not be forced to bear the burden of what was essentially a "political problem."

The same year, a Detroit fact-finding panel described as "a self-imposed inability" the city's contention that it lacked the necessary funds to meet policemen's pay demands. In this instance, the fact finders recommended ways to finance reasonable and needed increases. Instead of raising the property tax to the legal maximum, the city had chosen to authorize bonds against the maximum. While the panel did not question the use of bonds for capital improvements, it noted that some of these improvements could be deferred and that the property tax could have been made to yield some part or all of the funds needed for the policemen's raise.

Arnold M. Zack, a fact finder appointed by the Massachusetts Board of Conciliation and Arbitration to recommend a settlement between the New Bedford Teachers Association and the city's School Committee in 1968 observed that a municipality's ability to pay wages can no longer be the only criterion on which to base the amount of those wages. Mr. Zack's reasoning posed the following question:

> Are teachers and other public servants to be expected to subsidize governmental operations if sufficient funds are not provided through tax revenues? The school committee and indeed the city itself do not seek discounts from vendors of building and other materials they purchase in the open market . . . . Why then, if they are willing to pay the going competitive rates for goods and personnel provided by outsiders, should they seek to reduce below comparable standards the compensation they pay to their own employees, who live and work and spend their income within the community itself?

Nor are fact finders the sole source of pressure on local governments to find revenue to meet contract demands. Responding to a complaint by Local 1198 of the International Association of Fire Fighters, the Connecticut Board of Labor Relations ordered the town of West Haven to implement within 30 days an agreement reached in August 1967 between the union and the Board of Fire Commissioners. The decision was, in effect, an order to the town to secure the funds to fulfill the contract.

The Role of the Finance Officer

As one might expect, collective bargaining has had an impact on the role of the chief municipal finance officer. The extent to which he participates directly in negotiations varies considerably, but the direction is toward a greater involvement of the finance officer or budget director in the bargaining process. In Philadelphia the Finance Director, as a member of the negotiating team, is directly involved in the bargaining process. During the Wagner era in New York City, the Budget Director and Personnel Director held the major responsibility for the conduct of collective bargaining. Under Mayor Lindsay, the Director of Labor Relations has the responsibility, with the Budget Director acting as a member of a labor advisory council to assist him.

Accurate cost assessments are needed to gauge the full implications of employee demands. Therefore, finance officers may expect to be asked to collect, prepare, and present supporting financial data for city negotiators and to interpret city finances to employee organizations, the communications media, and the general public. Wages, fringe benefits, and operational changes are invariably central issues in collective bargaining.

Well-organized employee groups with competent research staffs besiege the finance officer, desiring to study executive proposals before they reach the legislative body. These efforts have intensified, leading some cities to conceal information as to what they expect to pay out in new collective bargaining agreements. Instead, the cities' strategy is to obscure its intentions within departmental estimates. They had learned that the amounts indicated in budget-line items tended to become a floor rather than a ceiling for militant employee groups.

Sometimes finance officers are accused of hiding funds as a defensive move; and sometimes the finance officer openly invites union auditors to "examine the city books." In any event, city representatives are becoming more inclined to present figures showing the fiscal impact of employee demands on the city's financial structure.

The bargaining process inexorably leads to the development of more sophisticated bargaining machinery both by unions and by government. Technical know-how is indispensable to effective bargaining. In one city, union leaders reported in an interview that their first round of negotiations "was like taking candy away from a baby." They added that as the city's bargainers became more experienced, the quality of bargaining shifted the balance of power to the side of the city.

Coordination between the budgetary and bargaining processes is also clearly required for effective municipal government. Failure to achieve a contract agreement before the budget is approved may necessitate awkward and financially cumbersome stopgap measures, including the use of open-end budgeting and the setting up of contingency funds to handle anticipated pay increases.

Settlements negotiated without the assistance of competent financial and legal advice run the risk of producing agreements that destroy the integrity of the appropriations process. Limitations on the tax powers of local units may be upset in bargaining. The time period for negotiations, the length of the contract period, and the correlation of contract periods with the government's fiscal year are closely related to effective municipal budgetary projections.

Evaluation of the Impact on Municipal Budgets

A municipal budget is not devised in a vacuum, nor is it written on a clean slate. The adopted budget reflects an amalgam of forces of which collective bargaining is but one important factor. Public employee organizations are not unchecked forces but operate within the general economic setting, responding to the expansions and contractions of a tax dollar.

Collective bargaining affects the city budget, but contract work performed for the city by private industry, whose costs are partially determined by collective bargaining between the contractor and his employees, likewise affects the city budget. Furthermore, it is unrealistic to assume that costs can be suppressed in the public sector when the free flow of market forces permits employee gains in private industry. Public employees no longer consider a governmental employer to be entitled to special privileges or rights when it comes to bread-and-butter issues.

The pattern of bargaining is a natural one. Unions will search for any fat in the proposed budget of the executive. Already having exerted such influence as they could bring to bear, they seek further modification of programs in their interest. If the slight modification of a tentative program is likely to bring more state or federal funds into play, the employee group will attempt to have the savings diverted to fulfill unachieved union goals.

Unions are afflicted with "me-tooism," and a desire to leapfrog competitor groups. They are also aware, however, of the economic and political environment in which they are operating. Their research departments try to project available revenues, the possibilities of more state or federal assistance, the likelihood of voter approval or rejection of pending bond issues or special tax levies; and the activities of competitive groups. Comparability with the private sector is only one edge of the sword; to outstrip by a wide margin the privately employed would impair the union image and arouse public resentment. Responsible elements within unions realize that despite initial exorbitant demands, the final terms must be realistic.

Employee groups are cognizant of the fact that budget officials refrain—as part of their game plan—from revealing their estimates of what they expect to pay out as a result of forth-coming agreements. While total amounts are included in proposed budgets, city officials appropriately camouflage dollar figures within departmental estimates. Experience has demonstrated that employee groups have tended to consider the estimates a floor rather than a ceiling when devising their demands.

Total costs of settlements vary, but the nature of the settlements remains similar. A city cannot realistically hope to grant an early retirement to some employee groups and expect to deny it to other groups with any organizational strength. Likewise, the granting of benefits is difficult to reverse, even though the reason for the initial concession is no longer valid. In the days before the widespread use of air conditioning, New York City employees were granted shorter summer hours. Successive city bargaining efforts to change the practice have met with union responses such as "over our dead bodies," and many New York City employees still retain the right to an earlier quitting time.

Gains achieved by one bloc of employees swiftly spread to other units, and the ripple effect has state-wide and sometimes national consequences. Soon after New York City concluded a new retirement plan with its employees, state employees expressed in letters to the press strong resentment at the gap between the city and state retirement plans.[16]

Statistical evidence adduced to demonstrate that collective bargaining has increased municipal budgets misses the point. The important fact is that collective bargaining exists and will become an ever more powerful influence. This fact spurs the need for more constructive, cooperative bargaining policies and procedures.

While public employee organizations should be viewed as one more pressure group, public officials cannot, in fear of their political lives, either ignore them or simply retreat to even higher taxes and service charges. By the early 1970's the demands of some well-established employee organizations .had reached awesome proportions, and capitulation would destroy the purpose of a budget-making process designed to assure fiscal responsibility.

236

Larger cities, as we have noted, have begun to develop more sophisticated machinery and personnel to achieve common sense agreements fair to both the employee and the public. Though the road is increasingly traveled, there is still a long way to go, as public employee strikes or threats of strikes are used increasingly to get both deserved and undeserved gains from the public treasury and as the cities feel the strangling impact of limited resources and unlimited demands.

Notes

1. U.S. Department of Commerce, *Statistical Abstract of the United States*, Washington, D.C. 1969, p. 430.
2. U.S. Department of Commerce, *Public Employment in 1967*, Washington, D.C.
3. James A. Craft, "Firefighter Militancy and Wage Disparity," *Labor Law Journal*, December, 1970, pp. 7-14 ff.
4. Illuminating sidelights on the politics of the parity issue in New York and the struggle of three of the country's leading arbitrators, David Cole, Arthur Goldberg, and Theodore Kheel, to reconcile the inter and intra-departmental ratios may be found in a paper by A. H. Raskin delivered at the American Management Association Conference in New York City, May 1971.
5. Stephen H. Perloff, "Comparing Municipal Salaries with Industry and Federal Pay," *Monthly Labor Review*, October 1971, p. 46.
6. Orley Ashenfelter, "The Effect of Unionization of Wages in the Public Sector: The Case of Fire Fighters," *Industrial and Labor Relations Review*, January 1971, pp. 191-203. This study, replete with figures and mathematical formulae, demonstrates the effect of unionization and reducing hours for fire fighters.
7. The NEA reported that the purported 65.6 percent increase actually amounted to an increase of 37.8 percent. *Economic Status of the Teaching Profession*, Report, National Education Association, Washington, D.C., 1969.
8. The data is based on a survey reported by the Personnel Department of Washington, D.C., in 1969.
9. Charles M. Rehmus and Evan Wilner, *The Economic Results of Teacher Bargaining: Michigan's First Two Years* (Ann Arbor, Mich.: Institute of Labor and Industrial Relations, 1968).
10. U.S. Department of Labor, *BLS Report 352, Employee Compensation in Selected Industries*.
11. Rosaline Levenson, "Municipal Fringe Benefit Pattern Shows Stability in Connecticut," *Local Government Newsletter* (Storrs, Conn.: Institute of Public Service, University of Connecticut, May 1967).
12. A.H. Raskin, "A New Pattern on Pensions," New York *Times*, January 7, 1968.

13. Growing Burden on Taxpayers: Public Employee Pensions," *U.S. News and World Report*, July 19, 1971, pp. 24-26.

14. Aaron Wildavsky, *The Politics of the Budgetary Process* (Boston: Little, Brown, 1964), p. 178.

15. Rehmus and Wilner, op. cit.

16. See New York *Post*, March 12, 1968.

10   The Strike Issue

The strike issue is the most controversial, urgent, and misunderstood problem of labor relations in public employment. Discussion of the subject mainly revolves about the propriety of its use and the question of whether the current legal approach encourages rather than deters public employee strikes. Cities and states have failed to come to grips with the central issue: whether it is sound public policy to guarantee workers the right to strike in the most socially vital sectors of private industry yet deny *all* public employees the same right, regardless of the importance of the function performed or the impact a stoppage might have on the public.

Several additional questions may be raised. If the absolute ban on public employee strikes is eliminated or loosened, how can the public be protected when strikes interrupt services vital to the health, safety, and welfare of the city? If existing legal bans are maintained, what steps should be taken to protect public employees against an arbitrary employer who uses his sovereign rights to implement personnel policies unilaterally and paternalistically? If government takes the position that privately employed workers *need* the strike weapon to secure justice and freedom, how can they justify its denial to *all* public employees without providing meaningful and effective substitutes? Is it preferable to rescind legal prohibitions or to continue to countenance the repeated violations of law that have in fact taken place.

The strike fever has already made public employee strikes a reality in the municipal services. The postal employees brush-fire strike of March 1970, along with the strike of air traffic controllers, may be construed as a danger signal that the strike contagion will eventually infect all government services. At the very least, public employee strikes inconvenience the public. In some cases they have imperiled communities. Their effects have both immediate and long-range implications. How to achieve the uninterrupted functioning of the essential services of government has clearly become a problem of magnitude and urgency.

The Right to Strike

The right to strike by privately employed individuals is now legally protected and is accepted as a fundamental right of workers. But this was not always the case. In the early decades of the 19th century strikes were regarded as illegal conspiracies. Only the persistent resort to work stoppages and political action over succeeding decades led the government to a change in attitude. This change was eventually reflected in legislation such as the Norris-LaGuardia Act of 1932 and the National Labor Relations Act of 1935. In the private sector the law now sanctions an area of "permissive economic warfare," in sharp contrast to the prior case law, which held illegal the deliberate commission of harm to another without justification recognized by law.

The Private Sector

In the private sector, employees may freely abandon their employment as means of compelling or attempting to compel their employers to accede to demands for better terms or conditions of employment. Yet, this right is by no means an absolute one. For example, any strike in the private sector may still be enjoined when the public safety is imperiled; and strikes that paralyze the normal activities of an entire commonwealth can be stopped by court injunctions.[1] Strikes for illegal objectives are not protected by law; and even assuming the objective is legal, an individual may seek judicial relief where the strike is accompanied by violence, fraud, or other illegal acts.

Yet, the government has trod cautiously in prohibiting strikes in private industry, regardless of the social importance of the service interrupted. In December 1968, New York City was subjected to

240

strikes by employees of the Consolidated Edison Company and by fuel oil deliverers. Despite the obvious importance of electricity and fuel during the winter season, the strikes were permitted to continue. A nationwide copper strike in 1968 was allowed to continue for months, and in 1969 the General Electric Company was subjected to a stoppage for months. New York City tolerated a tugboat strike for weeks in 1970, even though the city's residents were inconvenienced. Similarly, the city authorities made no effort to break a strike by gravediggers which compounded the grief of families, some of whom buried their own dead.

In each of these cases the authorities have rarely gone beyond attempting to discourage, postpone, or aid in the settlement of such strikes. Federal legislation authorizes the government to seek an injunction to postpone a strike for 80 days where national interests are involved, but the ultimate right to strike is guaranteed. Even in wartime the government has shown reluctance to curtail the right to strike.[2]

A major exception, however, has been the case of the railroads, where Congress has stopped strike action. When a nationwide strike was threatened in 1962, President Kennedy obtained passage of a compulsory arbitration law limited in time and coverage. When faced with a similar situation in 1967, after twice extending a no-strike waiting period, Congress passed legislation intended as a goad to a negotiated settlement with the possibility of an ultimate imposed solution. Again in 1970 the Congress patiently tried to postpone strike action and encourage peaceful resolution. Finally, the Congress was impelled to impose a settlement rather than tolerate in effect, a disruption of the nation's rail system.

The Public Sector

The hesitancy of government to curtail the right to strike in the private sector does not extend to its own employees. The government now applies its no-strike policy to every category of employee, with a few minor exceptions to be noted later. The no-strike policy, which began with the rise in the postal service of organizations composed wholly of federal employees, represented a departure from labor policies prevailing in federal industrial plants. There the resort to strikes by government workers, organized along with private employees in particular crafts, was taken for granted.

Despite the fact that strikes occurred as early as the administration of Andrew Jackson, no federal legislation explicitly forbade strikes by federal employees until the end of World War II. The federal policy regarding strikes, however, long antedated the legislation passed in 1946 (in appropriations bills) and the statute of 1955.[3] Every administration since that of Theodore Roosevelt had by Presidential statement or departmental order denied the right to strike. A similar situation prevailed with state and local governments, which prior to the Boston police strike of 1919 relied principally on case law as the basis of a no-strike policy in state and local employment.

Union Position on Strikes

Early Attitudes—The Official Line

A significant aspect of the civil service no-strike policy is the extent to which it was and is accepted by unions of federal employees. Virtually every organization is committed to a no-strike policy by constitutional provision or tradition; and this situation was characterized as "a principal characteristic of federal employment . . . based on law."[4] This view is still the prevailing one at the federal level, despite the recent rumblings reverberating as a result of the strike of postal employees in March 1970.

Likewise, municipal employee unions generally adopted a no-strike policy prior to the 1960's. The Committee on Employee Relations in the Public Service in 1942 concluded that general unions of strictly governmental employees were unanimous in their renunciation of the strike: "The NFFE, AFGE, and SCMWA have constitutional prohibition of strikes. The UFW and the AFSCME have stated officially that they do not strike."[5] The AFGE, which at one time included a large component of municipal employees, stated that it was "unequivocally opposed to and will not tolerate strikes, picketing or other public acts against governmental authority which have the effect of embarrassing the government."[6] The IAFF constitution was also clear: "We shall not strike or take active part in any sympathetic strike as our position is peculiar to most organized workers. We are formed to protect the lives and property of communities in case of fire or other serious hazard."[7] In 1940 David Ziskind noted that the American Federation of Teachers had maintained its no-strike policy since 1918 and had declared that none of its locals had gone on strike.[8] The NEA for decades urged its local affiliates not to strike.

Two of the major unions operative at the municipal level in the 1940's equivocated. Although SCMWA's constitution stated, "It shall not be the policy of this organization to engage in strikes as a means of achieving its objectives," the constitution also noted a procedure for "rules and regulations governing strike procedure."[9]

SCMWA President Abe Flaxer assumed a conservative stance even earlier, writing: "We are confident that we can employ these methods [legislation, education, and negotiations] with sufficient force and effectiveness to forward the interest of our membership without having to resort to strikes." [10] In a similar fashion The president of the rival AFSCME, Arnold Zander, stated that his union recognized that "the use of the strike weapon would be fatal to accomplishment in public employee organizations. Therefore, the strike is not used." [11]

Policy and Practice

Notwithstanding such official pronouncements, unions at the state and local level did on occasion assert the *right* to strike and did in fact strike. Careful reading of the Flaxer and Zander statements indicates that they were careful not to renounce the strike but believed that the strike was not as effective as other measures then available. However, federal unions, such as the United Public Workers of America, emphasized that any inclination to strike would be directed against state or local jurisdictions. Congressmen were informed that authorization for strike action in federal agencies had never been given "and never will be given." A major exception to the official no-strike policy was the craft unions, largely because most of the membership in such unions was privately employed and there was no need to place special restraints regarding strikes.

Few significant strikes occurred prior to World War II. Only in the wake of the rapid organization of local employees after the war was there an upsurge in strikes in municipal government. The public employee labor movement was still recovering from the jolt of the Boston Police strike of 1919, and the economic depression of the 1930's dampened the ardor for such extreme measures. Thus, the absence of the widespread use of the strike technique was in part due to the fact that such tactics were deemed ineffective or inimical to organizational welfare, rather than improper. [12]

The Current Position

In the 1970's leaders of municipal employee organizations virtually unanimously denounce legislative or any other type of restrictions on the *right* of civil servants to strike. They refuse to regard their strikes as a defiance of public authority but instead visualize the strike as a legitimate as well as useful weapon in a labor dispute. They object vociferously to surrendering the right merely because the government, in its dual role of lawmaker and employer, has clothed itself with special privileges. Their feelings were expressed in the following resolution adopted by three major New York City unions:

> That no one, no body of legislators or government officials can take from us our rights as free men and women to leave our jobs when sufficiently aggrieved; when a group of our members are so aggrieved, then indeed they will strike. [13]

Furthermore, they look upon antistrike legislation as the expression of a discriminatory policy that arbitrarily relegates them to second-class status by denying them rights guaranteed to all other workers in society. As early as 1963 AFSCME's President explained, "There is no logic in depriving an employee of his right to strike simply because he is employed by governmental unit." Union leaders condemn as unworthy of dignity the singling out public employees and hiding behind sovereignty. The right to strike is held to distinguish the free worker from the slaves. Without the right to strike, negotiations are viewed as no more than formalized petitioning and "collective begging." In this sense, all other rights are regarded as of minimal value without the right to strike.

The highly legalistic approach is singled out as futile. Zander argued. "To outlaw strikes will not eliminate them, bona fide negotiations will. . ." The former leader of the Uniformed Firefighters Association in New York City commented, "Even if the Condon-Wadlin Law were a workable piece of legislation, we would have to defy it." [14] Albert Shanker, President of New York City's United Federation of Teachers, was equally blunt: "Now we are beyond abstract lessons in legality . . .. Perhaps it is a bad lesson to learn, but the City has convinced us that striking brings us gains we need and cannot get any other way." [15]

Such statements led to the reversal of the official no-strike policy of many important unions. In 1963 Zander had written, "We oppose strikes; they should not be necessary." [16] His successor, Jerry Wurf, took a stronger line, reasoning that unions do not want the right to strike "just for the privilege of walking around a building, [but] . . . so long as workers sit at the bargaining table they must have something to deal with, something that will impress the boss." [17] The subsequent AFSCME policy statement, issued in July 1966, flatly insisted "upon the right of public employees—except for police and other law enforcement officers—to strike." [18]

The National Education Association followed suit in 1967, declaring that it would give support to the strike actions undertaken by its state and local affiliates. The same year the Civil Service Employees Association in New York State rescinded its 19-year-old no-strike pledge. By an overwhelming voice vote, the International Association of Fire Fighters' 960 delegates removed the no-strike clause from the union's constitution in August 1968. Even the American Nursing Association was unable to stem the tide and announced that strike actions were best left in the hands of state and local affiliates. A number of the state and local affiliates of other unions followed the lead of their national organizations and repealed no-strike provisions.

The reversal of such long-standing policies was characteristic of the militant mood of civil servants. Yet, the actions are not as "radical" as they appear at first sight. The leadership in each case only espoused the use of the strike as a weapon of last resort. In some instances the leaders explained that arbitrary officials, knowing the union's reluctance to strike, had exploited the situation—in effect daring the union to strike.

AFSCME stressed that in any event its national union could not call a strike, since the decision to strike or not strike resided with the local union. AFSCME was attacking, in particular, the traditional public-private dichotomy. Illustrative is the July 1966 policy statement, which stressed that "the prohibition on the use of the strike weapon by police and other law enforcement officers is, in this union, absolute." The statement cautioned the union's local police affiliates that their charters "will be revoked immediately if the members. . . call or participate in a strike or refuse in concert to perform their duties." On a few occasions since 1966, the national leadership has kept its pledge to "take the most drastic measures to stop the strike." In May 1970, AFSCME's 18th Biennial Convention, the delegates voted to eliminate its constitutional ban on strikes by police affiliates.

Nevertheless, the strike theoretically remains a weapon of last resort, to be used only under intolerable conditions. Not all strikes are defended by these reversals in policy. Rather an attempt is made to distinguish first between the right to strike and its use. For example, AFSCME's former ban on police strikes was "absolute," but it was self-imposed. A statement by AFSCME President Wurf in 1971 is illustrative:

> I am opposed to strikes. I don't want strikes. They're bad. They are hard on the city; they're even harder on the workers. I'll fight bitterly for the right to strike—the right to strike. But I don't think there is any principle involved in striking. Striking is a tactic to persuade an employer to deal with us. If it can be avoided almost any price ought to be paid in order to avoid a strike.

Second, the actions taken supported the notion that strike policy should be based on the nature of the job and its impact on the public rather than the public or private status of the employer. Basically, unions admonished government that a more realistic and flexible position was essential to the resolution of the issue of public employee strikes. Finally, the adoption of such positions in no way negated the right and duty of the government to take the action necessary to deal with strikes that imperiled the public health or safety.

Strikes in the Public Sector

The increase in the number of strikes is indicative of the growing power of public employee organizations. Thus, it is no coincidence that the wider acceptance of collective bargaining and more strikes have been simultaneous developments. In the absence of collective bargaining, unions for many years had concentrated on the use of political pressure almost solely through legislative lobbying and political alliances with local party machines. As municipal employee organizations grew stronger, the strikes became an additional form of political pressure.

Strikes by Local Public Employees

Following the pattern of developments in private industry, strikes in local governments became a serious problem only in the wake of rapid organization of local government employees. As shown in Chapters 1 and 2, organization of local government employees proceeded slowly for many years, with minor spurts in the late 1930's and 1940's, but with no real acceleration until the late 1950's, after which it proceeded very rapidly.

David Ziskind, in his study *One Thousand Strikes by Government Employees,* [19] listed more than 1,000 recorded strikes by public workers from 1835 to 1938. At least 36 of these strikes took place in public agencies concerned with public protection; 114 involved publicly owned utility operations; 94 occurred in public health and sanitation agencies; and 18 included workers in public parks and recreation facilities. Most of the strikes were by workers on emergency relief programs in the 1930's and thus did not involve municipal services.

Significant strikes by municipal employees prior to World War II, however, were few. The Cincinnati police strike of 1918 was followed by the Boston police strike of 1919. Firemen were involved in 30 strikes, resignations, or lockouts in 1918 and 1919. No further important work stoppages took place in municipal governments until after World War II.

The immediate postwar years were marked by unrest among municipal workers. In 1946 there were 43 strikes against the government in cities of over 10,000 population and numerous threats of strikes. The sudden outbreak of municipal strikes in 1946 led to the enactment of antistrike legislation in Texas, Washington, Nebraska, Missouri, New York, Pennsylvania, Michigan, and Ohio in 1947. New York State's Condon-Wadlin Act was the most drastic of these laws. Municipal unions were not strong enough to combat the restrictive legislation.

While some strikes by local government employees occurred in the 1950's, the number and scope of municipal employee strikes did not reach serious proportions until the mid-1960's, following several years of intensive organization of local government employees. More than twice as many work stoppages by public employees (mostly of local governments) occurred in 1966-1968 as in 1958-1965, when 244 were recorded. In 1968 alone there were 254 such stoppages.

While the figures for the public sector seem spectacular, until the 1960's the municipal sector was relatively quiescent by comparison with private industry, where an average of more than 3,000 strikes occurred annually and yearly figures of 4,000 and 5,000 strikes were not uncommon. In the municipal services strikes actually declined from 1960 to 1963, increased slightly in the following two years, and accelerated greatly from 1966 to 1968. More significant than the raw number of employee strikes was the fact that the number of public employees involved increased sharply, from 102,000 in 1966 to 190,000 in 1968, and the man days lost during the same period skyrocketed from 449,000 to 2,497,800.

Work Groups Involved

During the late 1960's virtually every municipal service suffered strikes. Striking public school teachers led the parade. Teacher strikes in 1968 ranged from a strike in a one-teacher school in Maine to the massive state-wide strike conducted by Florida teachers of the NEA and the UFT strikes in New York City involving 57,000 teachers and in excess of 1.1 million school children. In Ohio, NEA affiliates left their jobs on eight occasions to hold "professional meetings." The Colorado and the Idaho Education Association voted state-wide sanctions. Teacher strikes continued unabated in 1969, although the strikes were not so spectacular as in 1968. New

247

York City's UFT had engaged in two strikes prior to its walkout in 1967, but it was the three strikes in 1968 over decentralization and community control that involved issues beyond salaries. Basic rights of tenure and due process in transfers, dismissals, and guarantees of personal safety were the major issues that kept teachers away from their classes for many weeks. Problems of race relations dominated the whole unfortunate affair.

Nor do absolute figures fully indicate the extent of the militancy of public school teachers. When not striking, teachers have carried their picket signs to City Hall, held mass rallies and demonstrations, threatened to carry out mass resignations, and invoked what the NEA calls "professional sanctions," advising its membership not to accept jobs in certain school systems. To meet the organizational challenges of affiliates of the AFT, the NEA was constrained in 1967 to terminate its long-standing policy against strikes. In March 1968 the AFT announced the establishment of a "million-dollar militancy fund" to support teacher strikes and lobbying activities. In the same month, a one-day state-wide teacher strike in Indiana, led by the Indiana Teachers' Association, protested the legislature's inaction on a teacher-pay-raise bill. Milwaukee's first teacher strike, in May 1968, continued despite a circuit court judge's temporary restraining order against teacher involvement in strikes.

Sanitation workers, with almost 200 strikes, followed the educational workers in the number of strikes in the 1960's. In a strike of Refuse Department workers in Waterbury, Conn., in 1966, the membership returned to work immediately when they won a lighter work load, although other issues were also in dispute. Sanitationmen in communities as far apart as Scranton, Pa., where the demand was for the union shop, and Shreveport, La., where the union was seeking recognition, went on strike in 1968, as did sanitationmen in Roanoke, Va., who sat down on their jobs for a day. These strikes were significant because for the most part they involved low-paid workers, many of them members of minority groups, whose usual demands for higher pay were often accompanied by demands for union recognition.

Two of the most notable of the 1968 strikes of sanitation workers were those in New York City and Memphis, Tenn. The New York strike got caught up in national politics when New York's Governor Rockefeller, a candidate for the Republican nomination for President of the United States, denied Republican Mayor Lindsay's request to call out the National Guard after the union continued the strike in defiance of an injunction. Governor Rockefeller then took over negotiations himself and persuaded the city and the union to submit to "voluntary" arbitration, which led to the final settlement.

248

Striking Professionals

The new militancy of professional and other specialized workers was one of the most notable developments in local government labor relations in the 1960's. The teachers led the way. Firemen and policemen engaged in job actions of various kinds and on some occasions did not hesitate to strike. The Atlanta, Ga., firemen struck in 1966 for recognition as well as wages and shorter hours. They stayed out for two days, in defiance of a court order, until a mediator was agreed upon. First gaining only "informal recognition," they walked out a second time, seeking formal recognition, a signed contract, and higher wages. Firemen in Rockford, Ill., struck for higher pay in 1968. In Gary, Ind., in 1969 firemen remained on strike while a major fire blazed; the "red rash" afflicted fire departments in Lima, Ohio, and in Shelby and Kalamazoo, Mich. Policemen in Indiana, Pa., walked out in 1968 because the City Council would not meet their demands for higher wages. As previously mentioned, Detroit's police force encountered a siege of the "blue flu" in 1967, and in 1968 New York's police force was afflicted with a mass "Hong Kong flu" epidemic. New York's policemen also engaged in a slowdown in 1968 during which they refused to ticket traffic violators, and parkway policemen in Nassau County, in New York State, went on a "superenforcement" campaign to exert a different kind of pressure. "Sick calls" hampered the police department of Elizabeth, N.J., Middletown, Ohio, and three suburbs of Chicago in 1969.

Welfare workers in Lake County, in Indiana, quit work in 1969 to protest the firing of their local union President as a result of his participation and leadership in demonstrations over contract talks. The United Welfare Workers of Allegheny County, in Pennsylvania, staged a 20-day strike in March, 1969. The strike was followed a month later by a march on the state capitol by welfare workers from 40 of the state's 60 counties to demand union recognition and improved working conditions. The UWW was joined by Philadelphia-based Local 123 of AFSCME in sponsoring the march.

In September 1969 a threatened strike by the Doctors' Association of the New York City Department of Health was narrowly averted when the association ratified a contract raising the minimum salary and continuing job security provisions for part-time doctors.

In March and in May of 1969 San Francisco probation officers struck, protesting heavy case loads. In 1969 a strike threat by 22 Philadelphia Municipal Court judges was withdrawn when they received assurances that an appropriation bill providing increases in their salaries was scheduled for early release by the Pennsylvania State Senate Judiciary Committee.

Organized nurses have undergone a most tradition-shattering transformation. In 1966 nurses engaged in six strikes—in New York City, San Francisco; Chicago; Youngstown, Ohio; Kellogg, Idaho; and Richmond, Calif. In other cities—El Paso, Colo.; Jersey City, N.J.; Minneapolis; and St. Paul—nurses resigned, threatened to submit resignations, or called in sick in large numbers. Mental health nurses in Illinois took part in vigils and wore black-bordered badges to protest a new state-wide pay scale.

The wave of militancy was probably largely stimulated by actions of New York City nurses in 1965 and 1966. After months of fruitless talks, which had begun during the fall of 1965, and after the failure of mediation, nurses in the Bronx Municipal Hospital voted on April 14, 1966, in favor of mass resignations effective May 23. The chain reaction was swift. Within two weeks approximately half the city's nurses had tendered their resignations. Prior to the effective date of the resignations, fact finding culminated in a settlement with salary increases.

In April 1968 the New York State Nurses' Association demanded a pay increase plus an agreement that the pay of city-employed nurses be maintained at 15 percent above the salaries paid in private hospitals. The "parity provision," it was argued, was necessary to solve the nursing shortage in municipally owned hospitals. Resorting again to the submission of resignations, the nurses achieved a pay increase in August, along with a contract provision that future increases were in part dependent on the movement of salaries in private hospitals. Effective January 1, 1969, the city agreed to review nurses' salaries every three months.

Nurses' strikes continued in 1969. Nurses at Wayne County (Michigan) General Hospital ended a two-day "white flu" epidemic in September, after they were assured by the county Labor Relations Director that their grievances would receive attention. The work stoppage was in protest over the refusal of the hospital administration, the Civil Service Commission, and the county Labor Relations Board to negotiate grievances with the hospital nurses' association. The nurses were also demanding salary increases.

Causes of Strikes

Few strikes are based on a single issue. The announced goals often obscure the underlying causes, which may be interunion rivalries, intraorganization politics, the need for greater union security, or just plain catharsis. Strikes may be a manifestation of weakness, as well as a demonstration of power. An organization may, in its earlier stages, desire to prove its trade union virility, or its institutional needs may galvanize efforts to achieve greater unity.

Furthermore, strikes may be a manifestation of deep-rooted social as well as economic conditions: a struggle over issues such as community control and decentralization, a protest over legislative or executive inaction; or they may merely reflect the municipal political scene. Wages, however, are usually the prevailing surface issue. Disputes over recognition and the establishment of collective bargaining procedures also remain a major cause of strikes. Working conditions—particularly in the case of professional employees—and agency policies have increasingly played a role in motivating strikes. As "protest by provocation" and "politics by confrontation" increase, it may be anticipated that more stoppages will result from dismissals or other disciplinary actions.

Ziskind listed seven causes of strikes prior to 1938, and he concluded that the lag between wages and the rising cost of living appeared as the most frequent motive. Complaints regarding hours of work, working conditions, and methods of dealing with the employer were also prominent causes. Although the bread-and-butter issues have not lost their force, the most significant change is the increase in the number of strikes in which other issues played a primary role.

More frequently than not a host of issues are involved, as initial demands by employee groups range in the hundreds. Additional factors may complicate the numerous items to be negotiated. The New York City transit strike of 1966 was in part caused by the change in Mayor from Robert F. Wagner, Jr., to John V. Lindsay. Mike Quill, the TWU leader, who was a former ally of Wagner, had reason to test the mettle of the "new boy in town," as well as to embarrass him politically. The change to textbook-type bargaining patterns also annoyed the fiery union leader. It appeared that there would no longer be the "public agreement supplemented by private arrangements." When the new Mayor excoriated the established mode of bargaining, he soon found himself in a hornet's nest; other union leaders also mocked the suave Mayor, one of them, in a reference to the Mayor's Ivy League background, "My men understand Yale locks, not Yale men."

While strikes are not necessarily caused by ideological or personality differences, they are complicated by, and perhaps prolonged by, such differences. The New York City Sanitation strike was surely exacerbated by the personalities and contrasting political styles of the Mayor and the Governor. Mayor Lindsay assumed the stance of the proud defender of principle—young, idealistic, independent, and at times patronizing and short-tempered. Governor Nelson

Rockefeller, equally strong-willed, preserved a congenial, compromising, and pragmatic approach—so much so that he was accused of being a power-broker, primarily interested in humiliating the Mayor.

Racial elements are involved in an increasing number of strikes. The Birmingham, Ala. sanitation strike of 1960 was but a precursor of the Memphis, Tenn., sanitation strike of 1968 (during which Dr. Martin Luther King was assassinated) and the Charleston, S.C., hospital strike of 1969. The Detroit school teachers strike of 1966 and the strike of the New York City public health nurses were preliminary to the main bout fought by New York City school teachers in three strikes in 1968. As of 1970 New York City teachers and ghetto communities had achieved only a truce rather than a harmonious settlement.

The parallel between the assertion of individual rights through the civil rights movement and the struggle to achieve gains through collective bargaining is obvious. Infusing civil rights zeal into public employee militancy is also understandable. The problem arises where natural allies confront each other in clashes in which neither can win anything but a Pyrrhic victory.

Political Implications of Strikes

The political environment in which public employee-management relations are carried on differs from that of the private sector. In the private domain strikes are primarily a contest over economic stakes; in the public sector the strike threat and the strike itself are forms of political pressure utilized to supplement the bargaining process.

A strike against the Jersey City, N.J. Incinerator Authority in 1960 demonstrated how a strike could be used to embarrass or to neutralize an opponent politically. Likewise, the fire fighter strike of 1966 in Kansas City, Mo., was clouded by the Mayor's charge that the strike was, in part, an effort to discredit him by the lawyer of the striking union, the lawyer having been a former member of the City Council who had lost the mayoralty race.

When Mayor Lindsay took a hard line in the sanitation strike of 1968, the union drum-beaters hailed the men who daily conquered New York City's "Mount Everest of Garbage" as unsung heroes. Some of the sanitationmen remarked: "Let Lindsay stand in garbage up to his ears. See if it's Fun City when the rats pop out of the cans."

When the Mayor indicated that he would call out the National Guard, there were rumblings of "general strike!" by the Central

Labor Council, and there were charges of union busting. The Mayor countered with Coolidge-style rhetoric:

> Now is the time, and here is the place, for the city to determine what it is made of; whether it will bow to unlawful force or whether it will resist with all the courage that eight million people can find within themselves. . . I believe the people of this city will stand together. . .
>
> The central issue in this reprehensible strike is whether New York City can be blackjacked into awarding exorbitant contract demands to a union simply because that union is willing to break the law, threaten the health, safety, and welfare of eight million people and disgrace an entire city.

The Mayor was hailed in some quarters for his show of courage, leadership, and support of public interest over the reckless abuse of union power. Others assailed Lindsay for his elevation of politics over public welfare, with the public being the chief victim. There were charges that this "Coolidge stance" was a public relations stratagem, that Lindsay overplayed reliance on "principle," showed an excess of self-righteousness, was petulant, and was motivated by his rivalry with the Governor. Critics pointed to prior negotiations with striking teachers and transit workers to show that the Mayor was inconsistent in his new tough policy.

The Governor was also plagued with criticism: that he was motivated to repay the political support that the striking sanitation workers had previously rendered him; that he had demeaned the Mayor and undercut the city's bargaining position in a cavalier manner; that he had sabotaged the state law against strikes. Many praised the Governor for his realistic settlement, which they said evidenced political courage rather than cowardice. As for his refusal to call out the National Guard, he had calmed the frustrations, pressures, and tensions of a city on the brink of chaos.

The political overtones were clear. Neither the Mayor nor the Governor escaped entirely unscathed as the columnists had a field day. The late Drew Pearson wrote: "Rockefeller emerged as man kowtowing to a racket-ridden union which ignored all reasonable attempts to mediate." [20] William F. Buckley noted that Lindsay took the right position but wasn't convincing, "because his entire public record is one of arduous sycophancy to the labor unions." [21] Perhaps the most sage comment was made by Walter Lippman, who concluded that the strike showed the "vulnerability of urban living," with the city caught between the intolerable and the impossible in a problem that could not be solved on principle but could only be managed. The ultimate defenselessness of the modern city had ominous overtones. [22]

253

Other executives have felt the horns of the dilemma of action or inaction. During the Ecorse, Mich., teachers strike of 1966, Governor George Romney's inaction led to charges that he was "bucking for the Presidency." But on occasion a Mayor can make political capital by his involvement. Mayor Richard J. Daley of Chicago attempted to improve his political image by his mediative efforts in the Cook County Junior College strike of 1967. The same year Mayor Tate of Philadelphia found a good deal of political value in a work stoppage by civil servants seeking improved benefits. Despite charges that he was "buying labor's vote" with the impending election in mind, the Mayor sanctioned the walk-out and was victorious in his electoral campaign.

Strikes and the Law

The increasing acceptance and use of the strike as a legitimate step in the bargaining process have caused no corresponding loosening of legislative prohibitions applicable to public employee strikes. Although many states have statutes dealing with the employment relationship, only a minority have mandated collective bargaining by municipalities. Only Pennsylvania and Hawaii have legislation granting a limited right to strike to most categories of municipal employees. With the exception of these two statutes, enacted in 1970, public employee strikes are still generally illegal in the United States. Their legal prohibition takes many forms, including statutes, attorney-general opinions, municipal ordinances, judicial decisions, and administrative bans.

Antistrike Legislation

Most state statutes are silent on the subject, but as of February 1969, 18 states had enacted legislation specifically forbidding all public employees—state and local—the use of the strike weapon. Additional states prohibit strikes by state employees or have laws on the books directly related to specific categories of employees, such as municipal policemen or public school teachers.

As late as the early 1930's some authorities questioned the state of the law regarding such strikes. Beyer commented:

> Still less clear is the right of municipal employees to strike. Of legislation there is very little to throw light on this question. . . In this state of public opinion municipal employees cannot be said to have a recognized right to strike. Perhaps the most that can be said is that, when they do strike, they violate no law. [23]

This statement failed to note the distinction between "law" and legislation. The former term includes case law, which "from time immemorial" in the words of some courts, clearly stood as a barrier against public employee strikes. Mr. Beyer was correct, however, in noting the paucity of specific legislation on the subject. Even as late as 1942, the Committee on Employee Relations in the Public Service stated, "Laws directly forbidding strikes are probably in force in a few local governments, but no complete list is available." [24]

Actually, most legislation was a direct result of militant employee action and thus took the form of crisis enactments following strikes. The first wave followed the Boston police strike of 1919, and the second legislative wave followed World War II. For example, in the winter of 1919-20 Congress quickly passed a law applicable to police and firemen in the District of Columbia which made it a misdemeanor to strike. A number of municipalities either passed ordinances forbidding strikes, declared strikes to be considered a resignation, or forbade efforts to organize or affiliate in the hopes of preventing strikes. Salt Lake City, Utah; Macon, Ga.; Roanoke, Va.; San Antonio, Texas; Philadelphia; Chicago; Detroit; Los Angeles; Wichita, Kan.; and Dallas, Texas, were among the municipalities that enacted legislation prior to World War II. In some of these cities the action was taken in the form of an administrative ban rather than a local ordinance.

A sudden wave of strikes in 1946 led to the first state-wide antistrike legislation. In 1946 Virginia led the way, and in 1947 Texas, Washington, Nebraska, Missouri, New York, Pennsylvania, Ohio and Michigan followed suit. The most drastic and spectacular legislation was New York's Condon-Wadlin Law, enacted after a strike of Buffalo school teachers that had attracted nationwide attention. Providing for heavy penalties against individual strikers and including a strike definition so broad that an individual action could be construed as a strike, the statute, it was believed, armed department heads with a powerful weapon to oppose the activities of employee leaders.

After this, enactment of state legislation was minimal until the mid-1960's and the next great wave of strikes. In each new case of restrictive legislation the expectation that it alone would curtail strikes was doomed at the moment of enactment.

Attorney General Opinions and Administrative Bans

In at least five states, there is reliance on opinions of the Attorney General that forbid strikes. Some of these opinions take on the character and tone of a relatively recent opinion by the Attorney

General of Nevada in 1968, which states, "In every case reported, the right of employees to strike is denied unless otherwise authorized by statute. We have no such statutory authorization in Nevada." [25] Generally speaking, the opinions recite ad infinitum a list of court decisions that deny the legality of strikes.

Recent trends indicate a great diversity in the impact of such opinions. On occasion the opinion ranges beyond the strike issue and extends to such matters as the right to organize, recognition, affiliation, and bargaining. This was the case in the Nevada Opinion 494, which "outlawed" the American Federation of Teachers less than a year before the state legislature accorded it bargaining rights.

In 1966 Atlanta, Ga., fire fighters struck, and the Attorney General ruled that the city was not obligated to negotiate with the union. Nevertheless, the city agreed to union demands for an "independent" arbitrator.

An opinion of the Attorney General is not as effective as a statute. But the tendency to treat collective bargaining as a question of law rather than a question of public policy has caused great weight to be given to the Attorney General's opinion. Both attorneys general and city corporation counsels, who are the public employer's lawyers, reflect the employers' mood and attitude. In Oregon the Attorney General had ruled that the law mandated public employers to bargain. A court test resulted in a judicial decision that interpreted the statute in such a manner as to leave the decision to bargain optional on the part of the employer. In another instance, the 1959 statute enacted by Wisconsin also evoked a legal opinion that the statute did not provide bargaining rights. The legislature reacted swiftly, and in 1961 municipal employees were accorded the right to bargain. As a result, such opinions as related to the strike issue remain a fragile barrier to employee strike action.

Administrative bans are based on the premise that the acceptance of public employment implies agreement that a public employee will not engage in strikes and that the sovereign, through delegation, has entrusted officials with the right and duty to assure the continued functioning of government. Under such authority administrators and civil service commissions have promulgated bans on strikes. Again, the repeated statements of Presidents, Governors, and Mayors utilized to buttress such administrative actions stood as fragile reeds in the strike winds of the 1960's.

The Courts and Public Employee Strikes

Courts remain a primary bastion against strikes. In 1953 the authoritative American Law Reports concluded that "*in every case that has been reported, the right of public employees to strike is emphatically denied [emphasis added]."* [26] While this statement is no longer accurate, no highest state court has as yet directly stated that municipal employees have the right to strike. Indeed, several courts have recently reaffirmed the proposition that public employees do not have a right to strike.[27]

The Connecticut Supreme Court, in the Norwalk case in 1951, commented that ". . . to say [that public employees] can strike is the equivalent of saying they can deny the authority of government." [28] New York courts have taken a similar line of reasoning: to admit that a strike may halt operations until demands are met is to transfer to employees all legislative, executive, and judicial powers; strikes demonstrate the "intolerable outrage" of a public employee turning on his government; employee actions may constitute a form of blackmail or extortion. [29]

Courts have tended to view public employee strikes as an invasion of sovereignty and a challenge to governmental authority and to regard them as examples of outrageous conduct contravening the public welfare. Even in the absence of legislative prohibitions, courts have perceived strikes as more than a struggle over conditions of labor. Where court orders have been ignored and strikes continue, the strike is seen as a seditious attempt against the life of the courts. Therefore, if not from "time immemorial," it has long been the case law rule in most states that public employees may not strike.

But courts have not been unanimous in their attitude toward strikes. In 1957 a trial judge in Minnesota denied an injunction and stated that to assert that a public employee could not strike was "to indulge in the expression of a personal belief and then ascribe to it legality on some tenuous theory of sovereignty." [30]

More than a decade passed before another judge, in vacating a temporary restraining order against a union, faced the strike issue squarely. Judge Hugo Fisher stated that the case was "limited to the bald proposition of whether or not a public employee has the right to strike under the case and statute law of California." [31]

The same year the Chief Justice of the Indiana Supreme Court wrote a vigorous dissent to the majority three-to-two Anderson ruling of the court, which he stated offered "absolutely no justification for its holding that every strike by any public employees, including teachers, is illegal, and therefore enjoinable regardless of how peaceful and non-disruptive the strike is." [32] Rejecting the notion that a strike against government is in all cases unthinkable, the Chief Justice viewed such reasons as not a rational argument but a technique to avoid dealing with the merits of a dispute: "In the case of a peaceful strike and no major disruption of the community," said the Justice, "I find it very easy to think of a strike against the sovereign *and* to justify it."

While few judges have gone as far as Judge Fisher or Justice De Bruler, there are signs that some courts will uphold the no-strike principle and yet allow a strike to continue. The cases have generally involved public authorities that operated under special statutes. Still other courts have begun to question sharply the continued reliance on the doctrine of sovereignty to escape responsibility or have noted that the common law doctrine prohibiting strikes could be modified by legislation. [33]

The greatest movement has been made in the area of injunctions. By refusing to issue an injunction or by vacating an injunction, a court is able to allow concerted employee action to continue and still not affirm strikes in principle. For example, in 1968 the Michigan Supreme Court vacated the issuance of an injunction on the ground that the only harm shown was that schools would be closed and not open the fall term on time. [34] The same year a California court found that the injunctive proscriptions that had been imposed were broad enough to encroach upon constitutionally protected free speech and were violative of due process. By this type of action, the court assumed, but did not find, that a public employee strike could be enjoined. [35] The Wisconsin Circuit Court in 1971 refused to grant a temporary injunction in a suburban Milwaukee school stoppage. The court reasoned that the teachers had not presented their side of the dispute and noted that no disorder or threat to the public safety had been raised. [36]

The refusal to issue injunctions in cases similar to those noted above has been the exception rather than the rule. Courts generally have staunchly supported the constitutionality of no-strike laws and have proclaimed the common law as a barrier where no legislation exists; and higher courts have tended to move in a direction opposite to that of the opinions issued by Judge Fisher and Justice De Bruler.

Other courts have utilized different techniques to ease penalties. In 1971 a trial court found that the Michigan Employment Relations Commission exceeded its authority in ordering a check-off suspension rather than the withdrawal of recognition in the case of a striking union. In this instance, the Michigan Court of Appeals upheld the ruling. Similarly, the Ohio Supreme Court set aside strike penalties imposed in 1971, reversing a prior appellate ruling. The court reasoned that the Ferguson Act penalties were not automatic, and the city had failed to send notices required by the statute. [37]

Despite the above trends, it remains clear that there is no legal right to strike by public employees in the absence of a legislative grant. In 1971 the U.S. Supreme Court affirmed a lower court ruling that upheld the constitutionality of the federal law forbidding strikes by all employees of the federal government. [38] The same year the court upheld the constitutionality of the provision of New York's Taylor Law requiring a no-strike pledge from any union representing state employees. [39]

The Injunctive Process

Traditionally, the labor movement, both in the private and public sectors, has vehemently opposed the injunction. An injunction may be used either to restrain or to compel the performance of an act. As a legal device to avoid the threat, or the continuance of an irreparable injury, injunctions, once considered an "extraordinary remedy," were used so frequently that the procedure became America's most distinctive contribution in the application of law to industrial strife. [40]

Private employers used it as a device to hinder unionization. Frankfurter and Greene, in their authoritative study, which led to statutory restrictions on the use of the injunction in labor disputes in private industry, pinpointed what was wrong with the indiscriminate use of a potentially useful legal tool:

> To sanction vague and undefined terminology in "drag-net" clauses largely unenforceable, and certainly unenforced, is to distort the injunction into a "scarecrow" device for curbing the economic pressure of a strike and thereby discredit equity's function in law enforcement. To approve decrees that in form are like the idiot's tale, full of sound and fury, signifying nothing, each decree the replica of another and usually the partisan phrasing of counsel, but in substance compendia of legal rules purporting minutely to regularize conduct, is to raise faith in a cabala. [41]

The abusive and widespread use of injunctions in private industry was curtailed by the Norris-LaGuardia Act in 1932. But this statute in no way limited the use of the injunction by government employers. Municipal governments have clutched at the injunctive power to prevent or end strikes. From 1960 through May 1967 approximately one fifth of all public employee work stoppages were enjoined by the courts. A recent study indicated that the majority of strikes end within two days after the issuance of a court order, including those in which there is defiance. [42] This suggests that the reliance on the effectiveness of the injunction as an antistrike weapon may be useful in municipal government. Yet, during the past five years teacher groups have defied approximately 40 percent of the injunctions issued against them.

The crux, as in the case of strike bans, is in the enforcement. Courts in the United States have almost universally excoriated strikes that continue in defiance of court orders. Within a period of three months in 1968, public employee union leaders in New York City, Woodbridge, N.J., and Memphis, Tenn., were judged guilty of criminal contempt, fined, and sentenced to jail terms.

Although the sentences were mild—less than a month—the response of organized labor was instantaneous and vehement. Albert Shanker, President of the New York City affiliate of the AFT, denounced the sentences on television as "outrageous, vindictive, and antilabor." The Woodbridge teachers' union reminded the public that "injunctions and jail sentences will not teach children." By the time the court acted in the Woodbridge case, the mediation efforts of Theodore Kheel had borne fruit. Both the local school board and the union were eager to conclude a face-saving agreement and have the teachers return to work in a happy frame of mind. Indeed, representatives of the school board and Mr. Kheel requested leniency of the court in imposing punishment, but the court ignored the pleas.

When an injunction is defied, courts may respond with contempt-of-court penalties, including fines and the imposition of jail sentences. So many teachers had been jailed by 1970 that the AFT launched a campaign to end the use of ex parte injunctions.

The AFT charged that it is a simple matter for any administrator to get an injunction by dispatching a private messenger to a judge, who need only glance at the paper and sign, taking less than half a minute to enjoin a strike. This may be done at any time of the day or night, at any place—home, office, or club. The union likened the process to a judicial slot machine, producing injunctions without a hearing, trial, or any opportunity for the union to offer evidence to the contrary. For the foregoing reasons, unions promote changes in legislation that would authorize the issuance of injunctions only where a clear and present danger to the health, safety, and security of the community exists.

The reality is that such ex parte injunctions are temporary moves until the court can schedule a hearing as to whether a preliminary or permanent order shall be issued. Some judges clearly point out that they are aware of the contemporary social problems concerning public service bargaining but state that as judges they must remind public employees that the interests of unionism do not justify standing in defiance of law. Thus, if they condone contemptuous and illegal conduct, meekly acceding to requests under pressure, it would erode and ultimately destroy the high place in public esteem that unions enjoy in our society.

Awareness of the difficulties inherent in the use of the injunction in labor disputes is apparent in the report of the Advisory Committee on Public Employee Relations created by Governor Romney of Michigan in 1967. The committee favored the injunctive remedy under "appropriate circumstances" but warned that indiscriminate use would be "unduly punitive or impractical, damaging to the collective bargaining process." Judiciously rejecting the view that injunctions should be sought under all conditions and always issued by the courts when asked, regardless of circumstances, the committee also condemned a fixed scale of fines, "never to be forgiven," for violations of court orders. It carried flexibility to such a point that under certain circumstances the fine could be "forgiven" in the interest of harmony. The committee argued that injunctive relief should be mandatory when a strike occurs before the required statutory bargaining and other settlement procedures have been exhausted. In stoppages of truly critical functions, such as fire fighting and police service, the committee agreed that when requested by legal authorities the courts should issue an injunction.[43]

The points made by the Michigan study are not new, but they are realistic. There is a legitimate role for injunctions in labor relations. What is called for is a more flexible approach to the use of the injunction, the wisdom of which depends on the total circumstances and equities in each instance. Use of the injunction to protect society from a critical work stoppage is one thing; use of the injunction to spare the public employer inconvenience or to cater to his reluctance to deal with a new force in labor relations is another. This is especially grievous if the government official is inept or incapable or if political motives are obscured under the mantle of sovereignty.

The collective bargaining statute should limit the issuance of injunctions to situations that pose a clear and present danger to the community. The courts are in the best position to weigh the conflicting claims of the parties. In critical cases involving functions such as fire fighting, police, and prison guard service, the danger is obvious, and therefore the statute should provide for immediate issuance of a restraining order.

When collective bargaining results in an impasse, the injunction, appropriately used to protect the public health and safety, remains the most flexible legal tool to gain time in emergency disputes.

Procedures for enforcing strike bans extend beyond the injunctive process, and these procedures are primarily set forth in state legislation. At varying stages, however, the executive, the courts, special state agencies, and local administrators may be involved. The approach to penalties may be mandatory or optional. The penalties may be imposed against the union as an entity, against the leadership of the striking organization, or against individual strikers, or there may be a combination of such penalties. Types of penalties currently range from reprimand to criminal penalties including fines and/or imprisonment.

The penalties against individual strikers include reprimand, suspension, demotion, loss of civil service status, dismissal, probation, loss of professional certification, fines, and imprisonment. The leadership are subject to fines, imprisonment, and other penalties for defiance of court injunctions. Recently, as in the case of the Taylor Law prior to its amendment in 1969, the thrust was to penalize the union as an entity by such actions as decertification, loss of representation rights, suspension of check-off privileges, and heavy fines.

Specific penalties for violating strike bans are mandated by law in Georgia, Virginia, and Ohio. The Georgia statute provides that striking state employees must be discharged and cannot be rehired for three years. Moreover, in a clause aimed at union organizers, union leaders, and "outside agitators," the law provides that any person not a state employee who knowingly incites, influences, or persuades or pickets so as to urge a state employee to strike is guilty of a misdemeanor and upon conviction may be imprisoned up to a year and/or fined up to $1,000.

Other state laws vary somewhat in regard to mandatory dismissal. The length of time before a striking employee becomes eligible for rehiring varies, as does the period during which salaries are frozen and the amount of time a re-employed striker is to be on probation. In Ohio and Pennsylvania, for example, the law authorizes rehiring the moment the strike is terminated; the Virginia statute prescribes re-employment eligibility after one year.

The difficulties of enforcing such punitive measures caused the repeal of similar laws in Michigan and New York. These statutes have strong labor movements, which have been a factor both in the successful evasion of penalties by striking municipal employees and in securing repeal of statutes prescribing severe penalties. Michigan in 1965 repealed the automatic termination of employment and the "forfeiture of all benefits" provisions of the state's Hutchinson Act.

The amended act still permits discharge and other disciplinary action against the strikers, but enforcement is now discretionary on the part of the municipal employer.

The Taylor Law

New York's Taylor Law, enacted in 1967, is an outstanding illustration of the discretionary approach. The 1967 law contained no provision for penalties for individual strikers, other than a general statement that "a public employee who violates the [strike ban] shall be subject to the disciplinary penalties provided by law for misconduct in accordance with procedures established by law."[44] The law provided further that additional penalties—decertification or the suspension of the union's right to check-off or dues—might or might not be applied against the union, at the discretion of a court of competent jurisdiction or of the state Public Employee Relations Board, charged with this duty under the statute. In 1969 the Taylor Law was amended. Revisions provided for a loss of two days' pay for each day an employee is on strike, the loss of job tenure for striking, "unlimited" fines against unions and unlimited suspension of the check-off. The severity of the revisions led George W. Taylor, who had headed the study commission that preceded enactment of the original statute, to comment in a speech before the American Management Association in June 1969 that the amendments might be "unduly harsh."

The Taylor law is flexible in approach, and it contains one novel sanction. Section 211 requires the chief legal officer of the institution whose employees are on strike to seek injunctive relief in a court of competent jurisdiction when an employee organization "threatens, or is about to do, or is doing an act in violation" of the strike ban. If there is defiance of the injunction, the law directs the court to consider whether the public employer or its representative "engaged in such acts of extreme provocation as to detract from the responsibility of the employee organization for the strike." Then the court may determine the extent of fiscal and criminal contempt penalties, within statutory limits.

Despite a clear violation of the strike prohibition in the Taylor Law by firemen in Troy, the PERB in November 1969 for the first time declined, to order the forfeiture of dues check-off privileges, finding "extreme provocation" in the public employer's lack of good faith in bargaining. This indicates serious intent to place on the employer as well as the employee the obligation for responsible bargaining.

263

The extreme difficulty in enforcing strike bans has led to some relaxation in enforcement where extenuating circumstances exist. This is the clear signal of the refusal to issue injunctions noted above and of the actions of the New York PERB in refusing to apply the available penalties of the law where the strike was provoked by the employer.

Vermont was the first state to move in the direction of easing legislative bans. A Vermont law in 1967 left it for the courts to determine if any teacher-representative action "poses a clear and present danger to a sound program of education which in the light of all relevant circumstances it is in the public interest to prevent." [45] In 1969 the Montana legislature amended its bargaining law for nurses to permit strikes by employees in public and private hospitals unless "there is another strike in effect at another health care facility within a radius of 150 miles." In 1971 the state enacted a law authorizing school teachers to bargain, but withheld from teachers the right to strike. Thus, Montana now has legislatively declared its willingness to tolerate a strike by nurses, under certain conditions, but not one by teachers.

It seems likely that the next few years will result in a greater easing of the bans as currently written. Hawaii and Pennsylvania have already enacted laws authorizing strikes subject to limitations provided in the statute. In the absence of an irresponsible wave of public employee strikes, other states are likely to follow the lead of Pennsylvania and Hawaii. Politicians, however, are anxious to appear to be protecting the public interest, and consequently they are reluctant to experiment with relaxation.

Public opinion polls are far from conclusive on the strike issue. A Louis Harris poll of October 1967 found that the American people stood firmly opposed to strikes of teachers, firemen, and police. Yet, of the group polled, 41 percent, 35 percent, and 36 percent, respectively, favored the right to strike for the three categories. In 1969 another Harris poll indicated that a lesser percentage (35 percent) favored the right of teachers to strike. A similar percentage drop occurred when the question was posed "Should police and firemen be permitted to strike, or not?" Only 30 percent responded "yes." During the New York City sanitation strike of 1968, a New York *Times* survey of 1,010 persons indicated that 57 percent favored a strike ban. In the case of labor union households, only 47 percent favored a strike ban. A 1971 poll of high school teachers and students indicated that more than one half of both teachers and students believed public employees should have the right to strike. [46]

Specific strikes generate powerful but sometimes ephemeral public responses—the resentment subsides as emotions and wounds are healed by time. While strikes tend to generate legislative repression, it is sensible to consider carefully the case against *all* public employee strikes.

Pro and Con Regarding the Right to Strike

Those who oppose all public employee strikes suggest a number of reasons why strikes in the public domain should be prohibited. Strikes are considered a challenge to the authority of government and thereby an invasion of the sovereign's prerogatives. To submit to such strikes, they contend, would be to submit to illegal coercion, would be an abdication of responsibility entrusted to public officials by the people, and would contravene the public welfare.

The Sovereignty Argument

The sovereign state is held to possess the right to judge the merit of conflicting claims, including those disputes in which the government itself is a party. The absence of such rights, it is argued, would lead to insurrection, rebellion, and eventual anarchy. Public employee strikes are regarded not as pure labor disputes but as a direct defiance of governmental authority.

Trade unionists oppose construing all strikes by government workers as an assault on sovereignty. They maintain that it is ridiculous to equate a strike by window washers, city parking lot attendants, greenskeepers on a municipal golf course, or referees at a high school game as an assault on the sovereign.

What is objected to most is the use of the doctrine of sovereignty to create a specious rationale to prohibit *all* categories of employees from striking, instead of a logical classification. They assert that it is not common sense to consider a strike by publicly employed grass cutters or leaf pickers a crime when the government upholds the right of a private employee to diminish the free flow of food, fuel and other necessities of life until they actually imperil society.

The doctrine of sovereignty is seen as a legal ruse to justify the public employer's right to act unilaterally, paternalistically, and at times irresponsibly in its determination of employment relationships. The cloak of sovereignty is thus a convenient concept to clothe the public employer with special rights and privileges that foster inept administrators, blind the vision of competent ones, and allow arbitrary and capricious managers to escape responsibility.

Proponents of an absolute strike ban denounce strikes as an attempt to force legally vested public officials to abdicate or share with outsiders the responsibility for decision-making.

The nondelegation doctrine referred to in many judicial decisions, unions protest, is more illusion than reality. As originally stated, the doctrine prohibited the transfer of legislative powers to the executive and his appointed administrators. More recent decisions of the courts have upheld delegations of authority accompanied by criteria, standards, reasonable norms, or an intelligible principle to guide administrative actions. Public officials are in no way compelled to accede to employee demands. Indeed, the law and the courts stand as formidable barriers against dereliction of responsibility. Furthermore, in most cases it is sound public policy to consult and cooperate with public employee groups in the decision-making processes of government.

Strikes Are Coercive

When Franklin D. Roosevelt stated that a work stoppage by public employees "manifests nothing less than an intent on their part to prevent or obstruct the operations of government until their demands are satisfied," he injected the element of illegal coercion. Others added that the more vital the service controlled, the more likely the community was to capitulate.

Proponents of change concede that an element of "coercion" is involved in strikes, but they declare that the strike is an indispensable ingredient of free collective bargaining and, as described by Archibald Cox, "the motive power which makes collective bargaining operate." To the extent that the prospect of a strike is coercive, this form of coercion is deemed an essential part of a process recognized as a desirable and mutually beneficial component of a democratic society. Thus, to deny the strike to a substantial segment of society is, in itself, undemocratic.

Interference with Political Processes

The test of strength implicit in all strikes is also opposed as likely to impede the normal operations of the political process. Under the law budgetary responsibility is vested in public officials. The authorization of paralyzing strikes is considered tantamount to abandonment of the democratic processes in the setting of legislative and budgetary priorities. In the private sector the necessity of preventing goods and services from being priced out of the market has a deterrent effect. No such market restraints exist in the public sector, point out the defenders of the status quo.

Advocates of change deny that there are no countervailing forces to curb the public employee unions. The absence of the profit motive in government is in part compensated for by the constant pressure for greater economy. The standard record on which politicians run includes a balanced budget, economies achieved, and a promise of no tax increases. Giving over the keys of the public treasury to city workers would only serve to antagonize a larger public and result in political retribution.

The Model Employer Argument

It is also assumed by defenders of the strike ban that since the government is a "model employer," with no profit motives, the public employee is a member of a "privileged class," who are beneficiaries of job security, pensions, decent wages, and good working conditions. As the embodiment of the people, the public employer would by no stretch of the imagination deliberately exploit its employees. There is the persisting picture of government service as a complex of boondoggles grossly overmanned by political hangers-on who "swill at the public trough," collecting high pay and lavish fringe benefits.

Defenders of the right to strike note that relatively few people were aware of the financial plight of the postal workers until their problems were dramatically portrayed by television during the work stoppage of 1970, casting doubt on the notion that all governmental employers are per se, model employers. The concept of special benefits injuring to city employees, they point out, was largely a myth. Even a cursory glance at the salary scales of teachers, firemen, police, and nurses prior to the recent surge of collective bargaining reveals that wages and fringe benefits in government had lagged behind those achieved by privately employed workers subsequent to the passage of the National Labor Relations Act.

The Theory of Special Responsibility

A theory of "special responsibility" was also invoked to condemn strikes. Public employees were held to perform services for the public at large and to assume as a condition of employment the obligation not to strike or even falter in the performance of their duties. Patriotism and undivided loyalty were introduced into the strike issue by assertions that a good citizen would endure any hardships of government service—the "mere thought of a strike against his government would be repugnant to every true patriot." As early as 1909, Nicholas Murray Butler, President of Columbia University, intoned: "In my judgment loyalty and treason ought to mean the same thing in the civil service that they do in the military or naval service." Franklin D. Roosevelt stressed the special-obligation concept, asserting, ". . . looking toward the paralysis of government by those who have sworn to uphold it is unthinkable and intolerable."[47]

Unions respond that every occupation has its special responsibility corresponding to its nature. The government employer's contention is that *all* government jobs are endowed with a special responsibility to the employer because it is the government. The doctrine of special responsibility is looked upon merely as the summation of the state's claim to special rights as an employer and rests on the basic assumption that government employees constitute a special class, apart from all other workers in society. The unions ask, "Does a professor employed by a private university have less responsibility to his profession, students, and employer than a professor employed by a state university?" There are few jobs in the public sector without their counterparts in private industry.

The Public Welfare

In recent years defenders of the absolute ban on all public employee strikes have tried to escape resting their case on concepts of sovereignty or special status. They insist that strikes contravene the public welfare and that attempts to create different categories by which some employees are authorized to strike would not be feasible. A clearly stated legal ban is essential. According to this view, governments are established to provide services, to protect the community, and to promote the general welfare. Governments cannot go out of business, stock pile goods in advance or lock out employees, as in the case in private industry.

They add that many public employee strikes affect the public in an immediate, dramatic, and obvious manner. In large cities a transit strike compels thousands of people to seek alternate ways of getting to work. Business in the central city suffers serious economic losses, and the income of many—often those located in disadvantaged areas and least able to afford it—is seriously curtailed.

Garbage strikes of prolonged duration leave thousands of tons of garbage strewn on the streets, posing a serious health hazard. Teacher strikes not only deprive children of their right to an education but in some large urban centers stoke the fires of smoldering antiwhite and anti-Semitic sentiments in impoverished ghettoes. When welfare case workers strike, an even greater strain is placed on families living desperate lives. Hospital strikes place an added burden on the seriously ill.

Strikes by police, fire fighters, and prison guards pose the possibility of rampant lawlessness or a holocaust in which thousands may lose their lives. Strikes in these three services are considered equivalent to playing "Russian roulette" with the safety of the community, which includes the wives, children, and relatives of the strikers.

Proponents of an absolute ban on strikes concede that all strikes do not directly imperil the public safety. They argue that it is impractical and inappropriate to permit some strikes and forbid others only because certain specific functions are more immediate and drastic in their impact than others. Attempts to draw a line of demarcation would be futile and the subject of never ending controversy, as each employee group would seek to be included within the privileged categories authorized to strike. Furthermore, the mere existence of an essential-nonessential test would pressure leaders to become even more militant. Finally, it is claimed that the test itself is "vitiated by inherent procedural difficulties as to who may strike, when, and for how long." To avoid endless wrangling, a clear cut prohibition is the only way out.

Advocates of change rail at the attempt to obscure the fact that the defenders of the ban still cling to a legalistic approach, since transit, hospital, garbage collection, teaching, and other functions are also performed by private institutions. In each case the privately employed worker is guaranteed the right to strike by law. The legal emphasis, in the unions' view, continues to hide the simple fact that a strike is not "a matter of right but a brutal and spontaneous fact precipitated by events." [48] Claims of the sovereign enacted into law miss the point:

> . . . it is apparent why it is absurd to "forbid" the strike of civil servants. It is as absurd as to declare a revolution unconstitutional, or to outlaw war. On the contrary, none of these events can be "legalized"; they show that every legal order rests upon a fact of nature, a social reality beyond all law; namely, the group of human beings to which it applies. [49]

The legalistic public-private dichotomy has little relevance to the municipal employee. He has the same dreams, desires, fears, frustrations, problems and hopes as his counterpart in private industry. Excessive theorizing falls on deaf ears, as the municipal worker pays the same taxes, buys the same food and shelter, and has no more immunity from disease than a private employee.

Public Officials and Study Commissions

Despite the protestations of those who desire a change in the law, most public officials have followed the lead of Governor Coolidge during the Boston Police Strike by 1919. Mr. Coolidge's dictum, "There is no right to strike against the public safety by anybody, anywhere, at any time," has been echoed by countless mayors, governors, and presidents. During the Boston police strike President Wilson stated that leaving a city "at the mercy of an army of thugs is a crime against civilization." In 1937 President Roosevelt declared public employee strikes "intolerable and unthinkable." Governor Dewey of New York spoke of a state of anarchy in which liberties become useless when government is paralyzed by strikes; and Governor Rockefeller termed such strikes "utterly wrong in principle." Mayor Fiorello LaGuardia of New York City stated in 1941, "The city does not and cannot recognize the right of any group to strike against the city." Mayor John V. Lindsay resorted to Rooseveltian terms when he referred to a job action by fire fighters in 1967 as "indefensible, unconscionable, unthinkable, and illegal." [50]

Of the several state and privately sponsored study commissions that have examined labor relations in state and local government, the overwhelming majority have favored the retention of the absolute ban on public employee strikes. [51] Only the Pennsylvania Commission specifically advocated a relaxation of the existing ban on all public employee strikes. Looking upon a limited and carefully defined right to strike as a safety valve that might in fact prevent strikes, the Commission made a recommendation that provided the basis of legislation enacted in 1970. Recommendation No. 4 read, in part:

> Except for policemen and firemen, a limited right to strike should be recognized subject to these safeguards: (a) No strike shall be permitted for any reason whatsoever until all the collective bargaining procedures. . . have been fully complied with; (b) No strike should be permitted to begin or continue where the health, safety or welfare of the general public is in danger; (c) Unlawful strikes should be subject to injunctions, and violations thereof enforced by penalties that will

be effective against the bargaining agent or individual employees or both.[52]

The Maryland Commission in 1969, while not going as far as the Pennsylvania Commission, stopped short of a recommendation to continue the existing absolute ban. Recognizing the existence of two viewpoints—the second of which "advocates a limited right to strike among groups of public employees in work which has been described as 'noncritical'—the Commission recommended that "no strike should be permitted where the health and safety of the general public is in danger. . ."[53]

With increasing frequency study commissions, academicians, labor consultants, and even some public officials are recommending or forecasting the easing of strike bans. For example, in 1971 the American Assembly gave several reasons for refusing to support a total prohibition on strikes. Its report noted that such a ban gives rise to unequal treatment of public and private workers doing similar tasks; that the ban relies on the mistaken view that every strike by governmental workers affects public health and safety; that disrespect for law is encouraged; that the ban does not guarantee there will be no strikes; and that it fails to recognize the realities of public employment labor relations.[54]

Robert G. Howlett, Chairman of the Michigan Employment Relations Commission, predicts that the public employee's right to strike will be increasingly recognized by statute and judicial decision in the 1970's.[55] This raises the basic issue—how best to resolve impasses in order to prevent a strike, shorten its duration, or minimize its impact on the public interest and yet not treat the public employee like a "second-class citizen."

Notes

1. See *American Jurisprudence,* Vol. 31, Sec. 383, and *American Law Reports,* Vol. 25, p. 1245.
2. The War Labor Disputes Act, passed during World War II, provided for waiting periods and government-supervised strike votes but did not deny the right to strike after these procedures were exhausted. However, there were seizures of strike-impeded operations during World War II under the Selective Service Act. See Albert A. Blum, "Work or Fight: The Use of The Draft as a Manpower Sanction During the Second World War," *Industrial and Labor Relations Review,* April 1963, pp. 366ff; see also John L. Blackman, *Presidential Seizures in Labor Disputes* (Cambridge, Mass.: Harvard University Press, 1967).
3. Public Law 410, 1946; Public Law 663, 1946; and Public Law 330, 1955.
4. John W. Macy, Jr. "Employee-Management Cooperation in the Federal

Service," *Proceedings of the Industrial Relations Research Association,* 1966, p. 62.

5. Gordon R. Clapp, *Report to the Civil Service Assembly,* (Chicago, 1942), p. 113. Hereafter cited as *Civil Service Assembly Report.*

6. AFGE Constitution, Article 2, Section 3.

7. IAFF Constitution, Article 3, Section 2.

8. David Ziskind, *One Thousand Strikes of Government Employees* (New York: Columbia University Press, 1940), p. 3.

9. SCMWA Constitution, Article 2, Section 2 and Article 8, Section 15.

10. Abe Flaxer, *Public Management,* September, 1937, p. 264.

11. Arnold Zander, *Public Management* September 1937, p. 260.

12. Morton R. Godine, *Labor Relations in the Public Service* (Cambridge, Mass.: Harvard University Press, 1961), p. 166.

13. *A Declaration of Rights of Public Employees,* Adopted at Madison Square Garden Rally, New York City, May 23, 1967.

14. New York *Times,* March 27, 1967.

15. New York *Times,* September 11, 1967.

16. Zander, "A Union View of Collective Bargaining in the Public Service," *Public Administration Review,* Winter 1962, p. 8.

17. AFSCME, *Proceedings of the Sixteenth International Convention,* Washington, D.C., April 25-29, 1966, pp. 116-17.

18. AFSCME, *Policy Statement of July 26, 1966,* Washington, D.C.

19. Ziskind, op. cit., p. 3.

20. New York *Post,* February 19, 1968.

21. New York *Post, February 20, 1968.*

22. *Newsweek,* February 26, 1968, p. 16.

23. William C. Beyer, "Municipal Civil Service in the United States," in Carl J. Friedrich et al., eds., *Problems of the American Public Service* (New York: McGraw-Hill, 1935), p. 153.

24. *Civil Service Assembly Report,* op. cit., p. 110.

25. Attorney General, Nevada, Opinion No. 494, March 4, 1968.

26. American Law Reports, Vol. 31, Sec. 11, p. 1159.

27. The Supreme Court of Indiana, in *AFT v. School, City of Anderson,* 251 N.E. 2d 15 (1969), cites a number of cases to support this view. In 1970 the U.S. Supreme Court declined to review the decision.

28. *Norwalk Teachers Association v. Board of Education,* 138 Conn. 269; 83 A. 2d 482 (1951); 31 A.L.R. 2d 1142.

29. *See Railway Mail Association v. Murphy,* 44 N.Y.S. 2d 601 (1943); *City of New York v. Social Service Employees Union,* 266 N.Y.S. 2d 277 (1965); New York *Times,* February 6, 1968.

30. *Board of Education v. Public School Employees Union,* 45 N.W. 2d 797 (1957). On appeal the Supreme Court of Minnesota upheld the court's order but conveniently ignored the dictum concerning the right to strike, which was not essential to the decision.

31. *City of San Diego v. AFSCME, Local 127.* No written opinion was issued. Because of the widespread interest in the ruling, *Government Employee Relations Reports* reprinted the reporter's transcript in September, 1969. Subsequent California decisions have clearly held that in the

272

absence of a clear legislative grant, public employees have no right to strike.

32. *AFT v. School, City of Anderson,* supra, dissenting opinion of Chief Justice De Bruler.

33. In *Hargrove v. Town of Cocoa Beach,* 97 So. 2d 130 (1957), the Florida Supreme Court stated that to continue to endow the city with "sovereign divinity" appears "to predicate the laws of the twentieth century upon an eighteenth century anachronism." The New Hampshire Supreme Court, in *City of Manchester v. Manchester Teachers Guild,* 131 A. 2d 59, 60 (1957), reminded the legislature that collective bargaining or strike rights could be provided by statute.

34. City of Holland v. Holland Education Association, 157 N.W. 2d 206 (1968). The court held that it was insufficient to show mere prohibited action, since it was contrary to public policy in Michigan to issue injunctions in labor disputes absent a showing of violence, irreparable injury, or breach of the peace.

35. *In re Berry et al.,* 436 P. 2d 273 (1968).

36. *Government Employee Relations Reports,* No. 387 (1971) B-18.

37. See *Government Employee Relations Reports,* No. 398 (1971) F-1 and No. 408 (1971) E-1.

38. *United Federation of Postal Clerks v. Blount,* No. 70-328 (1971), 325 F. Supp. 879.

39. *Rodoff v. Anderson,* No. 71-197 (1971).

40. Felix Frankfurter and Nathan Greene, *The Labor Injunction* (New York: Macmillan, 1930); Charles O. Gregory, *Labor and the Law* (New York: Norton, 1949), pp. 95ff.

41. Frankfurter and Greene, op. cit., pp. 47-53, 105-22.

42. Douglas Routh and Richard Rous, "Strikes in the Public Service, 1960-1967," unpublished thesis, Graduate School of Public Administration, New York University, 1968, p. 108.

43. *Smith Report,* pp. 14-15.

44. New York, *Public Employees' Fair Employment Act,* Law of New York, 1967, Section 210.2

45. *Government Employee Relations Reports,* May 19, 1969.

46. *Government Employee Relations Reports,* No. 406 (1971) B-19.

47. Letter to Luther C. Steward, August 16, 1937

48. Cahen, "Les Fonctionnaires," quoted in Godine, op. cit., p. 164.

49. Carl J. Friedrich and Taylor Cole, *Responsible Bureaucracy* (Cambridge: Harvard University Press, 1932), p. 86.

50. With the notable exception of Mayor James H. Tate of Philadelphia, most mayors have emulated the Roosevelt stance. Mayor Tate suggested that the existing policy was a "double standard" and noted the "evil irony" in a viewpoint which insists that those who dare disrupt the smallest routines of public service to seek parity as first-class citizens are criminals: "They see the naked form of second-class citizenship through a swindle clad as law." Address, Federal Bar Association Conference, March 28, 1968.

51. See *Taylor Committee,* p. 82; *Illinois Report,* p. 27; *Smith Report,* p. 13; *Governors Conference Task Force Report,* Part I, p. 5 and Part II, pp. 36-49; and *ACIR Report,* Recommendation 2.

52. *Report and Recommendations of the Governor's Commission to Revise the Public Employee Law of Pennsylvania,* Harrisburg, June, 1968, Recommendation No. 4.
53. *Governor's Task Force on Public Employee Labor Relations,* Maryland, Recommendation No. 13, 1969.
54. *Collective Bargaining in American Government,* Report of the Fortieth American Assembly, Columbia University, New York, October 28-31, 1971, pp. 6-7.
55. Address before Chicago Bar Association, March 25, 1971, reprinted by Bureau of National Affairs, Washington, D.C., April, 1971.

11   Resolution of Impasses

Unit determination, representation rights, recognition, unfair labor practices, grievances, the negotiation of original or new collective bargaining agreements—anyone of these issues may result in an impasse, a deadlock between the parties. Diverse issues, such as representation, the interpretation and implementation of existing contract provisions, and the substantive provisions of a new contract, require different machinery and procedures to settle the impasse.

In each instance the basic question is how to forestall a strike or, if a strike occurs, how to restore services by achieving agreement between the parties. All steps taken must be directed toward the twin goals of fair treatment of employees and the upholding of the public interest. What course of action to pursue when an impasse occurs is, therefore, a crucial issue. We are here concerned with deadlocks that occur while negotiating a contract.

Several time-honored courses of action—mediation, fact finding, advisory or binding arbitration—tried in private labor disputes have also been attempted in municipal labor disputes. Variations of these—"mediation to finality," "mediation from initiation," compulsory arbitration, labor courts, "the last best offer," and other methods—have been suggested as alternatives. In each case the ultimate objective is the achievement of a contract that the parties can live with in a semblance of harmony by some form of third party intervention.

The Mediation Process

Mediation involves introducing a third party, often a professional, into an impasse. A mediator or panel of mediators attempts to bring about an agreement voluntarily acceptable to both parties. The purpose is not to introduce a foreign element into the bargaining process or to displace direct bargaining but to encourage and facilitate it. Mediation's primary aim is to seek an agreement by guiding the negotiations along a path that will allow both sides to save face and come out feeling like a winner.

The Mediator

A mediator, as a neutral, diligently seeks to bring the parties together to find a common ground on which they can both stand. He may be called in before an impasse develops or when direct bargaining has failed. If called in before a deadlock, he tries to help facilitate an agreement. The process becomes one of stimulation rather than substitution. When bargaining has broken down, his objective is to restore communication. Usually, he is totally without legal power. He cannot dictate but only suggest and advise. Therefore, tolerance, skill, and coolness under fire are essential qualities for the successful mediator.

Mediators are generally available upon the request of the bargainers in a number of highly industrialized states, such as California, Connecticut, Michigan, Minnesota, New Jersey, New York, Oregon, Pennsylvania, Rhode Island, and Wisconsin, which have established boards staffed with full-time personnel. A few states have provided mediation services for decades, Massachusetts having set up its board as early as 1886. Professional organizations also provide mediators upon request, and in some major cities local agencies have assembled panels of mediators.

The Mediator in Action

The methods utilized by a mediator vary with the issues, organizations, and personalities involved and ranging from persuasion to pressure. His objective is to achieve agreement rather than to concentrate on a fair and equitable award according to the merits of the dispute or even his personal perception of the issues.

276

His role varies as circumstances dictate. Whether the situation calls for a conciliator, counselor, teacher, director, moderator, or buffer or an analyst to sort out and frame core issues, the mediator cannot compel agreement but can only assist. He may cajole, advise, suggest, and, it is to be hoped, persuade.

Some mediators, in practice, have "twisted a few arms" in the process, but acting like a good "con man" is extraneous to the fact that he is a neutral presence attempting to bring about an agreement that is fully understood and freely accepted by both parties. Otherwise, the "settlement" will continue controversy rather than achieve labor peace.

Regardless of his methods, the mediator must command the respect and confidence of the bargainers. Meeting separately with each side, the adept mediator is able to challenge rigid and un-compromising positions. He is able to say and be told things that cannot be said or admitted at the bargaining table. A good mediator unswervingly follows what has been popularly referred to as Kheel's First Commandment: "Thou shalt not disclose the bargaining positions or make public proposals to solve the dispute." Only under such conditions of trust and confidence would the bargainers be willing to state candidly how far they would move from their prior, publicly stated positions. Therefore, the effectiveness of an individual mediator has a direct relationship to his ability to determine, to some degree, how the critical issues are viewed by each side. In some instances the public stands of the parties conceal the real issues, and the mediator may be able to inject proposals or alternatives to get one or both sides "off the hook."

The initial mediation sessions involve a presentation of the positions of the parties, with the mediator attempting at some point to achieve a clarification of the issues. Subsequently separate caucuses may be held, with the mediator serving as the communications link. In these separate sessions the mediator can utilize his knowledge to deflate extreme positions, play the role of sympathizer, or initiate moves toward joint sessions when he believes progress can be made. His objective remains to maximize bargaining by the parties.

It is when the mediator meets jointly with the parties that his baptism of fire is most acute, because misunderstandings, personality conflicts, and external pressures add to already complicated substantive issues. Ostensibly, direct bargaining had brought the parties to a situation where they could not yield one more inch. This is the primary reason some mediators do not generally meet with both sides in plenary session during the early stages of the process.

The mediator may or may not have induced enough flexibility to impel the parties to a settlement. Since the parties engage in a game of bluff and bluster publicly while the real negotiations are being carried on in private, the mediator must be most careful in his statements to the ubiquitous news media carefully following the progress of negotiations. Nothing should be said that would tend to exacerbate already tense and inflammatory bargaining. On occasion, his measured tones will convey the picture of a grave situation, which may or may not be part of the bargaining script. Aware of the course of negotiations, the mediator may be preparing the public for what management will eventually do or bolstering the chances of membership ratification of the position the union will adopt. If necessary to achieve agreement, the mediator may offer himself as the "sacrificial lamb"; in other cases, mediators will withdraw—for they have egos too.

At some point the mediator and the parties, having explored a wide variety of possible solutions, will either conclude an agreement or reach a deadlock. It is then decided whether additional steps are needed to resolve the remaining issues on which the parties cannot agree.

"Mediation to Finality" and "Mediation from Initiation"

The usual form of mediation has often failed to achieve results. This has led to suggestions for variations of the process many believe to be essential to the retention of free collective bargaining. One proposal has been described as "meditation to finality." In essence, additional mediators or a new panel of mediators are called in, and they take over and stick with the problem until it becomes apparent that the positions have hardened and a settlement must be imposed by a form of third-party intervention. In most cases the tendency is to adopt or substantially follow the proposed settlement of the mediators. It might be argued that where the same individuals who are involved as mediators finally "decide," the initial mediative role was unnecessarily complicated. However, during mediation, theoretically the parties make the decisions.

Another suggestion has been that the mediator should be present at the onset of bargaining rather than being called in only when an impasse develops.[1] Professor J. H. Foegen recommends that by mutual consent the independent third party would potentially play three different and sequential roles: monitor, mediator, and arbitrator.

Essentially, observing the procedure from the beginning allows the neutral party to get a "feel" for the situation, and alleviates objections of both parties to outsiders who come in on short notice, hand down a determination, and leave the parties to live with the agreement. There remains, of course, the difficult problem of deciding the precise moment when the third party should shift roles, not to mention the distinct possibility that his mediative role would be hampered when the parties knew in advance that the "mediator" could compel an agreement as arbitrator.

Mediation in the Public Service: An Evaluation

Mediation remains the most common, most flexible, and most successful form of third-party intervention in labor disputes. Although meaningful statistics are not available, Chairman R. Stutz of the Connecticut Board of Mediation and Arbitration stated in 1969 that over 50 percent of the impasses referred to state boards in Wisconsin, New York, and Connecticut were resolved by mediation.

Statistics are highly persuasive in attesting to the success of mediative efforts. Stutz's study indicated that mediation (which sometimes evolved into fact finding) resulted stoppages in only 1.3 percent of the more than 15,700 negotiations in the public service.[2] Nevertheless, the present emphasis on mediation and fact finding may not suffice to cope with the increasing number of negotiations that will take place in small cities unaccustomed to collective negotiations. Even the number of current negotiations have taxed the supply of competent neutrals.

New York City's Office of Collective Bargaining noted that during 1968 mediation produced contract settlements covering thousands of employees in a great variety of jobs: detectives, market inspectors, park attendants, nurses, and medical interns and residents. A strike by city lifeguards was averted on Fourth of July eve, after round-the-clock mediation. Agreement was reached with nurses after all-night mediation, and mediation efforts averted a slowdown by firemen and fire officers. Settlement was reached between the City Housing Authority and a union representing 5,800 employees after 33 hours of continuous mediation. Perhaps the most significant success was the city-wide agreement on pensions and other nonsalary items covering 120,000 employees reached after 18 mediation sessions.

The transit negotiations in New York City for years exemplified the successful use of mediation in the public service. As each round of negotiations built up to a crisis, the well-known labor mediator Theodore Kheel waited in the wings for his entrance at the proper psychological moment. Both Mayor Wagner and President Quill of the Transport Workers Union regarded Kheel as the "savior" who would prevent the strike.

Before Mayor-elect Lindsay assumed office, the transit negotiations of 1965 were underway, and the outgoing Mayor Wagner asked Lindsay to enter the negotiations. Wagner, as well as Quill, had wanted to secure the services of Kheel as the mediator. The Mayor-elect denounced "power brokers," and hesitated to seek Kheel's services, insisting that the parties to the negotiations were the Transit Authority and the TWU.

Since Kheel did not appear acceptable, Wagner requested Lindsay to draw up a list of negotiators, and Kheel was not on the list. Quill promptly threatened a strike in advance of the deadline, in an obvious ploy to get Kheel into the negotiations. As a compromise, Lindsay agreed to a three-man panel including Kheel, who, after the snub, was reluctant to join in the talks. His belated entrance, was, in part, the cause of the 13-day transit strike, which started five hours after the new Mayor took office. When the 1967 transit negotiations began, the Mayor approached Kheel early, and once again Kheel's mediative efforts saved New Yorkers from a New Year's Day strike.

In each major city a few mediators hold the enviable position of being called in to mediate the major disputes. Some unions appear to be drawn to particular mediators whom they feel will give labor its "fair shake."

Mediation succeeds best when the mediator is acceptable to both parties as a father figure whose credentials of neutrality are unimpeachable. This is seen in cases where an outstanding mediator is called in to resolve the irresolvable. It would take the mediator considerable time to study the dispute, which has raged bitterly, yet a settlement may be quickly achieved. It seems sensible, therefore, to conclude that, rather than magical intervention, the parties want a settlement. A mediator is needed to "save face" and put his stamp of approval on the settlement.

There have been few attempts to identify effective mediators.[3] The task of the mediator varies from situation to situation; there is no typical case; scientific standards are difficult to establish and even more difficult to apply in concrete instances. Nevertheless, McClellan and Obermeyer have recently suggested three performance criteria: the identification of individual mediators' stature within the profession, the analysis of work stoppages, and the extent of professional involvement. After an evaluation of ten standards, they concluded that there exists an "informal system of ranking" and that the process of mediation may still be more art than science. As indicated, the search for an ideal mediator may be an endless journey, with the ideal mediator being "several men."

Mediation is a flexible tool to resolve impasses. Even when mediation has not accomplished agreement, it still may have served a useful purpose. It remains an effective technique to reconcile conflict, when carried out by a skilled, respected, and knowledgeable individual.

Mediators in public sector disputes operate under restraints not operative in private industrial conflicts. Their effectiveness is partially impaired because the pressure leverage of a strike is theoretically absent. Furthermore, the parties are aware that they may have the legal right to resort to fact finding and, in some cases, arbitration. For example, in 1970 an AFSCME police affiliate in Marquette, Mich., exercised its right to binding arbitration within four days of the onset of mediation.

Still other factors militate against effective mediation. City-state relationships, legislative-executive competition, and budgeting restraints complicated by state aid or federal grants-in-aid all present problems evolving out of a highly political and legal context. Whether it is successful or not at the outset, mediation is a pervasive as well as a persuasive process, academic distinctions notwithstanding. The reality is that there is a tenuous line between mediation and the fact-finding process, which is often the next step taken to resolve public employment disputes.

The Fact-Finding Process

For any number of reasons, mediation efforts may fail to bring about an agreement. With positions hardened and sometimes a virtual halt in negotiations, one or both parties may request fact finding; or this may be the next form of third-party intervention required by law. New York's Taylor Act mandates a specific timetable to resolve impasses. Wisconsin, Michigan, Massachusetts and other states also provide for fact-finding at various stages of negotiation.

Fact finding is an attempt to discover the "true facts" in a labor dispute or to clarify the facts in order to generate adequate public pressure and thus compel the parties to end the dispute. Fact finding may or may not be accompanied by recommendations, and no decisions are imposed on the contending parties. In some cases fact finders first present their findings privately to the deadlocked parties; in other instances the law requires that the findings and recommendations be made public within a stipulated period of time.

Fact Finding and Mediation: A Tenuous Distinction

The line between mediation and fact finding is tenuous. In each case a neutral third party is involved. Both adopt "acceptablity" as the standard by which the settlement is judged; and neither mediation nor fact finding results in a final decision unless, in the latter case, the parties agree in advance to accept the recommendations of the fact finders.

Despite the reality that both mediators and fact finders are interested in sorting out the facts and issues, there is a considerable difference in the tone and character of the proceedings. The mediator has much more flexibility in "hearing the facts" or viewpoints of both parties in private sessions. While the degree of formality that occurs in fact finding is determined by the fact finders and the participants, the process is adversary and semijudicial in nature, in contrast to mediation, where the goal is to get the parties to agree without the trappings of formalized procedures.

In some states, for example, Wisconsin and Michigan, fact finding has become an elaborate quasi-judicial procedure. Testimony is given, written briefs may be submitted, oral argument and rebuttal are permitted, and the fact finders hand down signed reports resembling judicial opinions in style and tone. Fact finders are not necessarily limited to the "evidence" presented but may take "judicial notice" of extra-record information.

Fact finding has gained rapid acceptance as a technique to resolve public service impasses, with some states even underwriting the costs of the fact finding. William E. Simkin has argued that mediation is preferable to fact finding, since the objective of bargaining is agreement and agreements are often consummated in spite of the facts.

> The words—fact finding—conjure up notions of preciseness, of objectivity, of virtue. They even have a Godlike quality. Who can disagree with facts?
>
> In contrast, the word—mediation—that I do espouse, tends to have an aura of compromise, of slipperiness, of furtiveness.
>
> Since these are frequent impressions, why prefer the vulgar to the sublime?

The actual functioning of fact finders and mediators indicates that the labels are ancillary to the issues, the parties, and the individuals named as fact finders or mediators. As Simkin indicated, facts can be a potent weapon in the hands of a skilled mediator. Conversely, successful fact finders have mediated, sometimes deliberately and at other times instructively or surreptitiously.

The Fact-Finding Game

Finding the facts is not as antiseptic or easy as would appear. There is inevitably a tendency for each side to present only those facts favorable to it. If the issues involved are complex, the plethora of facts produced may well overwhelm the fact finders. Furthermore, the statistical evidence produced by one side is inexorably controverted by statistics elicited from the other side. And all the facts are presented in a judicial atmosphere wafted about by political breezes from the outside.

Theodore Kheel, with candor, has explained some of the difficulties of the process:

> There is a tendency, and it is very prevalent under the Railway Labor Act, for the fact-finders and recommenders to act in such a proceeding exactly as if they were arbitrators. A record is made, millions of exhibits are put in, a transcript is kept.
>
> My experience with the boards under the Railway Labor Act on which I have served is that, if I were able or if I undertook to read all the materials that were submitted, I would have absolutely no time to come to a decision. Indeed, it is impossible to read all the material submitted, which leads me to the conclusion that what is intended by fact-finding is the recommendations, which are the important part— not the facts, which should not be in conflict. My experience is that, as a result this is a kind of a game called "fact-finding."
>
> The parties undertake to hide the facts and the fact finders are given thirty days to try to find them. If you are good, you may be able to find them. If you are not, they will be lost perhaps forever. One thing is sure, the facts will not be in the record. You can't find them in the record and, to the extent that you proceed as if this were a judicial proceeding, your chances of finding the facts are, to that extent, diminished.[6]

The fact is that the "facts" are selected and slanted to gain a favored position with the fact finders. Each side alleges its facts to be the true facts. It becomes a partisan game, with the reality being that the union position may well be, "Who gives a damn about the facts; we must bring home the bacon to our membership." One union leader stated, "You are holding things back so that the fact finders can find leeway to make his decision." Another indicated his impatience with facts by stating, "You can spend an eternity in this procedure." The facts, sometimes obscure and generally entangled in the political thicket, are the means to an end.

The Issue of Public Recommendations

There are two principal types of fact finding: with and without recommendations. A more controversial question is whether the recommendations should be made public. Some statutes require that the facts and/or recommendations be made public if the dispute is not resolved within a stipulated period of time.

The purpose of fact finding is to generate public pressure for a settlement based on the facts. Public pressure, of course, could hardly be effective unless the facts are made public. The Taylor Committee reasoned that such reports provide a basis "to inform and crystallize thoughtful public opinion and news media comment,"[7] and the Committee believed that the public had a special right to be informed on the issues, contentions, and merits of disputes involving public employees. Moreover, a prime advantage of fact finding is that unsubstantiated or extreme demands tend to lose their force and status in this forum.

Study commissions in Michigan and Illinois also visualized public opinion as a focal point in the fact finding process. The Michigan commission suggested that recommendations be made public if the dispute remained unsettled within a stipulated period but urged prior mediation efforts by the fact finders, including the making of private and tentative recommendations to the parties.[8] The Illinois Commission urged a rigid time schedule, noting that "such publicity may be especially effective in the public sector, since the availability of funds will usually depend on legislative action with respect to such matters as budgets and taxation."[9]

Undoubtedly, the fact that the parties are obligated to react to proposals encourages them to scrutinize their prior positions and operates as a supplement to existing political pressures and possibly tips the balance of forces one way or the other. A more realistic appraisal, however, is that the public often has neither the time not the capacity to evaluate effectively the merits of a fact finding report where complex issues are involved. Certainly, the premature or automatic release of tentative findings and recommendations would tend to harden positions and increase the possibility of a strike.

Both labor leaders and administrators interviewed suggested that most labor disputes were so complicated that a mere portrayal of the facts as found was of little value, one labor leader contending that "the public couldn't care less." Therefore, the mere publication of facts is of primary value to opinion-makers such as editorialists, columnists, and radio and television commentators.

Neither side is legally compelled to accept the findings or conclusions as presented. In one case, the inflexibility of the mandate requiring public release of recommendations raised the hackles of Theodore Kheel to such an extent that he protested that "fact finding with an obligation to make public recommendations was the most difficult and dangerous kind of third-party procedure."[10] When requested to help resolve the impasse in transit negotiations,

Kheel made it a condition that he not be bound by procedures as public recommendations, which constitute a mild form of compulsion.

During the 1967 New York City teachers' strike, a fact-finding panel chaired by Archibald Cox publicly announced recommendations without giving the United Federation of Teachers an opportunity to study the proposals. Chances for resolution of the dispute were thus lessened. Not only did the UFT summarily reject the panel's findings as "a rotten offer," but it castigated the Cox panel as "stooges for the Mayor."

Fact finding without recommendations has been described as "an exercise in futility." Simkin has pointed out the dangers in assuming that recommendations flow automatically out of the facts as found. Indeed, the recommendations are not facts and may not even be primarily based on the facts, particularly where highly emotional issues, personality conflicts, or a serious imbalance of power is involved.

Aside from the general issue of recommendations, the mandating of public issuance is a sticky and dangerous procedure, bringing fact finding close to de facto advisory arbitration.

Experience with Fact Finding in Public Employment

In contrast to the private sector, the public sector had limited experience with fact finding prior to 1960's. But, by 1966, 14 states had adopted statutes providing for findings of fact and nonbinding recommendations for some of their public employees.[11] Some states provided general coverage, and in other states there was special coverage for particular occupational groups. Since 1966 the several states that have passed statutes applicable to public employees have provided for fact-finding procedures. Connecticut, Massachusetts, Michigan, Minnesota, Nebraska, New York, Vermont, and Wisconsin have all made fairly extensive use of this form of third-party intervention.

James L. Stern concluded, after a study of fact finding in Wisconsin, that it has made a substantial contribution to the improvement of collective bargaining among public employees.[12] He stated that it had become the preferred procedure for settling impasses in the public sphere. Acceptance of fact finding depends on a number of factors, including the power of the union, the quality of the panel, agreement between the parties as to the composition of the panel, the manner in which the process is implemented, the rendering of equitable and reasoned proposals, the attitude of the new media, and the political and social environment in which the panel carries out its work. [13]

The Stern study revealed that during the first three years that the Wisconsin statute was in operation, 73 petitions for fact finding were filed. Thirty-five of the petitions were settled at informal hearings, and only 28 went to actual fact finding, the remainder being dismissed. Over 70 percent of the reports served as the basis of settlement. The high percentage of acceptance justified Stern's conclusion that "political pressures may offer an effective substitute for the conventional economic pressures in securing acceptance of positions arrived at by collective bargaining procedures." The greatest weakness, however, was that the likelihood of acceptance by the city depended heavily on the political influence of the labor union involved in the dispute.

New York's experience with fact finding, under the Taylor Law, is not as extensive as Wisconsin's. An examination of the first year's operation of the Law showed heavy reliance on fact finding by school districts. Two reasons account for this. The time factor motivated many parties to bypass mediation in order to meet budget deadlines; and the inexperience of the parties had created difficulties in formulating positions and achieving solutions during the first round of bargaining under the statute. [14]

In the first nine months of the statute's operation, approximately 284 disputes were brought before the Public Employment Relations Board. Settlements were achieved in 157 cases. Mediation achieved favorable results in 85 cases; fact finding was the settlement process in 63 cases. Of the open cases, 58 were in mediation and 69 were in fact finding.

In March 1972 PERB reported that over the four-year span 1968-1971 an increased number of cases went directly to fact finding (bypassing mediation) but that fact finders frequently mediated disputes without the necessity of issuing a fact-finding report. This occurred in 23.6 percent of the impasses that went to fact finding. PERB also noted that the parties made increased use of the fact-finding report as "a guide rather than a blueprint." Thus, in 46.5 percent of the cases that went to fact finding, where a report was issued the report was modified by the parties through further negotiations. In short, of the 385 cases that went to fact finding during the four-year period, 23 percent were settled by "mediation" during fact finding, 30 percent accepted the reports, and 47 per cent modified the report before settling.

A recent study of the fact-finding procedures in New York and Wisconsin also concluded that fact finding was successful in resolving disputes; in over 90 percent of the impasses in which recommendations were written, agreements resulted.[16]

Fact Finding: An Evaluation

Unquestionably, fact finding is a useful tool as a supplement to mediation. There are potential advantages for unions as well as management in the process. In the view of Sam Zagoria, former member of the National Labor Relations Board, strengthening fact finding, is a more attractive alternative that others that have been suggested, because it puts emphasis "on cold facts rather than hot tempers," and brings "the public, which consumes the services and pays the bills, into the bargaining picture with a chance to achieve fair play." It helps the administrator convince the budgetmaker and the legislature that "he did not lose his head; he used it."[17] For the public to gauge the fairness of the demands and settlements and to exert pressure, some such type of procedure may be advisable in many cases, whether or not public opinion was able to influence the settlement.

William R. Word indicated that one or both parties rejected the fact-finding recommendations in 39 percent of the cases studied; the fact finders in Wisconsin and New York expressed uncertainty about the adequacy of the process; and that more of the employee groups surveyed preferred compulsory arbitration to fact finding.[18] This indicates a lack of the needed element of finality in fact finding, especially where the protective services are involved.

In sum, to view fact finding as a simon-pure, objective, reasoned process is to ignore reality. Fact finders operate in a political environment, and the practical problem remains how to find out "who is lying the most" in order to get some "icing on the cake." Fact finding may hinder or bolster the collective bargaining process, depending on a variety of factors for success. The evidence to date militates against rigid statutory prescriptions as to its use, especially with regard to the necessity of issuing public recommendations according to a statutory timetable. The major exception would be in the case of stoppages creating an immediate or imminent peril to the public safety.

Compulsory Arbitration

Compulsory arbitration as a means to resolve impasses has been the bete noire of both unions and public officials. Few issues, excepting the right to strike, have aroused more controversy or sparked more polemics in the field of labor relations. Yet, discussion of this subject has been marked by far too much mythology and far too few facts.

The Process

Simply stated, compulsory arbitration is the legally mandated submission of a dispute for resolution by a third party, resulting in a final and binding determination of the issues. It is distinguished from voluntary arbitration in that external legal compulsion is involved, requiring submission of the dispute irrespective of the will of the parties. Unlike advisory arbitration, the award by the arbitrators is usually legally binding upon both parties.

Arbitration, like fact finding, is basically quasi-judicial in nature. Each party presents oral evidence and submits exhibits and briefs in support of its position. The arbitrators or arbitration panel then renders an "award," much as a judge hands down an order or judgment at the conclusion of a trial.

In fact finding, the basic thrust is toward researching the facts and presenting to the parties, and in some cases the public, recommendations that the parties are free to accept or reject. Furthermore, the prime standard by which fact finders are theoretically guided is "acceptability of the recommendations." In the case of arbitration, the process is a *de novo* decision-making process, in which the "equity" of the claims is the basic issue before the arbitrator, who reaches a "just" and "correct" award.

But is one obliged to visualize compulsory arbitration in exactly this form? The usual response is that there are clear-cut distinctions between mediation, fact-finding, and the various types of arbitration—and that the distinctions are more than a matter of semantics. In practice, it is unusual for the process to operate in the juristic sense of a *de novo* examination of an impasse in a sterile atmosphere. Experienced and skilled arbitrators, during interviews, conceded that they were aware that any awards granted must be attuned to reality. Arbitrators strain to achieve a decision that both parties can live with, if not applaud.

The third party appreciates the fact that far more is involved than technical wage determination or even specific policy issues and will do his utmost not to alienate the permanent relationship that must continue with a reasonable degree of harmony after the decision in rendered. There must be a mutual satisfaction of needs by persons whose capacities supplement each other. In weighing the "justice" of an award, arbitrators will seek a bond that will hold the conflicting parts in some approximation of harmonious union. Since the decision must be capable of enforcement, arbitrators of course, aware of the political winds. Arbitrators are expected to demonstrate the wisdom of a Solomon, but they can hardly avoid abuse—feigned and real—from both sides.

The form of the "abuse" may be subtle. Arvid Anderson has described one form of pressure exerted on third-party neutrals:

> ... all too often they have come before a neutral and said, in effect, "Our hearts are pure. Our cause is just. You have been mutually selected and mutually paid by the parties. We know you'd like to serve again—do right! Do right by the employees or do right in view of the fiscal plight of the public employer. [19]

Furthermore, the words "final determination" cannot be taken literally. No third-party decision, by definition, can be superior to the sovereign authority of the people to override even the actions of a legislature. Legislatures, obviously, can amend or repeal statutes; third-party decisions that flagrantly and irresponsibly ignore a carefully defined role prescribed by statute are obviously subject to the same judicial check as are the actions of other public officials.

In sum, theoretical distinctions should not obscure the reality that there are "mediative" and fact-finding elements present in the process of arbitration.

Applicability to the Public Sector: Early Decisions

Many vigorous supporters of arbitration for the settlement of labor disputes in private enterprise question the applicability of the process in the public service as an abdication of the sovereign's prerogative. Numerous court decisions and the opinions of city and state attorneys have held that compulsory, binding arbitration constitutes an illegal delegation of authority vested by law in public officials. The law forbids submitting to arbitration any matter entrusted to their discretion, and they cannot bargain away authority confided in them by law or consent to arrangements contravening their authority.

Early judicial decisions were pointedly clear on the legal issues involved. In *Mann v. Richardson* the Illinois Supreme Court in 1873 flatly rejected arbitration, stating, "Where the law imposes a personal duty upon an officer in relation to a matter of public interest, he cannot delegate it to others, and therefore such officer cannot submit such matters to arbitration. [20] Almost 75 years later a Baltimore Circuit Court added: ". . . the authority of municipal officers may not be diminished or impaired by agreement to arbitration or by any other device."[21]

An even broader condemnation of arbitration was enunciated by an Ohio court in 1948, when it expressed the view that "no state has adopted laws applying the principle of compulsory arbitration to contracts such as we are considering here." The court went on, "In view of the overwhelming weight of authority, the court holds that, assuming the Board has power to enter into a contract with a union or association of employees, a provision for compulsory arbitration would be illegal."[22]

The Attorney General of Minnesota and the city attorneys of Bloomington, Ind., and Miami, Fla., took a similar position and held that the submission of disagreements between labor unions and public agencies was an illegal surrender of public power to a private group.[23]

But undue emphasis may have been placed in these earlier Detroit, and Tennessee Valley Authority and Canadian municipalities, reported, "In fact, voluntary arbitration has been the recourse in some governmental units . . ."[24] The report indicated that despite the legal questions involved in arbitration, many municipalities and unions have voluntarily agreed to accept arbitration awards as final and binding.

A 1951 Connecticut Supreme Court decision departed somewhat from the generally prevailing judicial attitude toward arbitration when it ruled that "arbitration may be a permissible method as to certain specific arbitrable disputes."[25] The decision was limited, however, with the court noting that the Board of Education had entered into a contract to arbitrate a specific dispute and had reserved the privilege of deciding whether it would arbitrate other questions within its power. The court ruled that any general agreement to arbitrate "all disputes" might constitute a surrender of the broad discretion and responsibility reposed in the agency by law and that the agency's "power to submit to arbitration would not extend to questions of policy." It reasoned that the government was exercising its sovereign power, rather than giving it up, in deciding to agree voluntarily to arbitration.

A 1954 Minnesota Supreme Court decision upheld a statute requiring compulsory arbitration of unsettled disputes involving maximum hours of work and minimum wage rates for "charitable hospitals," including within this definition all state, county, and municipal hospitals. The court rejected the union's claims that the statute constituted an illegal delegation of power, that it was vague and indefinite, and that it denied due process and the equal protection of the law. Reasoning that the compulsory arbitration provision limited the bargaining power of both parties and that the statute provided basic policy and rules of action to guide the arbitrators' exercise of power, the court rejected the contentions of the union. [26]

The question remains whether it would be legal to submit *all* matters involving contract negotiations to arbitration. The Task Force Report on Employee Management in the Federal Service in 1962 stressed that the final authority and responsibility of agency heads for their operations should not be undermined. The Taylor Committee in New York in 1967 rejected compulsory arbitration, stating, "There is serious doubt whether it would be legal because of the obligation of the designated executive heads of government departments not to delegate certain fiscal and other duties." [27]

Kheel has also suggested some legal obstacles to compulsory arbitration. At the 1968 Industrial and Labor Relations Conference, held under the sponsorship of Cornell University, he observed, "It cannot be that such an agency, so empowered by the legislature, can delegate its responsibilities for running the system to some third party. . . .It may well be that such delegation. . . .may be provided with regard to financial matters, but I have reservations about that." [28] Mr. Kheel was making the point that school board negotiations embrace a variety of matters, such as educational programs, class size, and other policy matters legally vested in the Board of Education.

The Taylor Committee also had legal doubts about "compulsion." The Committee concluded:

> There is serious doubt whether [compulsory arbitration] would be legal because of the obligation of designated executive heads of government departments or agencies not to delegate certain fiscal and other duties. No particular legal obstacle, however, stands in the way of the use of voluntary arbitration on an ad hoc basic, which the Committee termed a "desirable course" . . . although it also leads to binding decisions. [29]

George Taylor added, "What happens, if the legislative body won't provide the funds?"

Recent State Legislation and Court Decisions

Several states have mandated compulsory arbitration as the final stage in resolving impasses in disputes involving firemen and/or police. Rhode Island, Missouri, Pennsylvania, Maine, Nebraska,

Michigan, South Dakota, Vermont, and Wyoming are currently testing such procedures. Additional states have taken steps toward compulsory arbitration. Oklahoma in 1970 enacted a statute that required arbitration but did not make the award binding unless accepted by the employer. Georgia in 1971 authorized cities over 20,000 population to adopt advisory arbitration procedures. Both Denver and Los Angeles took action the same year to implement a measure of arbitration of police and fire disputes. In 1971 New York State amended its Taylor Law to legalize voluntary arbitration of collective bargaining impasses. In addition, the Public Employee Relations Act of Pennsylvania in 1968, covering employees other than firemen and police, did not provide for compulsory arbitration of all disputes that involved establishing the terms and conditions of employment not previously settled by fact finding but suggested voluntary arbitration.

The basic legal arguments against binding arbitration are that the legislative power and administrative discretion delegated to public officials cannot be surrendered to outsiders and that final and binding arbitration contravenes essential elements of the doctrine of sovereignty.

A significant recent decision on this precise point is the *Warwick* ruling handed down in 1969 by the Supreme Court of Rhode Island upholding the Firefighters Arbitration Act. The ruling bluntly stated, "A majority decision of the arbitrators shall be binding upon both the bargaining agent and the corporate authorities." The lower court had specifically ruled that the pertinent statutory provisions constituted an invalid delegation by failing to provide sufficient standards and an attempt to delegate a portion of the legislative power to private persons.

The appellate court reversed the judgment and held that "the standards clearly are sufficient to meet the constitutional requirement that the delegated power be confined by reasonable norms or standards." On the second issue, that of delegation of legislative power to private persons, the court ruled that "an arbitrator appointed under the pertinent provisions. . . is a public officer and that collectively the three constitute a public board or agency."[30]

The importance of the *Warwick* case lies more in the rationale for the decision. Indeed, the philosophical base of the decision was that the state legislature made a policy decision to entrust part of the legislative authority to arbitrators in order to make its statutory will operative. Nevertheless, safeguards retained all the essential elements of sovereignty, since the delegation was not unconditional. There were expressly defined channels, and such agencies operate as agents subject to judicial check against "irresponsible action." Thus, compulsory arbitration was upheld, but the "sovereign right to override" remained intact.

Other recent cases in state jurisdictions also support the legality of binding arbitration. In 1968 the New Hampshire Supreme Court upheld a clause providing for a decision that would be final and binding on the parties as not an unlawful delegation of the city's authority to control the police department.[31]

Perhaps the most significant recent case, aside from the *Warwick* decision discussed above, is the *City of Washington* decision of the Supreme Court of Pennsylvania.[32] The city appealed from an award stemming from binding arbitration between the city and its policemen. The Pennsylvania statute attempted to curb appeals to the court from arbitration awards. The court agreed that a public employer may not hide behind self-imposed legal restrictions and that an arbitration award that dealt only with proper terms and conditions of employment served as a mandate requiring affirmative action on the part of the legislature, if within its power.

Thus, the opinion of the court supported the aims and purposes of the statute, which was not struck down on the grounds of an illegal delegation of authority. The court, however, indicated its readiness to hear appeals on "review of jurisdiction, regularity of proceedings, excess in exercise of powers, and constitutional questions." The court then proceeded to modify the arbitration award to exclude the requirement that the city pay premiums on hospitalization insurance covering persons other than employees—in this instance members of the families of employees. The significance of the case is that the courts remain as an effective check on the scope of issues submitted to arbitrators, since the courts decide the meaning of "legitimate terms and conditions of employment."

Some jurisdictions continue to resist binding arbitration—even of employee grievances—as exemplified in an opinion of the Los Angeles City Attorney in 1971. The ruling asserted that the proposed arbitration ordinance would constitute an unlawful delegation of the authority vested in local officials under state law. Similarly, a 1971 opinion of a Superior Court in Indiana decided that until the state legislature further delineated the powers of state and local employees to engage in collective bargaining in the classical sense, the School Board of Gary, Indiana was without authority to enter into an agreement to provide for binding arbitration, compulsory or voluntary, in grievance procedures.

The legal challenges have also extended to specific aspects of arbitration awards, even where a statute exists providing for arbitration of contract disputes. In 1971 Allegheny County, in Pennsylvania, contested an award that included an agency shop provision and raised the possible illegality of the binding arbitration of firemen's grievances. In this instance the county commissioners voted to submit the two contested points of the award for reconsideration by the arbitration panel.

To all intents and purposes, however, the legal validity of compulsory arbitration is increasingly accepted, even by those who oppose its routine use on the grounds that arbitrators have no power to bind the decision-making prerogatives of the sovereign. Despite Kheel's "reservations" expressed above, he unequivocally stated in the *Travia Report*: "Recent experience indicates that where the issues are carefully framed and authority delegated explicitly, arbitration is feasible and permissible . . . Arbitration properly constructed is then a lawful technique for resolving disputes. [34]

In August 1969 New York's Mayor Lindsay called for new legislation to authorize the city's Office of Collective Bargaining to make "final and binding" decisions if mediation and fact finding failed to resolve contract disputes. Two years passed before the City Council granted the Mayor's request. Notably, Victor Gotbaum, Executive Director of AFSCME District Council 37 had stated that he "reluctantly supported" the Mayor's proposal. [35] The reported statement of the AFSCME leader was a major departure from AFSCME's view on arbitration, which has been illustrative of the labor movement's desire to emphasize the voluntary element rather than the compulsory:

> We believe there is a place for arbitration of disputes, but that place is the voluntary use of such procedures to settle disputes over the meaning or the application of the provisions of an existing collective bargaining agreement or in the final settlement of grievances which may arise under the terms of an agreement. [36]

Approximately five years after the issuance of the AFSCME policy statement in 1966, the union's President, Jerry Wurf, discussed compulsory arbitration at the Secretary of Labor's Conference on State and Local Government Relations, held in Washington. Wurf said in part:

> The position of most employers is clear. You say there should be no right to strike. Many agree with you. We are concerned about compulsory arbitration. Many think that it will be a simple and easy way to solve the problems in the public sector, although many employers have clearly said they prefer the right to strike to compulsory arbitration. Some day the unions might horrify you by lobbying for

compulsory arbitration . . . The public is inclined toward compulsory arbitration. It appears an easy way of eliminating strikes as long as we cannot agree on appropriate impasse procedures. The public may be totally justified in demanding a third-party neutral. Let me add that in spite of our concern about compulsory arbitration we have been impressed by the awards it has produced for employees and hostility it has brought from employers.

In the light of Wurf's remarks, it is interesting to note that in Quebec the awards of arbitrators under compulsory arbitration had become so extravagant that the city authorities became alarmed and asked for the restoration of the right to strike.

Impact on the Bargaining Process

The arguments against compulsory arbitration are both endless and, at first glance, plausible. It is asserted that the process destroys free collective bargaining, the indispensable element of a free labor movement. Additionally, it is argued that negotiations would become a charade, that there are insurmountable procedural difficulties and ominous long-range implications. Variants on the main theme mix in a good deal of mythology based on *a priori* judgments that "it can't work" and too few solid facts capable of empirical verification.

The primary argument stems from the belief that compulsory arbitration will inevitably destroy free collective bargaining. According to this line of reasoning, it is the possibility of a strike that induces the compromise; and with the power aspects reduced, there is less incentive to agree and the prospects of an early settlement are diminished. Furthermore, opponents insist that labor should not and could not be compelled to give up its most valuable weapon, the loss of which would constitute involuntary servitude. Since it is generally agreed that it is healthier for issues to be settled by direct negotiations and mutual acceptance of the results, the loyalty of the parties to the integrity of the bargaining process is an important ingredient.

At the very least, the argument runs, good faith bargaining would be subverted, if not replaced by a charade. Frustrated bargainers would tend to formulate exorbitant demands and unrealistic counter proposals, with the later step of arbitration in mind. Compulsory arbitration would become a crutch, as well as a stimulus to cling to fixed positions to the bitter end. Public agencies would have to assume that its "final offer" was merely a floor to be jacked up by the arbitrators. Internal problems besetting a union leader would encourage him to exploit the process by taking a militant, unyielding posture and later denouncing a settlement which had been "jammed down the throats" of his membership. Moreover, both sides of the table would tend to resent the wear and tear of bargaining and avoid unpleasant decisions by dumping them into the laps of the readily available third parties. [37]

Procedural Difficulties: Standards, Selection, Neutrality, and Implementation

Nor can a number of procedural difficulties be entirely discounted. For years students of labor relations have been plagued with the problem of the definition, and the application to specific cases, of standards for the arbitration of disputes. Precise, logically tight, and objective standards being difficult to formulate, there is the possibility that arbitrators will probably "split the difference" rather than examine *de novo* the merits of the dispute.

Further complications are produced by an approach essentially quasi-judicial in nature, with the main thrust being to reach a decision on the merits rather than attempt to reconcile and harmonize adverse positions by mutual agreement. While a legal approach tends to produce a clear victory for one side and defeat for the other, "the decision may unsettle more than it settles." [38] When one appreciates that even under the most favorable circumstances arbitration resembles the dictating of the terms of a treaty of peace more nearly than it does a strictly judicial process, the problem is obvious. [39] As a result, there is considerable difference of opinion as to the precise role of an arbitrator.

Even the method used to select arbitrators is a problem. Both sides resent placing key decisions in the hands of people who may not have the technical capacity or may lack the experience necessary to understand the consequences of their actions. The problem is compounded when some public officials privately express doubts as to the objectivity and neutrality of particular arbitrators, and union leaders castigate others as "stooges of the boss." In any event, the decision is taken out of the hands of those most deeply concerned.

Among the discernible long-range implications is another procedural aspect—the difficulty of implementing an award under given circumstances may cause stress and strain. Compulsory arbitration is basically a legal solution to a complex problem in human relations, and trying to "legislate a little bit of compulsion" is a complicated and dangerous business. Although compulsory arbitration posits a final binding decision, in practice the decision may be neither final nor binding, and sanctions to assure compliance would possibly entail the use of the police powers of the state.

Where the union membership feels that vital interests are unfairly dealt with, it may be anticipated that a series of slowdowns, wildcat strikes, and sick calls could still disrupt services. Government would be constrained to legislate more and more compulsion. Ill will on the part of administrators would encourage attempts to sabotage implementation of the award.

There are other implications. Where one political party is dominant over an extended period of time, there is danger that the decisions would reflect the political climate of the municipality. Still another argument is the potential impact on the entire wage and position-classification structure. There is some evidence that an award for one category of employees has a ripple effect on the entire community. Nor would the impact be confined to the public sector. Some administrators have gone so far as to regard an occasional strike as less disruptive to administration than frequent references of wage disputes to arbitration boards. Ironically, other critics maintain that the efficacy of the procedure will increase the number of impasses.

But the simplest, clearest, and most compelling argument is easily stated: compulsory arbitration does not deal with or remove the causes of impasses. Instead of a mutual agreement, you have an award that inevitably leaves one party with a feeling of dissatisfaction and frustration. If sufficient ill will is created at the moment of decision, the *revanchists* have had their case reinforced. The power contest and irresponsibility were not eliminated but only suspended, and legally mandated peace may well have bred further irresponsibility by having removed responsibility for reaching a mutually acceptable decision.

These are persuasive arguments voiced by government officials and union leaders, as well as many study groups composed of labor experts and distinguished scholars.

The Experience with Arbitration and Its Viability

Notwithstanding these forceful evaluations, there is a necessary quid pro quo whenever a strike ban exists. When strikes, all or some, are declared illegal, a form of compulsory decision-making is the only possible way of reaching agreements. To date, it is difficult to find anyone willing to tolerate strikes by fire fighters and police, including powerful unions such as AFSCME, which prior to its 1970 convention imposed an absolute ban on strikes by police affiliates.

297

Given the fundamental premise that collective bargaining is a mutually desirable, beneficial, and educative process, there is no equally effective substitute. But a compulsory process terminating in a final and binding decision in specific instances should be viewed as an unavoidable supplement and complement to collective bargaining. Indeed, the law should require that good faith bargaining precede the ultimate use of arbitration as additional leverage to the collective bargaining process.

Even Kheel, who argues that "collective bargaining, true joint determination, cannot exist without the prospect of a strike or lockout," concedes that "strikes by public workers that jeopardize the public welfare are intolerable and must be deterred" and "the right to strike no matter how important to labor must be subordinated to the superior public interest." [40] Therefore, by definition, the only alternative is some process of compulsory decision to prevent a senseless test of strength whenever any strike, public or private, constitutes a "clear and present danger to society."

There is no conclusive evidence that good faith bargaining will, ipso facto, not occur where compulsory arbitration is the "ultimate" step. The very possibility of its use may provide a stimulus to bargaining, because each side dislikes the uncertainty and risk involved when other parties enter the scene with authority to act.

In the Canadian federal experience, where employees are given a choice of the strike route or the arbitration route to resolve new contract terms, 100 out of 114 units chose the arbitration route. But during the three-year period 1967-1970, 108 contracts were concluded, with only eight references to arbitration, covering some 11 bargaining units; and only two were settled by the award process. [41]

Although Pennsylvania had in 1968 adopted mandatory compulsory arbitration where initial police and fire fighter negotiations failed to produce an agreement, in 1969 both the Philadelphia police and fire fighter units concluded their agreements through collective bargaining. In 1970, however, both the Fraternal Order of Police and the Fire Fighters Association invoked mandatory arbitration. Each employee unit secured more substantial increases than in any prior year excepting 1966-1967, when pension benefits were renegotiated. [42]

Since 1968, there have been 218 requests for arbitration in police disputes but only 118 awards, with the balance of cases settled, withdrawn, or pending; in fire fighter disputes there were 38 requests, 23 awards, 13 settlements, and two pending. [43] While there has been considerable use of the process during this brief span of time, there have been no strikes in the fire and police services that engaged in arbitration. Lowenberg also found that compulsory arbitration had played a significant role during the first year following the passage of the law, 66 awards having been issued. In the major cities more than one half invoked arbitration (and the larger city was more likely to be involved that the smaller municipalities) with the request usually coming from the employee organization. [44]

Similarly, the experience in Michigan has not been such as to justify the dire predictions of earlier years. Some estimates indicate that in at least half of the cases where mediation was involved, agreements were achieved without the necessity of going to arbitration.

Actually, there are mutually advantageous elements in process. From labor's standpoint, management cannot stall interminably or sit tight on its sovereign prerogative, neither accepting nor rejecting labor's claim where a strike is clearly inconceivable. Labor needs some form of recourse against arbitrary, unreasonable, and capricious actions by administrators or political leaders. The responsible union leader unwillingly pushed into an ultramilitant stance should welcome the opportunity to get the leadership off the hook. The leader's first instinct is to preserve his position of leadership and at the same time be able to champion the just causes of his membership yet not subject his constituency to the needless hardship of a strike.

The consequences of an arbitration award from the union's vantage point have been probed by Donald J. Petersen. The award may have an impact on future contract negotiations, on the rank and file's perception of the desirability of the process, and on the union leadership. [45] While the 400 cases studied concerned contract implementation rather than contract negotiation, the author's findings indicated that the membership seldom held their leaders responsible for a negative result. Adverse awards did not appear to stimulate a significant amount of dissatisfaction with the arbitration process itself. The influence was the greatest in the impact on future negotiations, where in 22 percent of the sample cases unions attempted to amend their agreements as a result of an adverse award.

The face-saving element is not confined to labor. The political reality is that the politician is confronted by a politically powerful force, and in some cases public officials find themselves virtually helpless at the bargaining table. Political deals seem to be the only way out, especially in election years. In such an environment a possible strike is one more form of political pressure.

Because of the relative newness of compulsory arbitration legislation, there have been few objective studies of how the laws have worked. In 1971 the Michigan Department of Labor summarized the 37 awards issued from October 1969 through March 1971. According to the report, 17 of the 37 awards were unanimous decisions. The city involved concurred in the decision as reached in about two thirds of the cases, and the union agreed in 28 cases.

For several decades unions screamed the loudest that compulsory arbitration would not work and would destroy the collective bargaining process. Yet, in major jurisdictions the recent trend has been for unions to support the continuance of compulsory arbitration where it has been experimented with. In Michigan the presidents of the Police Officers Association of Michigan and the Michigan Fire Fighters argued in favor of extending the law. During legislative hearings in 1971, representatives of the Police Office Research Association of California and the Federation of Firefighters of California strongly supported a bill providing for the binding arbitration of police and fire disputes.

To date, the major impact of compulsory arbitration statutes has evidenced itself in four ways. When the employee organization fails to achieve its goals by direct bargaining or with the help of mediation and fact finding, it has sought arbitration to improve its position. Second, some unions, such as AFSCME District Council 33 in Philadelphia, have awaited the outcome of police and fire arbitration proceedings in order to assess their potential gains. Third, some unions have quickly gone through earlier required steps to get to arbitration. Finally, although fewer strikes have occurred, some elected officials and administrators have been very unhappy with the results.

The California League of Cities suggested in 1971 that it virtually favored the right of police and firemen to strike in preference to the extreme alternative of compulsory arbitration, "which takes the final decision out of the hands of the local government." Insisting that "you can't do that because it changes the form of government," the League argued that arbitration would not prevent strikes and that they would reluctantly prefer to grant the right to strike rather than be legally bound by such awards.

Similarly, the Michigan Municipal League opposed the extension of Michigan's Act 312, which became law in 1969. After two years experience with the law, the League opposed making the law a permanent statute in 1971. The Michigan group argued that the two-year test had not prevented police or fire strikes and that the law had inhibited collective bargaining by encouraging unions to slide through mediation with the intent of going into arbitration.

Administrators argued that compulsory arbitration laws did not create a deadline for bargaining but provided a "starting time for arbitration." They insisted that the law infringed on their taxing power and failed to consider the ability of the city to pay.

A process of compulsory decision need not be based upon legalistic abstractions and hastily contrived legislation that provides inflexible procedures and elaborate machinery. On the other hand, reliance on a few "super mediators," without machinery, is not the answer. Compulsory decisions should be reserved for those cases where the bargaining process has already collapsed; and its scope could be carefully circumscribed. There should be no pretense that all prior events will be ignored and a decision handed down from Mount Olympus, with no regard for the feelings of the parties but a sole concern for the technical merits of the case. Joseph Loewenberg has suggested that the third, "neutral" member "injects a good deal of negotiating into the arbitral process." Some arbiters interviewed conceded that they informally requested that the parties resume bargaining, or attempted "to feel out what the parties would be satisfied with."

Nor are the procedural difficulties insurmountable as more experience is gained with the process. Courts in Pennsylvania, Michigan, Rhode Island, and Wyoming have upheld the constitutionality of statutes and have maintained the principle of judicial check. This indicates that the legal challenges can be overcome. The problem of statutory criteria to guide the arbitrators is a thorny one. Some statutes have not gone beyond a broad intelligible principle. No decision criteria set forth in the Pennsylvania and Wyoming laws. Other statutes have stipulated criteria such as wage and hour comparisons, the interest and welfare of the public, and "comparisons of peculiarities" of employment. Michigan has written nine basic criteria into its statutes. With a wide range of literature to draw upon, the problem can be solved. [46]

Probably the most controversial issue with regard to criteria involves whether the arbitrators should give greater weight to "the ability of a city to pay" vis a vis what may be considered a fair wage. This problem is especially difficult when a small, well-organized unit's settlement may well form the pattern for other, larger blocs of employees. Russell A. Smith and Meyer S. Ryder suggested that the Michigan experience showed that arbitrators did not consider ability to pay to be "the paramount consideration." Arnold Zack, an experienced arbitrator, posed the issue in these terms during the 1971 conference of the National Academy of Arbitrators:

> Although troublesome and foreign for many neutrals . . . such inquiry into financial data is an essential responsibility when a claim of inability to pay is challenged. Maybe it requires a new breed of

neutrals with public finance or economic experience. If he is required to determine terms, it is incumbent on the neutral to determine to his satisfaction whether the government's fiscal position precludes the demands.

Closely related to the problem of ability to pay is the issue that, the city argues, is a public policy question and nonnegotiable. Noting the reluctance of some arbitrators to consider questions of public policy in deciding labor-management disputes, Jean T. McKelvey suggests further training of arbitrators "to face the challenge of accommodating an older and valuable institution to the new movements for social change." This is more than a problem of expertise and competence of arbitrators, and the courts serve as the ultimate bastion against far-out decisions in policy areas. To date statutes have not been so loosely drawn as to imperil management rights.

The problem of the competence and neutrality of arbitrators is elusive and subjective. Some experienced in labor relations have called for elimination of reasoned opinions justifying the award. While fairness and reasonableness are nebulous concepts, the participants and the public are entitled to a written justification of the award. Courts and regulatory agencies assume the same type of responsibility, and there is no legitimate reason to exempt arbitrators. The mere requirement that an arbitrator explain his decision will compel him to subject his reasoning to the test of a written justification. Judicial decisions have utilized equally vague criteria—the rational basis test, substantial evidence, etc.—and to suggest the elimination of opinion writing would be considered sheer lunacy.

The limited experience with compulsory arbitration in the public sector has not shown signs of subverting collective bargaining. Nor can we expect that the process will become a panacea and prevent all strikes. Compulsory arbitration continues to pose philosophical as well as legal questions. After analyzing the first use of binding arbitration procedures by a public agency in the state of Oregon the Assistant Executive Secretary of the League of Oregon Cities posed the following questions: "If two parties are deadlocked, is it good public policy for a dispute to be resolved by a disinterested third party when the third party would have no responsibility to the voters but would have the power to determine the level and type of public services through the allocation of tax dollars? On the other hand, can meaningful collective bargaining occur if one of the parties has the authority to make a unilateral and final decision when the dispute cannot be resolved through negotiation?"[47]

Ultimately, true collective bargaining depends on the respect of the parties for the integrity of the bargaining process. A union leader does not want his influence diminished; nor does an administrator desire the substitution of an arbitrator's decision for his managerial authority. We can no longer afford to accept the reflexive response that a process of compulsory decision will not work. Finally, it would be equally naive to believe that any magic formula will prevent all strikes even where vital services are concerned.

More than two decades ago the continuing dilemma was posed:

> The issue admits of no final solution but only of working arrangements which leave intact the basic claims of each party. If government presses its sovereign authority to its logical end, it may destroy freedom. If the employees of government fully exercise their collective pressure in their own behalf, they may undermine the public security upon which freedom rests. The life of a free society depends upon the maintenance of freedom and authority in delicate balance. The preservation of this balance depends in turn upon mutual restraint on the part of both government and its employees founded upon the recognition of the fact that in real life there is neither complete liberty nor absolute sovereignty. [48]

This mutual restraint is best demonstrated by good faith bargaining, more frequent use of voluntary arbitration and compulsory decision in deadlocks creating a danger, rather than a temporary inconvenience, to society.

The "Last Best Offer"

Arbitrators have been criticized on the grounds that what they do is merely "split the difference" between the two final offers of the bargainers. A recent proposal termed the "Last Best Offer" is an attempt to overcome this major criticism of the arbitration. Arbitrators about to make their decision request the parties to submit their last best offer. Upon receiving the offers, the arbitrators are required to select, but not alter, one of the offers.

The last best offer was suggested as a means of reducing the authority of arbitrators and was intended to encourage realistic bargaining positions. The concept would provide an incentive to break deadlocks, since the only chance to win is to submit a reasonable offer. Each side is faced with the distinct possibility that the agreement will be concluded on the basis of his opponent's proposals. To submit an unrealistic offer would raise the possibility that an inadequate offer on the other side would be selected even though it failed to provide that measure of equity achieved during arbitration.

Roulette or Merit?

At first sight the Last Best Offer concept is intriguing. Yet many troublesome issues are implicit in the proposal. Each offer may tend to become a gamble tantamount to roulette, with each side guessing how far it should go. The labor team could decide to add a little "surplus" to its final offer, on the assumption that the public employer will go as far as it can and labor would have nothing to lose. The labor leader would certainly have more trouble justifying his low position than would the elected official, who could pass the buck to the arbitrator while posing as a staunch defender of the public purse.

While the Last Best Offer is a variation of arbitration, it is repugnant to arbitration's basic premise—a decision based on the merits. The requirement to choose between two offers, neither of which may be equitable, may force the choice of an offer that will exacerbate the deadlock rather than resolve it. Competent and experienced arbitrators perceive that the "truth" generally lies somewhere between the final offers. The leeway provided by arbitration may assure the acceptance that is the ultimate goal. To restrict arbitrators to the degree suggested destroys the degree of flexibility and may swing the disputed issues to a strike. One side clearly loses under the Last Best Offer; under arbitration, a compromise may be effected. Judicial review remains a sufficiently effective check against capricious actions of arbitrators.

In 1971 Salem, Ore., introduced the Last Best Offer concept into municipal bargaining. No decisions have as yet been issued. Undoubtedly, the experience of Salem will have a major influence on its introduction elsewhere.

New York City's Office of Collective Bargaining

The establishment of tripartite agencies—consisting of representatives of labor, management, and the public—is another approach for resolving impasses. Such agencies were extensively used by the War Labor Board during World War II, but their application in the public sector is presently unique to New York city. Under the local-procedures section of the Taylor Law, New York City was authorized to develop its own dispute-settlement machinery. [49] The result was the establishment in 1967 of the tripartite Office of Collective Bargaining, charged with, among other duties, the administration of procedures to resolve deadlocks in labor negotiations. The city act encourages a "consensual relationship" between unions, the public, and city officials, but participation is strictly voluntary. Under the New York system, two of the seven-member board are selected by participating labor unions and two by the city. There are three public members, one of whom is designated the Chairman, who are selected by the unanimous consent of the members previously designated by the city and the unions.

New York City's most powerful unions, including the Patrolmen's Benevolent Association, the Uniformed Firefighters Association, and AFSCME District Council 37 in particular, hailed the action as a step toward a "new era" in labor relations and the end of the myth of government as a disinterested third party in public employment. The only major union that failed to subscribe to the procedures was the Uniformed Sanitationmen's Association. Some of the smaller unions, such as the Social Service Employees Union (before it merged with AFSCME) also rejected the plan, largely because they expected it to work to the benefit of the rival AFSCME. This has impaired, but not seriously crippled, the OCB's operations and scope of action. It is expected that eventually all the unions in the city will participate and fully test the usefulness of tripartism.

OCB operating procedures provide that at least 90 but not more than 120 days prior to the termination of a contract, participating parties shall file a bargaining notice with it. The Chairman of the OCB maintains communication with the parties to insure than they are fulfilling their obligations and providing relevant information. Mediation is provided by the OCB on the request of either party or on the initiative of the chairman not less than 30 days after the start of negotiations.

In the event that mediation fails to resolve the issues, dispute panels may be invoked, on the request of the parties or on the motion of the chairman. Such panels are empowered to mediate, hold hearings, and take other action, including fact finding, to settle the dispute. If an agreement is not reached, the panel is authorized to formulate recommendations, which are submitted to the Chairman and the disputing parties. Such findings are to be made public within seven days.

The OCB has had a measure of success, but the lack of finality in its procedures finally led the City Council in November 1971 to enact binding arbitration for most categories of city employees. It is notable that employee organizations have not made a strong fight against the measure.

From time to time, proposals to establish a system of labor courts to resolve impasses in public employment are proposed and, generally, quickly rejected. For very much the same reasons that the labor movement has opposed compulsory arbitration, they even more vehemently oppose labor courts. When Kansas established its Court of Industrial Relations, Samuel Gompers noted in an address before the New Jersey state legislature in March 1920 that "there are some things which are worse than strikes—a degraded, demoralized and servile manhood."[50] Although today's opponents of compulsory decisions in labor disputes no longer hurl the epithet that such legislators would be "engaged in a Bolshevist manufacturing establishment," they oppose labor courts as antithetical to the concept of free labor, whether in private or public employment.

Nevertheless, the labor court continues to be proposed. As early as 1946, Fiorello La Guardia, Mayor of New York City, publicly proposed a system of separate labor courts. More recently, Judge Samuel I. Rosenman detailed a system of labor courts in a statement before Congress. Neither La Guardia nor Rosenman can be dismissed as reactionary baiters of labor and thus the Rosenman proposals should be carefully considered.

The Rosenman thesis is, essentially, that with equality now reached by labor in private industry, the right to strike should be curtailed when in conflict with the public interest in certain well-defined industries and in essential public, municipal, and state services, with some form of final, compulsory decision provided.

But by "compulsory decision," it is not intended to convey the usual ad hoc board of arbitrators but a separate labor judiciary, with the sole and exclusive function of deciding labor disputes that the parties cannot settle themselves. Nor would the Rosenman proposal urge that expedients such as cooling-off periods, mediation, conciliation, fact finding, and voluntary arbitration be abandoned or curtailed.

Collective bargaining would operate freely except where the public interest is jeopardized. To labor's argument that their right to strike would be cut off, the response is that in two of three major areas of industrial strife—unfair labor practices and grievances—labor has already, voluntarily or without much opposition given up the right to strike. The only remaining category involves the making of a new contract.

Basically, proponents of labor courts contend that the arguments used by unions and management would not have the same force against a system of labor courts. Both sides of the bargaining table are reluctant to place their fate in the hands of ad hoc arbitrators appointed for one specific case. Management, further, privately expresses the fear that some of these ad hoc appointments are partial to labor in most cases.

Nor would bargaining be destroyed. "For every case actually tried in our courts," states Rosenman, "scores are settled before litigation, during litigation, and even in the course of trial—right up to the time of verdict!" And these civil settlements are all the results of vigorous bargaining. As for the argument that courts would tend to "split the difference" as do arbitrators, Rosenman replies that this has not been the experience of Australian labor courts and "constitutes a libel on our judicial tradition."

Procedural difficulties are not viewed as insurmountable, since the criteria known by economists to fix wages are more reliable than criteria presently available to the courts in fixing personal injury damages. Furthermore, some method of adjudication must be created to bind government as well as unions, to eliminate the justified complaint of government employees that only they are bound. Finally, the fact that a court stands ready to decide does not prevent full bargaining on all issues by all parties, and labor courts merely substitute reasoned and considered judgment for a result based on comparative strength and resources.

A variation of the labor court is the plan suggested by Vincent McDonnell, Chairman of the New York State Mediation Board, in April 1970. McDonnell proposes the establishment of a labor court to determine if a public employee strike is justified. If the strike is deemed justified, the court would issue an injunction, pending the outcome of a jury trial on the issues. On the conclusion of the trial, a judge or panel of judges would decide the contract terms in dispute, subject to approval by a majority of a jury. Where the jury failed to approve, the judge would proceed to work out a compromise acceptable to a majority of the jury. In the case of strikes deemed unjustified, judicial penalties would be involved if a work stoppage actually takes place.

It is doubtful that the labor movement would view McDonnell's plan as either broadening their right to strike or providing equity. Jurors impaneled under the regular jury system are not likely to have the expertise sufficient to cope with labor court judges and would tend to be lost in the complexities of the single case they would hear. It remains doubtful whether the addition of jurors would add to the feasibility of labor courts.

Again, as in the case of compulsory arbitration, the labor court concept has appeal as a simple and easy solution to strikes. Our legal system is primarily geared to cope with individual violations of law.

When sufficiently aggrieved, large groups of public employees have already shown an inclination to ignore the rulings of courts. Having waged an enduring struggle to achieve bargaining rights, employee unions are likely to resist the imposition of judicial decrees and regard the labor court as a masquerade devised to protect the sovereign's rights to a privileged status. Because of earlier decisions of the courts, union leaders are not as sanguine about the judicial system as is Judge Rosenman. The Judge's shotgun approach, which would include such wide categories of employees within the no-strike ban, raises suspicion in the labor community that the real purpose is to prevent all strikes.

Seeds of distrust have been sown by the earlier resort to a legal approach to a complex problem in human relations. Constitutional changes of such broad import should not be abruptly instituted. For the present, the labor court would appear to be too radical a shift in policy. If current trends persist, however, we may well come to the point of establishing labor courts to cope with strikes in critical services.

Notes

1. J. H. Foegen, "Mediation from Initiation: Hope for Public Labor Relations," *Public Personnel Review,* January, 1970, pp. 7-12.
2. R. Stutz, Address, American Bar Association, Dallas, Texas, August 13, 1969.
3. Bureau of National Affairs, "Performance Standards for Mediators," *Labor Relations Yearbook—1969;* Henry Landsberger, *"A Final Report to Participants in the Mediation Project,* N.Y. State School of Industrial and Labor Relations at Cornell, 1959; and Larkin W. McClellan and Peter E. Obermeyer, "Science of Art?: Performance Standards for Mediators," *Labor Law Journal,* September, 1970 pp. 591-95.
4. Julius J. Manson, "Mediators and Their Qualifications," *Labor Law Journal,* October 1958, p. 755.
5. William E. Simkin, "Fact Finding—Its Values and Limitations," Address, Convention of the National Academy of Arbitrators, 1970.
6. Theodore Kheel, "Impasse Procedures in Public Employment," in Edward Levin, ed., *New York State Public Employment Relations* (Ithaca, N.Y.: New York State School of Industrial and Labor Relations, Cornell University, April 1968, pp. 21-22.
7. *Final Report of the Governor's Committee on Public Employee Relations,* State of New York, Albany, March 31, 1966, p. 37. (cited hereafter as *Taylor Report.)*
8. *Report to Governor George Romney, Advisory Committee on Public Employee Relations,* State of Michigan, Lansing, February 15, 1967, p. 11 (cited hereafter as *Smith Report).*
9. *Report and Recommendations: Governor's Advisory Commission on*

Labor Management Policy for Public Employees, State of Illinois, Springfield, March, 1967, p. 31 (cited hereafter as *Illinois Report*).
10. Report to Speaker Anthony J. Travia on the Taylor Law, February 21, 1968, p. 33.
11. Edward B. Krinsky, "Public Employment Fact Finding in Fourteen States," *Labor Law Journal*, September 1966, pp. 532-40.
12. James L. Stern, "The Wisconsin Public-Employee Fact Finding Procedure," *Industrial and Labor Relations Review*, October 1966, p. 3, 19.
13. Ibid.
14. *Year One of the Taylor Law* (September 1, 1967-August 31, 1968).
15. *PERB News*, vol 5, no. 3 (March 1972).
16. William R. Word, "Fact Finding: Complement or Substitute for Collective Bargaining in Public Employment," unpublished doctoral dissertation, University of Tennessee, 1970.
17. Sam Zagoria, "A New Frontier in Collective Bargaining: Public Workers and Citizen Bosses," Address, Labor Law Institute, Federal Bar Association, Columbus, Ohio, Chapter, May 17, 1968.
18. Word, "Impasse Resolution in the Public Sector," Address, Southeastern Conference on Current Trends in Collective Bargaining, November, 1970.
19. Arvid Anderson, "Collective Bargaining in Municipal and State Sectors," *Good Government*, Summer, 1971, p. 4.
20. 66 Ill. 481 (1873).
21. *Mugford v. Mayor et al*, 185 Md. 206, 44 A. 2d 745 (1945).
22. *Cleveland v. Division 268*, 84 Ohio App. 43, 81 NE 2d 310 (1948).
23. Charles S. Rhyne, *Labor Unions and Municipal Employee Law*, National Institute of Law Officers, Washington, D.C., 1946, p. 140.
24. *Report on a Program of Labor Relation for New York City Employees*, 1957.
25. *Norwalk Teachers Association v. Board of Education*, 138 Conn. 269, (2d) 482 (1951).
26. *Fairview Hospital Association v. Public Service and Hospital Employees Union, Local 113*, 214 Minn. 523, 64 N.W. 2d 16 (1954).
27. *Taylor Report*, op. cit., p. 67.
28. Kheel, op. cit., p. 20.
29. *Taylor Report*, pp. 67 and 68.
30. *City of Warwick v. Warwick Regular Firemen's Association*, Rhode Island Supreme Court, 256 A. 2d 206 (1969).
31. *Tremblay v. Berlin Police Union*, 237 A. 2d 668 (1968). The Tremblay decision, however, adds little legal support for compulsory arbitration of new contracts, since it was a grievance-procedure clause of the agreement that was attacked as an unlawful delegation of authority.
32. *City of Washington v. Police Department*, 436 Pa. 168, 259 A. 2d 437 (1969). See *Harney v. Russo et al*, 435 Pa. 183, 255 A. 2d 560 (1968), in re the constitutional issue.
33. *School, City of Gary, Indiana, et al. v. Gary Teachers Union, Local 4*, Lake Superior Court of Indiana, No. 370-3429, decided July 6, 1971.
34. *Travia Report*, p. 37.

35. New York *Times*, August 2, 1969.

36. *AFSCME Policy Statement*, July 26, 1966.

37. Both the New York and Illinois reports argued that compulsion would involve the "risk of chilling negotiations," particularly in the public sector, where mature bargaining has not yet developed. It would also reduce the prospects of early settlement by encouraging extreme demands. See *Taylor Report*, pp. 67-68, and *Illinois Report*, p. 32.

38. Herman Gray, "The Nature and Scope of Arbitration and Arbitration Clauses," *New York University Conference on Labor*, 1948.

39. See Emmanuel Stein, "Problem Areas in Labor Arbitration," *Proceedings*, Third New York University Labor Conference, 1950, pp. 167-168.

40. *Travia Report*, op. cit. p. 15.

41. Anderson, op. cit., p. 2. See also J. Douglas Muir, "Canada's Experience with the Right of Public Employees to Strike," *Monthly Labor Review*, July 1969, p. 57, in support of the proposition that most agreements have been reached without referral to arbitration.

42. Lennox L. Moak, "The Philadelphia Experience," *Unionization of Municipal Employees*, Proceedings of the Academy of Political Science, Columbia, University, New York, 1971, p. 128.

43. Anderson, op. cit., p. 3.

44. Joseph J. Loewenberg, "Compulsory Arbitration for Police and Firefighters in Pennsylvania in 1968," *Industrial and Labor Relations Review*, April, 1970, pp. 367-80. Some 198 larger cities were surveyed, and 132 arrived at an agreement by negotiation.

45. Donald J. Petersen, "Consequences of the Arbitration Award for Unions," *Labor Law Journal*, September 1970, pp. 613-17.

46. One excellent example is Emmanuel Stein's "Criteria in Wage Arbitration," *New York University Law Review*, October 1950, pp. 727-36.

47. Karl A. Van Asselt, "Binding Arbitration: A Recent Experience," *Public Personnel Review*, July, 1971, pp. 141-42.

48. Sterling D. Spero, *Government as Employer* (New York: Remsen Press, 1948), p. 487.

49. The local-procedures section of the Taylor Law authorized other local units to develop impasse procedures. As of September 1, 1968, the State PERB had approved the local procedures of 26 jurisdictions, leading to the establishment of local agencies to deal with collective bargaining problems.

50. Samuel Gompers, "The Kansas Court of Industrial Relations Law," Address before a joint session of the New Jersey state legislature, March 20, 1920.

51. Rosenman suggests police, fire, education, sanitation, subways, buses, hospitals, public health and welfare agencies as illustrative examples. Samuel I. Rosenman, "A Better Way to Handle Strikes," *The Record*, New York Association of the Bar of the City of New York.

12 Constructive Labor Relations or Bureaucratic Independence?

Substitution of bilateral agreement through collective bargaining for unilateral employer determination of governmental working conditions will not usher in the millennium. It may, however, open possibilities for harmonious equitable employment relationships, as it has in some private industries.

The objectives sought—equity for public employees, cities free from crippling strikes, a politically impartial civil service, and preservation of a merit system—are clear. Disagreement begins with the problem of how these objectives can be best secured.

Collective Bargaining and the Public Interest

It has been generally presumed that the adoption of collective bargaining was intended to promote the public interest. The National Labor Relations Act, state laws governing employment relationships in the public service, and Presidential Executive Orders 10988 and 11491 all include statements of policy that advance collective bargaining and recognize the process as a positive factor benefiting both sides of the employer-employee relationship.

Yet, some recent manifestations of public collective bargaining tend to shake assumptions regarding the process as a promoter of the public interest. Strikes continue to plague cities, cutting off essential services on which the safety and convenience of the urban population depend. There are bargaining delays that end in eleventh-hour settlements because of initial exorbitant demands by unions and the withholding of counter offers by public employers. Excessive wage settlements, irresponsible union leaders, and supermilitant rank and filers, as well as highhanded and stubborn employing authorities, test the citizenry's tolerance and strain the social fabric. Nor are these shortcomings confined to the public sector.

The Public-Private Dichotomy

Several key factors should be considered in relation to the public strike problem. First, the problem transcends government employment: it extends to all services that vitally affect the public health and safety. To date, government employers have relied without success on unrealistic attempts to apply an absolute ban on all public employee strikes, at the same time upholding the right to strike of employees in private industry. The public interest is not served by perpetuation of the myth that every public employee strike constitutes an intolerable assault on public authority.

Although distinguishing characteristics may be enumerated, there are actually more similarities than differences between the great majority of public and private employees. The traditional public-private dichotomy lacks validity in today's complex world, in which the roles of the public and private sector are intertwined. Government depends on the private sector for goods and services; the latter could not function without the services and orderly environment government makes possible.

Nothing has so confused, befogged, and frustrated the modernization of public employment relations as the tendency to view the problem as a question of law rather than an issue of public policy. The roots of this confusion lie in the doctrine of the sovereign state, which as far as employment relations are concerned is summed up in the maxim "The State determines its relations with its servants." This has been a sort of shorthand rationalization for the right of government in its capacity as employer to fix unilaterally the working conditions of those hired to carry on its functions.

Government is the legal instrument of the sovereign people, possessing limited powers derived from the people pursuant to the constitution. The prevailing view of the courts is that an individual's constitutional rights may not be *unreasonably* diminished as a price or condition of public employment.

312

This legal proposition was reflected years ago in congressional legislation invalidating executive orders of Presidents Theodore Roosevelt and Taft that forbade federal employees, individually or through associations, to seek to influence legislation affecting their interests. This legislation, known as the Lloyd-LaFollette Act, recognized the right of federal employees to organize, lobby, and affiliate with the organized labor movement. [1]

This federal legislation eventually influenced the passage of legislation by the New York State legislature that invalidated provisions in the New York City Charter forbidding policemen, fire fighters, and school system employees "to join or contribute to any organization intended to effect legislation concerning them." The New York law guaranteed civil service employees the right to appeal for redress of grievances to the legislature or any "public body." [2]

The public employer, no longer able to issue executive or charter "gag" rules as demonstrations of its sovereign prerogatives, now makes the appeal to sovereignty serve as a convenient technique to avoid dealing with the merits of issues in disputes with its employees. This technique appears most clearly in the case of strikes, where the employers' tactic has been to submerge the issues underlying the dispute and make the strike itself the sole issue, with the employer playing the role of the aggrieved party warding off an assault upon the very nature of the state.

When strikes occur, as they do regularly, their permissibility should be judged by the nature and impact of the function involved rather than by the identity of the employer, whether public or private. The public-private dichotomy fails to distinguish between necessity and convenience and takes no notice of the critical or noncritical character of the service.

The persisting opponents of all government service strikes have often relied on blunderbuss legislation, with heavy penalties that amount to a legislative burning at the stake. Such laws have proved futile if not actually counterproductive. The assumption that every public employee strike is a seditious act threatening the foundations of society ignores the fact that strikes in many private sector operations, where the right to strike is guaranteed, can interfere with essential governmental activities more seriously than some stoppages by public employees.

Many services provided by government are identical with those provided by private employers. There are publicly and privately operated schools and publicly and privately owned transit systems, sometimes existing side by side. Hospital, utility, and welfare services may be found under public and under private ownership and operation. Indeed, since the late 1880's the government has moved

313

into many areas hitherto considered the preserve of private industry. In some states bottled liquor is sold exclusively in state-owned and -operated stores, and a whole host of other activities now performed by government are characterized as "proprietary functions" by the courts.

Many operations carried out by government are less vital than some services provided by private industry. Private trucking companies, railroads, airlines, and maritime fleets are of crucial importance to the economy. And the government itself is dependent on private industry for vital utilities and supplies. The nation's security depends more on work performed by private industry than on the maintenance of public golf courses or the sweeping of public office buildings by public employees.

It is sometimes argued that the strike ban in the public sector serves as the equivalent of the "market restraints" operative in the private sector. While government cannot very well go out of business, neither as a practical matter can the Consolidated Edison Company or the American Telephone and Telegraph Company. The likelihood is that the government would not permit such companies to cease operations. Other industries closely associated with the national economy security system would hardly be allowed to stop operating, as has been demonstrated by governmental efforts in 1970 to rescue the Lockheed Aircraft Company from financial difficulties and to keep the Penn Central Railroad Company running despite its bankruptcy. Although governments, as such, cannot go out of business, they can and do contract out specific functions. This possibility of contracting out may serve as a restraining influence on union demands similar to the market restraint in the private sector.

A multitude of legal, political, and economic restraints weigh on public employees' demands. Their leaders are well aware of the budgetary processes, of the total "economic pie" that is available, and of the years in which the political in-fighting for funds will be especially acute. They know about constitutional debt limits and statutory tax ceilings. Ultimately, the tax-paying citizen will judge just how tough the political leadership has been in its dealings with employee organizations; and this, too, serves as a restraint.

Labor peace "involves elements of balance that elude final statement." A strictly legal approach based on an absolute strike ban fails because it attempts to create a logically tight system based on abstract and theoretical considerations that simply do not work in the real world. In this sense, the proponents of the absolute ban deviate from the traditional case-by-case approach, which has been a principal pillar of strength of our legal system.

Legal prohibitions have thus far failed—laws will not prevent

314

strikes where intolerable conditions exist and the employees feel sufficiently aggrieved or strong enough to take the risks for the possible gains.

In the United States support for the law is dependent on mass acceptance, and we have yet to discover a way to cope legally with mass or group defiance in a democratic society. Recent history notably demonstrates the powerlessness of statutes in the face of great popular movements. Law tends to follow popular sentiment rather than create it; and the modern disparity has been noticeably widened simply because jurists have been working with instruments of an earlier time. [3]

The dictum, "One cannot strike against the government," may no longer be regarded as an article of faith. Actually, the violations of the faith have become so frequent that strike laws have prolonged strikes until employees could either bargain away the penalties or obtain legislative forgiveness. Public employee unions rely on the probability that the need to restore essential services will outweigh the desire of management to inflict the penalties provided by law. Many examples demonstrate an official unwillingness or practical inability to implement prescribed sanctions.

Following a strike by the fire fighters of Atlanta, Ga., in 1966, the city agreed to administer no reprisals and to end all pending court action against the union.

The same year, sanitation workers in York, Pa., struck, and the City Council voted a pay increase despite a legal prohibition on such action. Press accounts implied that state officials recognized the illegality but "in the circumstances no court would accept a taxpayer's suit against the Mayor."

In New York State legislation was enacted to exempt transit workers from the statutory sanctions of the Condon-Wadlin Law of 1946, after a taxpayer's suit demanded executive implementation of the law.

In Dayton, Ohio, Public Service Union strikers were permitted to return to their jobs despite the clear words of the state law requiring dismissal of strikers.

Illegal strikes doubly damage the respect for law and authority of government that the very denial of the right to strike seeks to preserve. The existing state of the law presents officials with a "Hobson's choice": to maintain their authority in the face of an illegal strike, they must execute the law as written, using all their available powers to restore services; if they countenance illegal actions, the failure to enforce the law encourages strikes and breeds further contempt for the law. By automatically considering all stoppages a challenge to the sovereign's rights, strict interpretation of the law may defeat the restoration of services, which might have been achieved by handling the matter as a simple labor dispute.

The basic problem is restoration of services without denigrating the law; but the law, by concentrating on punishment, defeats the prime objective of restoration. Recent court decisions in a few instances have taken notice of this fact. Some courts have, as indicated previously, ignored the absolute ban in extenuating circumstances and have refused to issue injunctions. Other courts have shown a reluctance to mete out penalties, delaying action in the hope that the combatants will come to agreement. Some judges have delayed action to "read the riot act" to city officials and union leaders, in the hope of spurring a settlement.

Government, of course, has the right to use all its power when the necessity of maintaining its existence and preserving public order and safety require it. But situations requiring such strong steps may just as well arise out of stoppages in private enterprise. For example, the Coolidge dictum, "There is no right to strike against the public safety by anybody, anywhere, anytime," would not be seriously contested by anyone concerned with the preservation of society. Yet, the statement, applying to a group of public employees, is broad enough to be applicable to strikes in the private sector. Absolute legal bans are negative approaches to complex problems in human relations.

The Strike Plan

The extraordinary concern with civil service strikes has led to a search for a foolproof formula to preserve the special claims of the state employer and protect him from the alleged threat to his sovereign authority. The result has been the enactment of a spate of unenforceable laws and regulations, which have in effect substituted incantations against evil in place of a search for practical efforts toward solution.

Suggestions to classify public employees on the basis of the "social importance" of their functions are futile, because time and circumstances may quickly render such a priori classification obsolete or unworkable. Thus, in 1946 a tugboat strike created a major crisis in New York City, curtailing all services dependent upon continuing supplies of fuel oil. New methods of fuel delivery have now enabled the city to weather similar strikes for an extended period without undue hardship.

Before modern refrigeration, a strike of the handlers of perishable foods could quickly cause harm to the people of a large city. Today such a strike could go on for some time before a crisis resulted. Some years ago a national strike of gasoline filling stations employees could readily have been weathered. Now such a strike could paralyze the country in short order. The impact of a telephone operators' strike would have been immediate a few years ago. Then government communications, including police and fire services, was affected, as well as everyday private business. The modern automated system can now keep communications going until the progressive breakdown of the delicate machinery could make itself felt. Thus, what might have been a serious emergency strike at one time may at a later day readily be taken in stride. Or, conversely, a strike that might have been easily tolerable at one time might be a serious threat today.

It is ironic that in antistatist America, where nationalization is a naughty word and governmental activity is widely decried, the legal ban on the public service strike is still almost universal, while other democratic countries—including France, Italy, Sweden, Canada, and Great Britain—do not ban all government employee strikes. In Canada, both federal and provincial laws specifically permit some government employees to strike. Great Britain permits strikes in her nationalized industries, and the nation experienced long postal strikes in 1964 and 1969. Canada has experienced several public services strikes.

Despite searches by "blue ribbon" panels, public and private, made up of labor relation specialists, no one has come up with the desired magic formula, for the simple reason that there is none. No mechanism or procedure will guarantee strike-free public services in the United States, any more than in other democratic countries, which have decided to face the situation realistically and have given up the futile search for antistrike magic.

The first requirement for progress would seem to be liquidation of the widespread attitude that special horrors inhere in the public service strike. All disputes that vitally affect the public health and safety, whether in public or private employment, should be regarded and treated in the same way.

An initial step (already effected by the settlement of the postal strike in the spring of 1970 and included in the Postal Reorganization Act, signed into law in August of the same year) would be to place the administration of all regulatory labor relations laws within agencies that have jurisdiction in private industry, i.e., the National Labor Relations Board for national problems and similar state boards for matters within their jurisdictions. Such agencies can search out ways of handling the great variety of special public service problems, as they have already found ways of handling the great variety of specialized complex problems in the private sector of American industry.

A break in the hitherto solid American barrier outlawing all public service strikes already has occurred through some court decisions and even more significantly through laws passed in 1970 in Hawaii and Pennsylvania, guaranteeing bargaining rights and limited strike rights to most public employees.

Another essential step toward realistic handling of public service disputes would be the application to government services of the principle of the "cooling-off" period provided in the Taft-Hartley Act, initiated by a restraining order applied for by the responsible authority of the jurisdiction concerned, when such authority decides that the strike at issue in public or private employment actually affects the public health and safety and not merely the public convenience. The court would then proceed to hear the evidence and decide whether or not the issuance of a restraining order is warranted. If the court grants the order, it should simultaneously direct intensive collective bargaining in good faith, with such mediative assistance as the parties may consider necessary or desirable. The progress of negotiations should be presented to the court at a given time during the cooling-off period. If no satisfactory progress is indicated, the court should order the appointment of one or more fact finders, chosen from a previously agreed upon panel. At a given time prior to the expiration of the cooling-off period, the fact finders should, when they consider the situation appropriate, report their findings privately to the parties for further negotiation. If agreement still fails to be reached during the no-strike period, the situation should be reported to the court, which, with the technical assistance of two experts, one from a management panel and one from a union panel would adjudicate the fact finders' report in conference with the disputants and attempt to effect a settlement, or if none could be reached, make a final and binding decision.

In the case of public safety forces—police, fire fighters, and prison guards—if no new contract has been concluded 15 days prior to the expiration of the existing agreement, the procedures outlined from the initial injunction to final disposition would go into effect immediately. Complete cessation of such services could spell disaster for the community.

Reality Replaces Legalistic Abstractions

The above plan abandons the negative policies of the past and replaces them with a positive policy of encouraging the process of collective bargaining. It recognizes that no talismanic formula can apply to all categories of employees in all circumstances. Solutions inevitably involve good faith acceptance of mutual obligations, consultation, and cooperation. The crucial element is to avoid the events and attitudes that precipitate strikes—statutory changes are only the beginning and can only eliminate the artificial legalisms that currently impinge on the public employment relationships.

Procedures alone will not suffice, but the more equitable, bilateral, and cooperative they are, the greater will be the opportunity to avert most strikes. The spirit of these proposals is to encourage, enhance, and supplement the bargaining process at every stage in the dispute.

While the emphasis on mediation and fact finding is retained, the proposed arbitral elements warrant testing. In this instance, however, it is not suggested that all that has gone before should be ignored and a *de novo* decision imposed in some rarified quasi-judicial atmosphere removed from reality. Many past proposals have failed to take account of the basic problem involved in implementation of the agreement. The spirit of mediation fuses with the last-resort "arbitral" step, and the strictures on its use are intended to add leverage to bolster the collective bargaining process. Furthermore, the right to strike is preserved, in the words of Archibald Cox, as "the motive power behind collective bargaining." Also, the cooling-off period, reserved for authentic emergency strikes, is utilized as a time for the encouragement of an agreed settlement instead of serving merely as an empty waiting period that, experience has shown, the parties sit out until the strike can legally be resumed.

This suggested process is not infallible; it will not prevent all public employee strikes. It does, however, bring additional elements of fairness into play and would generate powerful public support toward reaching acceptable results without resort to the ultimate strike weapon by unions.

The Public Employer's Responsibility

Government employers all too often appear to assume that the avoidance of a strike fulfills their obligation to the public. With far too great frequency the accustomed "hard line" enunciated by them on approaching the bargaining table gives way to timidity in the face of a threatened strike. Sensitive to the role-playing threats in the union script and fearing the political backlash if a strike should occur, employing officials often cave in and succumb to union demands.

Resort to the strike, with all the dire predictions surrounding it, has tended to obscure the fact that aside from the vital protective services, many public strikes can be taken in their stride by the community and may have less social impact than strikes in the private sector.

Employing officials should realize that strikes are not always won by strikers and that by risking the temporary inconvenience and deprivation of a strike the public employer may actually be defending the long term public interest.

When public labor relations attain a greater degree of maturity, public employing authorities may come to realize that there are circumstances when the wisest policy will lie in their readiness to resist employee demands and accept a strike.

The federal government claims to have contingency plans to meet a strike. It is incumbent on local governments to have similar plans. The New York police strike of 1971 demonstrated that with a substantial minority of the force remaining on duty good management gave the community effective protection. [4]

Municipal governments and employee unions have a history of mutual suspicion to overcome. Public officials must rid themselves of the notion that collective bargaining is a necessary evil threatening their prerogatives. Both management and unions must make a reality of the assumption that constructive collective bargaining is a mutually beneficial relationship.

Testimony to this effect comes from public executives who have had long experience with collective bargaining. The Director of Personnel Administration of the United States Department of the Interior, Newell B. Terry, declared:

> The procedures of collective bargaining have fulfilled a definite need in Interior. . . our labor agreements have proved to be an effective means of communication between management and its employees. Through these agreements employees find recognition of their role in the missions of government . . . . The agreements have provided a set of "ground rules" outlining the place of management and labor in the effective prosecution of our work operations, giving both a greater sense of security, [and have] resulted in a definite improvement in employment morale. Collective bargaining is now an internal part of personnel management in the department. [5]

Some years prior to Mr. Terry's statement, two directors of the TVA said privately that "collective bargaining buttressed by the power to strike should keep management on its toes and promote its effectiveness."

320

Trade Union Responsibility

The public has become increasingly impatient with public employee strikes; the labor, highly conscious of its public image, is well aware that there are voices questioning the strike as an outworn weapon in present-day society. The strike, except where regarded as a "dress rehearsal for revolution," is considered labor's weapon of last resort. Unfortunately, some employee groups have not conserved their "strike capital" for authentic impasses, using it rather as a weapon of first instance.

There is an influential body of public opinion that holds that however illogical present antistrike policies confined to public employees may be, they are, nevertheless a legal fact. Therefore, bitter attacks by some union leaders against antistrike prohibitions accompanied by threats to defy the law and statements impugning the integrity of the courts hurt the cause of labor. Unions, they hold, cannot defy one set of laws and simultaneously urge the passage of laws promoting ever more security and gains for labor.

This attitude runs counter to over a century and three quarters of American tradition of defiance of discriminatory laws accompanied by a willingness to accept the penalties for their violation.

After the strike in the summer of 1971 when New York bridge tenders opened the drawbridges, removed essential operating mechanisms, and blocked the flow of traffic into the city, a union leader involved in the strike declared that as head of the union he was responsible for breaking the law and was ready to take the consequences.

Since the current demonstrations of public union militancy, literally scores of national and local union leaders and active rank and filers have been sent to prison. In Newark, N.J., after the long and bitter teacher strikes in 1970, some judges went on what has been described as "a virtual jailing binge," which only served to exacerbate the already explosive situation.

In addition to the jailings in Newark, union leaders have been sent to prison in Cicero, Ill., Minot, N.D., Cincinnati, Chicago, and New York City for varying terms. Two prominent national leaders, David Selden of the AFT and Jerry Wurf of AFSCME, were among those sentenced for defying court orders. All of these sentences were accepted proudly and defiantly.

The American tradition of defiance of discriminatory laws is regarded in labor circles as a demonstration of good citizenship and respect for law in its highest sense as a nondiscriminatory instrument.

Both labor leaders and some academic students of the labor

movement suggest that without the strikes defying the conspiracy acts, the laws might still be on the books. Without the defiance of injuctions, which was strongly supported by Samuel Gompers, President of the AFL, there might still be no Norris-La Guardia Act. One prominent trade union leader declared that "willingness to take the consequences of challenging discriminatory laws without childish demands for amnesty represents dramatic action against abuses of power within the general framework of law."

Contract Rejections and Membership Responsibility

The responsibilities of a trade union are not limited to the leadership. Well-meaning legislative attempts to inject more democratic process into union operations have led to unintended results. The widely believed myth that union leaders exploit the membership has been swept aside in the wave of contract rejections by supermilitant rank and filers. Union leaders under today's conditions have difficulty in pledging the action of the membership. While there have been many disturbing contract rejections in the public service, their proportion has been far smaller than in private industry, where reliable sources placed the number at 1,000 or more in 1970. The industry experience has had its effect on the public sector, where restless memberships have also shown a willingness to yield to the leaders of opposition factions and shout down negotiated agreements, demanding that the officers try again for more.

AFL-CIO President George Meany has proposed that union leaders be granted the legal authority to conclude binding agreements. Several responsible and experienced union officials have differed strongly with Mr. Meany's proposal. The consensus among them was that a labor leader to be successful must get "the feel of his membership" and be guided by it in negotiations and in all other union activity.

The issue underscores the whole problem of internal union government, which requires a search for procedures whereby officers may be held responsible to their memberships, with frequent elections under some recognized party system operating in ways analogous to parliamentary government.

Collective Bargaining and the Administrative Process

In the United States tendencies toward bureaucratic autonomy, as indicated in Chapter 7, have been confined largely to professional employees bringing their "craft" concepts with them into the public

322

service. The interests of the rank-and-file American public workers are centered on bread-and-butter issues except in extraordinary cases such as the prison guards at the Attica facility in upstate New York. Here prison reform, higher standards for correctional service personnel, and more humane treatment of inmates coincided with the welfare and safety of the correctional employees represented by the union. When similar relationships between service policy and employee welfare develop, as they may in many branches of government activity, employee organizations will doubtless tend to show increasing interest in operational policy. Thus, union trends toward involvement with substantive programs and issues of public policy are by-products of traditional union concerns. These trends, which appear to be the likely accompaniments of the growth of collective bargaining, will pose increasingly delicate problems for responsible public administrators. They entail what is perhaps the most difficult adjustments that unionization and collective bargaining bring to the public administrator.

The basic problem of adjustment for the administrator has been the necessity to accept collective bargaining, which compelled him to share his accustomed sole authority and to deal with his organized employees on a basis of equality.

The greatest changes have of course been in the area of personnel administration. Here the methods and procedures that constitute the personnel officers or civil service commissioner's professional techniques are being increasingly transferred to the bargaining table.

Public administrators on all levels, from local supervisors to chief executives, will have to acquaint themselves with the nature of the labor movement and the broader aspects of collective bargaining, even though they may not have to function as negotiating technicians. They will have to become more conversant with the labor costs of their agencies, including the hidden costs involved in benefits and the underutilization of the work force, as well as the more obvious costs of wages and salaries. They will have to make efforts to compete effectively with their union opposites in presenting a strong case to the public, because public opinion carries weight in labor disputes—especially in the public sector, where services rather than manufactured items are involved.

Competent labor relations staffs, often aided by outside consultants, will become equal partners of traditional "scientific" personnel officers, who must learn to function openly as instruments of management rather than as tightrope walkers attempting to be impartial friends of both sides.

Collective bargaining may force some restructuring of our local governments. It should at the very least bring about the establishment of regional centers for the advisement of smaller governmental units and the exchange and clearance of data and experience. If it does not bring about some merger and consolidation among the thousands of smaller governmental units, it may well encourage the establishment of regional administrations with adequate powers. But before such changes take place, associations of local units, analogous to trade associations of smaller businesses, may well be formed so that smaller and weaker units will be in a better position to deal with strong national unions, in the way in which the small-shop needle trades industries have associated to bargain with the strong unions in their field. In some areas of municipal administration, especially education and welfare, local negotiation may have to give way to negotiation on a state-wide basis. Some union leaders have indicated that they would welcome changes that would make it possible to deal with fewer units.

The Federal Interest

It should be noted that a substantial federal involvement already exists in local government administration. President Johnson attacked the settlement of the New York Transit strike of 1965 as exceeding federal wage guidelines. The President's vigorous television statement was widely regarded as a political attack on New York's new Mayor, who was then of the opposite political party. Federal involvement in local administration is also manifested by the merit system requirements for grant-in-aid programs and the restrictions on the political activity of local government employees under provisions of the Hatch Act, affecting employees of local agencies who are paid in part by federal funds.

It is to be hoped that both the teachers and AFSCME will give second thought to their proposal for federal legislation guaranteeing the right to organize and bargain. From a public policy viewpoint this represents a highly undesirable degree of centralization. From a union viewpoint it will represent legislation at the level of the lowest common denominator and the loss of much of the progress that local experimentation has achieved.

Balance Sheet and Outlook

The expanding unionization of public employees has brought about changes in the conduct of local government that would have been regarded as "impossible" before the 1960's. Municipal employees have, with few exceptions, not only closed the gap between their economic status and that of private employees but actually forged ahead of the latter in some respects. Also, according to testimony of experienced officials, good faith bargaining has proved to be an effective means of communication between public employers and employees.

Public administrators, however, not only have lost a substantial portion of their unilateral management rights but have also been obliged to share with the unions an increasing degree of their decisive powers over important aspects of public policy. Government, many have warned, must resist unreasonable incursion into its legal rights to determine public policy. Implementation of this warning, however, depends on the definition of "unreasonable." It is easy to say that internal democracy within the administrative process must not be permitted to erode responsible constitutional political democracy. But the roots of the problem lie in differentiating between "legitimate" bargaining issues of working conditions and questions of public policy in the constitutional domain of the political authorities and their legally designated agents.

Realistically, the process of managing can no longer be separated from the concept of cooperation with employee organizations, which must recognize that all employment relationships cannot entail collective bargaining. A clear line demarking the respective spheres of bargaining rights and managerial prerogative defies solution. It cannot be resolved by rhetoric or strained definitions. A modus vivendi might be found in mutual restraint and growing maturity of the parties. But public employment relations do not operate in a Utopian vacuum. They operate in an environment the very essence of which is politics. This more than all else determines the nature and direction of public employer-employee relations.

While the strike is the most dramatic issue, equally important is the rising extent of codetermination of policy in the public administrative process, now widely referred to as participative decision-making. The ultimate effect of these tendencies raise serious questions, the answers to which cannot be foreseen. Will they spell basic changes in the traditional balance of political power and create a new force strong enough to subordinate constitutional organs, transferring decisive public power beyond the reach of our normal political processes? Or will unionized public employees in association with millions of fellow citizens in a common labor movement enhance representative government by breaching the barriers between the bureaucracies and the people?

Notes

1. 37 Statute 555, August 24, 1912.
2. State of New York, Chapter 805, 1920.
3. Harold J. Laski, *Authority in the Modern State* (New Haven: Yale University Press, 1927), p. 379.
4. This was unlike the situation in the famous Boston police strike of 1919, where, either through the deliberate duplicity or gross mismanagement of the Police Commissioner and Governor Collidge's repeated evasion of responsibility, the nonstriking police and a specially organized emergency force were not used and disorder occurred. For a fully documented account of the tragic and unnecessary Boston strike, see Sterling D. Spero, *Government as Employer* (New York: Remsen Press, 1948).
5. Newell B. Terry, "Collective Bargaining in the U.S. Department of Interior," *Public Administration Review*, Winter 1962, p. 23.

Bibliography

Books and Monographs

Anderson, Howard J. *Public Employee Organization and Bargaining*. Washington, D.C.: Bureau of National Affairs, 1968.

Banfield, Edward C. *Big City Politics*. New York: Random House, 1966.

————, ed. *Urban Government*. New York: Free Press of Glencoe, 1961.

————, and James Q. Wilson. *City Politics*. Cambridge: Harvard University Press, 1963.

Barbash, Jack, ed. *Unions and Union Leadership*. New York: Harper & Row, 1959.

————. *The Practice of Unionism*. New York: Harper & Row, 1956.

Belasco, James A. *Public Employee Dispute Settlement: The Wisconsin Experience; Collective Bargaining in City X*. Ithaca: New York School of Industrial and Labor Relations Reprint No. 188, 1966.

Blackman, John L. *Presidential Seizures in Labor Disputes*. Cambridge: Harvard University Press, 1967.

Blum, Albert A. *Management and the White-Collar Union*. New York: American Management Association Research Study No. 63, 1964.

Bok, Derek C., and Dunlop, John T. *Labor and the American Community*. New York: Simon and Schuster, 1970.

Case, Harry L. *Personnel Policy in a Public Agency: The TVA Experience*. New York: Harper & Row, 1955.

Chalmers, W. Ellison, and Gerald W. McCormick, eds. *Racial Conflict and Negotiations: Perspectives and First Case Studies*. Ann Arbor, Mich.: Institute of Labor and Industrial Relations, 1971.

Champlain, Neil W., and J. W. Kuhn. *Collective Bargaining*. New York: McGraw-Hill, 1965.

Coddington, Alan. *Theories of the Bargaining Process*. London: Allan and Unwin, 1968.

Committee on Employee Relations in the Public Service, *Report to the Civil Service Assembly*. Chicago, 1942.

Connery, Robert H., and William V. Farr. *Unionization of Municipal Employees*. Proceedings of the Academy of Political Science, Columbia University, New York, 1970. Vol. 30, No. 2.

Cook, Alice H. *Adaptations of Union Structure for Municipal Collective Bargaining*. Reprint Series No. 198. Ithaca, N. Y.: New York State School of Industrial and Labor Relations, Cornell University.

Corcoran, John D. "An Agency Shop for Public Employees in New York City," *District Council 37, AFSCME, 1968*. Mimeo.

Crispo, John H. S., ed. *Collective Bargaining and the Professional Employee*. Toronto: Centre for Industrial Relations, University of Toronto, 1966.

Dahl, Robert A. *Who Governs*. New Haven: Yale University Press, 1961.

Doherty, Robert E., ed. *Employer-Employee Relations in the Public Schools*. Ithaca: New York State School of Industrial and Labor Relations, Cornell University, 1967.

Dunhill, Frank. *The Civil Service*. London: Allyn and Unwin, 1956.

Dunlop, John T. *Industrial Relations Systems*. New York: Holt, Rinehart and Winston, 1958.

Drachman, Allan W. *Municipal Negotiations: From Differences to Agreement*. Labor-Management Relations Service, Washington, D.C., 1970.

Eaton, William J. *A Look at Public Employee Unions*. Labor-Management Relations Service, Washington, D.C., Pub. No. 4, September 1970.

Finer, Herman. *Theory and Practice of Modern Government*. New York: Holt, 1949.

Ford, Pamela S. *Political Activities of the Public Service: A Continuing Problem*. Berkeley, Calif.: Institute of Governmental Studies, 1963.

Frankel, Saul J., and R. C. Pratt. *Municipal Labor Relations in Canada*. Montreal: Canadian Federation of Mayors and Municipalities, 1954.

Frankfurter, Felix, and Nathan Greene. *The Labor Injunction*. New York: Macmillan, 1930.

Friedrich, Carl J., and Taylor Cole. *Responsible Bureaucracy*. Cambridge: Harvard University Press, 1932.

Godine, Morton R. *The Labor Problem in the Public Service: A Study in Political Pluralism*. Cambridge, Mass.: Harvard University Press, 1951.

Goldstein, Bernard. *The Perspective of Unionized Professionals*. New Brunswick: Rutgers–The State University, Institute of Management and Labor Relations, Reprint No. 7, 1959.

Gray, Kenneth E. *"A Report on Politics in Cincinnati."* Cambridge, Mass.: Joint Center for Urban Studies, 1959. Mimeo.

Greenstone, David. *A Report on the Politics of Detroit*. Cambridge, Mass.: Joint Center for Urban Studies, 1961. Mimeo.

Gregory, Charles O. *Labor and the Law*. New York: W. W. Norton, 1949.

Hagburg, Eugene C., ed. *Problems Confront Union Organization in Public Employment*. Columbus: Ohio State University, Labor Education and Research Service, 1966.

Hanslowe, Kurt L. *The Emerging Law of Labor Relations in Public Employment*. Ithaca: New York State School of Industrial and Labor Relations, Cornell University, 1967.

Hanson, Bertil. *A Report on the Politics of Milwaukee*. Cambridge: Joint Center for Urban Studies, 1961. Mimeo.

Hart, Wilson R. *Collective Bargaining in the Federal Civil Service*. New York: Harper & Row, 1961.

Heisel, W. D., and J. D. Hallihan. *Questions and Answers on Public Employee Negotiation*. Chicago: Public Personnel Association.

Institute of Collective Bargaining and Group Relations. *Collective Bargaining Today*, Washington, D.C.: Bureau of National Affairs, 1970.

Kheel, Theodore. *The Pros and Cons of Compulsory Arbitration*. New York Chamber of Commerce Pamphlet, March 1961.

Klaus, Ida. "Collective Bargaining by Government Employees," in *Conference on Labor*. Proceedings. New York University, 1959, pp. 21-38.

————. *Collective Bargaining Will Help Staff Morale*. New York: Society for the Experimental Study of Education, Yearbook, 1963.

Kramer, Leo. *Labor's Paradox: The American Federation of State, County and Municipal Employees, AFL-CIO*. New York: Wiley, 1962. Studies of Comparative Union Governments.

Kruger, Daniel H., and Charles T. Schmidt. *Collective Bargaining in the Public Service*. New York: Random House, 1969. Paperback.

Landsberger, Henry. *A Final Report to Participants in the Mediation Project*. Ithaca: New York State School of Industrial and Labor Relations, Cornell University, 1959.

Laski, Harold. *Authority in the Modern State*. New Haven, Conn.: Yale University Press, 1918.

Lazarus, Herman, and Joseph P. Goldberg. *The Role of Collective Bargaining in a Democracy*, Report No. 3. Washington, D.C.: The Public Affairs Institute, 1949.

Levin, Edward, ed. *New York State Public Employment Labor Relations.* Ithaca: New York State School of Industrial and Labor Relations, Cornell University, 1968.

Lieberman, Myron, and Michael H. Moskow. *Collective Negotiations for Teachers.* Chicago: Rand McNally, 1966.

Long, William A. *The Development and Techniques of Collective Bargaining in the Municipal Service.* Washington, D.C.: International Association of Fire Fighters, 1966.

Marini, Frank., ed. *Toward a New Public Administration.* Scranton, Pa.: Chandler, 1970.

Mosher, Frederick C. *Democracy in the Public Service.* New York: Oxford University Press, 1968.

Moskow, Michael H., J. Joseph Loewenberg, and Edward C. Kozaria. *Collective Bargaining in Public Employment.* New York: Random House, 1970.

————. *Teachers and Unions.* Philadelphia: University of Pennsylvania, 1966.

Ocheltree, Kenneth, ed. *Government Labor Relations in Transition.* Chicago: Public Personnel Association, 1966.

Olson, Mancur. *The Logic of Collective Action: Public Goals and the Theory of Groups.* Cambridge, Mass.: Harvard University Press, 1965.

Pickets at City Hall, Report and Recommendations of the Twentieth Century Fund Task Force on Labor Disputes in Public Employment. New York: Twentieth Century Fund, 1970.

Polisar, Eric. *Strikes and Solutions.* Chicago: Public Personnel Association, 1968.

Rayback, Joseph G. *A History of American Labor.* New York: Macmillan, 1961.

Roberts, Harold S. *Labor-Management Relations in the Public Service.* Industrial Relations Center, University of Hawaii, August 1968. (A good list of references for material prior to 1969.)

Rehmus, Charles M., and Evan Wilner. *The Economic Results of Teacher Bargainings: Michigan's First Two Years.* Ann Arbor: Institute of Labor and Industrial Relations, University of Michigan–Wayne State University, 1968.

Rhyme, Charles S. *Labor Unions and Municipal Employee Law.* Washington, D.C.: National Institute of Law Officers, 1956.

Rothman, Edwin. *Philadelphia Government.* 6th ed. Philadelphia: Pennsylvania Economy League, in association with the Bureau of Municipal Research, 1963.

Rubin, Richard S. *A Summary of State Collective Bargaining Law in Public Employment.* Public Employee Relations Report No. 3. Ithaca: New York State School of Industrial and Labor Relations, Cornell University, 1968.

Rustein, Jacob J. *Survey of Current Personnel Systems in State and Local Governments.* Good Government National Civil Service League, 1971.

Saso, Carmen D. *Coping With Public Employee Strikes.* Chicago: Public Personnel Association, 1970.

Sayre, Wallace S., and H. Kaufman. *Governing New York City.* New York: Russell Sage Foundation, 1960.

Shils, Edward B., and C. Taylor Whittier. *Teachers, Administrators, and Collective Bargaining.* New York: Crowell, 1968.

331

Simkin, William. *Mediation and the Dynamics of Labor Relations.* Washington, D.C.: Bureau of National Affairs, 1972.

Solomon, Benjamin. *Teachers and Nurses: The Issue of Group Power for Professional Employees.* Chicago: University of Chicago, Industrial Relations Center, 1966.

Spero, Sterling D. *Government as Employer.* New York: Remsen Press, 1948.

————. *The Labor Movement in a Government Industry.* New York: George D. Doran Co., 1924.

————. *Labor Relations in British Nationalized Industry.* New York: New York University Press, 1955.

Stahl, Glenn O. *Public Personnel Administration.* 6th ed. New York: Harper & Row, 1971.

Stanley, David. *Managing Local Government Under Union Pressure.* Washington, D.C.: The Brookings Institution, 1971.

————. *Professional Personnel for the City of New York.* Washington, D.C.: The Brookings Institution, 1963.

Stinnett, T. M., Jack Kleinmann, and Martha Ware. *Professional Negotiation in Public Education.* New York: Macmillan, 1966.

Straetz, Ralph A. *PR Politics in Cincinnati.* New York: New York University Press, 1958.

Stutz, Robert L. *Collective Dealing by Units of Local Government in Connecticut.* Storrs, Conn.: University of Connecticut, Labor Management Institute, 1960.

Thomson, Andrew J. *Unit Determination in Public Employment.* Public Employee Relations Report No. 1. Ithaca: New York State School of Industrial and Labor Relations, Cornell University, 1967.

————. *Strikes and Strike Penalties in Public Employment,* Public Employee Relations Report No. 2. Ithaca: New York State School of Industrial and Labor Relations, Cornell University, 1967.

Voslos, William B. *Collective Bargaining in the United States Federal Civil Service.* Chicago: Public Personnel Association, 1966.

Warner, Kenneth O., ed. *Collective Bargaining in the Public Service: Theory and Practice.* Chicago: Public Personnel Association, 1967.

————, and Mary L. Hennessey. *Public Management at the Bargaining Table.* Chicago: Public Personnel Association, 1967. (Pp. 28-31 and 220-24 deal with independent associations.)

Weber, Arnold R., ed. *The Structure of Collective Bargaining.* Glencoe, Ill.: Free Press, 1961.

Weiford, Douglas. *Public Management,* May 1963.

Wellington, Harry H., and Ralph K. Winter, Jr. *The Unions and the Cities.* Washington, D.C.: The Brookings Institution, 1971.

Wike, Leroy E. *Police Unions.* Washington, D.C.: International Association of Chiefs of Police, 1958.

Wildavsky, Aaron. *The Politics of the Budgetary Process.* Boston: Little, Brown, 1964.

Wildman, Wesley A. *Implications of Teacher Bargaining for School Administration.* Chicago: University of Chicago, Industrial Relations Center, 1964.

Williams, David G., and Don C. Hall. *The Legal Status of Public Employee Strikes and Collective Bargaining in West Virginia.* Pub. No. 68 Bureau for Government Research. Morgantown: West Virginia University, December 1970.

332

Woodworth, Robert. *Collective Negotiations for Public and Professional Employees.* Glenview, Ill.: Scott, Foresman, 1967.

Zeidler, Frank P. *New Roles for Public Officials in Labor Relations,* PHRL, No. 23, Public Personnel Association, Chicago, 1970.

———, Felix A. Nigro, J. D. Love, and W. D. Heisel. *Rethinking the Philosophy of Employee Relations in the Public Service.* Chicago, Ill.: Public Personnel Association, 1968.

Ziskind, David. *One Thousand Strikes of Government Employees.* New York: Columbia University Press, 1940.

Articles and Addresses

Agger, Carol. "The Government and Its Employees." *Yale Law Journal,* May 1938, pp. 1109-35.

Anderson, Arvid. "Selection and Certification of Representatives." Address, *Twentieth Annual Conference on Labor,* New York University, April 18, 1967. Mimeo.

———. "Labor Relations in the Public Service." *Wisconsin Law Review,* July 1961. (Reprinted in *Labor Law Journal,* November 1961.)

———. "The New York City Office of Collective Bargaining," in Edwin Levin, ed., *New York State Public Employment Labor Relations, Conference, November 15, 1967.* Ithaca, New York: New York State School of Industrial and Labor Relations, Cornell University, 1968, pp. 7-11.

———. "Labor Relations in the Public Service: Analysis of the Present Status of Public Employee Unions," *Labor Law Journal,* vol. 12 (November 1961), pp. 1069-94.

———. "Labor Relations in the Public Service," *Wisconsin Law Review,* July 1961.

———. "Public Employees and Collective Bargaining: Comparative and Local Experience," *Proceedings of the 21st Annual Conference on Labor,* New York University, New York, 1969.

———. "Collective Bargaining in Municipal and State Sectors," *Good Government, Summer, 1971.*

Ashenfelter, Orley. "The Effect of Unionization on Wages in the Public Sector: The Case of Fire Fighters," *Industrial and Labor Relations Review,* January 1971, pp. 191-203.

Baird, William B. "Barriers to Collective Bargaining in Registered Nursing," *Labor Law Journal,* January 1969, pp. 42-47.

Balik, Al. "Toward Public Sector Equality: Extending the Strike Privilege," *Labor Law Journal,* June 1970, pp. 338-57.

Barbash, Jack. "Bargaining for Professionals and Public Employees," *American Teachers Magazine,* April 1959.

Barboff, Bernard, and Lily Mary David. "Collective Bargaining and Work Stoppages Involving Teachers", *Monthly Labor Review,* May 1953.

Belasco, James. "Resolving Disputes Over Contract Terms in the State Public Service: An Analysis," *Labor Law Journal,* September 1965, pp. 533-44.

Berger, Harriet F. "Grievance Process in the Philadelphia Public Service," *Industrial and Labor Relations Review,* vol. 13, July 1960, pp. 568-80.

———. "The Old Order Giveth Way to the New: A Comparison of

333

Executive Order 10988 with Executive Order 11491," *Labor Law Journal,* February 1970, pp. 79-88.

Berrodin, Eugene F. "Cross-Currents in Public Employee Bargaining," *Public Personnel Review,* October 1968, pp. 217-22.

Beyer, William C. "Municipal Civil Service in the United States," in Carl J. Friedrich, *et al., Problems of the American Public Service.* New York: McGraw-Hill, 1935.

Blank, Blanche D. "Topics: Civil Services as a Victim," *The New York Times,* March 4, 1967.

Bloedorn, John. "The Strike and the Public Sector," *Labor Law Journal,* March 1969, pp. 151-61.

Blum, Albert A. "Work or Fight: The Use of the Draft as a Manpower Sanction During the Second World War," *Industrial and Labor Relations Review,* April 1963.

Bodenhimer, Richard. "D.C. 37 Wins Agreement," *The Chief,* March 5, 1969.

Brooks, Thomas R. "Labor: Transit Rank-and-File Revolt," *Dun's Review and Modern Industry,* March 1965, pp. 34-35, 63-68.

—————. "Collective Bargaining in Education," *Dissent,* vol. 13, May-June 1966, pp. 306-11.

Brown, George W. "Teacher Power Techniques: Serious New Problems," *American School Board Journal,* vol. 152, February 1966.

Burns, John E. "The Professional Employee Dilemma and the Appropriate Bargaining Unit," *Labor Law Journal,* April 1961.

Capozzola, John M. "Citizen's Concern With Municipal Collective Bargaining," in Robert E. Walsh, ed., *Sorry . . . No Government Today: Unions vs. City Hall.* Boston: Beacon Press, 1969.

—————. "Compulsory Arbitration: Too Much Mythology and Too Few Facts." Address, National Conference on Government, Philadelphia, November 12, 1969.

—————. "Public Personnel Law: Its Meaning for Teacher Unions in the United States." Address, American Educational Research Association, Chicago, 1968.

—————. "Union Bargaining Hits City Budgets," *National Civic Review,* December 1967.

Catlin, Robert E. "Should Public Employees Have the Right to Strike?" *Public Personnel Review,* January 1968, pp. 2-7.

Chisholm, Allan D. "Mediating the Public Employee Dispute," *Labor Law Journal,* January 1961.

Clark, R. Theodore, Jr. "Public Employee Labor Legislation: A Study of the Unsuccessful Attempt to Enact a Public Employee Bargaining Statute in Illinois," *Labor Law Journal,* vol. 20, March 1969, pp. 164-73.

Cohen, Frederick. "Legal Aspects of Unionization Among Public Employees," *Temple Law Quarterly,* vol. 30, Winter 1957, pp. 187-98.

Cook, Alice H. "Union Structure in Municipal Collective Bargaining," *Monthly Labor Review,* vol. 79, June 1965, pp. 606-08.

—————. "Public Employee Bargaining in New York City," *Industrial Relations,* May 1970.

Costikyan, Edward N. "Who Runs the City Government?" *New York Magazine,* May 26, 1969.

Coutourier, Jean J. "Crisis, Conflict, and Change: The Future of Collective Bargaining in Public Service," *Good Government,* Spring 1969, pp. 7-12. (Concise and superbly handled overview.)

————. "Patronage Versus Performance—The Balance Sheet of Civil Service Reform," *Good Government,* Fall 1967.

Craft, James A. "Fire Fighter Militancy and Wage Disparity," *Labor Law Journal,* December 1970, pp. 794-807.

Crichton, Edward E. "Arbitration Practices in the Australian Public Service," *Public Personnel Review,* April 1965, pp. 88-93.

Crowley, Joseph R. "The Resolution of Representation Disputes Under the Taylor Law," *Fordham Law Review,* May 1969.

Daly, Ronald O. "New Directions for Professional Negotiation," *National Education Association Journal,* October 1966.

Dean, Lois R. "Union Activity and Dual Loyalty," *Industrial and Labor Relations Review,* July 1954.

Derber, Milton. "Labor Management Policy for Public Employees in Illinois: The Experience of the Governor's Commission, 1966-1967," *Industrial and Labor Relations Review,* vol. 21, no. 4, July 1968, pp. 541-58.

Dewald, Franklin K. "Bargaining—Unit Relationships in Public Service," *"Personnel Administration,* vol. 33, no. 1, January-February 1967, pp. 40-42.

Dewey, Allen C. "Labor Law—Collective Bargaining—Right or Power of Municipalities to Engage in Collective Bargaining," *Michigan Law Review,* vol. 56, February 1958, pp. 615-18.

Doherty, Robert E. "Determination of Bargaining Units and Election Procedures in Public School Teacher Representation Election," *Industrial and Labor Relations Review,* vol. 19, July 1966, pp. 573-95.

————. "Labor Relations Negotiators on Bargaining Factories vs. the Schools," *ISR Journal,* vol. 1, no. 1 Winter 1969, pp. 5-14.

————. "Law and Collective Bargaining for Teachers," *Teachers College Record,* vol. 68, October 1966, pp. 1-12.

Donoian, Harry A. "Organizational Problems of Government Employee Unions," *Labor Law Journal,* vol. 18, March 1967, pp. 137-144.

————. "Recognition and Collective Bargaining Agreements of Federal Employee Unions—1963-1969," *Labor Law Journal,* September 1970, pp. 597-607.

Dotson, Arch. "The Emerging Doctrine of Privilege in Public Employment," *Public Administration Review,* Spring, 1955, p. 77.

————. "A General Theory of Public Employment," *Public Administration Review,* Spring 1956.

Eaton, William J. *A Look at Public Employee Unions.* Washington, D.C.: Labor Management Relations Service, 1970.

Egan, Cy. "Police Talk Tough at Convention," *New York Post,* July 21, 1970.

Elam, Stanley M. "NEA-AFT Merger—and Related Matters," *Phi Delta Kappan,* vol. 47, February 1966, pp. 285-86.

————. "Rift Without Differences," *The Nation,* October 18, 1965, pp. 247-49.

————. "Union or Guild," *The Nation,* June 29, 1964, pp. 651-53.

Eisner, J. Michael. "First Amendment Right of Association for Public Employee Union Members," *Labor Law Journal,* July 1969, pp. 438-45.

Fallon, William J. "For Some Order in Public Employee Bargaining," *Labor Law Journal,* July 1970, pp. 434-38.

"Feinsinger Gives Plan on Strikes," *Milwaukee Journal,* May 21, 1967.

Flagler, William J. "Preparation for Negotiation," *Ideas . . . Employee-*

Management Cooperation. Washington, D.C.: U.S. Department of Agriculture, 1963.

Foegen, J. H. "Mediation from Initiation," *Public Personnel Review,* January 1970, pp. 7-13.

————. "The Partial Strike: A Solution in Public Employment," *Public Personnel Review,* April 1969, pp. 83-88.

Foltman, Felician F. "Implications of Fringe Benefits in the 1970's," *Arizona Review,* June-July 1968.

Forkosch, Morris D. "Boulwarism: Will Labor-Management Relations Take It or Leave It?" *Catholic University of America Law Review,* Spring 1970.

Frederickson, H. George. "Public Employee Militancy: Attitudes, Politics, and Bargaining." Proceedings of the American Political Science Association, Washington, D.C., 1968.

French, Wendell L., and Richard Robinson. "Collective Bargaining by Nurses and Other Professionals: Anomaly or Trend?" *Labor Law Journal,* October 1964.

Graham, Jean C. "Patronage—Fact and Fancy," *Public Personnel Review,* April 1962.

Gray, Herman A. "Topics: The City Unions Need One Bargaining Table," New York *Times,* December 16, 1967.

————. "The Nature and Scope of Arbitration and Arbitration Clauses." Address, New York University Conference on Labor, 1948.

Gromfine, I. J. "Union Security Clauses in Public Employment." Address, Twenty Second Conference on Labor, New York University, June 11, 1969.

Hamilton, Randy H. "The New Militancy of Public Employees," *Public Affairs Report,* vol. 8, no. 4, Berkeley: Institute of Governmental Studies, University of California, August 1967, p. 6.

Harris, Richard L. "Independent Municipal Employee Associations in California," in Kenneth O. Warner, ed., *Management Relations with Organized Public Employees.* Chicago: Public Personnel Association, 1963. pp. 194-202.

Hastings, Robert H. "How to Bargain in the Public Service," *Good Government,* Winter 1970, pp. 8-15.

Heisel, W. Donald. "Anatomy of a Strike," *Public Personnel Review,* October .1969, pp. 226-33.

————, and J. P. Santa Emma. "Unions in City Government: The Cincinnati Story," *Public Personnel Review,* January 1971, pp. 35-39.

Helburn, I. B., and Stephen R. Zimmer. "The Federal Supervisor: A Comment on Executive Order 11491," *Public Personnel Review,* January 1971, pp. 2-8.

Hellriegel, Don, et. al. "Collective Negotiations and Teachers: A Behavioral Analysis," *Industrial and Labor Relations Review,* April 1970.

Hepbron, James M. "Police Unionization Means Disorganization," *American City,* vol. 73, November 1958, pp. 131-32.

Herzog, Donald R. "Fringe Benefits: The Federal Government v. Private Industry," *Labor Law Journal,* February 1971, pp. 89-100.

Hoffman, Herbert. "Right of Public Employees to Strike," *De Paul Law Review,* vol. 10 no. 2, Autumn-Winter 1966, pp. 815-839.

Hoffman, Robert B. "The Union-Employee Communication Gap," *Labor Law Journal,* April 1970, pp. 231-40.

Holland, Thomas W. "When You Meet With the Union," Unpublished address delivered at the Regional Staff Committee Conference on Employee-Management Cooperation. U.S. Department of Labor, Washington, D.C., June 1963.

Hustad, Fred. "Legal Conflict Between Civil Service and Collective Bargaining in Michigan," *Public Personnel Review,* October 1970, pp. 269-73.

Jensen, Vernon H. "The Process of Collective Bargaining and the Question of Its Obsolescence," *Industrial and Labor Relations Review,* July 1963.

Kahn, Tom. "Teacher Unions and Politics: Some Thoughts for Labor Day," New York *Times,* September 5, 1971.

Kaplan, H. Eliot. "Political Neutrality of the Civil Service," *Public Personnel Review,* April 1940.

Kasper, Hirschel. "The Effects of Collective Bargaining on Public School Teachers' Salaries," *Industrial and Labor Relations Review,* October 1970, pp. 57-73.

Kassalow, Everett M. "Public Employee Bargaining in Europe: What Lessons for the United States," *Proceedings of the Twenty-First Annual Meeting, Industrial Relations Research Association,* Madison, Wisc., 1969, pp. 48-58.

—————. "Trade Unionism Goes Public," *The Public Interest,* Winter 1969.

Kelly, Matthew. "The Contract Rejection Problem: A Positive Labor-Management Approach," *Labor Law Journal,* July 1969, pp. 404-16.

Kheel, Theodore, "Impasse Procedures in Public Employment." in Edwin Levin, ed., *New York State Public Employment Labor Relations.* Conference, November 15, 1967, New York State School of Industrial and Labor Relations. Ithaca: Cornell University, 1968, pp. 19-22.

—————. "How to Prevent Strikes by Public Employees," *Proceedings of the 21st Annual Conference on Labor,* New York University, 1969.

Kiely, Terrence. "Right of Public Employees to Strike," *De Paul Review,* vol. 16, Autumn-Winter 1966, pp. 151-65.

Kieta, Joseph E. "The Strike and Its Alternatives in Public Employment," *Public Personnel Review,* October 1970, pp. 226-31.

Killingsworth, Charles C. "Grievance Adjudication in Public Employment," *American Arbitration Journal,* vol. 13, no. 1, pp. 3-15.

Kingston, Paul J. "Check-off—Does It Ever Die?" *Labor Law Journal,* March 1970, pp. 159-67.

Klaus, Ida. "Labor Relations in the Public Service: Exploration and Experiment," *Syracuse Law Review,* vol. 10, Spring 1959, pp. 183-202.

—————. *Collective Bargaining Will Help Staff Morale.* New York: Society for the Experimental Study of Education, 1963.

—————. "The Emerging Relationship." Address, Conference on Public Employment and Collective Bargaining, University of Chicago, February 5, 1965.

Klein, Paul E., and Janet Axelbrod. "The Taylor Law and Public Schools: A Look at Some Areas of Representation and Improper Practices," *Labor Law Journal,* July 1970, pp. 420-34.

Kleingartner, Archie. "Nurses, Collective Bargaining and Labor Legislation," *Labor Law Journal,* vol. 18, April 1967, pp. 236-45.

Knowlton, Thomas A. "Is Collective Bargaining the Answer? Comments on a Municipal Labor Crisis (New York City)," *Arbitration Journal,* vol. 21, no. 2 (1966), pp. 93-97.

Krinsky, Edward B. "Public Employment Fact Finding in Fourteen States," *Labor Law Journal,* September 1966, pp. 532-40.

Krislov, Joseph. "The Independent Public Employee Association: Characteristics and Functions," *Industrial and Labor Relations Review*, July 1962, pp. 41-57.

————. "The Union Shop, Employment Security and Municipal Workers," *Industrial and Labor Relations Review*, January 1959.

Krouse, Robert D. "The Short Troubled History of Wisconsin's New Labor Law," *Public Administration Review*, December 1965, pp. 302-7.

Kuhn, James W. "A New View of Boulwarism: The Significance of the GE Strike," *Labor Law Journal*, September 1970, pp. 582-91.

Lahne, Herbert J. "Contract Negotiations: Who Speaks for the Union?" *Labor Law Journal*, May 1969, pp. 259-64.

Levenson, Rosaline. "Municipal Fringe Benefit Pattern Shows Stability in Connecticut," *Local Government Newsletter*, Storrs, Conn., Institute of Public Service, May 1967.

Levine, Marvin J. "Collective Bargaining in the Federal Government," *Public Personnel Review*, July 1969, pp. 164-69.

Lieberman, Myron. "Battle for New York City's Teachers," *Phi Delta Kappan*, vol. 43, October 1961, pp. 2-8.

————. "Teacher Strikes: An Analysis of the Issues," *Harvard Educational Review*, vol. 81, Winter 1956, pp. 39-70.

————. "Teachers' Strikes: Acceptable Strategy," *Phi Delta Kappan*, vol. 46, January 1965, pp. 237-240.

Loeb, Louis S. "Public Employees and Political Activity: New Realities Require Fresh Approaches," *Good Government*, Winter 1967, p. 8.

Loewenberg, J. Joseph. "Compulsory Arbitration for Police and Fire Fighters in Pennsylvania in 1968," *Industrial and Labor Relations Review*, April 1970, pp. 367-80.

————. "Development of the Federal Labor-Management Relations Program: Executive Order 10988 and Executive Order 11491," *Labor Law Journal*, February 1970, pp. 73-79.

Long, Norton. "Public Policy and Administration: The Goals of Rationality and Responsibility," *Public Administration Review*, Winter 1954.

Love, Thomas M. "Municipal Employment Relations in Wisconsin: Administration," *Wisconsin Law Review*, Summer 1965, pp. 652-70.

Lovell, Hugh G. "The Pressure Lever in Mediation," *Industrial and Labor Relations Review*, October 1952.

Madden, John V. "To Strike or Not To Strike: Does the Government Already Have an Alternative?" *Labor Law Journal*, May 1970, pp. 310-18.

Madden, Richard L. "Lindsay Finds Capitol Lobby Success," *New York Times*, February 13, 1970.

Manson, Julius J. "Mediators and Their Qualifications," *Labor Law Journal*, October 1958.

McCafferty, Bart. "Unionized Municipal Employees: Financial Aspects," *Municipal Finance*, vol. 33, November 1960, pp. 98-103.

McLennan, Kenneth, and Michael H. Moskow. "Multilateral Bargaining in the Public Sector," *Twenty-First Annual Proceedings, Industrial Relations Research Association*, Madison, Wisc., 1969, pp. 31-40.

McClellan, Larkin W., and Peter E. Obermeyer. "Science or Art? Performance Standards for Mediators," *Labor Law Journal*, September 1970, pp. 591-97.

McKelvey, Jean. "Cook County Commissioners' Fact Finding Board Report on Collective Bargaining and County Public Aid Employees," *Industrial and Labor Relations Review*, vol. 20, no. 3, April 1967, pp. 457-77.

————. "Fact Finding in Public Employment Disputes: Promise or Illusion," *Twenty-First Annual Proceedings, Industrial Relations Research Association,* Madison, Wisc., 1969, pp. 41-47.

————. "The Role of State Agencies in Public Employee Labor Relations," *Industrial and Labor Relations Review,* vol. 20, no. 2, January 1967, pp. 179-97.

————. "The American City and Its Public Employee Unions." *Proceedings of the Industrial Relations Research Association, Spring Meeting, 1966.*

McLaughlin, Richard P. "Collective Bargaining Suggestions for the Public Sector," *Labor Law Journal,* March 1969, pp. 131-38.

Meller, Norman. "Executive-Legislative Conflict and the Personnel Administrator," *Public Personnel Review,* April 1966.

Miller, Arwood M. "The Personnel Officer—Between the Devil and the Deep," *Public Personnel Review,* January 1962.

Miller, Norman C. "Lobby in Action," *Wall Street Journal,* January 20, 1970.

Moberly, Robert B. "Causes of Impasse in School Board–Teacher Negotiations," *Labor Law Journal,* October 1970, pp. 668-78.

————. "The Strike and Its Alternatives in Public Employment," *Wisconsin Law Review,* vol. 17, Spring 1966, pp. 549-82.

Morse, Muriel M. "Shall We Bargain Away the Merit System?" *Public Personnel Review,* 1963, pp. 239-43.

Mortier, James F. "The Experience in Milwaukee," in *The City Prepares for Labor Relations,* Labor Management Relations Service, Washington, D.C., 1970.

Moskow, Michael H. "Collective Bargaining for Public School Teachers," *Labor Law Journal,* vol. 15, no. 12, December 1964, pp. 787-94.

Muir, J. Douglas. "The Strike as a Professional Sanction: The Changing Attitude of the National Education Association," *Labor Law Journal,* October 1968, pp. 615-27.

————. "Canada's Experience With the Right of Public Employees to Strike," *Monthly Labor Review,* July 1969.

Mulcahy, Charles. "A Municipality's Rights and Responsibilities Under The Wisconsin Municipal Labor Law," *Marquette Law Review,* vol. 49, no. 3, February 1966, pp. 512-32.

Mustafa, Husain. "Cost Implications of Public Labor-Management Cooperation," *Labor Law Journal,* October 1970, pp. 654-63.

Mysliwiec, Frank A. "Municipal Employees' Unions: The Climb Up Labor's Ladder," *Duquesne University Law Review,* vol. 4, no. 1, Fall 1965, pp. 137-45.

"New Opportunities Greet School Lunch, School Aides," *Public Employee,* vol. 9, no. 5, May 8, 1968.

Nigro, Felix A., ed. "A Symposium: Collective Negotiations in the Public Service," *Public Administration Review,* vol. 27, March-April 1968, pp. 11-147.

————. "Unions and New Careers," *Good Government,* Fall 1970, pp. 10-12.

————. "What Every Civil Service Commissioner Needs to Know About Labor Relations," *Good Government,* Spring 1969, pp. 3-7.

"Nurses' Aides: Up, Up, Up the Career Ladder," *Public Employee,* vol. 9, no. 5, May 8, 1969.

339

Parker, Hyman. "Performance Standards for Mediators," *Labor Law Journal,* November 1970, pp. 738-45.
Parks, Michael. "Cities on Strike," *American,* vol. 115, October 15, 1966, pp. 455-57.
Patrick, Floyd R. "Organized Labor's Role in American Politics," *Labor Law Journal,* vol. 28, no. 5, May 1967, pp. 274-77.
Pearlman, David. "The Surge of Public Employee Unionism," *The American Federationist,* June 1971.
Perloff, Stephen H. "Comparing Municipal Salaries with Industry and Federal Pay," *Monthly Labor Review,* October 1971.
Peterson, Donald J. "Consequences of the Arbitration Award for Unions," *Labor Law Journal,* September 1970, pp. 613-18.
Phelps, Orme W. "Compulsory Arbitration: Some Perspectives," *Industrial and Labor Relations Review,* vol. 18, October 1964, pp. 81-91.
Posey, Rollin B. "The Negotiating Session," *Public Personnel Review,* April 1965, pp. 73-78.
Presondorf, Anthony. "A Political Machine in Wheels," *New York Post,* February 24, 1968.
Pressman, William B. "Place of the Agency Shop," *The Chief.* Letters to the Editor, March 5, 1969.
Prevo, Randall M. "Unions and the Personnel Officer," *Public Personnel Review,* April 1970.
Putnam, Robert D. "Political Attitudes and the Local Community," *American Political Science Review,* September 1966.
Rains, Harry H. "Collective Bargaining in Public Employment," *Labor Law Journal,* vol. 8, pp. 548-50.
————. "New York Public Employee Relations Laws," *Labor Law Journal,* May 1969, pp. 264-93.
Raskin, A. H. "A New Pattern on Pensions," New York *Times,* January 7, 1946.
————. "Do Public Strikes Violate Public Trust?" *New York Times Magazine,* January 5, 1961.
————. "He Leads His Teachers Up the Down Staircase," *New York Times Magazine,* September 3, 1967.
————. "Politics Up-Ends the Bargaining Table." Address, Conference of American Management Association, New York, March 22-24, 1971.
————. "Strikes by Public Employees," *The Atlantic,* vol. 201, no. 1, January 1968, pp. 46-51.
Rehnquist, William H. "Public Dissent and the Public Employee," *Civil Service Journal,* vol. 11, no. 3, January-March 1971, pp. 7-16.
Rich, J. M. "Civil Disobedience and Teacher Strikes," *Phi Delta Kappan,* vol. 45, December 1963, pp. 151-54.
Rick, Michael B. "Labor Law: Public Employees' Right to Picket," *Marquette Law Review,* vol. 50, April 1967, pp. 541-49.
Rock, Eli. "Practical Labor in the Public Service," *Public Personnel Review,* vol. 18, April 1957, pp. 71-80.
————. "Research on Municipal Collective Bargaining," *Monthly Labor Review,* vol. 89, no. 6, June 1966, pp. 615-16.
————. "Role of the Neutral in Grievance Arbitration in Public Employment." Address to the 20th Annual Meeting of the National Academy of Arbitrators, reprinted in *Government Employees Relations Report,* no. 191, May 8, 1967, pp. D-1–D-11.

Rosenman, Samuel I. "A Better Way to Handle Strikes," *The Record,* Association of the Bar of the City of New York, January 1968.

Roser, Foster B. "Collective Bargaining in Philadelphia," in Kenneth O. Warner, *Management Relations with Organized Public Employees.* Chicago: Public Personnel Association, 1963.

——————. "The Philadelphia Story," *The Public Employee,* April 1960.

Ross, David B. "The Arbitration of Public Employee Wage Disputes," *Industrial and Labor Relations Review,* October 1969, pp. 3-15.

Ross, Irwin. "The Newly Militant Government Workers," *Fortune,* vol. 78, no. 2, August 1968, pp. 104-07, 131.

Rowlands, David D., and Jerry Wurf. "Unions Enter City Hall," *Public Management,* vol. 48, September 1966, pp. 244-52.

Rubenstein, Harvey B. "The Merit System and Collective Bargaining in Delaware, *Labor Law Journal,* March 1969, pp. 161-64.

Salisburg, Sidney. *The Check-off of Union Dues in Municipal Government,* New York City Department of Labor, 1956.

Sanford, David. "Our Uncivil Servants," *The New Republic,* April 1968, pp. 8-9.

Santos, C. R. "The Political Neutrality of the Civil Service Re-examined," *Public Personnel Review,* January 1969, pp. 9-15.

Saso, Carmen D. "Massachusetts Local Government Goes to the Bargaining Table," *Public Personnel Review,* vol. 28, July 1967, pp. 146-52.

Seidman, Joel. "The Trend Among Professional Groups Today," *American Journal of Nursing,* vol. 65, no. 1, January 1965, pp. 72-78.

Selden, David. "Class Size and the New York Contract. *Phi Delta Kappan,* March 1964, pp. 283-87.

——————. "Why the AFT Maintains its AFL-CIO Affiliation," *Phi Delta Kappan,* February 1966, pp. 298-300.

Seymour, Whitney N., Jr. "Must Civil Servants Be Politicians Too?" *Good Government,* Winter 1967, p. 11.

Shair, David I. "The Mythology of Labor Contract Rejections," *Labor Law Journal,* February 1970, pp. 88-95.

Shenton, David G. "Compulsory Arbitration in the Public Service," *Labor Law Journal,* vol. 17, March 1966, pp. 138-47.

Sharpe, Carleton F., and Elisha C. Freedman, "Collective Bargaining in a Nonpartisan, Council-Manager City," *Public Administration Review,* vol. 22, Winter 1962, pp. 13-18.

Sibley, John. "Training Program is Urged to Put More Nurses in City Hospitals," New York *Times,* June 10, 1970.

Simkin, William E. "Fact Finding—Its Values and Limitations." Address, Convention of National Academy of Arbitrators, 1970.

Sloan, Stanley. "Democracy in a Public Employee Union," *Public Personnel Review,* October 1969, pp. 194-99.

Smith, Oscar S. "Are Public Service Strikes Necessary?" *Public Personnel Review,* July 1960.

Smythe, Cyrus F., Jr. "Pragmatic Approach to Public Employee Labor Legislation," *Public Personnel Review,* October 1970, pp. 265-69.

Spero, Sterling D. "Arbitration in the American Public Service," *The Arbitration Journal,* October 1938.

——————. "Collective Bargaining in the Public Service," *Public Administration Review,* Winter 1962.

——————. "May Unions Strike Against the Government?" *Civil Service Leader,* April 9, 1940.

341

Stahl, O. Glen. "Strikes and Society," *Good Government,* Winter 1970, pp. 15-20.

Stanley, David T. "What Unions are Doing to the Merit System," *Public Personnel Review,* April 1970.

Staudohar, Paul D. "Compulsory Arbitration of Interests Disputes in the Protective Services," *Labor Law Journal,* November 1970, pp. 708-16.

Stieber, Jack. "A New Approach to Strikes in Public Employment, *MSU Business Topics,* October 1967, pp. 67-71. Published by Michigan State University.

————. "Collective Bargaining in the Public Sector," in *Challenges to Collective Bargaining,* American Assembly, Lloyd Ulman, ed. Englewood, N. J.: Prentice-Hall, 1967, pp. 65-88.

Stein, Emmanuel. "Criteria in Wage Arbitration," *New York University Law Review,* October 1950.

————. "Problem Areas in Labor Arbitration," *Proceedings of the Third Annual Conference on Labor,* New York University, 1950.

Steiner, Peter O. "Collective Bargaining and the Public Interest," *Labor Law Journal,* June 1953.

Stern, James L. "The Wisconsin Public-Employee Fact Finding Procedure," *Industrial and Labor Relations Review,* October 1966.

Stetson, Damon. "Rebellion on Contracts," New York *Times,* December 2, 1968.

Stevens, Carl M. "Is Compulsory Arbitration Compatible with Bargaining?" *Industrial Relations,* vol. 5, February 1966, pp. 38-52.

Strieff, Dean E. "Implications of Collective Bargaining for Public Personnel Management," *Good Government,* Fall 1968, pp. 11-15.

Stutz, Robert L. "Collective Bargaining by City Employees," *Labor Law Journal,* November 1964.

Sullivan, Daniel P. "How Can the Problem of the Public Employees' Strike Be Resolved?" *Oklahoma Law Review,* vol. 19, November 1966, pp. 365-85.

Summers, Clyde W. "Collective Agreements and the Law of Contracts," *Yale Law Journal,* March 1969, pp. 323-38.

Taylor, George W. "Public Employment: Strikes or Procedures?" *Industrial and Labor Relations Review,* July 1967.

Terry, Newell B. "Collective Bargaining in the U.S. Department of the Interior," *Public Administration Review,* vol. 22, Winter 1962, pp. 19-23.

"The Teaching and Practice of Politics," *NEA Journal,* October 1961.

Thompson, Helen. "Atlanta's Segregated Approach to Integrated Employment," *Public Personnel Review,* April 1962.

Van Asselt, Karl A. "Binding Arbitration: A Recent Experience," *Public Personnel Review,* July 1971, pp. 138-43.

Wakefield, Joseph C. "Expanding Functions of State and Local Governments," *Monthly Labor Review,* vol. 10, July 1967, pp. 9-14.

Ward, Douglas. "Union Security in Teacher Contract," *Labor Law Journal,* March 1971, pp. 157-73.

Weber, Arnold. "Paradise Lost: Or Whatever Happened to the Chicago Social Workers?" *Industrial and Labor Relations Review,* April 1969.

Wellington, Harry H., and Ralph K. Winter, Jr. "The Limits of Collective Bargaining in Public Employment," *Yale Law Journal,* vol. 78, no. 7, June 1969, pp. 1107-27.

White, Donald J. "Rights and Responsibilities in Municipal Collective Bargaining," *Arbitration Journal,* vol. 22, no. 1, 1967, pp. 31-39.

Wildman, Wesley A. "Collective Action by Public School Teachers," *Industrial and Labor Relations Review,* vol. 18, October 1964, pp. 3-19.

————. "Conflict Issues in Negotiations," *Monthly Labor Review,* vol. 89, June 1966, pp. 617-620.

————. "Implications of Teacher Bargaining for School Administration," *Phi Delta Kappa,* December 1964, reprint series 120.

Wirtz, W. Willard. "Local Government and its Employees: Four Guidelines for a Durable Truce," *American County Government,* vol. 31, December 1966, pp. 13-15.

Wollett, Donald H. "The Public Employee at the Bargaining Table: Promise or Illusion?" *Labor Law Journal,* vol. 15, January 1964, pp. 8-15.

Wurf, Jerry. "Personnel Opinions," *Public Personnel Review,* vol. 89, no. 1, January 1966, pp. 52-53.

————. "Unions Enter City Hall," *Public Management,* vol. 27, no. 9, September 1966, pp. 224-252.

————. "The Case Against Compulsory Arbitration," *The Public Employee,* March 1966.

Young, Dallas M., and James D. Brown, Jr. "Two Views on the Right to Strike," *Personnel,* July-August 1967, pp. 34-43.

Zack, Arnold M. "Are Strikes of Public Employees Necessary?" *American Bar Association Journal,* vol. 53, September 1967, pp. 808-10.

Zack, Arnold M. "Improving Mediation and Fact Finding in the Public Sector," *Labor Law Journal,* May 1970, pp. 259-74.

Zagoria, Sam. "A New Frontier in Collective Bargaining: Public Workers and Citizen Bosses." Address, Labor Law Institute, Federal Bar Association, Columbus Ohio Chapter, May 17, 1968.

Zander, Arnold S. "A Union View of Collective Bargaining," *Public Administration Review,* Winter 1962.

Zwakman, John C. "Municipal Employment Relations in Wisconsin: The Extension of Private Labor Relations Devices into Municipal Employment," *Wisconsin Law Review,* Summer 1965, pp. 691-701.

Public Documents and Reports

City of New York. Board of Estimate. *Resolution—Payroll Check-off of Employee Organization Dues.* Cal. 127, January 12, 1956.

————. Board of Estimate. *Resolution Covering Conduct of Labor Resolutions Between the City of New York and Its Employees.* Cal. 134, August 23, 1962.

————. *City Charter.*

————. Civil Service Commission. *Procedures for Collective Bargaining on Group Classification Matters.* December 28, 1961.

————. Council of City of New York. *Local Law 53—1967—Office of Collective Bargaining.* September 1, 1967.

————. Department of Labor. *Announcement of Procedures for Joint Collective Bargaining with the Budget Director and the Personnel Director Under Executive Order 49.* May 28, 1960.

————. Department of Labor. *Rules and Regulations Governing the Determination of the Representation Status of Labor Organizations of the City Employees.* May 28, 1970.

————. Department of Labor. *Report on Program of Labor Relations for New York City Employees.* June 1957.

This report represented and summarized the collective thinking of the following eight monographs published by the Department of Labor between 1955 and 1957: (1) Klaus, Ida. *The Right of Public Employees to Organize—In Theory and Practice;* (2) Klaus, Ida. *Recognition of Organized Groups of Public Employees;* (3) Salsburg, Sidney. *Extent of Recognition and the Bargaining Unit in Public Employment;* (4) Karph, Estelle. *The Ascertainment of Representative Status for Organizations of Public Employees;* (5) *Organization and Recognition of Supervisors in Public Employment;* (6) *The Collective Bargaining Process in Public Employment;* (7) *Government as Employer—Participation in the Collective Dealing Process;* and (8) *Unresolved Disputes in Public Employment.*

————. Department of Labor and Department of Personnel. *New York City–Employee Relations Program.* 1963.

————. Department of Personnel and Civil Service Commission. *Annual Report.* 1964, 1965, 1966, 1967, 1968.

————. Department of Personnel and Civil Service Commission. *Regulations Governing Performance Ratings.* March 7, 1967.

————. Mayor's Committee on Management Survey. Griffenhagen and Associates. *Classification of the Service of the City of New York.* 4 vols. 1951.

————. Office of Collective Bargaining. *Annual Report of the Office of Collective Bargaining.* 1968, 1969, 1970.

————. Office of Labor Relations. *City-Wide Contract Between the City of New York and District Council 37, AFSCME, AFL-CIO,* for the period July 1, 1967, to June 30, 1970.

————. Office of Labor Relations. *Contract Between the City of New York and District Council 37, AFSCME, AFL-CIO, Covering Certain Clerical-Administrative Employees of the City of New York,* for the period January 1, 1969, to June 30, 1971.

————. Office of Labor Relations. *Contract Between the City of New York and District Council 37, AFSCME, AFL-CIO, Covering Certain Hospital Aides and Technician Employees of the City of New York* for the period January 1, 1969, to June 30, 1971.

————. Office of the Mayor. *Interim Order on the Conduct of Labor Relations Between the City of New York and Its Employees.* July 21, 1954.

————. Office of the Mayor. *Executive Order 38—Time Spent on the Conduct of Labor Relations.* May 15, 1957.

————. Office of the Mayor. *Executive Order 49—On the Conduct of Labor Relations Between the City of New York and Its Employees.* March 31, 1958.

————. Office of the Mayor. *Executive Order on the Conduct of Labor Relations Between the City of New York and Members of the Police Force of the Police Department.* March 28, 1963

————. Office of the Mayor. *Executive Order 38—Duties, Responsibilities and Authority of the Director of Labor Relations.* February 7, 1967.

————. Office of the Mayor. *Executive Order 40—Exclusive Representation and Recognition Under City Employer Relations Program.* April 18, 1967.

————. Office of the Mayor. *Executive Order 52—The Conduct of Labor Relations Between the City of New York and Its Employees.* September 29, 1967.

344

————. Temporary Commission on City Finance. *Central Personnel Administration.* Staff Paper No. 2, May 1966.

————. Temporary Commission on City Finance. *Municipal Collective Bargaining.* Staff Paper No. 8, July 1966.

————. Tri-partite Panel to Improve Municipal Collective Bargaining Procedures. *Memorandum of Agreement,* March 31, 1966.

Commonwealth of Pennsylvania. Governor's Commission to Revise the Public Employee Law of Pennsylvania. *Report and Recommendations,* June 1968.

State of California. *Collective Bargaining and Right to Strike for Public Employees.* State Personnel Board Memorandum, June 16, 1966.

State of Connecticut. *Report of the Interior Commission to Study Collective Bargaining by Municipalities,* 1965.

State of Illinois. *Report and Recommendations.* Report prepared by the Governor's Advisory Commission on Labor-Management Policy for Public Employees, 1967.

State of Maine. *Report of the Legislative Research Committee on Collective Bargaining by Municipalities,* January 1968.

State of Maryland. Governor's Task Force on Public Employee Labor Relations, 1969.

State of Michigan. *Report to Governor George Romney.* A Report by the Advisory Committee on Public Employee Relations. Lansing, February 15, 1967.

State of Minnesota. *A Report by Governor's Committee on Public Employee Labor Relations Laws,* 1965.

State of New Jersey. Public and School Employees' Grievance Procedures Study Commission. *Final Report to the Governor and the Legislature.* Trenton: State House, January 9, 1968.

State of New York. Governor's Committee on Public Employee Relations. *Final Report,* March 13, 1966.

————. *Interim Report,* June 17, 1968.

————. *Report of January 23, 1969.*

————. *Report to Speaker Anthony J. Travia on the Taylor Law from Theodore W. Kheel,* February 21, 1968.

————. Temporary State Commission on the Constitutional Convention (Daniel L. Kurshan). *Background Paper on Public Employment,* January 31, 1967.

State of Nevada. *Attorney General's Opinion No. 494,* March 4, 1968.

————. "Attorney General's Opinion," *GERR,* no. 335, February 9, 1970.

State of Rhode Island. *Commission to Study Mediation and Arbitration,* February 1966.

State of Wisconsin. *Digest of Decision of the Wisconsin Employment Relations Board and the Courts Involving the Wisconsin Employment Peace Act and Section 111.70, Wisconsin Statutes (Municipal Employer-Employee Labor Relations Law.)* Vol. I, June 1, 1966.

U.S. Civil Service Commission. *Conducting Hearings on Employee Appeals.* Washington, D.C.: Government Printing Office, 1964.

————. *Employee Management Cooperation in the Federal Service.* Personnel Methods Series, No. 15, Washington, D.C.: Government Printing Office, 1962.

————. *Exclusive Recognition and Negotiated Agreements in Federal Agencies Under Executive Order 10988.* Washington, D.C.: Government Printing Office, 1971.

————. *Résumé of Collective Bargaining for Civil Servants in Canada,* 1966.

————. *Statistical Report of Exclusive Recognitions and Negotiated Agreements in the Federal Government Under Executive Order 10988.* Washington, D.C.: Government Printing Office, 1966.

U.S. Department of Commerce. *Statistical Abstract of the United States.* Washington, D.C.: Government Printing Office (published annually).

————. *Public Employment in 1970.* Washington, D.C.: Government Printing Office, 1970.

U.S. Department of Labor, *BLS Report 352, Employee Compensation in Selected Industries,* Washington, D.C., 1970.

————, Bureau of Labor Statistics. *Projections 1970.* Bulletin No. 1536, 1966.

————. Bureau of Labor Statistics, *Municipal Employee Associations,* August 1971.

————. *Work Stoppages in Government, 1958-1965,* May 1970.

————. *Work Stoppages: Government Employees, 1942-1961.* Bureau of Labor Statistics Report No. 247, 1963.

U.S. President. President's Task Force on Employee-Management Relations in the Federal Service. *A Policy for Employee-Management Cooperation in the Federal Service.* Washington, D.C.: Government Printing Office, 1961.

————. Executive Order 10988, January 17, 1962.

————. Executive Order 11491, October 29, 1969.

————. *Report of the Commission on Political Activity of Government Employees.* Washington, D.C.: Government Printing Office, 1963.

Reports

Advisory Commission on Intergovernmental Relations. *Labor Management Policies for State and Local Government.* Report A-35, Washington, D.C., September 1969.

American Bar Association. *Section of Labor Relations Law, 1963, 1964, 1965, 1966, 1967 Proceedings.* Report of the Committee Law of Government Relations. Chicago: The Association, 1964-1968.

————. *Report of the Committee on State Labor Law,* American Bar Association, Chicago: The Association, 1969, 1970, 1971.

American Civil Liberties Union. *Policy Statement on Civil Rights in Government Employment.* New York: American Civil Liberties Union, 1959.

American Law Reports, vol. 163, pp. 1363-70.

Arkansas Legislative Council. *The Right of Public Employees to Organize, Bargain Collectively, Picket and Strike Against Their Employer.* Little Rock: Arkansas Legislative Council, Research Department, 1963.

British Trade Union Congress, *Interim Report on Public Ownership,* 1953.

California. "The Generation Gap—Implications for Labor-Management Relations," *Proceedings of the Thirteenth Annual Research Conference in Industrial Relations.* Institute of Industrial Relations, University of California. L.A. 90024, 1971.

California State Employees Association. *37th General Council Annual Report.* Los Angeles: State Employees Association, 1967.

Canada. *Report of the Preparatory Committee on Collective Bargaining in the Public Service.* Ottawa: Roger Duhamel, Queen's Printer, 1965.

Connecticut Public Expenditure Council. *A Guide to Municipal Bargaining.* Hartford: August 1968.

Griffenhagen-Kroeger. *Employer-Employee Relations for the County of Sacramento, California.* A Report to the Board of Supervisors Through the Management Committee. Sacramento: Griffenhagen-Kroeger, Inc., August 1967.

International City Managers Association. *Negotiations with Municipal Employee Organizations.* MLS Report No. 176. Chicago: The Association, September 1958.

National Council of the Churches of Christ, Committee on the Church and Economic Life. *The Right to Strike and the General Welfare.* New York: Council Press, 1967.

National Education Association. *Economic Status of the Teaching Profession.* Washington, D.C., 1969.

————. *NEA Handbook.* Washington, D.C.: National Education Association (published annually).

National Governors' Conference. *Report of Task Force on State and Local Government and Labor Relations.* Chicago: Public Personnel Association, 1967.

————. *1968 Supplement to Report of Task Force on State and Local Government Labor Relations.* Chicago: Public Personnel Association, 1968.

Pennsylvania Economy League. *Union Shop for Philadelphia's City Employees?* Bureau of Municipal Research, 1960.

Public Personnel Association. *The Anatomy of a Comprehensive Employee Relation Program.* PERL Series no. 1. Chicago: Public Personnel Association, 1968.

————. *What Can Government Learn from Private Industry Bargaining Practices.* PERL Series no. 7. Chicago: Public Personnel Association, 1968.

————. *Making the Collective Bargaining Agreement Work.* PERL Series no. 10. Chicago: Public Personnel Association, 1968.

————. *Rethinking the Philosophy of Employee Relations in the Public Service.* PERL Series no. 1. Chicago: Public Personnel Association, 1969.

————. *Pioneer Collective Bargaining Laws for Public Employees.* PERL Series no. 4. Chicago: Public Personnel Association, 1969.

————. *Canadian Trailblazer—The New Collective Bargaining Law.* PERL Series no. 6. Chicago: Public Personnel Association, 1969.

Unpublished Theses and Doctoral Dissertations

Fleischman, William. "A Case Study of Collective Bargaining for Public School Teachers in Detroit." Unpublished doctoral dissertation, University of Michigan, 1971.

Routh, Douglas and Richard Rous. "Strikes in the Public Service, 1960-1967." Unpublished master's thesis, Graduate School of Public Administration, New York University, 1968.

Word, William R. "Fact Finding: Complement or Substitute for Collective Bargaining in Public Employment." Unpublished doctoral dissertation, University of Tennessee, 1970.

CASES

AFSCME v. Shapp, Pa. Sup. Ct., June 24, 1971. Reprinted in *GERR,* no. 409, E-1, July 5, 1971.

AFSCME v. Woodward, 406 F. 2d 137 (8th. Cir., 1969).

AFT Local 519 v. School, City of Anderson, 251 N.E. 2d 15 (1969). Affirmed by 399 U.S. 928, 90 Sup. Ct. 2243. (1970).

Atkins, et al., IAFF v. City of Charlotte, 296 F. Supp. 1068 (1969).

Bagley v. Washington Township Hospital District, 421 P. 2d 409 (1970).

Bauch v. The City of New York, 21 N.Y. 2d. 599, 237 N.E. 2d 211 (1968).

Board of Education, West Orange, v. Wilton, 57 N.J. 404, 273 A. 2d 76 (1971).

City of Holland v. Holland Education Association, 157 N.W. 2d 206 (1970).

City of Manchester v. Manchester Teachers Guild, 131 A. 2d 59 (1957).

City of New York v. De Lury, 23 N.Y. 2d 175, 243 N.E. 2d (1969). App. dismissed, 394 U.S. 455 (1969).

City of San Diego v. AFSCME, Local 127. Reporter's transcript reprinted by *GERR,* September 1969, because of widespread interest in Judge Fisher's ruling.

City of Warwick v. Warwick Firemen's Association. R.I. Sup. Ct., Appeal no. 616, 256 2d 206 (1969).

City of Washington v. Police Department. 259 A. 2d 437 (1969).

Clampitts v. Board of Education of Warren, Mich. 70 LRRM 2996 (1968).

Cleveland v. Division, 84 Ohio App. 43, 81 N.E. 2d 310 (1948).

Foltz v. City of Dayton, Ohio, 75 LRRM 2321, 22 Ohio Misc. 27 (1969).

Fort v. Civil Service Commission, 392 P. 2d 385 (1964).

Fairview Hospital Association v. Public Service and Hospital Employee Union, 64 N.W. 2d 16 (1954).

Goldberg v. Cincinnati, 26 Ohio St. 2d (1971). Reprinted in *GERR,* no. 408, E-1, July 7, 1971.

Goldberg v. City of Cincinnati, 23 Ohio App. 2d 97, 261 N.E. 2d 184 (1970).

Hagerman v. City of Dayton, 147 Ohio St. 313, 71 N.E. 246 (1947).

Hargrove v. Town of Cocoa Beach, 96 So. 2d 130 (1957).

Harney v. Russo, 345 Pa. 183, 225 A. 2d 560 (1969).

IBEW, Local 1536 v. City of Lincoln, Nebraska Court of Industrial Relations, Case no. 48, October 1971.

In re Berry et al., 436 P. 2d 273 (1968).

In re Hawaii State Teachers Association, Case no. Sf-05-1, October 27, 1971.

Keyishian v. New York Regents, 385 U.S. 589 (1967).

Los Angeles Teachers Union, AFT, Local 1021 v. Board of Education, Case no. 29637, Sup. Ct., June 30, 1969.

Mann v. Richardson, 66 Ill. 481 (1873).

McAuliffe v. Mayor of the City of New Bedford, 29 N.E. 517 (1890).

McLaughlin v. Tilendis, 398 F 2d 287 (7th Cir., 1968).

Melton, et al., v. City of Atlanta, Civil Action no. 14391, U.S. District Court, Northern District of Georgia, Atlanta Division, February 5, 1967.

Moes v. City of New Berlin, Wisconsin Employment Relations Board, Case IV, no. 9897-MP17, Decision no. 7293 (1967).

Mugford v. Mayor et al., 185 Md. 206, 44 A 2d 745 (1946).

Nagy v. City of Detroit, 71 LRRM 2362 (1969).

NLRB v. General Motors Corp., 373 U.S. 734 (1963).

Norwalk Teachers Association v. Board of Education, 138 Conn. 2d 269, 83 A. 2d (1951).

Oakland County Sheriffs v. Council 23 AFSCME, Michigan Labor Relations Board, Decision of January 8, 1968.

PBA of the City of New York v. City of New York, 27 N.Y. 2d 410, 318 N.Y.S. 2d 477, 267 N.E. 2d 259 (1971).

Pullen v. County of Wayne, Michigan Court of Appeals, no. 8201, Dec. 2, 1969.

Ritto v. Fink, 297 N.Y.S. 2d 407 (1969).

School City of Gary, Indiana, et al. v. Gary Teachers Union Local 4, Lake Superior Court of Indiana, no. 370-3429.

Smigel v. Southgate Community School District, 24 Mich. App. 179, 180 N.W. 2d 215 (1970).

Swartz Creek Community Schools v. Jackson, MERC, Case no. C69 G80, Decided July 29, 1971.

Tremblay v. Berlin Police Union, 108 N.H. 416, 237 A. 2d 668 (1968).

Shanker v. Rankin, 396 U.S. 120 (1969).

Index

City of New York
  interim executive order of 1954, 63
  Executive Order 49, 64
  Executive Order 38, 65
  Office of Collective Bargaining, 65-69
Civil Service Employees Association of California, 24, 148
Civil Service Employees Association of New York, 15, 24-26, 48, 88, 245
Civil Service Forum, 15-16, 63
Closed shop, 155-156
  private industry and, 155
  public sector and, 155-156
Coalitions. See Political activity, lobbying
Collective bargaining
  administrative machinery, 164
  Cincinnati, 51-52, 53-55
  City of New York, 64-65
  Detroit, 45-47
  Milwaukee, 60-62
  Philadelphia, 44
  administrative process, impact on, 322-324
  administrators and, 129
  budgetary process and, 215-225
  Bureaucracy and, 172
  capital improvements and, 229-230
  coalitions and, 127-128
  contract implementation, 117-120
  contract ratification, 115-117
  contract rejections, 322
  demonstrations, 127
  federal government, interest in local bargaining, 324
  fringe benefits, 223-225
  employer responsibility, 319-320
  end run, the, and, 130-134
  finance officers and, 234-235
  hours, wages and, 222-223
  "leap frog," the, and, 134-135
  "mee-tooism" and, 134
  municipal budgets, impact on, 229-237
  nature of, 107
  negotiating teams, 44, 45-46, 54, 64-65
  negotiations, early, 108-110
  pensions and, 225-229
  personnel directors and, 205-207, 210-211
  power brokers and, 112

pressure tactics, 126-135
public interest and, 311-312
public and private sector differences, 312-316
racial factors, 120-126
rank and file and, 112, 322
revenue sources and, 230-232
role playing, 108-110
Roosevelt, F. D. and, 5-6
scope of bargaining, 188-192
script, the, 107-112, 114
sovereignty and, 5
strike meetings, 128
supplemental arrangements, 112
third party intervention, 109, 275-308
Unions, and
  bargaining teams, 116-117
  demands, initial, 108-109
  institutional needs, 113
  leadership, role of, 113
  preparation for bargaining, 108-109
  responsibility to public, 320, 322
Wages, salaries and, 217-222
"Whipsawing," 134
Communism, 120-181
Compulsory arbitration, 287-303
  administrative opposition to, 300
  advisory arbitration, 288
  applicability to public sector disputes, 289-295
Arbitrators
  criteria to guide, 296, 301-302
  pressures on, 288-289
  selection and neutrality of, 296-302
Arguments against, 295-297
Arguments for, 297-303
Awards
  City's ability to pay, and, 301-302
  finality of, 289
  implementation of, 296-297
  ripple effect of, 297
  Union, consequences to, 299
California League of Cities, position on, 300
Canada, experience with, 298
City of New York adoption of, 306
City of Warwick, Conn., courts uphold, 292-293
criteria to guide arbitrators, 296, 301-302
defined, 288
distinguished from fact finding, 288

354

impact on bargaining process, 295-296, 302
judicial decisions, 289-295
earlier decisions against, 289-290
recent decisions upholding, 292-293
legislation mandating, 291-292
mediative and fact finding elements in, 289, 300-301
Michigan, experience with, 299, 300, 301
Michigan Municipal League, attitude, 300
nature of, 288
Pennsylvania, experience with, 298-299
policy issues and, 302
procedural difficulties of, 296
strikes, right to, and, 294-295, 297
theoretical premises, validity of, 288-289
union advantages, 299
union support of, 300
Condon-Wadlin Act, 7, 244, 315
Connecticut Municipal Employee Relations Act, 68
Connecticut State Employee Association, 80
Consultation, labor-management, 119, 194-195, 211, 325
Contracts
implementation of, 117-119
initial union demands, 108-109
ratification of, 115-117
rejections by membership, 322
Courts
Compulsory arbitration and, 289-295
dues checkoff and, 153-154
organize, right to, and, 16-17
political activity, right to, and, 78-79
Craft Unions, 23-24
Detroit
AFSCME contract, 188
internal bureaucratic rivalries, 47
Labor Relations Bureau, 45-46, 49-50
District Council 37, AFSCME, City of New York
advocacy of tripartitism, 305
agency shop and, 161
compulsory arbitration and, 294
merit system and, 209

pension negotiations and, 226, 228
political activity of, 94-95
social workers contract of 1970, 181
teacher strikes and, 122
training programs and, 212-213
Dues checkoff, 153-155
AFSCME and, the, 154
Detroit, 45
disadvantages of, 155
in municipal governments, 154
legality of in public sector, 154
Milwaukee, 60
suspension of, 154
New York, 157
Electoral activity, 90-101
Employee organizations, 17-31
Central Labor Council and, 83
coalitions and, 100-101
electoral activity and, 90-103
lobbying and, 84-89
political restrictions on, 79-80, 81
political tactics of, 81-89
types of, 17
"End-run," the, 130-134
Cincinnati police and, 131
Hartford, Conn., 69, 131-132
City of New York, 131
Exclusive recognition, 149-152
advantages of, 150-152
Cincinnati, 52
Philadelphia, 43
Executive Order 10988, 6, 138-139, 151, 311
Executive Order 11491, 139, 151, 311
Fact-finding, 281-287
appraisal of, 287
defined, 281
difficulties, 283
distinguished from mediation, 281-282
experience in public sector, 285-287
Michigan, 282
New York, 286-287
principal types of, 283
public recommendations, 283-286
Illinois commission on, 284
issue of, 283-285
Kheel, T. W. on, 284
rejection of by parties, 287
Simkin, W. on, 285
senior objections to, 283, 284
Wisconsin, 282, 285-287
Factionalism. *See* Union factionalism

Federal government
  interest in local bargaining, 324
  mediative role in Cincinnati, 56
Ferguson Act, 57
Finance. *See* Municipal finance
Firefighters
  coalition bargaining, 127-128
  endorsements, 102-103
  lobbying activities, 84, 89
  organizations, 27-28
  public policy and, 186-187
  racial dissension and, 124-125
  strike policy, 245
  strikes, 249
  union shop agreements, 156
Fraternal Order of Police, 28, 43
"Gag-Orders," 16, 76, 84
General strike, the, 104
Government Employee's Council, the,
  84
Grievance procedures, 66, 118-120,
  158
Hartford, Connecticut
  early de facto bargaining, 68
  merit system and bargaining, 206-
  207
  public policy and bargaining, 190
  supervisory personnel, 147
  union shop agreement, 156
Hatch Act, 76, 79. *See also* Political
  activity
Hutchinson Act, 44
Impasse resolution. *See* Compulsory
  arbitration, Fact finding, Mediation, Labor courts
Independent Associations, 24-26
Internal disputes plan, 32
International Association of Firefighters, 27-28, 186, 242, 245
International Brotherhood of Police
  Officers, 29
International Brotherhood of Teamsters, 20-21
  coalition lobbying and, 88
  expulsion from AFL-CIO, 36-37
  jurisdiction of, 20-21
  membership composition, 21
  police locals of, 29
  rivalry with AFSCME, 31-32
International Conference of Police
  Associations, 28, 103
Inter-Union Competition
  AFSCME v SCMWA, 18

AFSCME v SEIU, 32, 179-180
AFT v NEA, 30-31, 33-34
  encourages "leap frog," 134
  internal disputes plan, AFL-CIP, 32
  no-raiding agreements, 29
  police organizations and, 29
  unions and independent associations,
  24-27
  wage competition, 205
Jurisdictional Rivalries, 31-33
Labor Courts, 306-308
Laborers International Union, 21-22
  jurisdiction, 22
  membership, 22
  merit system, attitude toward, 207
Labor solidarity, 7, 35, 36, 127-128,
  135
Last best offer, the, 303-304
Leadership rivalry, 19
Leadership styles, 65-66, 129, 251
"Leap frog," the, 134-135
Lloyd-LaFollette Act, 16, 313
Lobbying, 83-89
  coalitions and, 88
  District Council 37, AFSCME, 94
  expenditures for, 87
  firefighters and, 84-85
  methods of, 88
  police and, 84-85, 184
  sanitationmen and, 92
  teachers and, 84-85, 86, 97-99, 175
Madison Square Garden Rally, 127
Maintenace of dues, 157
Maintenance of membership, 157
Managerial prerogatives, 48, 52, 66,
  82, 172-173, 176-177, 181, 188-
  192, 211, 324
Mediation, 276-281
  appraisal of, 279-281
  Connecticut, 279
  defined, 279
  fact finding, 282
  factors militating against, 281
  "mediation from initiation," 278-
  279
  "mediation to finality," 278
  mediators
  essential qualities for, 276
  performance standards for, 280
  techniques of, 276-278
  New York, 279-280
  Wisconsin, 279
Mergers, 26-27, 30, 121, 179

356